Inventing Languages

How are invented languages created? Artificially constructed languages ('conlangs') shed light on how we can apply the universal principles of language to produce whole new languages. Grounded on world building and linguistic typology, this engaging book provides a step-by-step guide to language invention, introducing the basic blocks of language building (such as sounds, morphemes and sentence structure) and demonstrating their use in both natural languages from English to Swahili, and invented languages from Esperanto to Klingon. An original conlang is developed throughout the book to bring the theory to life, accompanied with scaffolded, creative exercises that allow the reader to explore different linguistic options before incorporating them in their own conlang. Making conlanging accessible to readers with little or no background in linguistics, this guide is ideal for linguistics students, creative writers, and readers interested in language and language invention.

Carolina González is Professor of Spanish and Linguistics at Florida State University.

Inventing Languages
A Practical Introduction

Carolina González Florida State University

Shaftesbury Road, Cambridge CB2 8EA, United Kingdom

One Liberty Plaza, 20th Floor, New York, NY 10006, USA

477 Williamstown Road, Port Melbourne, VIC 3207, Australia

314–321, 3rd Floor, Plot 3, Splendor Forum, Jasola District Centre, New Delhi - 110025, India

103 Penang Road, #05-06/07, Visioncrest Commercial, Singapore 238467

Cambridge University Press is part of Cambridge University Press & Assessment, a department of the University of Cambridge.

We share the University's mission to contribute to society through the pursuit of education, learning and research at the highest international levels of excellence.

www.cambridge.org
Information on this title: www.cambridge.org/9781108836166

DOI: 10.1017/9781108864015

© Carolina González 2025

This publication is in copyright. Subject to statutory exception and to the provisions of relevant collective licensing agreements, no reproduction of any part may take place without the written permission of Cambridge University Press & Assessment.

When citing this work, please include a reference to the DOI: 10.1017/9781108864015

First published 2025

Cover image: Santif Map - Abdelatif Aguinini and Susan Cox

A catalogue record for this publication is available from the British Library.

Library of Congress Cataloging-in-Publication Data
Names: González, Carolina (Professor of Spanish and linguistics), author.
Title: Inventing languages : a practical introduction / Carolina González, Florida State University.
Description: Cambridge ; New York, NY : Cambridge University Press, 2025. | Includes bibliographical references and index.
Identifiers: LCCN 2024052521 | ISBN 9781108836166 (hardback) | ISBN 9781108799416 (paperback) | ISBN 9781108864015 (ebook)
Subjects: LCSH: Imaginary languages.
Classification: LCC P120.I53 G66 2025 | DDC 499/.99–dc23/eng/20241206
LC record available at https://lccn.loc.gov/2024052521

ISBN 978-1-108-83616-6 Hardback
ISBN 978-1-108-79941-6 Paperback

Cambridge University Press & Assessment has no responsibility for the persistence or accuracy of URLs for external or third-party internet websites referred to in this publication and does not guarantee that any content on such websites is, or will remain, accurate or appropriate.

For Eu product safety concerns, contact us at Calle José Abascal, 56, 1°, 28003 Madrid, Spain or e-mail eugpsr@cambridge.org

Contents

List of Figures	*page* x
List of Tables	xii
Preface	xv
Acknowledgments	xvi
Abbreviations and Glossing Conventions	xviii
IPA Alphabet	xxi

1 What Are Constructed Languages? — 1
- 1.1 What Are Constructed Languages? — 2
- 1.2 Slang, Secret Languages and Language Games — 5
- 1.3 Types of Conlangs — 6
- 1.4 Why Do People Invent Languages? — 8
- 1.5 How to Go About Constructing a Language — 10
- 1.6 Fictional Scenario — 11
- 1.7 Guided Conlanging Practice — 12
- 1.8 A Conlanging Blueprint — 16

2 World Building — 19
- 2.1 Language and Culture — 19
- 2.2 World Building — 23
- 2.3 Fictional Maps — 26
- 2.4 Crafting a Text — 32
- 2.5 Guide to Developing Your Fictional World — 34
- 2.6 The Salt People — 36

3 Designing Vowel Inventories — 40
- 3.1 Speech Sounds — 42
- 3.2 The International Phonetic Alphabet — 43
- 3.3 Basic Vowel Articulation — 45
- 3.4 Contrastive Sounds — 48
- 3.5 How Many Vowels? — 48
- 3.6 Building Vowel Inventories — 51
- 3.7 Vowel Frequency — 52
- 3.8 Additional Vowel Contrasts — 54
- 3.9 Conlanging Tips — 58

3.10	Conlanging Practice: The Languages of Ur	59
3.11	Vowels in the Salt Language	61
3.12	Guide to Developing Your Conlang Vowels	62
3.13	Conventions and Diacritics Introduced in This Chapter	62

4 Designing Consonant Inventories — 64

4.1	The Basics of Consonant Articulation	66
4.2	Consonant Inventories	73
4.3	Other Dimensions of Contrast	75
4.4	Conlanging Tips	82
4.5	Conlanging Practice: Consonants	85
4.6	Consonants in the Salt Language	87
4.7	Guide to Developing Your Conlang Consonants	89

5 From Sounds to Syllables — 91

5.1	What Are Syllables?	92
5.2	Syllabification	93
5.3	The Typology of Syllable Margins	95
5.4	The Typology of Nuclei	97
5.5	Phonotactics	99
5.6	Conlanging Practice: Syllabification in the Ur Languages	101
5.7	Syllables in the Salt Language	101
5.8	Guide to Developing Your Conlang Syllable Structure	103

6 Stress and Tone — 104

6.1	What Is Stress?	105
6.2	Stress Typology	107
6.3	What Is Tone?	110
6.4	Tone, Segments and Syllable Structure	112
6.5	Intonation	113
6.6	Stress and Tone in Conlangs	113
6.7	Conlanging Practice: Stress and Tone in the Ur Languages	114
6.8	Stress in the Salt Language	115
6.9	Guide to Developing Stress and Tone in Your Conlang	117

7 The Lexicon — 118

7.1	What Is the Lexicon?	120
7.2	Content Words	122
7.3	Grammatical Words	132
7.4	Developing the Lexicon	134
7.5	Conlanging Practice: The Lexicon in Ur Languages	140

7.6	The Muq Lexicon	141
7.7	Guide to Developing Your Conlang Lexicon	144

8 The Morphology of Nouns — 146

8.1	Inflectional Morphology	148
8.2	Glossing	150
8.3	Morphological Typology	151
8.4	Number	153
8.5	Gender	158
8.6	Case	161
8.7	Conlanging Practice: Number, Gender and Case in Deep Aqua	165
8.8	Nominal Morphology in Muq	166
8.9	Guide to Developing Nominal Morphology	169

9 The Morphology of Verbs — 171

9.1	Verbal Agreement	172
9.2	Tense	175
9.3	Aspect	178
9.4	Mood and Modality	181
9.5	Conlanging Practice: Tense, Aspect and Mood in the Moon Language	183
9.6	Verb Morphology in Muq	184
9.7	Guide to Developing Verbal Morphology	187

10 Word Order — 189

10.1	Utterances, Sentences and Clauses	190
10.2	Constituents	191
10.3	Basic Sentence Structure	194
10.4	Word Order Typology	196
10.5	Head-Initial and Head-Final Languages	197
10.6	Flexible Word Order	198
10.7	Word Order in Conlanging	200
10.8	Conlanging Practice: Word Order in the Ur Languages	201
10.9	Word Order in Muq	201
10.10	Developing Sentence Structure	202

11 Statements, Questions and Commands — 204

11.1	Statements	205
11.2	Questions	206
11.3	Commands	215
11.4	Conlanging Practice: Speech Acts in Deep Aqua	220

11.5	Speech Acts in Muq	220
11.6	Guide to Developing Statements, Questions and Commands	221

12 Negation and Evidentials 223

12.1	Negation	224
12.2	Evidentials	231
12.3	Conlanging Practice: Negation in Deep Aqua	235
12.4	Conlanging Practice: Evidentials in the Ur Languages	235
12.5	Negation and Evidentials in Muq	235
12.6	Guide to Developing Negation and Evidentials	237

13 Complex Sentences 238

13.1	Complex Sentences	239
13.2	Coordination	240
13.3	Subordination	246
13.4	Conlanging Practice: Dependent Clauses in Toki Pona	252
13.5	Complex Sentences in Muq	253
13.6	Guide to Developing Coordination and Subordination	254

14 Writing Systems 256

14.1	What Is Writing?	257
14.2	Logo-Syllabaries	258
14.3	Phonographic Systems	260
14.4	The Development of Writing	267
14.5	Conscripts	268
14.6	How to Design a Conscript	271
14.7	Conlanging Practice: Ur Scripts	275
14.8	The Muq Conscript	277
14.9	Guide to Developing Your Conscript	278

15 Semantics and Pragmatics 280

15.1	What Is Meaning?	281
15.2	How Many Meanings?	283
15.3	Metaphor and Multiplicity of Meaning	285
15.4	Word Networks: Semantic Fields	286
15.5	Meaning in Context	288
15.6	Conlanging Practice: Semantics and Pragmatics in the Ur Languages	295
15.7	Semantics and Pragmatics in Muq	295
15.8	Guide to Expanding Your Conlang Lexicon	298

16 Variation in Space and Time   301
   16.1   Dialects   302
   16.2   Gender Variation   305
   16.3   Variation in Conlanging: The Case of Klingon   307
   16.4   Language Change   308
   16.5   Conlangs and Historical Change   312
   16.6   Conlanging Practice: Variation in the Ur Languages   314
   16.7   Variation in the Salt Language   314
   16.8   Guide to Incorporating Variation in Your Conlang   316

17 Language Channels and Modalities   318
   17.1   Language Modalities   319
   17.2   Communication Channels in Spoken Languages   319
   17.3   Manual-Visual Languages   321
   17.4   Tactile Languages   325
   17.5   Plant Communication   326
   17.6   Animal Communication   327
   17.7   Xenolinguistics   328
   17.8   Conlanging Practice: Language Modalities and Speech Channels in the Ur Languages   329
   17.9   A Note on Language Channels in Muq   330
   17.10   Guide to Incorporating Language Channels and Modalities   330

18 Wrapping Up and Moving Forward   332
   18.1   What We Have Accomplished So Far   332
   18.2   Expanding Your Conlang   333
   18.3   A Final Question   338
   18.4   Translation of the Muq Fictional Text   339

Appendix A: Natlangs Mentioned   342
Appendix B: Conlangs Mentioned   350

   References   355
   Index   375

Figures

1.1	Conlanging motivations.	8
2.1	Map of Lokaria. Reproduced with permission from Daniel Bates.	29
2.2	Map of the Fairy Lands. Reproduced with permission from Sara Friedmeyer and Abigail Galbreath.	30
2.3	Map of Sushizu. Reproduced with permission from Gabrielle Isgar.	31
2.4	Map of Talasa by Robert Curran and Matt Anderson. Picture by Marcos Colón.	32
2.5	Map of the Salt People island.	37
3.1	Organs involved in the phonation and articulation of speech sounds.	42
3.2	Tongue height and vocalic aperture.	46
3.3	Vowel advancement.	47
3.4	Lip rounding.	47
3.5	Possible vowel contrasts.	59
4.1	Front view of the tongue.	66
4.2	Main places of articulation. Adapted from a diagram from Tavin.	70
4.3	Main pulmonic consonants.	74
4.4	Additional pulmonic consonants.	75
4.5	Non-pulmonic consonants.	82
4.6	Possible consonant contrasts.	82
14.1	Cherokee syllabary.	261
14.2	Nüshu written in the Nüshu script. Public domain.	262
14.3	Mandombé in Mandombé script. Public domain.	266
14.4	Toki pona logograms. Public domain. From Lang (2014: 104–110).	269
14.5	Toki Pona: *sitelen pona* 'good, simple writing,' in sitelen pona. Public domain.	270
14.6	Cirth /kirθ/ 'runes' in Angerthas script (Daeron mode). Public domain.	270
14.7	Tengwar /t ɛ ᵑgʷ a r/ 'letters' in Tengwar script. Public domain.	271

14.8	Shizu vowel graphemes (courtesy of Gabrielle Isgar).	275
14.9	Shizu tonal diacritics (courtesy of Gabrielle Isgar).	275
14.10	'Shizu' written in Shizu script (courtesy of Gabrielle Isgar).	275
14.11	Shizu script (courtesy of Gabrielle Isgar).	276

Tables

1.1	Some ways to describe how a language sounds.	13
1.2	Initial steps.	13
1.3	Vowels to choose from.	13
1.4	Consonants to choose from.	13
1.5	Initial words.	14
1.6	Compounds.	14
1.7	Additional compounds.	14
1.8	Adjectives and adverbs.	15
1.9	Tense.	15
1.10	Subject-verb order.	16
1.11	Sentence translations.	16
3.1	American English vowels.	50
3.2	British English vowels.	50
3.3	Typical vocalic inventories in natlangs.	51
3.4	Conlang vocalic inventories: Toki Pona, Esperanto, Klingon and Láadan.	52
3.5	Conlang vocalic inventories: Dothraki, Classical Sindarin and Na'vi.	53
3.6	Contrastive vowels and frequency in natlangs (based on Moran & McCloy 2019).	54
3.7	Most common long vowels in natlangs (based on Moran & McCloy 2019).	55
3.8	Short vs. long: possible and impossible vowel inventories.	55
3.9	Most common nasal vowels in natlangs (based on Moran & McCloy 2019).	56
3.10	Oral and nasal vowels: possible and impossible vowel inventories.	57
3.11	Modal and non-modal vowels: possible and impossible vowel inventories.	58
3.12	Possible vowel inventories for the Ur languages.	60
3.13	Contrastive vowels in the Salt language.	61
4.1	Contrastive consonants in English.	68
4.2	Most common geminates in natlangs (based on Moran & McCloy 2019).	76

List of Tables

4.3	Frequent consonants with secondary articulations (based on Moran & McCloy 2019).	78
4.4	Most frequent consonants in natlangs (based on Moran & McCloy 2019).	84
4.5	Toki Pona consonant inventory (based on Lang 2014:16).	85
4.6	Láadan consonant inventory (based on Elgin et al. 2020:15).	86
4.7	Ur inventory I.	86
4.8	Ur inventory II.	86
4.9	Ur Inventory III.	87
4.10	Contrastive consonants in the Salt language.	88
4.11	Muq lexicon so far.	89
5.1	Syllables: between sounds and words.	92
5.2	Simple syllable units.	92
5.3	Complex syllable units.	93
6.1	Most frequent tones in natlangs (based on Moran & McCloy 2019).	112
6.2	Muq stress.	115
7.1	List of word categories.	121
7.2	Some verb types and meanings.	124
7.3	Some adjective types and meanings.	126
7.4	Examples of adverb types and meanings.	129
7.5	Some interjection types and meanings.	131
7.6	Words 1–50 in the Leipzig–Jakarta list (Tadmor 2009).	136
7.7	Lexicon from fictional text in Salt language.	142
7.8	Salt language: adjectives.	143
7.9	Adjectives derived from abstract nouns in Salt language.	143
7.10	Color terms in muq.	143
8.1	Degree of synthesis: how many morphemes/roots per word?	152
8.2	Degree of exponence: how many meanings per morpheme?	152
8.3	Degree of fusion: what types of affixes are allowed?	153
8.4	Degree of flexion: how variable are morphemes?	153
8.5	Deep Aqua number.	165
8.6	Outline of nominal morphology in Salt language.	167
8.7	Fictional text: nominal morphology translation and gloss.	168
9.1	TAM in Moon.	183
9.2	Outline of verbal morphology in muq.	185
9.3	Fictional text: verbal morphology.	186
11.1	Interrogative words in English, Spanish and Basque.	212
13.1	Salt language: subordinate conjunctions.	254
14.1	Sketching a conscript.	273
14.2	Grapheme strokes and shapes.	274

14.3	Ur scripts.	276
14.4	Muq consonant graphemes.	277
14.5	Muq vowel graphemes.	277
14.6	Identical consonants.	278
14.7	Examples of muq writing.	278
15.1	English pronouns and case.	290
15.2	Esperanto pronouns in the nominative case (adapted from Kellerman Reed 2003).	290
15.3	Dothraki demonstrative pronouns (nominative; from Peterson 2014:81).	293
15.4	Textual deixis in Lojban (Cowan 2016:142; IPA).	294
15.5	Kinship terms.	297
15.6	Personal pronouns.	297
15.7	Spatial deixis.	298
15.8	Temporal adverbs.	298

Preface

The main goal of this book is to provide a step-by-step guide to language invention ('conlanging'). Its main audience are readers who are interested in languages and conlanging, particularly those with little or no background in these areas.

This book is grounded on world building and linguistic typology. It introduces the basic blocks of language building (such as sounds, morphemes and sentence structure) and exemplifies their use in natural languages from English to Swahili and in conlangs from Klingon to Toki Pona. The book includes scaffolded creative exercises to encourage the exploration of varied linguistic choices in conlanging. It also describes the step-by-step construction of an original language devised for this book (called 'muq' or 'the Salt language').

The book consists of eighteen chapters; each chapter begins with a short preview of its contents and a list of key words (which are bolded the first time they are used). Most chapters include a conlanging practice section and a section devoted to describing and illustrating a relevant aspect of the muq conlang. In addition, all chapters end with a set of guided conlanging questions and a list of resources to explore further.

This book can be used for self-study for readers interested in language, conlanging and/or creative writing. It can also be used as a primary or supplementary text in undergraduate or graduate courses focusing on conlanging and linguistic typology. A website with additional materials connected to the book is available from the publisher. Also available is an instructor's manual with sample answers to the exercises in the book and pedagogical suggestions on how to incorporate the book in language invention courses.

Acknowledgments

This book arises from my long-standing curiosity about languages generally and about conlangs specifically, which has led me to teach courses on language invention at Florida State University since 2015. It has been a joy to witness my students' creative achievements as they design original conlangs from the ground up. I am very thankful to my former and current students in these courses for their inspiration and for pushing my understanding of languages and conlanging further. I would like to acknowledge in particular Abdelatif Aguenini, James (Matt) Anderson, Daniel Bates, Juli Chicherelli, Susan Cox, Robert Curran, Nerea Delgado, Shannon Drizin, Alexis Finet, Sara Friedmeyer, Abigail Galbreath, Gabrielle Isgar, Carolina Macchi, Alexander Pollard and Dawn Rollings for their generosity in letting me share some aspects of their wonderful conlangs in this book.

My colleagues in the department of Modern Languages and Linguistics at FSU have been unfailingly supportive throughout my endeavor to write this book. I would like to thank Lara Reglero, Antje Muntendam and Marcos Colón for their thoughtful comments on various aspects of this book. Marcos also took the picture of the Talasa map in Chapter 2, which was no small feat! Grazie mille to Katy Prantil and Pietro Pesce for information on Italian, شكراً to Zafer Lababidi and Adam Gaiser for their help with Arabic, and Дякую to Robert Romanchuk for examples and discussion of Ukrainian and other languages. Outside my department, I am also grateful to Amanda Porterfield and Matthew Goff for their advice and encouragement on book writing and publishing, and to my friends, in particular Annie and Bill Giles, Diane Goff and Angie Standley, for bearing with me. I am also thankful to my late friend and mentor Jon Franco; it's no exaggeration to say that without Jon I would not be a linguist, and I would not have written this book.

I feel very lucky to have such a wonderful family on both sides of the Atlantic; the constant encouragement from my parents, siblings and in-laws while writing this book meant a lot and kept me going. Although she barely remembers it now, my daughter Adela provided helpful feedback on some of the illustrations and contributed some words for the Salt language. And certainly, my greatest debt is to my husband Adam, who has been enthusiastic about this book since the very beginning and who has remained supportive and incredibly patient during the long process of completing it. This book is dedicated to both of them.

I could not have written this book without the generous support from FSU, which granted me a sabbatical semester in spring 2022, a COFRS grant in summer 2021, and a Small Grant in spring 2023 to help me complete this book. As part of the latter, I was able to work with Gabrielle Isgar, who was instrumental in compiling the index and formatting the front matter, references and appendices. Gabrielle also provided excellent feedback on the content and structure of the final version of the manuscript. I would also like to acknowledge support from the FSU UROP and the InternFSU programs, which provided me with the opportunity to explore different aspects of conlanging with talented undergraduate students, including Elsie (Noelle) Day, Joseph Lefler and Xinran (Sisley) Luo.

Finally, I am extremely grateful to my editor Helen Barton and to Isabel Collins at Cambridge University Press for their guidance and support for this project, and to the anonymous reviewers of the original book proposal and the completed manuscript. This book is certainly stronger because of their insightful feedback and suggestions. Any errors are, of course, my responsibility.

Abbreviations and Glossing Conventions

A	Agent
ABL	Ablative
ABS	Absolutive
ACC	Accusative
ADVP	Adverbial phrase
ALL	Allative
AN	Animate
AP	Adjective phrase
ASC.PL	Associate plural
ASSUM	Assumptive
ASSUM.EV	Assumed evidential
AUD.EV	Auditory evidential
AVR	Aversive
BEN	Benefactive
CMPL	Completive
COL.PL	Collective plural
COM	Comitative
COMP	Complementizer
CONT	Continuative
CONTEM	Contemplative
DAT	Dative
DEF	Definite
DEC	Declarative
DED	Deductive
DIM	Diminutive
DIR	Directive
DIR.EV	Direct evidential
DIST	Distal/remote
DIST.FUT	Distant future
DIST.PST	Distant past
DU	Dual
ERG	Ergative
EV	Evidential
EXCL	Exclusive
F	Feminine

FAM	Familiar (informal)
FOC	Focus
FUT	Future
FUT.IMP	Distant imperative
GEN	Genitive
HAB	Habitual
HEST	Hesternal
HHON	Extra-polite
HOD	Hodiernal
HON	Honorific
HORT	Hortative
ILL	Illative
IMP	Imperative
IMPF	Imperfective
INAN	Inanimate
INCH	Inchoative
INCL	Inclusive
INDIR.EV	Indirect evidential
INFR.EV	Inferential evidential
INST	Instrumental
INT	Interrogative
IRR	Irrealis
ITER	Iterative
JUS	Jussive
LOC	Locative
M	Masculine
MAL	Malefactive
MS	Masculine speech
MED	Medial
N	Neutral
NAR	Narrative
NEG	Negation
NMZ	Nominalizer
NOM	Nominative
NONVIS.EV	Non-visual evidential
NP	Noun phrase
NPST	Non-past
OBJ	Object
P	Patient
PART	Participle
PAU	Paucal
PFV	Perfective

PL	Plural
PL.PL	Superplural
POL	Polite (formal)
PP	Prepositional phrase
PROG	Progressive
PROH	Prohibitive
PROX	Proximal
PRP	Purposive
PRS	Present
PRS.IMP	Near imperative
PST	Past
PTV	Partitive
QUOT.EV	Quotative evidential
REAL	Realis
REC.FUT	Near future
REC.PST	Recent past
REL	Relativizer
REM.FUT	Remote future
REM.PST	Remote past
SBJ	Subject
SEM	Semelfactive
SG	Singular
SPECL	Speculative
STRONG.PFV	Strong perfective
T/A	Tense/aspect
TNS	Tense
TOP	Topic
TRI	Trial
VIS.EV	Visual evidential
VOC	Vocative
VP	Verb phrase

IPA Alphabet

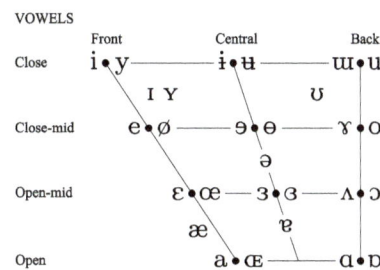

1 What Are Constructed Languages?

This book is intended for anyone interested in inventing languages. You don't need a previous background in linguistics or in language invention. Right now, you might not be confident about your ability to invent a language from scratch; but this book will help you reach this goal while learning a lot about languages along the way.

This chapter focuses on what language invention entails. Section 1.1 introduces constructed languages (such as Esperantor or Na'vi) in contrast to natural languages (such as Arabic or Cherokee). Section 1.2 distinguishes constructed languages from creative language forms such as slang and language games. This chapter also covers the main types of constructed languages and the key motivations underlying language invention (Sections 1.3, 1.4). Section 1.5 addresses some important considerations to keep in mind when creating a language, and Sections 1.6 and 1.7 walk you through a fictional scenario and a guided conlanging exercise. Section 1.8 previews the rest of the book, and Section 1.9 suggests additional sources if you want to learn more about the topics covered in this chapter.

Key Words

A priori conlangs
A posteriori conlangs
Alien languages (exolangs/xenolangs)
Alternative languages (altlangs)
Artistic languages (artlangs)
Auxiliary languages (auxlangs)
Compounds
Constructed languages (conlangs)
Engineered languages (engelangs)
Fictional languages
Grammar
   Descriptive grammar
   Prescriptive grammar
Language games (ludlings)
Linguistic systems

Logical languages (loglangs)
Morpheme
Morphology
Naming languages
Natural languages (natlangs)
Philosophical languages
Phonology
Secret languages
Slang
Syntax

1.1 What Are Constructed Languages?

If you were asked to provide an estimate of how many languages are spoken in the world today, what would be your guess? Although it's hard to pinpoint exactly, many researchers calculate that there are between 5,000 and 7,000 languages nowadays. Some, like English or Hindi, are used by millions of people. Others, such as Ainu or Yaaku, only have a handful of speakers. Regardless of the number of speakers, the geographical area where they are spoken and whether they have a writing system, English, Hindi, Ainu and Yaaku are **natural languages (natlangs)** that arose without conscious design. Natlangs spoken today vary greatly; but the rich variation in language they evidence is expanded even more when we consider invented languages, most commonly referred to as **constructed languages** or **conlangs**.

Unlike natlangs, constructed languages are designed consciously. Some are relatively well known, such as Esperanto or Klingon. Some are more obscure, such as Balaibalan or Volapük. Some constructed languages have been around for a while, like Esperanto, invented in the nineteenth century. Others, including Klingon or Dothraki, are more recent. Conlangs appear to be more pervasive now than a few decades ago, but it is important to note that language invention is not an exclusively recent phenomenon. In fact, more than 1,000 constructed languages have been documented since the twelfth century, and the number of conlangs keeps on growing every year.

Do constructed languages resemble natlangs? They do in many respects. All conlangs feature large vocabularies and have developed grammatical systems. The best of them, such as Tolkien's Quenya (High-Elven) and Sindarin (Grey-Elven), also include linguistic irregularities, ubiquitous in natlangs (unfortunately for adult learners). They also take into consideration how languages evolve through time.

Lingua Ignota ('unknown language' in Latin) is often considered the first documented conlang. It was devised by St. Hildegard von Bingen, a Benedictine abbess and polymath who lived in Germany in the twelfth century. St. Hildegard attributed the invention of Lingua Ignota to divine revelation. Lingua Ignota has 1,011 words, rendered in an invented alphabet composed of twenty-three *litterae ignotae* ('unknown letters'). Most of these words are nouns, although there are some adjectives as well; examples are given below. Note that here and throughout, italics are used for words from other languages, and quotation marks for their English translation.

(1) Lingua Ignota words   (from Higley 2007:205–230)
    a. *Aigonz*   'God'   d. *naurizin*   'ring'
    b. *diziama*   'licorice'   e. *ornalz*   'hair'
    c. *gulzianz* 'potter'   f. *razil*   'poison'

Having over 1,000 words is impressive, but this alone does not qualify Lingua Ignota as a language. This is because languages are not just collections of words; they are **linguistic systems** involving **grammar**, that is, systematic patterns that define how sounds, parts of words and words can combine in a given language.

Grammar is an often-maligned word, since it tends to be associated to restrictive, often out-of-touch language rules. If you went to school in an English-speaking country, you were probably told at some point that you should not end sentences with a preposition. In this view, common expressions such as *Where (are) you at?* or *What's up?* would not be grammatical. So would a sentence such as *My friend couldn't adopt the kitty she fell in love with*. This use of 'grammar' stands for **prescriptive grammar**. Prescriptive grammar is unavoidable in beginning language courses, or when you are learning to write formally in school. This book, however, focuses on **descriptive grammar**, which describes the ways in which sounds and words are organized in a language, irrespective of whether the language policy (typically self-appointed) decides if it's proper.

Coming back to Lingua Ignota, researcher Sarah Higley shows that in addition to having a sizable vocabulary, this language includes **morphemes** as well. Consider, for example, the similarity in shape and meaning of the Lingua Ignota words in (2).

(2) Lingua Ignota (II) (Higley 2007:102)
    a. *zaimzabuz*   'quince'
    b. *kisanzibuz*   'cotton tree'
    c. *scuanibuz*   'myrtle'
    d. *mizamabuz*   'mulberry tree'

You probably noticed that all words in (2) end in *-buz* and refer to bushes or trees. Because the same meaning patterns with a similar form, *-buz* 'bush, tree' is a **morpheme**, that is, a meaningful unit that cannot be divided further. Thus, since Lingua Ignota displays grammar, it can be considered a constructed language, albeit a primitive one.

Natlangs also have morphemes; consider, for example, the words in (3). The second verb in each example begins with *re-*, which adds the meaning 'again' to the basic verb form; thus *redo* is 'to do again,' *reconsider* is to consider again and so on. We conclude that *re-* is a morpheme in English. You can probably think of many other verbs in English carrying this morpheme.

(3) English verbs
    a. do   redo
    b. consider reconsider
    c. think   rethink
    d. write   rewrite

DID YOU KNOW?

The Lingua Ignota scholar Sarah Higley is also a language inventor and sci-fi writer under the pen name of Sally Caves. One of the languages she invented is Teonaht, spoken by the Teonim, who live in a region that floats over or submerges below the Caspian and Black seas. Teonaht was recognized with the 'Smiley Award' in 2007. This award, given by conlanger David Peterson between 2006 and 2020, recognized noteworthy conlangs described online during a given year. Other conlangs that received this recognition include Brithenig, Rickchik, Kēlen and Ithkuil. We will consider these and other noteworthy conlangs further throughout this book.

Lingua Ignota features some **morphology** but lacks a well-developed grammar. On the other hand, recent conlangs such as Esperanto, Quenya or Na'vi have fully developed grammatical systems including an inventory of sounds that can be combined in specific ways (**phonology**), a set of morphemes indicating distinctions such as singular vs. plural (**morphology**), and a way in which words combine within a sentence (**syntax**). We will explore the grammatical characteristics of these and other languages throughout this book – some might even serve as inspiration as you work on your own conlang.

1.2 Slang, Secret Languages and Language Games

Conlangs evidence creativity and love of language, but they are not the only outlet humans have to play with or modify language. Throughout history, people have invented and enjoyed **secret languages** and **language games (ludlings)**. Secret languages, codes or 'argots' are used by communities throughout the world to obscure meaning to outsiders and to foment a feeling of inclusiveness for those who are 'in.' Examples of secret languages include Lunfardo, used by criminals in Argentina from the late nineteenth century, and Polari, a secret gay language used in Britain in the 1960s–1970s. Some Polari words are given in (4):

(4)   Polari words   (Baker 2019:288–296)
     a. *polari*   'the gay language; to talk'
     b. *bona*   'good'
     c. *auntie*   'an older gay man'
     d. *dinarly*   'money'

Slang comprises words and phrases used informally by specific groups of people. It is also a creative form of language which sometimes derives from secret languages, although it emphasizes more the 'insider/outsider' perspective. Slang changes quickly and tends to be used mostly by younger speakers in casual contexts. You probably use slang with your peers; you might have noticed that other age groups use different slang words from you. Some well-known examples of slang include Valley Speak, which originated in California in the eighties, and which still lives on in expressions such as 'whatever' or 'totally.' Examples of fictional slang include Nadsat in *A Clockwork Orange*, and Slayer Slang in the *Buffy the Vampire Slayer* show.

Slang can overlap with language games, as in French 'Verlan,' based on syllable reversal ('verlan' is the reversed form of the French word *l'envers* 'reverse'; the 's' is silent). As shown in (5), in Verlan monosyllabic words, the consonant and vowel are switched. In longer words, syllables are reversed.

(5)   Verlan words

	Verlan	French	English translation
a.	*ouf*	fou	'mad'
b.	*looc*	cool	'cool'
c.	*céfran*	français	'French'
d.	*féca*	café	'coffee'

Language games also have secrecy and in-grouping as goals, but they tend to be used more for fun. They occur throughout the world and are particularly favored by children. If you grew up in an English-speaking country, you're probably familiar with Pig Latin. If you spoke Spanish as a child, you might have used or heard Jerizonga. Examples for both are given in (6). Can you figure out how they work?

(6) Pig Latin and Jerizonga words

	English word	Pig Latin	Spanish word	Jerizonga
a.	'sun'	unsay	*sol*	solpo
b.	'world'	orldway	*mundo*	munpudopo
c.	'night sky'	ightnay yskay	*firmamento*	firpimapamenpetopo
d.	'pulverize'	ulverizepay	*pulverizar*	pulpuveperipizarpa

Pig Latin and Jerizonga use specific 'rules' or patterns to obscure words. In Pig Latin, the word-initial consonant is moved to the end, followed by 'ay.' In Jerizonga, each syllable is followed by 'p' and a vowel identical to the one before.

Language games occur in other languages. For example, in Japanese Babigo the syllables 'ba, bi, bo, bu, be' are inserted after each syllable in the word (thus, the word *sushi* is pronounced 'subushibi'), and in Swedish Rövarspråket ('robber language'), each consonant is doubled and an 'o' is inserted between them (transforming *Ikea* into *Ikokea*, for example).

Are language games, secret languages and slang similar to conlangs? Like them, they are creative and evidence conscious design. Crucially, however, they lack a grammatical system different from the language they are associated with. Rather, they modify the ways that sounds and/or words are combined in a natlang to be playful or/and to make the meaning obscure to outsiders. Slang, secret languages and language games are certainly part of 'language play,' like puns and invented scripts, but they are not full languages.

1.3 Types of Conlangs

Several conlang types can be distinguished, beginning with **naming languages**, that is, conlangs consisting mostly of a list of words with little or no grammar. Examples of naming languages include Lapine, the rabbit language in Richard Adam's novel *Watership Down*, and the **alien languages** Runa and Jana'ata in Mary Doria Russell's novels *The Sparrow* and *Children of God*. Most scholars also consider Lingua Ignota a naming language as well since it has little morphology and no syntax.

Auxiliary languages (auxlangs) are conlangs designed to serve as common languages for people from diverse language backgrounds; they combine vocabulary and grammar from two or more languages. Some examples include Esperanto, based on Romance, Germanic and Slavic languages; Afrihili, building on Swahili, Akan and other African languages; and Guosa, combining aspects from Hausa, Yoruba and Igbo. The most successful auxlang to date is Esperanto. One of the reasons why it continues to be popular is that it is relatively easy to learn, particularly for speakers of Romance languages. Although Esperanto was more popular in the past, it still has a thriving community, particularly in Europe, and even hundreds of native speakers.

Artistic languages (artlangs) are designed for creative purposes. They are often connected to specific fictional groups. This is the case of Klingon, Na'vi and Quenya, developed for some of the fictional groups in *Star Trek*, *Avatar* and *Lord of the Rings*, respectively. Artlangs can also stand alone, as in Trent Pehrson's Idrani. **Fictional languages** are those existing in a fictional world; Dothraki and Láadan are examples, and so is Loxian, designed by Roma Ryan for Enya's albums *Amarantine* and *Dark Sky Island*. **Exolangs** (also referred to as **xenolangs** or **alien conlangs**) are languages used by fictional aliens. Examples include Klingon and Fith, spoken by centauroid sapient marsupials on the planet Fithia.

Engineered languages (engelangs) explore one or more properties of language and thus test the limits of how language works. Examples include Láadan and Kēlen. Láadan, created by Suzette Haden Elgin, explores how a language based on female experience would work. Kēlen, by Sylvia Sotomayor, explores what a language without verbs would be like. **Logical languages (loglangs)** aim to be logical and remove ambiguity from language. Well-known loglangs include Loglan, invented by James Cooke Brown, and its successor Lojban.

Other conlang types include **philosophical languages** and **alternative languages (altlangs)**. Philosophical languages are conlangs that aim at building perfect languages that reflect thought precisely. Philosophical languages had their heyday in the seventeenth century; one example is John Wilkinson's Philosophical Language. Altlangs are conlangs set in an alternative history. One example is Brithenig, invented by Andrew Smith; it explores what a Romance language in the British Isles would be like if it had displaced Celtic and undergone Celtic historical changes.

A conlang can belong to more than one category above. For example, John Quijada's Ithkuil is both an engelang and a philosophical language; Láadan is both an engelang and a fictional language (since it features in Elgin's *Native Trilogy* novels), and Heptapod B in Denis Villeneuve's movie *Arrival* can be considered an artlang, exolang and engelang.

It is also useful to distinguish between **a priori** and **a posteriori conlangs**. A priori conlangs are created from scratch, with no direct connection to other languages; examples include Láadan and Na'vi. A posteriori conlangs, on the other hand, are based on one or more languages. For example, Brithenig is based on Latin and Celtic languages, and Eskayan is based on Boholano, Spanish and English.

1.4 Why Do People Invent Languages?

Conlang classification takes into consideration the goals of language invention (Figure 1.1). Some conlangs aim to improve language and achieve a perfect connection with thought (philosophical languages); others have as goals to achieve international (or intercultural) communication (auxlangs). Some conlangs explore the limits of language or linguistic avenues not attested in natlangs (engelangs), while others are designed for artistic purposes (artlang) and/or to enrich a fictional world (fictional languages).

The paragraph above summarizes some of the main reasons why people throughout history, all around the world, decide or have decided to spend weeks, months or their whole lives to developing conlangs. But there are also other possible motivations underlying language invention, including pure fun or enjoyment.

In his 1931 talk 'The Secret Vice,' J. R. R. Tolkien comes out of the language inventor closet and addresses why he devoted so much time and effort to the invention of the languages featured in his literary works. Tolkien highlights artistic pleasure as his primary motivation. In fact, Tolkien wrote *The*

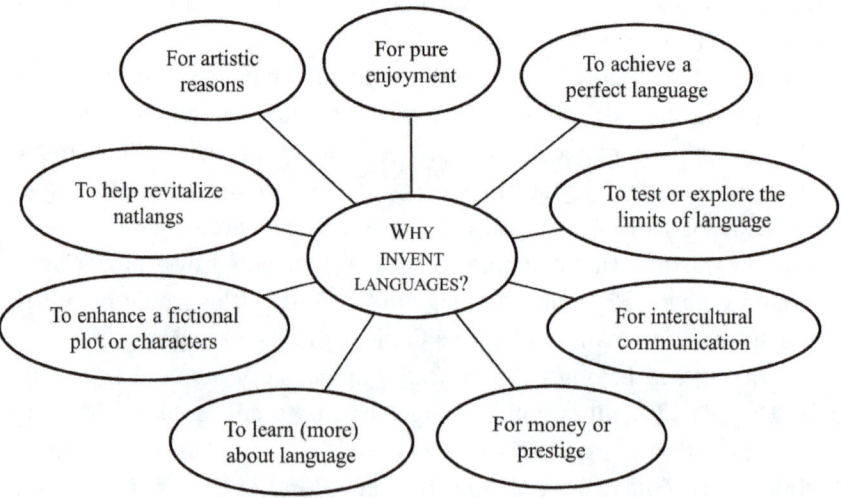

Figure 1.1 Conlanging motivations.

Hobbit, Lord of the Rings and *The Silmarillion* to provide a fictional world for his constructed languages – not the other way around.

> **DID YOU KNOW?**
>
> J. R. R. Tolkien was the first language inventor that incorporated linguistic irregularities and historical change in conlanging. Partly because of this, Tolkien is considered by many to be the first modern language inventor.

Some inventors create languages for other reasons, including fame and fortune. Two examples are Edward Rulloff (1819/1820–1871) and Charles Bliss (1897–1985). Rulloff funded his unrelenting efforts to develop a philosophical language through a notorious criminal career involving theft, fraud and even murder. Charles Bliss, the inventor of Blissymbolics, hoped to become famous in the academic world. When Blissymbolics was successfully adopted as a means of communication by the Ontario Crippled Children's Centre in the 1970s, Bliss sued the school. A settlement was reached, which Bliss used to print his own Blissymbolics teaching manual, all to become more famous.

Language invention can also be used to help revitalize declining or dormant languages. Some scholars consider Cornish, Hawaiian, Modern Hebrew and Maori to be invented in a way, since they involve conscious design of vocabulary and grammar, at least to some extent. More obvious examples include Patxohã and Houma. Patxohã is based on Pataxó, a language formerly spoken in Brazil. The revitalization of Patxohã is ongoing; much of its vocabulary was invented by the community, while its grammar is based on Portuguese and Maxakalí. For the dormant Muskogean language Houma, which appears to have been most closely related to Choctaw, there has been a community effort to reconstruct the language since 2013. Even communities that regularly use a language for everyday purposes regularly augment it by inventing new words in response to a changing world, as we will see in Chapter 16. Thus, the distinction between natlang and conlang is not absolute.

It is important to note that there might be more than one motivation at play in the invention of a given conlang. For example, Láadan was invented to explore what a female-centered language would be like; and to incorporate it into a fictional story. In addition, professional conlangers can be commissioned to invent a language for money; their conlangs certainly enrich the fictional world associated with them.

Some people think that language inventors are geeky; some might discount language invention as a waste of time. But as the documentary

Conlanguing: The Art of Crafting Tongues shows, not only is language inventing an old endeavor in the history of humankind, it is also harmless (unless funded by a career in crime, à la Rulloff) and can be extremely fulfilling.

There is one more possible reason to invent a language: to learn about how languages work. This is the main goal of this book: to serve as a guide to conlanging, while learning more about the languages of the world.

1.5 How to Go About Constructing a Language

This book provides step-by-step guidance in inventing an original conlang. Regardless of your goals and motivation, it's important (i) to avoid replicating languages you are familiar with; (ii) to be aware of which characteristics are unique, and which relatively common, in natlangs; and (iii) to strive to be consistent as you build your language from the bottom up.

It is extremely important to be aware of the linguistic characteristics of your native language so that you do not create a simplified or alternative version of it. This is a common pitfall for first-time language inventors. It also happened to me the first time I tried to invent a language. When I was twelve, inspired by Tolkien's Elvish languages in *Lord of the Rings*, I invented a language that, in hindsight, sounded somewhat like Hawaiian as it was based on Spanish but had a limited number of consonants and vowels. I tried to teach this language to my three best friends at the time under the pretense that the radio was broadcasting lessons in it. Because they were good friends, they put up with my attempts to teach them my conlang for a couple of weeks.

You might be multilingual or familiar with several natlangs (and perhaps some conlangs as well). In this case, you might be tempted to model your conlang on another language. But although natlangs and conlangs certainly can serve as inspiration, it is important not to be overly influenced by them, unless of course the conlang you are developing is a posteriori.

It is also important to learn about how natlangs work; specifically, which linguistic characteristics are relatively common in the thousands of languages currently spoken, and which are unique or relatively uncommon. This is crucial to make informed decisions about what you would like your conlang to be like. In general, while conlangs strive for originality and tend to feature unique linguistic patterns, auxlangs typically incorporate well-represented linguistic characteristics, as a compromise among different **linguistic systems** and vocabularies. The best auxlangs are also easy to learn, at least for the speakers of the languages they are based on.

Finally, it is essential to keep track of your choices as you work though designing a sound system, applying it to make up dozens or hundreds of words in your conlang, and developing the morphological and syntactic structure that will help communicate the concepts embodied by those words. It is important to apply the phonological, morphological and syntactic structures you decide upon systematically to keep the language as consistent as possible.

This book provides examples of how English works, since it assumes that you are a native or fluent speaker of this language. It also includes many examples from Spanish, my native language and one that many English speakers are familiar with, as well as from a wide array of languages spoken in different parts of the world. It is expected that this approach will help you make informed decisions about the linguistic aspects you would like to include in your conlang, without being overly influenced by languages you know well.

The book will also guide you step by step in the process of conlanging. As you advance through the book, you will be reminded to step back each time you add layers to your conlang to make sure your conlang is as consistent as possible.

1.6 Fictional Scenario

When building a conlang, you first need to decide who the language is for. Who are your conlang speakers? What are they like? Where do they live? What is their world like? Your answers will inspire you and guide your linguistic choices to some extent.

Perhaps you already have a clear idea of the fictional or non-fictional group you would like to focus on. Regardless, bear with me while considering the following fictional scenario:

> It is the year 3245. An apocalyptic disease (or a meteorite, or another civilization, or all three: your choice) has wiped out most of the population in the planet. The survivors need to come together to subsist/take their planet back. But the survivors come from linguistic communities speaking very dissimilar languages.

Do you envision this scenario applying to Earth? Another planet or moon? Was this planet or moon colonized by earthlings at some point? Or is it a fictional planet?

If you answered 'Earth,' or a real planet or moon overrun by earthlings, you need to decide which languages are spoken by most of the apocalyptic survivors, and a plausible reason why those languages survived. You could combine the characteristics of some of the surviving languages (as in Belter from *The Expanse*) or you could decide that the language spoken in this moon or planet is unrelated to any other language. Both are great choices, but your conlang approach will differ in each case. This book mostly focuses on inventing a language from scratch, but also provides you with some ideas and guidance of how to build a posteriori languages as well.

Inventing an auxlang might appear to be an easier endeavor than creating an a priori conlang, but in reality, it might be harder to invent an auxlang that is truly unique. The reason is that many auxlangs are based on well-known, widely spoken languages, mostly Indo-European. These include Romance languages (e.g., Spanish, French, Portuguese) or Germanic ones (e.g., English, German, Dutch). If you are interested in creating an original auxlang and do not wish to replicate Eurocentric ones such as Esperanto or Volapük, you should consider languages from other linguistic families and/or spoken in other areas of the world.

Considering current or plausible scenarios that result in bringing speakers of different languages together might inspire which languages to draw from. For example, the refugee crisis that started in 2011 as the result of the Syrian civil war inspired some of my students to develop an auxlang for refugee children and children living in the countries sheltering them. Before the COVID pandemic, another team of students devised a common language for a fictional medical community. We will consider some aspects of the latter conlang in Chapter 2.

1.7 Guided Conlanging Practice

To have a better idea of what conlanging entails, let's walk through devising a mini-conlang for a language spoken in the fictional world of Ur. Ur has separate but interconnected regions, and its population is divided into four main groups, as described in (7).

(7) The population of UR
   a. The *Aqua* people live deep under the ocean. They gather sea vegetables and shellfish. They are well known for their intricate dancing.
   b. The *Gem* people live underground. They dig for minerals and metals. They are master jewelers, and they love to sing, especially while they work.
   c. The *Grass* people are nomadic herders. They have a fierce reputation and trade all over Ur.
   d. The *Fog* people live in floating dwellings. They are the elite (philosophers, priestesses and royalty) and are fluent in all Ur languages.

1.7 Guided Conlanging Practice

How do you imagine the language for each group sounds? Powerful, whimsical, graceful? Table 1.1 lists some additional options: having a sense of how the language sounds might inspire you and guide some of your linguistic choices.

Table 1.1 Some ways to describe how a language sounds

airy	choppy	graceful	lofty	polite	rustic
archaic	elegant	guttural	melodic	proper	sumptuous
arrhythmic	flowing	harsh	mysterious	powerful	tempting
casual	formal	light	poetic	raspy	whimsical

Next, pick the Ur group that strikes you as the most intriguing or fun, and follow the steps below to flesh out a mini-language for it.

1.7.1 Design a Basic Sound System

In this step you will select some of the vowels and consonants for your selected Ur group. Before we begin, fill out Table 1.2.

Table 1.2 Initial steps

Your chosen group: [Aqua / Gem / Grass / Fog]
The language sounds ……………………………… (Pick some adjectives from Table 1.1)

1.7.1.1 Select the Vowels

Choose four–six vowels from Table 1.3. Decide how each vowel sounds; their pronunciations should differ from each other.

Table 1.3 Vowels to choose from

a	e	i	y
o	ö	u	ü

1.7.1.2 Select the Consonants

Choose nine–ten consonants from Table 1.4.

Table 1.4 Consonants to choose from

p	t	k	Note that:
b	d	g	– 'z' sounds like the first sound in 'zoo'
s	z	sh	– 'sh' sounds like the first sound in 'show'
m	n	l	r

1.7.2 Create Some Initial Words

Combine the vowels and consonants that you selected above to render the words in Table 1.5. The words you come up with can be short (e.g., 'zun') or long (e.g., 'meshitani'). Regardless, they should be pronounceable (i.e., avoid words like 'nkrtz' or 'uueiszsh').

Note that the words in Table 1.5 represent different word types (nouns, adjectives, verbs); you can choose to make each word type differ in your conlang if so you wish.

Table 1.5 Initial words

water	sky	dangerous	to eat
land	beautiful	safe	to sing
mountain	useful	to think	to work

1.7.3 Create Some Compounds

Now, translate the concepts listed in Table 1.6 by combining the words you invented in Section 1.7.2 into **compounds** (words combining two or more words, such as *playground*, *date night* and *well-known*). You can also include additional compounds of your choice in Table 1.7; make sure to indicate the concept that they correspond to in English.

Table 1.6 Compounds

Concept	Compound
'An object that is beautiful and useful'	....
'An idea that is dangerous to think about'	....
'The shore' (where water and land meet)	....
'The horizon' (where sky and land meet)	....

Table 1.7 Additional compounds (optional)

Concept	Compound
....	....
....	....
....	....

1.7.4 Provide Some Basic Morphology

In this step, you will develop morphology to derive adverbs from adjectives, and to inflect verbs in the past, present and future tense.

1.7.4.1 Derive Adverbs from Adjectives

In many languages, adjectives and adverbs differ morphologically. For example, in English the suffix *-ly* is added to adjectives to create adverbs: compare *beautiful* with *beautifully*, and *sad* with *sadly*. In the Ur conlang you are developing, you can form adverbs by adding a prefix to an adjective related in meaning. To do so, decide which is the adverbializing prefix; and then add it to the adjectives in Table 1.8 to form the corresponding adverbs.

Table 1.8 Adjectives and adverbs

Adjectives		Adverbs	
beautiful	....	Beautifully	....
useful	....	Usefully	....
dangerous	....	Dangerously	....

1.7.4.2 Inflect Verbs for Tense

Tense is often expressed morphologically on verbs. In this conlang, present, past and future tenses are conveyed by verb prefixes.

First, decide which prefixes indicate past, present and future; then, complete Table 1.9 to inflect the verb *to sing* in these three tenses.

Table 1.9 Tense

sing (present):	....
sing (past):	....
sing (future):	....

1.7.5 Decide the Word Order

In this step you will decide on the relative order between subject and verb, nouns and adjectives, and adverbs and verbs.

1.7.5.1 Subject–Verb Order

In many languages, including English, the subject (S) precedes the verb (V) in the sentence: *Paul sleeps*; *Brennan walks* (SV order). But in other languages such as Hawaiian, the subject follows the verb (VS order).

First, decide whether the conlang have SV or VS word order. Then, translate the sentences in Table 1.10 reflecting this word order. (Note that 'Shore' and 'Horizon' are popular names in Ur.)

1 What Are Constructed Languages?

Table 1.10 Subject-verb order

Shore eats.	....
Horizon thought.	....
Shore will work.	....

1.7.5.2 Adjective-Noun Order

Languages differ in whether adjectives precede nouns, as in English (*beautiful house*), or the other way around, as in Italian (*casa bella*). Indicate which order applies in your conlang: noun-adjective, or adjective-noun.

1.7.5.3 Verb-Adverb Order

Languages differ in whether adverbs precede verbs, or the other way around. Indicate which order applies in your conlang: verb-adverb, or adverb-verb.

1.7.6 Translate Some Sentences

Now, translate the sentences in Table 1.11 taking into consideration your word order choices above. You can also add some sentences of your own.

Table 1.11 Sentence translations

Horizon works dangerously.	....
Shore sang beautifully.	....
Horizon will do useful work.	....
....	....
....	....

1.8 A Conlanging Blueprint

The guided practice in Section 1.7 illustrates some steps involved in conlanging: from choosing a fictional group, to creating words, to deciding on morphemes and syntax that make it possible to build fully formed sentences. The following chapters expand on these and other components, guiding you toward designing a fully fledged conlang. To help you envision the overall process, this section previews the content of the remainder of the book.

Chapter 2 focuses on the creation of the fictional world, taking into consideration your conlanging goals and how you would like the conlang to sound. In addition to fleshing out some characteristics of the fictional world and the fictional conlang speakers, it provides guidance on how to sketch a fictional map and to compose a short text related to the fictional world. This chapter also introduces the fictional world of the 'Salt People,' whose language will be developed throughout the book.

Chapters 3–6 cover sounds. Chapter 3 introduces the basics of speech sounds and how to select vowels for a conlang, while Chapter 4 focuses on consonants. Chapter 5 shows how both can combine in languages, while Chapter 6 covers stress and tone. By the end of Chapter 6, you will already have constructed several words for your conlang.

Chapter 7 addresses how to build a conlang vocabulary. You will expand and/or refine the words you have already created and combine some of them into compounds. You will also begin to translate your fictional text from Chapter 2.

Chapters 8 and 9 cover morphology for nouns and verbs, respectively. You will decide the types of affixes your conlang will have and consider whether you want your conlang to express gender, tense and/or other meanings morphologically. You will also continue translating your fictional text, focusing on its morphological aspects.

Chapters 10–13 discuss syntax. You will consider which word order could work best in your conlang, how negation is expressed and how different sentence types (such as questions or commands) are structured. We will also cover how languages express the source of information, and how they build complex sentences. You will also continue to translate your fictional text, focusing on its syntactic aspects.

Chapters 14–18 discuss other areas that can add depth to your conlang, including designing a constructed script or 'conscript' (Chapter 14) and expanding the lexicon further by considering nuances of meaning (Chapter 15). Chapter 16 addresses dialectal variation and historical evolution, and Chapter 17 introduces additional modalities used in languages. Finally, Chapter 18 wraps up the book and provides an example of a translated text from the language of the Salt People.

To Learn More

This chapter draws in part from Okrent (2010), Adams (2011) and Sanders (2020); see also Goodall (2023). To learn more about Blissymbolics, see the 1974 documentary *Mr. Symbol Man* by Bob Kingsbury and Bruce Moir, available on You Tube (www.youtube.com/watch?v=HAjOJFEFbuI). To learn more about Edward Rulloff, Lingua Ignota and Eskayan, see Bailey (2003), Higley (2007) and Kelly (2022), respectively. Tolkien's essay 'The Secret Vice' is included in Fimi and Higgins (2016).

Lapine is featured in Richard Adam's novel *Watership Down* and its sequel *Tales from Watership Down*, and Runa and Jana'ata in Mary Doria Russell's novel *The Sparrow* and its sequel *Children of God*; all are highly recommended. To learn more about slang and secret languages, see Davie (2018) and Baker (2019); the latter focuses on Polari. For Buffy Speak, see Adams (2003).

McWhorter's TED talk 'Are Elvish, Klingon, Dothraki and Na'vi Real Languages?' is a great, short introduction to conlangs and their characteristics (http://ed.ted.com/lessons/are-elvish-klingon-dothraki-and-na-vi-real-languages-john-mcwhorter). The documentary *Conlanging: The Art of Crafting Tongues* (Britton Watkins 2017) is an informative, touching documentary on language inventors (a bonus feature titled *Even More Conlanging* is also available). You can learn more about philosophical languages in Eco (1997). For language play, see Crystal (1998) and Cook (2000).

A fun introduction on secret languages is Okrent's article 'The Pig Latins of 11 Other Languages' in *Mental Floss*, April 23, 2013 (http://mentalfloss.com/article/50242/pig-latins-11-other-languages). If you want to brush up on your Pig Latin, you can try a Pig Latin translator such as the one in https://lingojam.com/PigLatinTranslator.

The Language Creation Society supports conlangs and their inventors and offers a wealth of information about constructed languages: www.conlang.org. You can learn more about Teonaht on the Teonaht website (https://web.archive.org/web/20110608162956/ www.frontiernet.net/~scaves/teonaht.html) and about conlangs awarded the 'Smiley Award' by David Peterson here: http://dedalvs.com/smileys/. Fiat Lingua provides an archive of conlang languages: www.fiatlingua.org/. For a trove of information about auxiliary languages, see the International Auxiliary Languages website (http://interlanguages.net/).

We will return to many of the conlangs mentioned in this chapter later in the book. In addition, you can learn Esperanto, High Valyrian and Klingon in Duolingo; or Belter, Esperanto, Quenya, Lojban, Klingon, Na'vi and Interlingua in Memrise. To learn more about the reconstruction of the Houma language, see the Houma Language Project (www.houmalanguageproject.org/).

2 World Building

Many conlangs are connected to a fictional world, typically in the realm of fantasy or sci-fi. This chapter discusses world building in relationship to conlanging. Section 2.1 explores the connections between language and culture. Section 2.2 addresses world building and suggests aspects to incorporate in the development of a fictional world associated with your conlang. Fictional maps and texts can help in developing a conlang; they are covered in Sections 2.3 and 2.4 respectively. Section 2.5 provides you with a set of guided questions to develop your fictional world and conlang, and Section 2.6 introduces the fictional realm connected to the Salt Language, a conlang that will be developed throughout this book.

Key Words

Borrowing
Creole
Culture
Dystopia
Fantasy
Fictional map
Fictional world
Lexicon
Lingua franca
Linguistic relativity hypothesis (Sapir–Whorf hypothesis)
World building
Science fiction (sci-fi)
Utopia

2.1 Language and Culture

Culture comprises the beliefs, social norms and material characteristics associated with a specific group of people. **Culture** tends to be intangible; we usually don't reflect on the fact that we have one unless we encounter people from different regions, countries, ethnicities or faiths. Some of the most noticeable aspects of culture involve food differences, including foodstuffs that we are not used to, and different mealtimes and social norms related to eating. Other aspects involve differences in grooming, dress, religious beliefs and customs, accents and languages, and technology. But culture goes beyond this.

Linguistic anthropology considers that culture and language are inextricable. The **linguistic relativity hypothesis** (also known as the **Sapir–Whorf hypothesis**) states that the language you speak influences your thoughts (and by implication your culture and how you view the world). This is a controversial hypothesis in linguistics, but it is often taken as a starting point in conlanging. For example, it is the premise behind Láadan, which explores what a woman-centered language could be like, and behind Heptapod B in *Arrival*, which involves a nonlinear perception of time.

> **DID YOU KNOW?**
>
> *Arrival* is based on Ted Chiang's novella *The Story of Your Life*. Chiang's story introduces the difference between two language modalities used by giant seven-limbed aliens: Heptapod A (which is oral) and Heptapod B (which is written). The sounds of Heptapod A are impossible to decode, so efforts to communicate with the aliens focus on 'Heptapod B.' Both forms of Heptapod were further developed for the movie, with Dr. Jessica Coon from McGill University as a linguistic consultant. Dr. Morgan Sonderegger from McGill University helped develop Heptapod A using sounds emitted from whales and felines among others. For Heptapod B, circular symbols were devised by artist Martine Bertrand and production designer Patrice Vermette. We'll explore Heptapod B further in Chapter 14.

A weaker version of the linguistic relativity hypothesis states that culture seeps into language. This is evident in the coinage of words for technology: *blogger, viral, finsta*. But the relationship between culture and language can work both ways: continuous reliance on technology sometimes results in technology words crossing over, as with the term *unfriend*, for example. This word, used since the early 2000s in connection to Facebook (now Meta) is now used by some speakers to refer to cutting off friendships outside of virtual environments (i.e., in real life).

Conlangs can build on the connection of culture and language in different ways. Consider, for example, the Elves in Tolkien's Middle Earth; they are wise, lofty and connected to nature. They speak Sindarin and Quenya, melodic, poetic languages suited to their cultural traits. On the other hand, the warring Klingon and Dothraki in *Star Trek* and *Game of Thrones* speak languages that are harsh and forceful, reflecting an important cultural aspect.

How can cultural tendencies be conveyed in a conlang? One way to do so is to use sounds that suggest specific qualities. For example, Sindarin features many 'light' sounds such as 'l' or 'n,' while Klingon and Dothraki use guttural sounds suggesting force and aggressiveness (at least from the point of view of English speakers). However, the associations of certain sounds to specific cultural traits does not mean that Klingons don't appreciate poetry; or that Elves shun conflict. Elves are fierce fighters; their melodic language does not appear to hamper their prowess in war. And Klingons are very appreciative of literature: as the Klingon chancellor Gorkon stated in *Star Trek VI: The Undiscovered Country*: "you have not experienced Shakespeare until you have read him in the original Klingon."

The use of specific sound associations in conlanging, particularly when in connection to a movie or show, assumes that the target audience also shares them. But beauty (or its lack thereof) is in the eye of the beholder. The association between sounds and culture is not necessarily universal, or even consistent within a linguistic community. For example, guttural sounds might sound harsh and alien to many speakers of English, but not to speakers of languages that have them in their inventory (as in Arabic). We will explore sounds and sound associations in conlanging in more detail in the following chapters.

Another way to incorporate the connection between language and culture in conlanging is through culture-specific greetings and sayings. Natlangs have many examples; compare *goodbye* in English with the Pirahã night-time farewell *Don't sleep, there are snakes*. Conlangs usually feature culture-specific, idiosyncratic greetings or sayings. In Toki Pona, 'hello' is *toki*, which also translates as 'talk'; in Láadan it is *wil sha*, which translates as 'Let there be harmony.' In High Valyrian, a common saying is *Valar morghulis* or 'All men must die'; the proper reply is *Valar dohaeris*, 'all men must serve.'

The Quenyan greeting *Elen síla lúmenn' omentielvo*, which translates as 'A star shines on the hour of our meeting,' is highly poetic and fit for the Elves (and Elves' friends – Frodo uses it in *Lord of the Rings* to greet Gildor the Elf and his company). Notice that all the words in this greeting feature 'l' and/or nasal sounds ('m,' 'n'), which help convey the melodic flow of the language.

In Na'vi, one possible way to greet someone is *Oel ngati kameie*, rendered as 'I see you'; it is usually accompanied by a gesture from the forehead.

The verb *kame* in Na'vi conveys spiritual 'seeing' (the verb for physical seeing is *tse'a*); thus, this greeting conveys openness of heart and mind. In addition, the farewell *Eywa ngahu* means '(May) Eywa (be) with you.' The spiritual connection to the 'great mother' Eywa certainly reflects an important cultural aspect of the Na'vi.

In other conlangs, greetings, farewells and other sayings tend to reflect or emphasize culturally appreciated traits, including directness, assertiveness or respect. For example, in Klingon there is no equivalent to 'hello'; the closest is the question *nuqneH*, meaning 'What do you want?' Klingon also lacks an expression for thanks. In Dothraki, to say farewell, you can choose among *Hajas!* (literally 'Be strong!'); *Fonas chek!* (literally 'Hunt well') or *Dothras chek* ('Be cool', literally 'Ride well').

2.1.1 Culture in the Lexicon

The **lexicon** or vocabulary of a language can be associated with the environment and culture of the group that speaks it. Not all languages encode all possible concepts lexically. This is one factor that explains **borrowings**, that is, words or expressions from one language that are adopted into another. Examples of borrowings in English are *sushi*, *flan* or *spaghetti*, from Japanese, Spanish and Italian respectively. Other examples include *schadenfreude* from German (conveying 'enjoyment obtained from the troubles of others'), *hygge* from Danish and Norwegian, evoking both coziness and togetherness, and *Shinrin-yoku* (森 林 浴) 'forest-bath' from Japanese ('walking in the forest for its restorative and therapeutic benefits'). These borrowings are all culturally based.

The specific connection between words and culture is a great resource in conlanging and in the creation of imaginary worlds. For example, the Lapine lexicon includes rabbit-centered words like the following:

(1)   Lapine words (Adams 2005:475–476)
    a. *silflay*   'To go outside to feed.'
    b. *hrududu*   'A tractor, car or any motor vehicle.'
    c. *hrair*   'A great many; an uncountable number; any number above four.'
    d. *hlessi*   'A rabbit living above ground, without a regular hole or warren. A wandering rabbit, living in the open.'

Dothraki has many words and expressions centered on horse riding, crucial for this warrior culture, while Láadan features words and expressions associated with a female-centered view of the world. Some Láadan words are given below:

(2) Láadan words (from Elgin et al. 2020: 153, 162, 177)
    a. *Doroledim*   'Sublimation with food accompanied by guilt about depriving others of it.'
    b. *nithedimethóo*   'Refrigerator guest, a guest who shows up unannounced, comes on in and helps herself to whatever's in the fridge – and that's a good thing.'
    c. *Hatheril*   'Woman-time; marking the passage of time based on interpersonal relationships: births, deaths, relocations, marriages, etc.'
    d. *Hatherilid*   'Man-time; marking the passage of time based on important sporting events, wars, conquests, major disasters; the way time is marked in most late twentieth-century 'history' books.'

The connection between lexicon and culture also underlies semantic areas that are salient in a language. For example, a warrior culture will give more relevance to words related to war, a philosopher culture to words related to philosophical speculation and a rabbit world to words related to rabbit customs. The culture–language connection might also be reflected in morphology, syntax and even writing systems, as we will see throughout this book. It is also important to point out that not everything in a language must be culturally motivated or related to the fictional world. Natlangs continuously evolve, and cultural connections that might have been obvious in the past are often lost with the passage of time. The connection between language and culture is a great resource and can serve as inspiration as you develop your conlang; but it is not meant to constrain language invention. Some conlanging choices are just for fun, because the conlanger considers them pleasing, beautiful or cool.

2.2 World Building

World building refers to the development of a **fictional world** and its inhabitants. As we mentioned in the previous chapter, many conlangs are devised for artistic reasons, to explore certain aspects of language or to test its limits. Many conlangs are connected to fictional groups in books, television, movies or videogames. Broadly speaking, these fictional settings are associated with **fantasy** and/or **science fiction (sci-fi)**. Although the borders between these two genres can be blurry, fantasy involves scenarios that could not happen in our reality, and sci-fi involves those that are not currently possible, but that could be. **Fantasy** often focuses on pre-industrial worlds and frequently involves magic, while sci-fi typically features scientific or technological advancements. Thus, *Lord of the Rings*, *Harry Potter* and *Game of Thrones* involve fantasy worlds, and *Star Trek*, *Avatar* and *The Expanse* involve sci-fi worlds.

A **fictional world,** or fictional universe, refers to a made-up setting that differs from the real world in various respects. There are many types of fictional worlds. You can think about an imaginary or alternative world set on Earth, or in another planet or universe. You can envision a large fictional universe (as in *Dune* or *the Hitchhiker's Guide to the Galaxy*), a small fictional world (perhaps a small, isolated village) or something in between. Your fictional world could be a desert, forest, glacier, the underworld, the stratosphere, and so on. You could develop a **utopia** or ideal world, or a **dystopia** involving a terrible situation that causes suffering or injustice. Some possible situations you could explore involve environmental or nuclear disasters (as in Hugh Howey's *Silo* series), totalitarian societies characterized by governmental, technological or religious control (as in Orwell's *1984* or Murakami's *1Q84*), or other situations that could lead to loss of individuality and a focus on survival.

Thinking through some fictional scenarios might help you develop aspects of the fictional world and inspire your conlanging. For example, if there is an environmental disaster, what exactly caused it? What was the aftermath? How did it affect the linguistic situation in the fictional world? Some aspects of the fictional world will be related to your conlang. At the very least, your fictional world will help you decide on specific areas of vocabulary to develop. These can range from specific geographical and environmental terms to the types of activities favored by the fictional inhabitants (e.g., hunting, gathering, fishing, agriculture, herding, mining, weaving, trading, warfare, pirating) as well as objects, customs and events of cultural or historical significance.

After developing some aspects of the fictional world, you should consider its inhabitants. Perhaps your fictional world is populated by Elvish-like characters, evil unicorns or pirating mermaids. What are they like? To what extent do they resemble humans? In this book we assume that the speakers of your conlang are human-like in that they have a vocal tract able to produce the full range of sounds considered possible in natlangs. You can modify this assumption for fun or to connect it to the fictional world, but this might impact some of the characteristics of the conlang.

One interesting aspect to consider is the fictional speakers' sensory predilections, which can be connected to the fictional environment and might be reflected in the lexicon as well. One example is the sense of smell. Many, if not most, human communities are notoriously bad about naming and recognizing odors, but this is not because it is impossible for humans to recognize odors abstractly. Indeed, speakers of the Jahai language are excellent at naming and recognizing smell. Their language includes over a dozen verbs referring to olfactory qualities, including 'to be musty,' describing the smell of mushrooms, stale food and old dwellings, and 'to have a bloody smell that attracts tigers,' such as the smell of squirrel blood or crushed head lice. Subsistence and lifestyle contribute to the ability to name and recognize odors. Thus, if your fictional world involves hunting-gathering or places a high importance on activities where smell is highly relevant (perhaps cooking or potion making), you might want to include specific terms for culturally relevant odor qualities in your conlang lexicon.

Color is another example. Although human beings appear to perceive colors in similar ways, not all natlangs convey the same colors lexically or partition the color spectrum in the same way. Some natlangs just distinguish between 'white/light' and 'black/dark' colors (as in Jalé), while others distinguish multiple shades of colors (as in English). If the sense of vision is not vital in the fictional world, or if the fictional speakers perceive color differently from humans, some color terms might not be expressed in the lexicon. We will explore color terms further in Chapter 7.

Traditionally we are taught that we have five senses: touch, smell, hearing, vision and taste, but neuroscientists have identified additional ones, including the sense of balance ('equilibrioception'), the sense of heat/temperature ('thermoception') and the sense of time passing ('chronoception'). These or other senses might be relevant in your fictional world – and perhaps your conlang will include words or expressions reflecting their importance.

Another aspect you need to consider is how big the conlang speaking group is. Natlangs can have a wide range of speakers, from billions to a handful. Languages with large numbers of speakers tend to show dialectal variation. Even if you do not develop them in your conlang, you can acknowledge this fact, and think of how a profusion of dialects impacts the fictional world. For example: Klingon has eighty dialects; the official dialect depends on what the emperor speaks at the time. Often, Klingons speak several dialects, just in case the emperor dies; otherwise, they risk losing political influence. We will discuss dialectal variation in more detail in Chapter 16.

Languages spoken by a small number of speakers tend to show less dialectal variation; however, they tend to be endangered, that is, at risk of being lost. Even languages spoken by hundreds or thousands of speakers might be at risk if generational language transmission suffers (this tends to occur when children no longer learn the language). If your conlang is spoken by a few speakers, and/or if its generational transmission is threatened, consider how this is related to the fictional world (perhaps it is due to an invasion or colonization).

It is also useful to consider the relationship of the core fictional group to allies and enemies. Is the fictional group you're focusing on in close contact with other groups because of trading or conquest? Is it at war or in hiding? The contact and power relations between the groups in the fictional universe might be reflected in a **lingua franca**, that is, a language used for widespread communication by people speaking different languages. In natlangs, a lingua franca is a language that is used extensively. Swahili is a lingua franca in a large swath of Africa; English is also used as a lingua franca in many areas of the world. Fictional lingua francas include Hedgerow in *Watership Down*, and Westron or 'Common Speech' in *Lord of the Rings* (although Westron is really 'translated' into English in Tolkien's novels).

Alternatively, contact and power relations between two or more groups can be reflected in a **creole**, that is, a language that evolved naturally from close contact between groups speaking different languages. This is the case of Belter, developed by Nick Farmer for the show *The Expanse*. Belter is a fictional creole used for communication in the Asteroid Belt and the outer planets of the solar system. Belter is primarily based on English but has influences from other natlangs, including Arabic, Japanese, Zulu and Romance, Germanic and Slavic languages. A third option is to develop an auxlang. In this case, you will have to determine what led to certain languages (natural or fictional) to be combined.

Finally, you might find inspiration in real events and situations, or in fictional worlds featured in novels, shows or movies. Or you might want to provide a missing language for a fictional world based on a favorite book or movie (perhaps a classic, like *Narnia* or *the Neverending Story*). This is fine, as long as you acknowledge your inspirations.

2.3 Fictional Maps

Many fictional worlds include a map; well-known examples include the Marauder's map in *Harry Potter* and the map of the known world for the *Song of Ice and Fire* series and *Game of Thrones*. Maps can provide inspiration for a fictional world. For example, Robert Louis Stevenson drew the map of Treasure Island to entertain his nephew and then decided to write the novel *Treasure Island*. Tolkien first drew the map of Middle Earth and then made the story fit.

This section focuses on sketching a **fictional map**. If you are developing an auxlang you can still draw a map of the area where the auxlang would be spoken. This could be based on an actual territory on Earth, but you have creative license to modify it or highlight several aspects of the territory as you see fit.

You don't need to worry about drawing the map to scale (although of course you can if you so wish). Mapping in many cultures is not drawn to scale, instead emphasizing the cultural relevance of specific topographical terrain and relative distance. The latter could involve linear distance or the time and effort that it would take to reach a particular place, for example.

Although there is free software available to assist in map-making, you can sketch a map by hand. I recommend you do so first, even if you lack prior experience with map-making and/or think that you are not particularly good at drawing. You can use your creativity to sketch geographical features such as mountains, rivers, forests or lakes. Conveying these and other terrain features in map-making is cultural to a large extent; you might come up with unique ways to depict them that are also suited to the fictional world you are building. The following sections outline the steps needed to sketch a map and provide examples of hand-drawn maps based on these steps contributed by former conlanging students. When you are ready, get paper and pencil and let's begin!

2.3.1 Sketching Fictional Maps

There are nine easy steps involved in sketching a **fictional map** by hand.

Step 1: Draw a simple shape.
This can be a circular, oblong, rectangular shape, etc. You decide.
a. Is this an island? If so, decide whether this island is part of an archipelago, and/or whether this island is off a continent or another landmass.
b. Is this a continent? If so, decide whether there are islands off it.

Step 2: Add one or more lakes.
Draw one or more lakes. Keep in mind that lakes usually either lie in lowlands, and/or are surrounded by mountains. Consider whether these lakes are similar to the ones on Earth, or whether they are different (frozen, made out of chocolate or molten lava, etc.).

Step 3: Add one or more mountain ranges.
Consider placing a mountain range (or several) around the lake(s) you have sketched. Decide whether there are any other mountain ranges in other areas.

Step 4: Add woods.
Consider whether your fictional world has woods, marshes, deserts, swamps or other geological features; incorporate them as you see fit.

Step 5: Add a main river.
Typically, rivers come down mountain ranges and tend to end at a lake or at the coastline, but you can make the main river flow toward somewhere different.

Step 6: Add tributaries and/or other rivers.
Decide if the main river has streams or tributaries joining in different places. Consider including additional rivers.

Step 7: Decide the location of main towns.
Think of where your fictional group would settle. Groups might settle close to bodies of water since water is essential for life; water is usually also a food magnet and relevant for trading purposes. People might of course also live in woods, deserts, mountains or other areas. If there are different groups in your fictional world, they might inhabit different regions.

Step 8: Name the features in your map
You can begin to name the features in your map using English or another language you know. You can revise these names and translate them into your conlang later.

Step 9: Revise and update as needed!
This is a just a first draft of your fictional map. Like all aspects of world building and language invention, you can come back later and revise it.

2.3.2 Examples of Fictional Maps in Conlanging

This section provides examples of four fictional maps kindly contributed by former students in a conlanging course. They were first sketched following the steps above and underwent revision throughout the course.

Figure 2.1 shows the map of Lokaria, home to centaurs. The Lokaria centaurs are a sophisticated race whose lives are intertwined with nature and the cycles of the moon, planets and stars. Their language, Centauran, is inspired by centaur myths and by Heptapod B from *Arrival* (Denis Villeneuve, 2016).

Figure 2.2 shows the map of the Fairy Lands, home to several groups of fairies, including the Flower Fairies, which are matriarchal and polytheistic. Their primary occupations are writing and publishing. The Flower Fairies speak the Language of Flowers; their language and culture is under threat from the Volcano Fairies and their allies (the Fire and Cave Fairies). The map in Figure 2.2 and its associated fictional world was inspired by fairytales, the novel *Fourth Wing* by Rebecca Yarros and the movies *Barbie* (Greta Gerwig, 2023), *Barbie: Fairytopia* (Walter Martishius and William Lau, 2005) and *Tinker Bell* (Bradley Raymond, 2008).

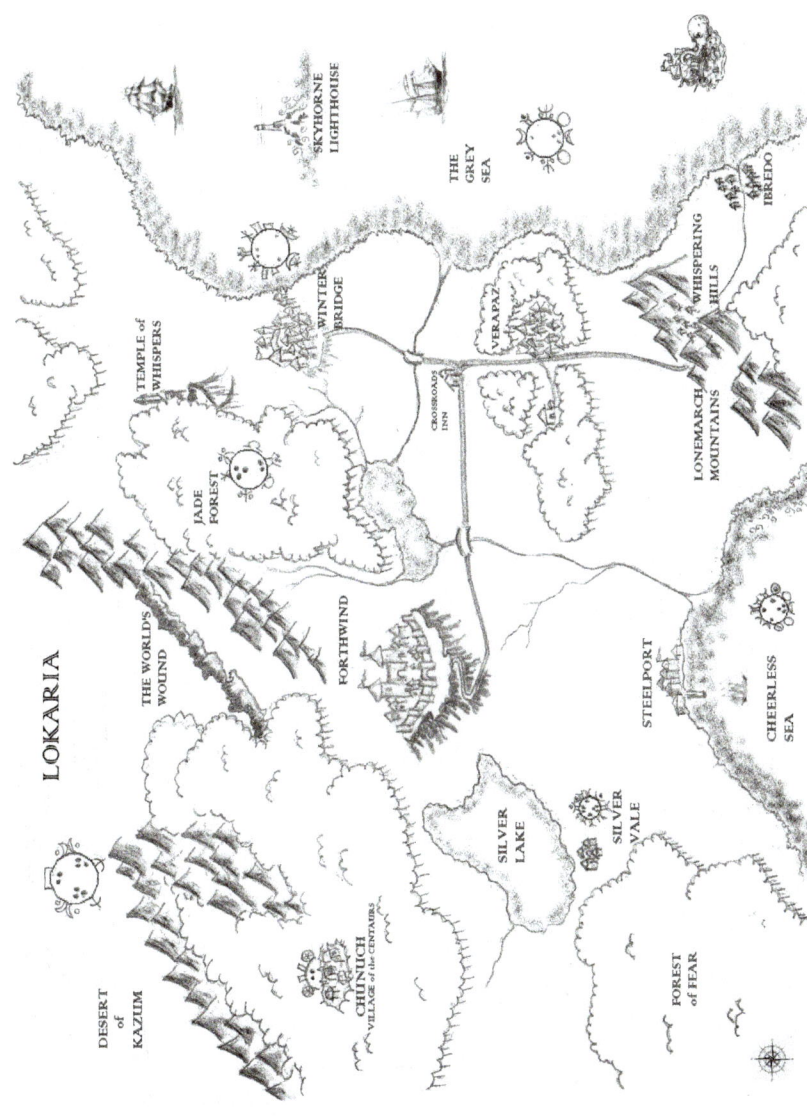

Figure 2.1 Map of Lokaria. Reproduced with permission from Daniel Bates.

Figure 2.2 Map of the Fairy Lands. Reproduced with permission from Sara Friedmeyer and Abigail Galbreath.

Figures 2.1 and 2.2 are very different in style, but both are excellent examples of fictional maps. Your own map might look simpler or more detailed; you could choose to color it, sketch it using materials other than pencil or ink, and/or draw it on specialty paper. You could also decide to create a less traditional map, as in Figure 2.3, depicting the planet Sushizu in the Krote galaxy. Three different groups live in this planet: the spirit guides, the technologists and the warrior leaders. All use the Shizu language as their lingua franca to communicate effectively in their defense from galactic invaders.

The fictional map in Figure 2.3 is figurative and minimalist. It prominently features triangles to convey the relevance of the three groups in Sushizu. As such, it is uniquely suited to the fictional world. This map exclusively features Shizu writing (which we describe in detail in Chapter 14) to convey the location of each group. The spirit guides live in the middle, in a flat land with lush and tropical forests (centered in the map to indicate its relevance). To the right is the abode of the warrior leaders; a mountainous, bleak, desert-like land. The leftmost area, heavily urban and featuring extensive transportation and architecture, is home to the technologists. Notice that

2.3 Fictional Maps

Figure 2.3 Map of Sushizu. Reproduced with permission from Gabrielle Isgar.

the map is represented as an open scroll, which is connected to the means of writing in the planet, as we'll see in Chapter 14.

The maps in Figures 2.1–2.3 present a bird's-eye view of the fictional world, emphasizing the horizontal scale, particularly in the first two cases. But you can choose to draw a map using a different perspective. In fact, people in different regions of the world have different mental atlases. For example, Sherpa children in Nepal tend to emphasize the vertical dimension when asked to draw a map of their surroundings, which is not surprising since altitude is essential for life in the Himalayas. In addition, some fictional maps emphasize the vertical aspect; examples include the nine circles of Hell in Dante's *The Divine Comedy*, the tree-map of the nine worlds in the *Runemarks* series by Joanne Harris, or the space elevator map in Jason M. Hough's *The Darwin Elevator*. If your fictional world centers around a tree or mountain range, or if it consists of vertical levels under or above ground, you might decide to emphasize this aspect in your fictional map.

You could also consider using a different medium, perhaps a three-dimensional one, as in the Talasa fictional map shown in Figure 2.4. Talasa is a frozen prison asteroid; its map was drawn on the near side of a blank moon lamp.

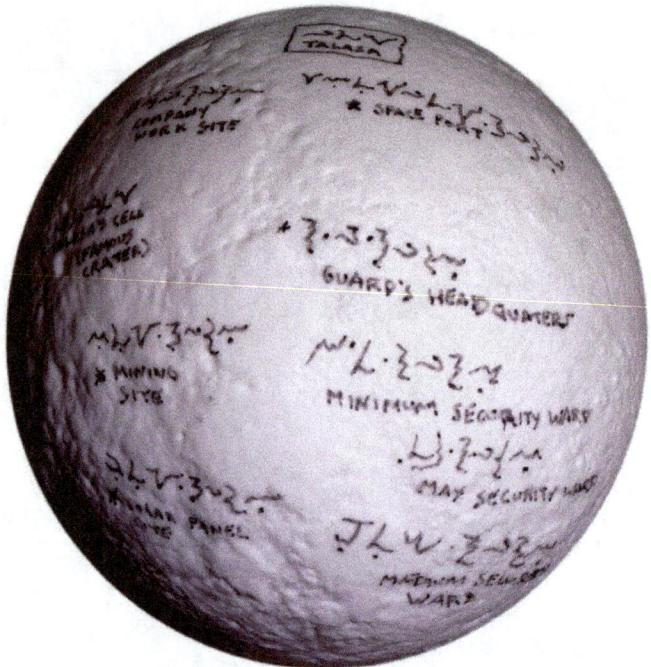

Figure 2.4 Map of Talasa by Robert Curran and Matt Anderson. Picture by Marcos Colón.

> **Your Turn**
>
> - Do you have a favorite fictional map connected to a work of art or fiction? What aspects of the map do you particularly like?
> - Which of the fictional maps in this section do you like the best, and why?
> - Consider redrawing the map you sketched in Section 2.3.1 taking into consideration the map-making ideas and examples covered in 2.3.2.

2.4 Crafting a Text

It can be useful to draft a short text (about one paragraph long) on an aspect related to the fictional world, such as a foundational myth or a description of a major historical event. Doing so might make you think more deeply about your conlang and associated fictional world. Below are examples of four short texts contributed by students taking a conlanging class. Texts were relatively short (75–100 words long); the genre and content were left up to the conlanger. Fictional texts were requested early in the course and served as a guide to developing vocabulary and grammar.

2.4 Crafting a Text

The first example is an origin myth for Yod Thalean (3), by Nerea Delgado and Alexis Finet. The Yod Thalean speak a language of the same name. It involves a sacred Tree, which the Yod Thalean are tasked to protect from non Yod-Thaleans. The tree sap would grant eternal life to whoever would feed on it:

(3) Yod Thalean creation myth (courtesy of Nerea Delgado and Alexis Finet)
At the beginning of time, the elements were in disarray; the wind played in a whirlwind; the fire fought to keep its embers alive; the earth shook and crumbled; the water drifted away from its course. When the wind met the earth, a seed was planted; when the seed met the water, it started to grow. When the fire came last, it gave the tree its blood. And this blood became the beginning of life.

This concise text provides an evocative account of the foundation of the Yod-Thalean world. This creation myth shows similarities to other fictional worlds, most notably to The Tree of Souls in *Avatar*'s Pandora; but as Nerea Delgado and Alexis Finet note, other cultures have similar myths.

Our second example (4) is from Axon, the lingua franca spoken by the imprisoned aliens in the Talasa artic prison moon depicted in Figure 2.4. This text lays out the expectations for Talasa prisoners; it serves as a survival blueprint, and it is modeled on the Ten Commandments.

(4) The Orders of Talasa (courtesy of Matt Anderson and Robert Curran)
  1. You must always respect you and I (the ones close to you).
  2. You must always resist the guards, even hurt them, if the mob bosses give you the orders.
  3. If they insult you, you must prove yourselves worthy.
  4. Always observe your times and spaces in great detail (have situational awareness).
  5. You must always respect allies; if they do not respect you, do not respect them.
  6. You must always fight in confrontations.
  7. You must always resist. You must never snitch.
  8. You must never steal allies' stuff.
  9. Never gamble if you have no stuff.
  10. The words of you prove your worth.

The third text (5) is a warning and a call to arms connected to the map of Shushizu from Figure 2.3. The text makes clear the relevance of 'the metal' in this world and mentions the three different cultural groups in the planet: warriors, spirit guides, and technologists.

(5) Shizu fictional text (courtesy of Gabrielle Isgar)
Warriors, spirits and technologists, it was heard that enemies have discovered the metal. They will attack Sushizu (planet) and they will conquer the metal. All must unite and defend Sushizu. Leaders will have jobs. Technologists will protect the technology. Warriors will defend the metal. Spirit guides will unite the allies. It is felt that the metal is ours. The enemies will not gain power. It is felt that all will have peace and all will accomplish unity [peace and unity for all].

Our final example (6) is an announcement warning of the spread of a dangerous virus in Maezu, a fictional world composed of fourteen geographically isolated nations, each of them with their own language. Note that Maezu was invented before Covid-19.

(6) Maezu fictional text (courtesy of Alex Pollard, Dawn Rollins and Shannon Drizin)
An outbreak of a new and contagious virus is spreading across southern Shuharia. Symptoms start with a red rash on the hands, neck and face. Within twenty-four hours of displaying the initial symptom the infected person will suddenly fall asleep. The sleep lasts for approximately thirty-six hours. When the affected person wakes up, all symptoms will quickly subside. The virus is dangerous because it is a possibility that those affected will suddenly fall asleep in a dangerous situation or a dangerous place. Public health officials are encouraging the population to take precautions against catching the virus and research will begin immediately for a vaccine to prevent future outbreaks.

Your Turn

- Consider the fictional texts in this section. Which do you consider more inspiring, and why?
- Which text might be harder to translate into a conlang?
- Which type of text do you envision drafting as a starting point for your conlang?

2.5 Guide to Developing Your Fictional World

This section provides a set of guided questions to help expand the characteristics of the fictional world and its associated conlang. Your answers are intended as a starting point in world building and conlanging; you can always revise and elaborate them later.

2.5.1 The Fictional World

1. Is the fictional world modeled on Earth or set in an alternative universe?
2. Is the fictional society predominantly urban or rural? How technologically advanced is it?
3. What is the geography like (e.g., mountainous, desertic, glacial, tropical, the underworld)?
4. Is the fictional world utopic or dystopic? What series of events caused this situation?
5. How are the utopic/dystopic aspects of the fictional world connected to your conlang?
6. What activities are predominant (e.g., hunting, gathering, fishing, trading, agriculture, weaving, warfare, pirating)?
7. What do the inhabitants look like? If they are very different from earthlings, discuss how their physical characteristics might shape their language.
8. Which senses are important in the fictional world?
9. Are there social hierarchies? For example, is there a divide among wealth, social class, gender, age, origin, ethnicity, religion, nationality, tribe, caste or political status?
10. What are your sources of inspiration for this fictional world?
11. Draft a short text (about one paragraph long) on the fictional world. Good options are myths, accounts of key historical events or a description of cultural practices.

2.5.2 Your Conlang

1. What is the conlang name? (it can be tentative).
2. What type is it (e.g., an artlang, engelang, auxlang)? What draws you to this conlang type?
3. What three adjectives come to mind when trying to describe your conlang?
4. Who speaks this language?
5. How many speakers are there? Is the language thriving or endangered? Why/how so?
6. Does the conlang serve as a lingua franca? If so, discuss how this came to be.
7. If the language has many speakers, indicate whether there are distinct dialects, and whether they are determined geographically or socially.
8. Will there be different forms of address for beings of different social status?

9. Does the fictional world encompass different languages? If so, provide a brief description.
10. What are your sources of inspiration for the conlang?

2.6 The Salt People

This section introduces the fictional world of the Salt People, whose language will be developed throughout this book. Section 2.6.1 describes the fictional world and Section 2.6.2 outlines some characteristics of the conlang. Section 2.6.3 acknowledges my sources of inspiration and offers some comments on the map-making process.

2.6.1 The Salt People: Fictional World

The Salt People live in a post-apocalyptic Earth. After decades of climate change and a collision with space debris, many people lost their lives, mostly in large urban centers. The main infrastructure of the world collapsed; the societies that survived were small. The Salt People have a relatively advanced knowledge of salt work. They live in a mountainous, volcanic region by the sea. The last eruption of one of the volcanoes sent lava down the valley, and the lava reached the ocean. The area where it cooled off is used by the Salt People to dry and harvest sea salt. A map of the fictional world is shown in Figure 2.5.

In the past, the Salt People were forced to work salt flats; they lived in dismal conditions while their overlords profited from the salt trade. However, the Salt people rebelled and killed their overlords with obsidian blades. At the time their language is documented, the Salt people enjoy peace and benefit from a profitable salt trade. Salt is a valuable commodity; the Salt People tend to keep away from foreigners to protect their secrets.

The Salt People are primarily dedicated to salt work, fishing and agriculture. Salt and fish are traded for other products, mostly foods and fabrics. Salt People are also artists; they create beautiful salt sculptures for ceremonial occasions such as coming of age and the end of the salt harvest.

Salt People have a main chief, usually a woman, and a council that includes old and young members of the community. At this point, I am undecided about social hierarchies. However, there are some differences in the speech of younger and older people in the community; this is understood as part of how things change but stay the same. There is a distinct ceremonial register used in council meetings and communications, in addition to ceremonial stories and songs.

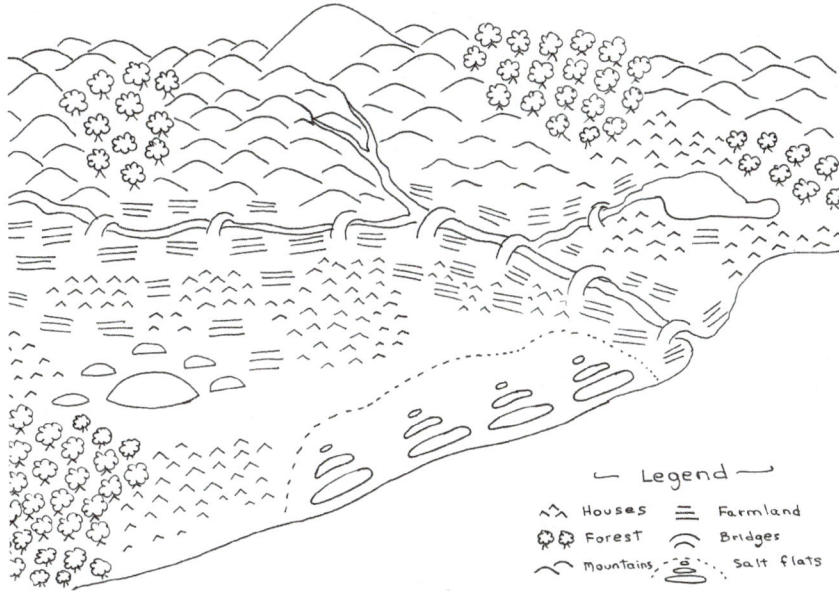

Figure 2.5 Map of the Salt People island.

A short text related to the fictional world is given in (9); it addresses how life began on the island where the Salt People live. Throughout the book, we will use this text to exemplify various aspects of the associated conlang.

(7) Fictional text: Salt People origin story
A long time ago the world slept; there was darkness. The wind was silent and the ocean whispered with sadness. Then the mountain screamed and spewed out fire, and the island burned. It burned and burned for many days. When it stopped burning, the island had changed. The ocean soothed the burning land and gave it some of its life force. The life force from the ocean destroyed the darkness and dawn returned. This is how life on our island started again.

2.6.2 The Salt Conlang

The Salt conlang is both a fictional language and an artlang. There are about 1,000 speakers of this language. The community tries to stay stable in number to avoid overwhelming the environment and depleting available natural resources. It is a tight community where loyalty is paramount. Traders travel to markets in the area a few times a year; they use a lingua franca to communicate with speakers of other languages in the region. Non-traders are typically not concerned with this lingua franca.

Although the number of people speaking the language is limited, within the fictional world the language is thriving, since the community passes the language on to the younger generation. The Salt People use writing, as we will see in Chapter 14.

2.6.3 Sources of Inspiration and Comments on the Map-Making Process

I decided to focus on a post-apocalyptic fictional group inspired by Ursula Le Guin's novel *Always Coming Home*. When I first thought of a fictional world for this book, I considered having it centered around a volcano. I'm intrigued by the different types of salt in the world, and one day it occurred to me that salt production and trading could be the basis of my fictional world. To learn more about this topic I read Kurlansky's (2003) book on salt in the history of the world, and I began exploring methods of salt production. The idea of salt sculptures was inspired by Motoi Yamamoto's work, in particular his book *Return to the Sea: Saltworks* (2012).

The map in Figure 2.5 was hand drawn and is the last of three map sketches made over several months. The first one was drawn by pencil on coral paper (for fun) and featured a volcano prominently in the middle. The second was sketched with pencil on white paper; the volcano receded into the distance, and the Salt land was depicted from an angle. The map in Figure 2.5 improved on the second primarily by focusing on geographical details such as forests and salt flats; it was drawn with a fine point marker and includes a legend.

To Learn More

Everett (2012) addresses the connection of culture and language; his view has been shaped by this study of Pirahã, which has some unusual cultural aspects, including no concern for past myths or where the Pirahã people came from, an emphasis in the here and now, and a lack of numbers, among others. You can read more about the Pirahã in Everett (2008).

The discussion of fantasy and sci-fi here is based on Mandala (2010). For a comprehensive discussion of aspects related to imaginary worlds, see Wolf (2018). Comins (2011, 2012) explains how differences in planet behavior relate to essential world aspects, from atmospheric events to geography and the development of civilizations. Each chapter begins with a gripping fictional scenario.

To learn more on odor naming in Jahai see Majid and Burenhult (2014). For odor naming and recognition in hunter-gatherer cultures, see Majid and Kruspe (2018). To learn more about human senses, see Higgins (2022). For Toki Pona, see Lang (2014).

For further discussion of the connection between map-making and culture, see the chapter 'An Atlas in the Mind' in Harrison (2007). The steps to sketch a map draw from Blando (2015). Jones (2020) is also recommended; it includes an overview of world building as well. Lewis-Jones (2018) is an excellent book on fictional maps. For vertical maps, see Burgess (2017). Many map-making resources are available online; if you are a Tolkien fan, you will probably enjoy the interactive LOTR Project website: http://lotrproject.com/.

J. R. R. Tolkien was a great artist in addition to a great novelist and conlanger; he began writing *The Hobbit* with the map of Thror. Early mapping was also crucial for *Lord of the Rings*. Later, the illustrator and cartographer Pauline Byrne was commissioned by Tolkien's publisher to make a poster version of Middle Earth and to work with Tolkien on maps/illustrations. Byrne also illustrated all of C. S. Lewis's Narnia stories. Tolkien's son Christopher also helped in some of the map-making involved for his father's fictional work. You can learn more about Tolkien's life, art, and map-making in McIlwaine (2018).

3

Designing Vowel Inventories

It is now time to begin designing your conlang. You might feel ready to start making up words; but before you do so, it is important to give some thought to which speech sounds you will use as your conlang building blocks. The information in this and the next chapter, addressing vowels and consonants respectively, might feel a bit dense, but it is essential to understand how sounds work before you combine them into words and eventually sentences.

This chapter begins by introducing speech sounds and how to transcribe them using the International Phonetic Alphabet (IPA) (Sections 3.1, 3.2). Section 3.3 covers basic vowel articulation, and Section 3.4 briefly discusses contrastive sounds. Sections 3.5–3.7 address how vowels are organized in languages, and Section 3.8 explores non-basic vowel contrasts.

The remaining sections focus on conlanging: Section 3.9 offers some conlanging tips on how to choose the vowels for your conlang, and Section 3.10 provides conlanging practice. Section 3.11 describes the vocalic inventory of the Salt language, and Section 3.12 provides a set of guided questions to facilitate the selection of your conlang vowels. The chapter ends with a list of the conventions introduced in this chapter (Section 3.13) and a list of resources to learn more.

Key Words

Corner vowels
Diphthong
Duration
International Phonetic Alphabet (IPA)
Long vowels ([V:])
Minimal pair
Minimal set
Monophthong
Nasalization
Nasal vowels ([Ṽ])
Near-minimal

One-to-one correspondence
Oral vowels
Peripheral vowels
Organs involved in speech
   Epiglottis
   Larynx (voice box)
   Lungs
   Nasal cavity
   Oral cavity
   Pharynx
   Trachea (windpipe)
   Vocal folds
Phoneme (//)
Romanization
Short vowels
Speech sound
   Articulation
   Initiation
   Phonation
     Modal
     Non-modal
Triphthong
Voice quality
   Breathy (murmured) ([V̤])
   Creaky/glottalized ([V̰])
   Vocalic inventory
     Average
     Large
     Small
   Voiced
   Voiceless ([V̥])
   Whispered ([V̥])Vowel
   Vowel classification
   Advancement (frontness/backness)
     Back
     Central
     Front
   Height
     High (close)
     Low (open)
     Mid
     Mid-high

Mid-low
Lip rounding
Rounded
Unrounded
Vowel dispersion

3.1 Speech Sounds

Speech sounds originate from air coming out from the **lungs**, moving up the **trachea (windpipe)** into the **larynx (voice box)**. This air passes through the **vocal folds**, which might vibrate or move in other ways, and afterwards reaches the **pharynx**, which leads into the **oral** and **nasal cavities**. The movement of parts of the throat, mouth and nose shapes the air into sounds that we recognize as speech.

The lungs and trachea are responsible for the **initiation** of speech sounds: the larynx, for **phonation** or the turning of air into speech sounds, and the pharynx, oral and nasal cavities, for their **articulation**. Sounds pronounced with air coming out of the lungs are pulmonic. Non-pulmonic sounds (such as clicks) are also possible in natlangs; we will cover them in Chapter 4. Figure 3.1 illustrates the main **organs involved in** the phonation and articulation of **speech** sounds.

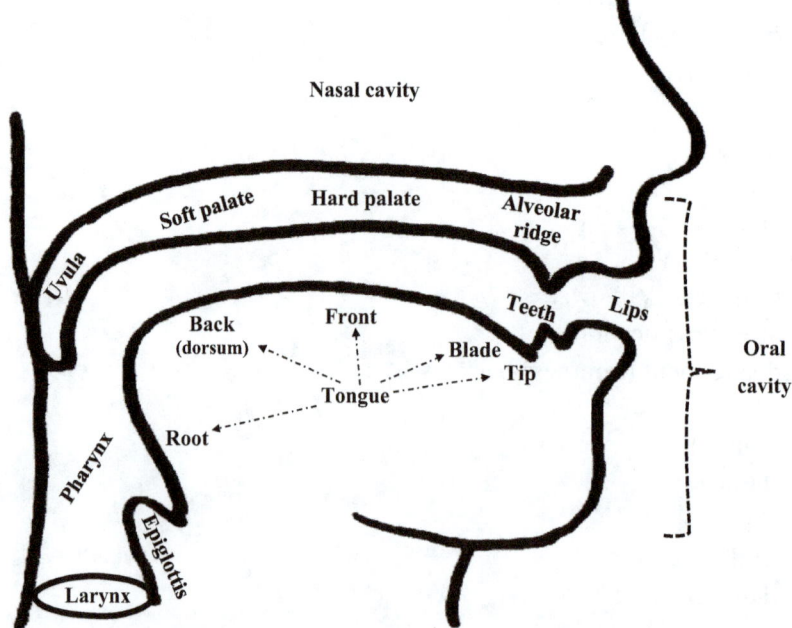

Figure 3.1 Organs involved in the phonation and articulation of speech sounds.

It is useful to introspect to get a better sense of how speech sounds are pronounced. Let's start by locating your Adam's apple (Eve's apple?) so that you can feel where the larynx is. Within the larynx sit the vocal folds, which shape air into speech sounds by moving in various ways. Most commonly, the vocal folds are either open, as in the first sounds in 'sit' or 'fault,' or close together so that they vibrate, as in the first sounds in 'zit' and 'vault.' Speech sounds produced with spread vocal folds are **voiceless**; those pronounced with vocal fold vibration are **voiced**. When the vocal folds are apart, the air coming from the lungs passes through unimpeded, resulting in voiceless sounds. When the vocal folds are close together, the air coming from the lungs pushes them apart, causing vibration that results in voiced sounds. You can check if a sound is voiceless or voiced by lightly placing a finger on your Adam's apple. If you feel vibration, as in the sound [n], the sound is voiced; if you don't, as in [s], the sound is voiceless.

Right above the larynx is the **epiglottis**; its most important role is lowering to prevent food from going into the larynx so that we don't choke (food goes through the esophagus into the digestive system; the esophagus is not depicted in Figure 3.1 since it is not part of the articulatory system). The epiglottis can also act as an articulator for speech sounds, as we will see in Chapter 4.

The pharynx, mouth and nose are involved in further shaping speech sounds. For vowels, the tongue and the lips are crucial, as we discuss in Section 3.3.

> ### Your Turn
>
> Indicate whether the initial sound in the following words is voiced or voiceless:
>
> hobbit   mead   vampire   elf   centaur   troll

3.2 The International Phonetic Alphabet

Grounding your conlang in a fictional world and having an idea of how you want it to sound will guide many of your conlanging choices. Whether a language sounds 'musical,' 'harsh' or 'happy' can be conveyed by certain sounds and sound combinations. Before discussing sounds further, however, it is essential to consider how to represent them.

One obvious option is to make use of our writing system. Representing sounds with the letters of the Latin (or Roman) alphabet is referred to as **romanization**. Many conlangs, from Toki Pona to Na'vi, are rendered this way. However, romanization can be problematic since sound–letter correspondences are not always straightforward. For example, letters might be 'silent,' that is, not pronounced (1a–c); two adjacent letters might correspond to one single sound (1d, e); and one single letter might correspond to two sounds (1f).

(1)　　English: Sound–letter discrepancies
    a. dune　　('e' is silent)
    b. knot　　('k' is silent)
    c. plight　　('g,' 'h' are silent)
    d. shire　　('sh' is pronounced as one sound)
    e. moon　　('oo' is pronounced as one sound)
    f. pixie　　('x' is pronounced as two sounds: [k] followed by [s])

> **Your Turn**
>
> Identify the sound–letter discrepancies in the following words:
>
> vampire　hobbit　troll　mead　centaur

To complicate matters further, one letter or letter combination might correspond to multiple sounds in different words. For example, 'th' is pronounced differently in *thin*, *these* and *Thompson*. Conversely, the same sound might be written down using a variety of letters or letter combinations. For example, the underlined letters in *phra__s__e*, *ma__z__e* and *__x__ylophone* are all pronounced in the same way.

In addition, different languages using similar writing systems might pronounce the same letters differently. For example, in English 'v' and 'b' represent different sounds (cf. *van* and *ban*). However, in Spanish, 'v,' 'b' typically sound the same; for most speakers, the verbs *bota* 'bounces' and *vota* 'votes' have identical pronunciations.

Using letters to represent sounds is thus not ideal. A better option to represent sounds is to employ a sound-based alphabet. The most widely used is the **International Phonetic Alphabet (IPA)**, reproduced at the beginning of the book. The IPA features a one-to-one association between symbols and sounds. For example, in IPA [v] and [b] represent the first sounds of English *van* and *ban*, respectively; the initial sound in Spanish words *bota* and *vota* is conveyed as [b]. Further, the first consonants in *thin*, *these* and *Thompson* would be transcribed as [θ], [ð] and [t]. Notice that the brackets around IPA symbols make it clear that we are referring to speech sounds rather than letters; the latter are represented with single quotation marks. The **one-to-one correspondence** between IPA symbols and specific sounds makes it possible to transcribe and refer to sounds consistently and unambiguously in natlangs and conlangs; we will be using this way to represent sounds throughout this book.

3.3 Basic Vowel Articulation

Two main types of sounds are attested in the world's languages: vowels and consonants. **Vowels** are the most open sounds; they are pronounced with a (relatively) open vocal tract. Compare the degree of aperture of your mouth when pronouncing the sounds in the word 'us': the vocal tract is much more open for the vowel than for the consonant. This also explains why when you go to a doctor to get your throat checked, you will never be asked to say 'ssss'!

Vowels are usually voiced; they are also the center of syllables, as we'll see in Chapter 5. Many natlangs have words consisting only of one vowel sound. Examples include *a* in English, *y* 'and' in Spanish and *eau* 'water' in French. Very few languages have syllables or words exclusively composed of a consonant. Thus, [f] cannot be a word in English or in most natlangs.

All vowels are produced by moving the tongue and the lips. Their articulation involves three basic parameters: (i) the vertical placement of the tongue (i.e., vowel **height**), (ii) the front/back position of the tongue (i.e., **vowel advancement**) and (iii) whether the lips are **rounded** or **unrounded** (i.e., **lip rounding**). All are essential in **vowel classification**, discussed below; additional articulatory actions are introduced in Section 3.6. Syllables can have one, two or three vowels sounds, which are referred to as **monophthongs** (as in 'sea'), **diphthongs** (as in 'sky') and **triphthongs**, respectively; an example of the latter, at least for some English speakers, is 'fire.' This chapter focuses mostly on monophthongs; diphthongs and triphthongs are discussed in Chapter 5.

3.3.1 Vowel Height

Vowel height refers to the position of the tongue relative to the palate (the roof of the mouth). Five different height levels are attested in natlangs (Figure 3.2). **High vowels** are pronounced with the tongue close to the palate, as in b*ee*t. In **mid vowels**, the tongue is neither high nor low in the vocal tract, as in the vowel in b*u*t. **Low vowels** are pronounced with the tongue low in the vocal tract, as in b*a*t. **Mid-high** vowels are intermediate between high and mid vowels (as in b*i*n), and **mid-low** vowels are intermediate between mid and low (as in b*e*nt).

It is hard to see the tongue move when pronouncing a vowel, but you can feel the vertical movement of the tongue from high to low (or from

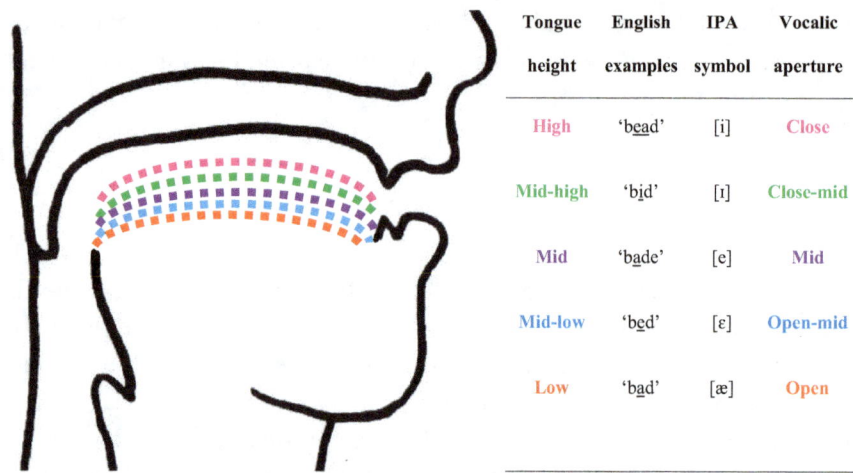

Figure 3.2 Tongue height and vocalic aperture.

low to high) if you place a flat lollipop on your tongue and pronounce each vowel slowly. You will notice that as the tongue goes down in height, the jaw drops and the mouth increasingly opens. High and low vowels are often referred to as **closed** and **open** respectively, referring to the relative opening of the vocal tract.

English is unusual in having all five degrees of vocalic height; most commonly, natlangs distinguish three (high, mid and low, as in Spanish). Natlangs with very few vowels typically just have a contrast between high and low (as in Quechua).

3.3.2   Vowel Advancement

Vowel **advancement** refers to the front or back position of the tongue (Figure 3.3). Natlangs distinguish up to three advancement levels. In **front vowels**, the tongue is in a forward position in the mouth (as in *beet* or *bet*). In **back vowels**, the tongue moves towards the back of the vocal tract (as in *boot* or *bot*). In **central vowels**, the tongue is neither forward nor back. You can feel the relative advancement of the tongue if you place a flat lollipop on your tongue and pronounce the vowels in *boo* and *bee*, or in *bot* and *bet* slowly. A three-way distinction in vowel advancement is common in natlangs.

3.3.3   Lip Rounding

Lip rounding refers to the configuration the lips adopt while articulating a sound. In rounded vowels, lips are rounded (as in *boo*). In unrounded vowels, lips are spread (as in *bee*) or held in a neutral position (as in *but*). Both options are illustrated in Figure 3.4.

3.3 Basic Vowel Articulation

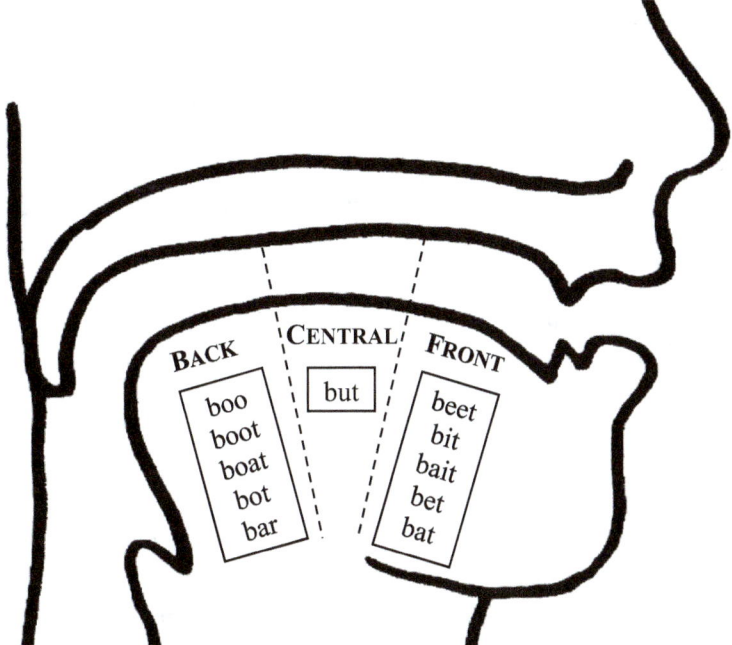

Figure 3.3 Vowel advancement.

Figure 3.4 Lip rounding.

In natlangs, front and central vowels tend to be unrounded, while back vowels tend to be rounded. This is mostly the case in English. One exception is the low back vowel in words like *park*, which is unrounded. In addition, many English speakers do not have lip rounding in the mid-high back vowels of words like *put* or *could*.

3.4 Contrastive Sounds

Sounds are highly variable; speakers do not always pronounce sounds such as [s] or [p] the same way for various reasons, including differences in the size of the vocal tract and dialectal variation, among others. Sound variability does not usually impact communication because speech sounds are the physical manifestation of **phonemes**, that is, contrastive segments that distinguish (but do not carry) meaning.

Let's consider one example. Regardless of whether an [i] sound is longer or shorter, or pronounced by a male or a female, it corresponds to the phoneme /i/ in English (phonemes are conveyed within slanted lines). If we replace [i] by [u] in a word, the meaning changes; cf. *bee* vs. *boo*, *heat* vs. *hoot*. Thus, in English both /i/ and /u/ are contrastive, that is, they are different phonemes.

Word pairs like *bee*/*boo* or *heat*/*hoot* are **minimal pairs**, that is, words with the same number of sounds and different meanings that diverge only in one sound. Other examples of minimal pairs in English include *meet*/*met*, *farm*/*harm* and *troll*/*droll*. **Minimal sets** comprise more than two words of this type, as in *farm*/*harm*/*charm* or *heat*/*hoot*/*hat*. Note that crucially, the sound that differs in minimal pairs and minimal sets needs to be in the same position across words.

> **Your Turn**
>
> a. Are the following minimal pairs in English? Explain why or why not.
>   farm, arm   troll, drill   best, belt   gloom, bloom
> b. Consider the Láadan word sets below (Elgin et al. 2020). Are they minimal sets?
>   [ɑl]   'toilet'   [ɛl]   'to make'   [ɪl]   'to see'
>   [ɛd]   'tool'   [ɪd]   'and then'   [ɪb]   'crime'
> c. Are the following Hawaiian words a minimal set?
>   [kaka] 'to rinse'   [keke] 'turnstone'   [koko] 'blood'

When building your conlang, you need to decide how many phonemes it has. You also need to provide minimal pairs or minimal sets exemplifying these contrasts. Developing minimal sets is also a way to increase your conlang lexicon, as we will see in later chapters.

3.5 How Many Vowels?

Languages have **vocalic inventories**, that is, sets of vowels used contrastively. Considering vowel height, advancement and lip rounding, vocalic inventories can range from two vowels (Yimas) to fourteen (German). The mean number of vowels in an inventory is five, as in Spanish or Hawaiian.

About 51% of natlangs have **average vowel inventories** of five–six vowels. **Small vowel inventories** comprising two–four vowels occur in 16% of natlangs; for example, Cherokee has three vowels and Shipibo-Konibo four. Approximately 33% of languages have **large vowel inventories** of seven–fourteen vowels; many are languages of northwestern Europe, including Danish (eleven vowels) and German (fourteen vowels).

English also has a large vowel inventory; depending on the dialect, it can have up to thirteen contrastive vowels. You might be surprised to learn this; after all, English vowels are written using six letters only ('a, e, i, o, u, y'). Remember, however, that the correspondence between sounds and letters is not perfect in English (or most natlangs). To find out how many vowels contrast in your English dialect, consider the words in (2). Do they correspond to a minimal set?

(2) English word set: vocalic contrasts
     beat   bit   bait   bet   bat   but
     boot   put   boat   bought   bot

Most of the words in (2) will probably constitute a minimal set for you (except for 'put,' since it begins with a different sound). In fact, the words in (2) exemplify a **near-minimal** set, since all words have different meanings, comprise the same number of sounds and have a similar sound structure. In the absence of a perfect minimal set, near-minimal sets are usually appropriate to establish contrasts in a language.

You probably have different vowels sounds for the words in the top row and the first four words in the second row. But if you are a speaker of American English, you might pronounce *bought* and *bot* with the same vowel sound. If you do, you distinguish ten contrastive vowels. If you pronounce *bought* and *bot* with different vowel sounds, you have eleven contrastive vowels.

We can chart the vowels of American English according to their height and advancement, as shown in Table 3.1. Note that high vowels are at the top of the chart, and low vowels at the bottom. In addition, front vowels are on the left-hand side, and back vowels on the right. You can observe also that going from high to low, vowels appear to gradually be less front or back. This reflects the articulatory tendency for vowels to have less extreme tongue advancement as they go down in height. Note also that although not all speakers might always contrast the back low and mid-low vowels in *bot* and *bought*, both are included in the chart; you probably have this contrast in word pairs such as *farm/form* and *park/pork*.

3 Designing Vowel Inventories

Table 3.1 American English vowels

Height	Front	Central	Back
High	/i/ 'beet'		'boot' /u/
Mid-high	/ɪ/ 'bit'		'put' /ʊ/
Mid	/e/ 'bait'	/ə/ 'but', 'cup'	'boat' /o/
Mid-low	/ɛ/ 'bet'		'bought,' 'form' /ɔ/
Low	/æ/ /bat/		'bot,' 'farm' /ɑ/

All front vowels in Table 3.1 are unrounded, and all back vowels rounded. The reason is perceptual: front vowels are more clearly recognized if they lack lip rounding, and the opposite is true for back vowels. The exception is the low back vowel /ɑ/, which is unrounded. Lip rounding is typologically rare for lower vowels, since the downward movement of the jaw involved in lowering the tongue stretches the lips vertically, making it hard for the lips to draw together.

As we mentioned earlier, the number of contrastive vowels differs across English dialects. Table 3.2 lists the contrastive vowels of standard British English (sometimes referred to as RP or received pronunciation). Unlike American English, standard British English has a mid-low unrounded central vowel /ɜ/ in words like *bird*, and a low back rounded vowel /ɒ/ in words like *hot*.

Table 3.2 British English vowels

Height	Front	Central	Back
High	/i/ 'beet'		'boot' /u/
Mid-high	/ɪ/ 'bit'		'put' /ʊ/
Mid	/e/ 'bait'	/ə/ 'but'	'boat' /o/
Mid-low	/ɛ/ 'bet'	/ɜ/ 'bird'	'bought' /ɔ/
Low	/æ/ /bat/		'farm' /ɑ/ /ɒ/ 'bot'

It is interesting that no natlang has more than fourteen basic vowel contrasts, since the combination of five height levels, three advancement levels and two lip position options results in thirty possible vocalic contrasts. We return to this point in Section 3.7.

3.6 Building Vowel Inventories

How are vowel inventories built? Table 3.3 illustrates the most frequent small, average, and large vowel inventories in the world's languages, consisting of three, five and seven vowels, respectively. Table 3.3 depicts tongue height from top to bottom, and advancement from front to back. Can you tell what these three inventories have in common?

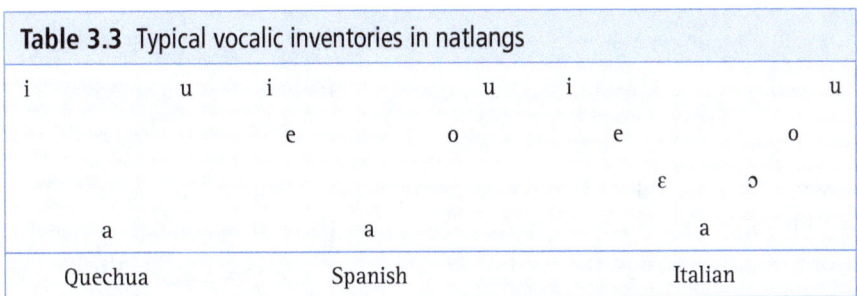

Table 3.3 Typical vocalic inventories in natlangs

i		u	i		u	i			u
			e		o	e			o
							ɛ	ɔ	
a				a			a		
Quechua				Spanish			Italian		

You probably noticed that (i) the vowels in these three inventories tend to be spread apart, and (ii) all have an odd number of vowels. Natlangs tend to maximally disperse vowels in the vowel space, since this has perceptual advantages. In small inventories, this tendency toward **vowel dispersion** results in a preference for **corner vowels** (/i a u/), thus called since they are articulated at the most fronted, lowest and most back position, respectively. In larger inventories, more vowels need to fit in the vocalic space; the front and back dimensions are typically filled before the central area of the vowel space.

The preference for odd-numbered vocalic inventories is connected to a tendency for symmetry across the front/back dimension in the mid and high areas of the vowel space, together with the anchoring of the vowel space by /a/, the lowest, most open vowel.

One of your first conlanging decisions will be the size of the vocalic inventory. Both small and large vocalic inventories are relatively uncommon in natlangs, and either might be a good option for unique or alien conlangs. For example, Dothraki has four vowels, Classical Sindarin has six and Na'vi seven (we'll explore these further in Section 3.7). A small or average vowel inventory might work well for simple or easy to learn conlangs, as in Esperanto, which has five vowels. However, these are only general suggestions; even average-sized vowel inventories can display unique patterns. Consider the two five-vowel inventories in Table 3.4; which one is [something is either unique or it isn't ...] unique?

3 Designing Vowel Inventories

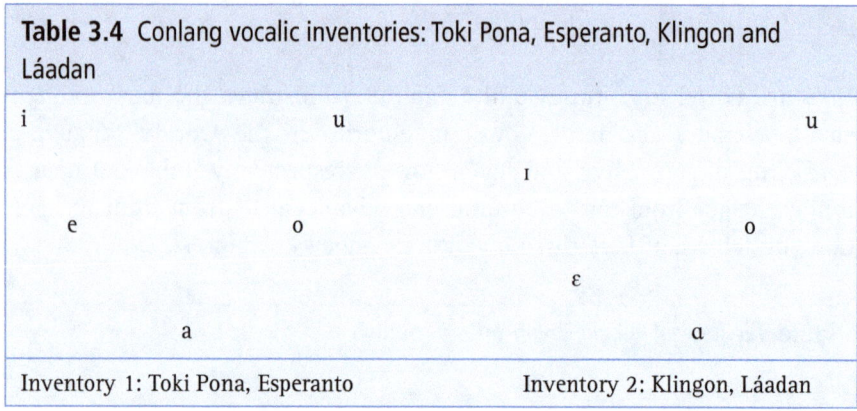

Table 3.4 Conlang vocalic inventories: Toki Pona, Esperanto, Klingon and Láadan

Inventory 1: Toki Pona, Esperanto   Inventory 2: Klingon, Láadan

Inventory 1 in Table 3.4 has three degrees of height and three degrees of advancement. Vowels are dispersed, and there is symmetry across the front/back dimension, with a low central vowel anchor. On the other hand, Inventory 2 has five degrees of height and two degrees of advancement; vowels are dispersed, but there is asymmetry in the front/back dimension. For these reasons, Inventory 2 is unique typologically.

Finally, tonal languages are likely to have larger vowel inventories than non-tonal languages. We will consider tone further in Chapter 6.

3.7 Vowel Frequency

To make your conlang vowel inventory unique, you can exclude some of the vowels in English, include vowels from other natlangs, or both. Some vowels attested in other languages are fronted rounded vowels; these occur in French and Turkish, for example. Both natlangs have a contrastive high, front rounded vowel /y/; it is pronounced like [i] in *beet*, but with lip rounding (try it: while holding the tongue articulation for [i] steady, round your lips; the result is [y]). French also has the rounded mid-front vowel /ø/ (pronounced like /e/ but with lip rounding) (3, 4a).

(3) Contrastive lip rounding in French vowels (Ladefoged & Ferrari Disner 2012)
    a. *lit*   /li/   'bed'   *lu*   /ly/   'read'
    b. *les*   /le/   'the (plural)'   *le*   /lø/   'the (masculine singular)'

(4) Contrastive lip rounding in Turkish vowels (Zimmer & Orgun 1992:44)
    a. /kil/   'clay'   /kyl/   'ashes'
    b. /kul/   'slave'   /kɯl/   'hair'

3.7 Vowel Frequency

Turkish also has a high, back unrounded vowel /ɯ/ (pronounced like /u/, but without lip rounding) (4b); this vowel is also found in Japanese among other languages. To pronounce it, begin with the sound [u] in words like *hoot* or *boot*, and then relax your lips so that they don't become rounded.

> **Your Turn**
>
> Consider the conlang vowel inventories in Table 3.5. How do they differ from typical small, average and large vowel inventories respectively? (Note: ~ indicates variation in pronunciation.)

Table 3.5 Conlang vocalic inventories: Dothraki, Classical Sindarin and Na'vi

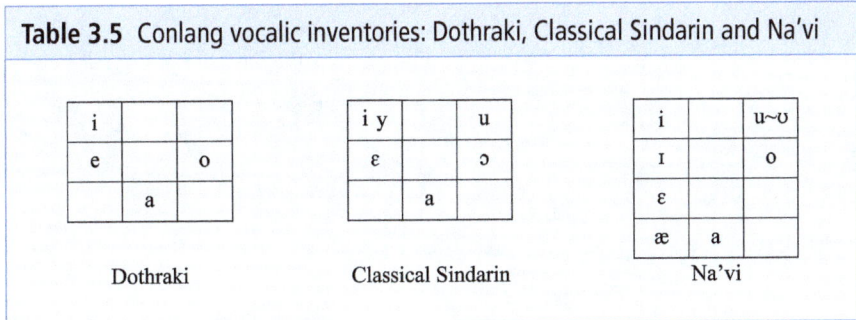

Table 3.6 provides information on the relative frequency in vowels in natlangs since this information can be useful to decide which vowels to include in your conlang. The frequency reported is from the PHOIBLE database, which includes phonological inventories from over 2,100 natlangs. Vowels occurring contrastively in at least 20 percent of natlangs are shaded.

Table 3.6 uses IPA symbols but deviates from the IPA vowel chart (reproduced at the beginning of the book) in a few ways. First, it includes only five levels of height, consistent with the vowel typology discussed in this chapter (the IPA vowel chart implies seven height distinctions; no natlang contrasts so many vowel heights). /æ/ and /ɐ/ are classified as low, and /a/ as central. The IPA does not specify rounding for /ɐ/, but PHOIBLE considers it as round, so it is included here as the rounded counterpart of /a/.

As you can see, the five most widely attested vowels in natlangs are /i u a e o/; these occur in at least 60% of natlangs. Next are /ɛ ɔ/, found in over a third of languages, and the mid central vowel [ə] (called 'schwa'), present in over 20% of natlangs. /ɨ ɪ ʊ/ are less frequent (16%–14% of natlangs). All other vowels occur in less than 7% of natlangs. **Peripheral vowels** (i.e., those that define the borders of the vowel space) are overall more frequent that central vowels, which are harder to perceive.

Table 3.6 Contrastive vowels and frequency in natlangs (based on Moran & McCloy 2019)

	Front		Central		Back	
	Unrounded	Rounded	Unrounded	Rounded	Unrounded	Rounded
High	i 92%	y 6%	ɨ 16%	ʉ 2%	ɯ 6%	u 88%
Mid-high	ɪ 15%	ʏ 1%	ɘ 1%	ɵ 1%		ʊ 14%
Mid	e 61%	ø 3%	ə 22%		ɤ 3%	o 60%
Mid-low	ɛ 37%	œ 3%	ɜ 1%	ɞ >1%	ʌ 4%	ɔ 35%
Low	æ 7%	ɶ >1%	a 86%	ɐ 2%	ɑ 7%	ɒ 2%

3.8 Additional Vowel Contrasts

Vowels differ in their tongue height, advancement and lip rounding. In natlangs, most vowels are voiced (i.e., pronounced with vocal fold vibration), **short** and **oral** (i.e., released through the oral tract). However, vowels can also be long, nasal and/or voiceless. We examine these 'not so basic' vowel contrasts next.

3.8.1 Duration

Around 30 percent of natlangs use **duration** to contrast vowels, distinguishing between **short (regular)** and **long vowels**, which are 1.5–3 times longer. One example is Korean (5); note that the IPA diacritic (symbol) [ː] after a sound indicates that it is long. Long vowels in Korean and other natlangs tend to be more peripheral than short vowels; the reason is that long vowels are held longer and thus pronounced with more articulatory effort.

(5)   Korean vowels (Lee 1999:121)
         a. /mal/   'horse'   /maːl/   'speech'
         b. /bʌl/   'punishment'   /bʌːl/   'bee'

Languages can use duration to contrast all vowels (as in Latin, which had five short vowels and five corresponding long vowels) or just a subset of vowels. Corner vowels tend to contrast in duration in about a third of natlangs; other long vowels are less common (Table 3.7). Note that all long vowels occurring in at least 10 percent of natlangs are peripheral.

3.8 Additional Vowel Contrasts

Table 3.7 Most common long vowels in natlangs (based on Moran & McCloy 2019)

Vowel	%	Vowel	%
iː	32	əː	4
aː	30	ɑː	3
uː	29	ɪː	3
eː	21	ʊː	3
oː	21	ïː	3
ɛː	11	æː	3
ɔː	10	yː	2

Table 3.8 Short vs. long: possible and impossible vowel inventories

i		u	i iː		u uː	iː		uː
e		o	e eː		o oː	eː		oː
	a			a aː			aː	
✓ Short vowels only			✓ Both short and long vowels			✗ Long vowels only		

Including long vowels in your inventory is one way to increase the number of contrastive vowels and to make your conlang unique. It is important to note, however, that while all natlangs have short vowels in their inventory, there are no languages that have only long vowels. This is probably because long vowels involve more articulatory effort than short vowels. Possible and non-possible inventories regarding vowel duration are outlined in Table 3.8, taking as an example a five-vowel inventory.

Duration in Conlanging

Like Latin, Quenya contrasts long and short vowels: /a e i o u/, /aː eː iː oː uː/. One example of a minimal pair is *cu* /ku/ 'dove' and *cú* /kuː/ 'crescent' (Fauskanger 2002:44). Short mid vowels are somewhat more open than their long counterparts, which means that the former can probably be transcribed as /ɛ ɔ/. This is consistent with the tendency for long vowels to be (more) peripheral than short vowels in natlangs.

High Valyrian also uses vowel duration, distinguishing /a e i y o u/ from /aː eː iː yː oː uː/. One example of a minimal pair is [kelin] 'I stop' vs. [keːlin] 'herd of cats' (Peterson 2015:44). This durational contrast was lost in modern Valyrian.

3.8.2 Nasality

The vowels we have described so far are **oral**, that is, they are realized with air released through the mouth. About a quarter of natlangs have **nasal vowels**, that is, vowels pronounced with air released through the oral and nasal cavities simultaneously. Examples of contrastive nasal and oral vowels in French are given below; the diacritic [˜] indicates that a sound is nasal.

(6) French vowels
    a. /pɛ/   *paix*   'peace'   /pɛ̃/   *pain*   'bread'
    b. /lɛ/   *laid*   'ugly'   /lɛ̃/   *lin*   'linen'

English does not contrast oral and nasal vowels, but vowels are nasalized in some contexts, as in the word 'Ann' (which would be transcribed [æ̃n]). Likewise, in some dialects of Spanish, particularly in the Caribbean, speakers often nasalize vowels in words such as *pan* [pãn] 'bread.'

Natlangs might have an equal number of contrastive oral and nasal vowels, as in Sedang, or just a subset of nasal vowels; this is the case in Portuguese, which has nine contrastive oral vowels, but only five nasal ones. The most common nasal vowels in natlangs are shown in Table 3.9. Note that the nasal vowels occurring in at least 15 percent of natlangs are corner vowels.

Table 3.9 also shows that natlangs can have long nasal vowels. One natlang that contrasts vowels in both duration and **nasality** is Apurinã. This language has twenty phonemic vowels: five short oral /i e ɨ a o/; five short nasal /ĩ ẽ ɨ̃ ã õ/; five long oral /i: e: ɨ: a: o:/ and five long nasal /ĩ: ẽ: ɨ̃: ã: õ:/ (Hajek 2013).

Including nasal vowels is another way to make your conlang vowel inventory unique. It is important to note, however, that while all natlangs

Table 3.9 Most common nasal vowels in natlangs (based on Moran & McCloy 2019)

Vowel	%	Vowel	%
ĩ	18	ɨ̃	4
ã	17	ɪ̃	3
ũ	16	ĩ:	3
õ	11	ũ:	3
ẽ	11	ʊ̃	3
ɛ̃	8	ɔ̃	3
ɔ̃	8	ã:	3

have oral vowels in their inventory, there are no languages that have only nasal vowels. The reason is that nasal vowels are more articulatorily complex and harder to perceive than oral vowels. Possible and non-possible vowel inventories regarding vowel nasality are outlined in Table 3.10.

Table 3.10 Oral and nasal vowels: possible and impossible vowel inventories

i	u	i ĩ	u ũ	ĩ	ũ
e	o	e ẽ	o õ	ẽ	õ
a		a ã		ã	
✓ Oral vowels only		✓ Both oral and nasal vowels		✗ Nasal vowels only	

3.8.3 Voice Quality

Voice quality refers to phonation, that is, the action of the vocal folds involved in the pronunciation of speech sounds. All natlangs have voiced (or **modal**) vowels, produced with regular vocal fold vibration. Some natlangs also have **non-modal** vowels involving different actions of the vocal folds. Within these we can distinguish voiceless, creaky and **breathy** vowels.

Voiceless or **whispered vowels** are pronounced without vocal fold vibration. Contrastive voiceless vowels are found only in a handful of natlangs, including Ik and Dafla. Voicelessness is transcribed in IPA with a circle under the relevant segment: [̥]. The most frequent voiceless vowels are /i̥ u̥/ – each is attested in five natlangs only.

Creaky vowels are pronounced with increased tension in the vocal folds. They are transcribed in IPA with a wavy line below the segment [̰]. The most frequent creaky vowels in natlangs are /a̰ ḭ ḛ ṵ o̰/; each occurs in 1 percent of natlangs. Natlangs that contrast creaky and voiced vowels include Jalapa Mazatec (7); the accent mark over the vowel indicates high tone.

(7) Creaky vowels in Jalapa Mazatec (Ladefoged & Maddieson 1996:317)
/já/ 'tree' /já̰/ 'he wears'

Breathy vowels, also known as **murmured vowels**, are pronounced with lax vocal folds, resulting in a sigh-like quality. They are transcribed with a dieresis under the relevant sound [̈]. The most frequent breathy vowels are /o̤ i̤ ṳ e̤ ɔ̤ a̤ ɛ̤/; each occurs in 1 percent of natlangs. Natlangs that contrast breathy and modal vowels include Gujarati (8).

(8) Breathy vowels in Gujarati (Ladefoged & Ferrari Disner 2012; Esposito et al. 2012)
/mɛl/ 'dirt' /mɛ̤l/ 'palace'
/baɾ/ 'outside' /ba̤ɾ/ 'twelve'

Although English lacks contrastive non-modal vowels, in certain contexts, vowels can be pronounced as voiceless (e.g., the first vowel in *potato*, which is pronounced voiceless since it's surrounded by voiceless consonants), creaky (e.g., the word *bye* at the end of a conversation; creaky voice can indicate the end of a conversational turn) or breathy (e.g., the first vowel in the word *darling*, for some speakers).

Including contrastive non-modal vowels in your inventory will certainly make your conlang sound unique, since they are so rare crosslinguistically. As with long and nasal vowels, all natlangs have modal vowels in their inventory, but only some have non-modal vowels as well. This is probably because non-modal vowels are harder to perceive than modal ones. Table 3.11 illustrates possible modal/non-modal vowel inventories, focusing on creaky vowels (inventories with other non-modal vowels would work in similar ways).

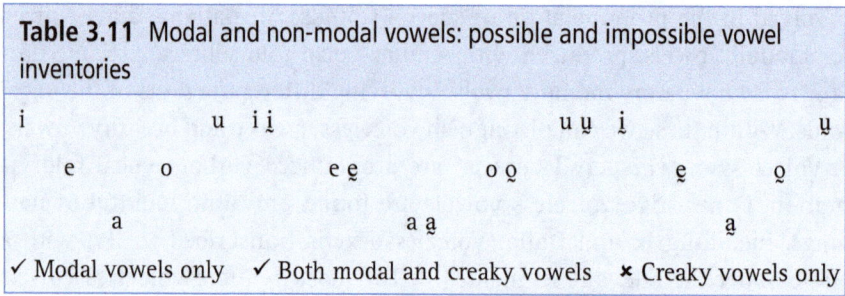

Table 3.11 Modal and non-modal vowels: possible and impossible vowel inventories

i		u	i ḭ			u ṵ	ḭ		ṵ
e		o	e ḛ		o o̰		ḛ		o̰
	a		a a̰				a̰		

✓ Modal vowels only   ✓ Both modal and creaky vowels   ✗ Creaky vowels only

DID YOU KNOW?

Sedang is the natlang with most contrastive vowels (24). It has seven voiced vowels /a ɛ e i ɔ o u/, seven nasal vowels /ã ɛ̃ ẽ ĩ ɔ̃ õ ũ/ and seven creaky vowels /a̰ ɛ̰ ḛ ḭ ɔ̰ o̰ ṵ/, in addition to three nasal creaky vowels /ḭ̃ ã̰ õ̰/.

3.9 Conlanging Tips

This chapter has gone over different options to build vowel inventories. While all languages have contrastive oral, short, voiced vowels involving a specific tongue height, advancement, and action of the lips, some natlangs also include vocalic contrasts involving duration, nasality and voice quality; these options are summarized in Figure 3.5. The information covered here does not exhaust all possible contrastive vowel types in natlangs.

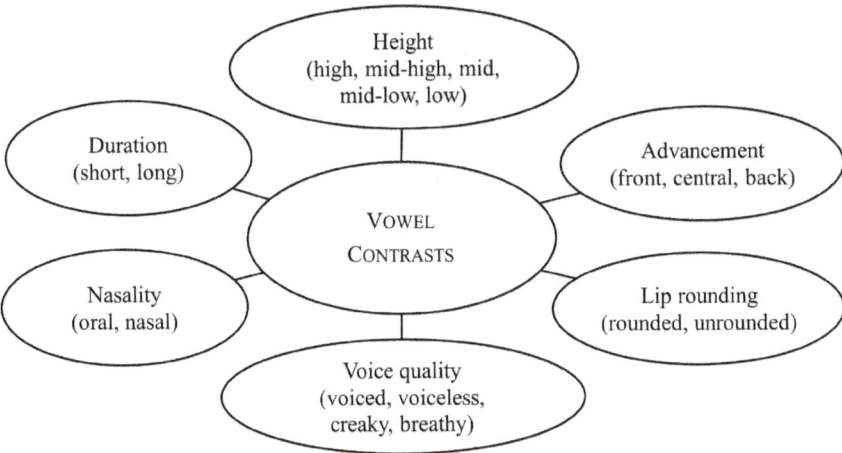

Figure 3.5 Possible vowel contrasts

If you are interested in exploring this topic further, you can check the resources listed at the end of the chapter.

Throughout this chapter, we have discussed frequency of occurrence of vowels in natlangs as a way to make your conlang unique. As you build your vowel inventory, it is important to mention that contrastive vowels tend to occur in sets regarding characteristics such as tongue height or advancement. For example, a typical five-vowel inventory such as that of Spanish (/a e i o u/) includes two front unrounded and two back rounded vowels. The inventory /a e y o u/ is not as naturalistic, since not all front vowels pattern similarly for rounding.

You might want to convey a specific sound quality in your conlang; one way to do this is to use specific vowels (consonants can also contribute to sound quality, as we will see in Chapter 4). Front vowels such as /e/ or /i/ are usually perceived as 'brighter' and back vowels such as /o/ or /u/ as 'darker.' Perhaps your inventory will favor front or back vowels depending on the effect you want to convey, or will feature both for balance. In any case, if you are unsure of how many vocalic contrasts to include, you can start with a few and add or revise them later. If so, remember to update your vowel chart and any words you have created in your conlang.

3.10 Conlanging Practice: The Languages of Ur

A. In your opinion, which vowel/vowel characteristics could help create the following effects?
- Smallness
- Cuteness

- Ugliness
- Raspiness
- Secrecy
- Elegance

B. Indicate which of the vowel inventories in Table 3.12 would fit well with any of the Ur languages (Aqua, Gem, Grass, Fog). Check your answers to 1.7; you can add or remove vowels to one or more of these inventories if you would like. Design an additional vowel inventory for the remaining Ur language.

Table 3.12 Possible vowel inventories for the Ur languages

i i:		u u:	i ḭ		u ṵ	i ĩ		u ũ
e e:		o o:	e ḛ		o o̰	e ẽ		o õ
	a a:			a a̰			a ã	
Long and short vowels			Voiced and creaky vowels			Oral and nasal vowels		

C. Ur has a small, inhabited moon. From Ur, this moon looks like a great ball of pink, because for centuries, the Moon people have grown a pink flower similar to the Earth rose at a great scale (legend has it that this started after the visit of a child prince from another planet, many ages ago). The Moon people are also great historians and storytellers. They spend most of their time watching the people of Ur, recording what they do and inventing stories about them. Moon people are in close contact with the Fog people, but they like the Grass people the best.

> What do you imagine the Moon language sounds like – lyrical, harsh, happy?

Some of the consonants in the Moon language are /s m f/. This language has a small vowel inventory of four contrastive vowels; one of them is /i/. In addition, the Moon language has four contrastive long vowels and four contrastive nasal vowels.

- What other three oral vowels are contrastive in Moon? Chart the four basic vowels. How is this system typical or atypical crosslinguistically?
- Add the long vowel counterparts to the chart (remember to use IPA conventions!).

- Include the nasal vowel counterparts in the chart as well.
- Provide minimal pairs or sets showcasing the contrastive vowels of this language (try to include all vowel contrasts; include the meaning for each word as well. You can use words that consist of one single vowel; or you can also use consonants /s m f/).
- Are any of the aspects of the vowel inventory in Moon related to a particular sound quality or to any characteristics of the fictional world? (You can 'fill-in' details about Moon culture, history, etc. as needed.)

3.11 Vowels in the Salt Language

The Salt language has a larger than average vocalic inventory, with nine basic contrastive vowels (Table 3.13). It contrasts three heights (high, mid, low) and three degrees of advancement (front, central, back). Note that vowels are spread out across the vowel space and occur in sets for advancement and height. Also, front vowels are unrounded, and back vowels rounded, except for /ɑ/.

Table 3.13 Contrastive vowels in the Salt language

	Front	Central	Back
High	i	ɨ	u
Mid	e	ə	o
Low	æ	a	ɑ

Because this inventory is larger than average, I do not feel a pressing need to include contrasts in duration, nasality or phonation, although I keep an open mind and I might reconsider this choice as I continue developing the language.

Minimal pairs exemplifying some of these contrasts are given in (9); note that they imply the consonants /k s t n m/ are present in the language (as we will see in Chapter 4). If you are not yet sure of which consonants you will include in your conlang, you can either think of words composed only of one vowel or wait until the next chapter to build minimal pairs.

(9) Minimal pairs in Salt
    a. /num/ 'to go' /nem/ 'below'
    b. /kost/ 'to understand' /kust/ 'salt, life force'

3.12 Guide to Developing Your Conlang Vowels

- What type of sound effect (if any) would you like your conlang to convey?
- Will your vowel inventory lean toward uniqueness or simplicity?
- List the basic vowel contrasts (tongue height, advancement, lip rounding) (see the resources listed at the end of the chapter for links to clickable IPA charts).
- List any contrasts in duration.
- List any contrasts in nasality.
- List any contrasts in voice quality.
- Do any of these vocalic contrasts relate to a specific sound effect?
- Draw a vowel chart with the contrastive vowels in your conlang (in IPA). If your inventory is asymmetric or features unusual vocalic patterns, indicate why this is the case.
- If there are contrastive long, nasal or non-modal vowels, you can also include them in the chart (see Tables 3.5–3.8 for examples).
- If your conlang has words consisting of only one vowel, transcribe them in IPA and indicate their meanings using quotation marks. For example, in Spanish we have the following minimal set:

    /i/   'and'   [a]   'to'   [o]   'or'

3.13 Conventions and Diacritics Introduced in This Chapter

Sounds are indicated with	[ ]	Phonemes are indicated with	/ /
Long sounds are transcribed	[ː]	Nasal vowels are transcribed	[˜]
Voiceless vowels are transcribed	[̥]	Glottalized vowels are transcribed	[̰]
Breathy vowels are transcribed	[̈]		

To Learn More

Many excellent resources on the IPA and the sounds of the world's languages can be found online. To listen to the different sounds of the world's languages and visualize their articulation using MRI, ultrasound and in some cases animation, go to Seeing Speech: www.seeingspeech.ac.uk/ (Lawson et al. 2018). Another great source providing real-time MRI videos of IPA sounds of the IPA is the SAIL (Signal Analysis and Interpretation Laboratory) database at the University of Southern California (https://sail

.usc.edu/span/rtmri_ipa/). Toutios et al. (2016) provides more information about this resource.

The 2020 version of the IPA chart is provided at the front of the book for reference. There are several options to type IPA symbols into your documents. One is to download a free, Unicode compliant IPA font such as IPA Doulos and add it to the font library of your computer (https://software.sil.org/doulos/). Another is to use online IPA keyboards such as Typeit (https://ipa.typeit.org/) or Lexilogos (www.lexilogos.com/keyboard/ipa.htm). A third option is to use the interactive resource from the International Phonetic Association, which permits you to both transcribe and listen to IPA sounds: www.internationalphoneticassociation.org/IPAcharts/inter_chart_2018/IPA_2018.html.

You can also download the free IPA phonetics app in your phone (see Coey et al. 2014 for more information). For information about vowels in natlangs, see chapter 8 in Maddieson (1984), chapter 9 in Ladefoged and Maddieson (1996) and Maddieson (2013a, b) and Hajek (2013) in the *World Atlas of Language Structures* (WALS). Many of the natlang examples in this chapter can be listened to at the UCLA Phonetics Lab Archive (http://phonetics.ucla.edu/) where you can search by language or by sound. The PHOIBLE database is very useful for exploring sound frequency and inventories in natlangs (Moran & McCloy 2019). The vowel chart for American English in Table 3.1 is based on Zsiga (2024:29), with the difference that the contrastive central vowel is rendered here as /ə/ rather than /ʌ/. This aligns better with IPA conventions (since [ʌ] stands for a mid-low back unrounded vowel, and [ə] for a mid-central unrounded one). For a detailed discussion of the transcription and contrastive status of central vowels in English, see Edwards (2003:246–269). We'll discuss English central vowels further in connection to stress in Chapter 6. Additional sources mentioned in this chapter are listed in the reference section at the end of this book.

4 Designing Consonant Inventories

This chapter focuses on choosing the contrastive consonants for your conlang. We begin by describing how consonants are pronounced (Section 4.1) before previewing consonantal inventories (Section 4.2). Section 4.3 discusses additional ways in which consonants can contrast, and Section 4.4 provides some tips in selecting consonants for your conlang. Section 4.5 includes conlanging practice, and Section 4.6 describes the consonants of the Salt language. The chapter ends with a guided set of questions to help you design your consonant inventory (Section 4.7) and offers a list of resources to explore further.

Key Words

Airstream mechanism
   Egressive
   Glottalic
   Ingressive
   Non-pulmonic
   Pulmonic
   Velaric
     Accompaniment
     Clicks
     Ejectives
     Implosives
Allophone
Articulators
   Active
   Passive
Consonant inventory
Consonants
Geminates (long consonants)
Manner of articulation
   Obstruents
     Affricate
     Fricative

    Sibilant
    Stop (plosive)
Phonation type
  Aspiration
  Breathy voice
  Creaky voice (Glottalization)
Phono-aesthetics
Place of articulation
  Alveolar
  Bilabial
  Coronal
  Dental
  Dorsal
  Epiglottal
  Glottal
  Interdental
  Labial
  Labiodental
  Labio-velar
  Laryngeal
  Radical
  Palatal
  Pharyngeal
  Post-alveolar (palato-alveolar; alveo-palatal)
  Retroflex
  Uvular
  Velar
Secondary articulation
  Labialization
  Palatalization
  Pharyngealization
  Velarization
Sonorants
  Approximant
  Central
  Lateral
  Nasal
  Rhotic
  Tap
  Trill

Voicing
Voiced consonants
Voiceless consonants

4.1 The Basics of Consonant Articulation

If vowels are the most open speech sounds, **consonants** are the most constricted. They typically precede or follow the nucleus in a syllable (a point we take up in Chapter 5). While vowels are classified by lip rounding and tongue height and advancement, consonants are distinguished by the degree and specific location of the narrowing in the vocal tract.

The parts of the vocal tract involved in phonation and articulation were shown in Figure 3.1. For some consonants, like [b] or [f], the lower lip moves toward the upper lip or teeth to produce a constriction. For others, a specific part of the tongue reaches toward the teeth (as in _th_espian), the roof of the mouth (as in [t] or [k]) and even the pharynx. Figure 4.1 shows a front view of the parts of the tongue most often involved in consonant articulation. For some consonants, the **articulator** is the larynx (as in [h]). Articulators that move toward others are **active articulators**; otherwise, they are **passive articulators**.

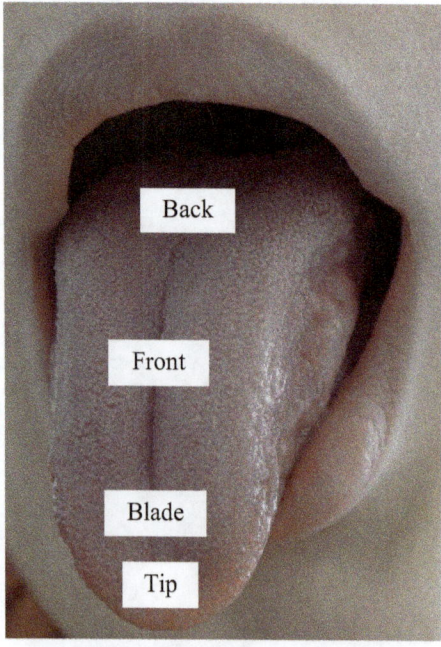

Figure 4.1 Front view of the tongue. Adapted from a picture by Lezlie Rewatch. Public domain.

Consonants contrast in **voicing**, **manner of articulation** (i.e., degree of vocal tract constriction), and **place of articulation** (i.e., the area where the constriction takes place). These are usually referred to as 'basic articulatory dimensions.' We will explore additional dimensions of consonantal contrast in Section 4.3.

4.1.1 Voicing

Voiced consonants are produced with vocal fold vibration, and **voiceless consonants** without. **Consonant inventories** tend to have both; for example, in English the consonants /f/ and /v/ (*fan*, *van*) and /s/ and /z/ (*seal*, *zeal*) differ in **voicing**. You can easily tell when a consonant is voiced if you place a finger on your Adam's apple while pronouncing it. For [v] or [z] there is vocal fold vibration, unlike for [f] or [s].

4.1.2 Manner of Articulation

Consonantal constrictions can be of different types. The most constricted is the **stop** or **plosive**, achieved when two articulators come in contact and temporarily stop airflow. This airflow builds up behind the constriction; when the obstruction is released, a small burst of air can be heard. This is what happens when you pronounce [p]: your lips come together, stopping airflow briefly before releasing it. /p t k/ are contrastive stops in English, as demonstrated by the minimal trio *pin, tin, kin*. So are /b d g/ (*boon, dune, goon*). /p t k/ are voiceless, while /b d g/ are voiced.

Fricatives involve partial obstruction; the articulators come near, narrowing the vocal tract so that airflow becomes turbulent. Examples of fricatives in English include /f v/ (*fan, van*), /s z/ (*Sue, zoo*) and /ʃ ʒ/ (*assure, azure*). English also contrasts /θ ð/ (*think, though*) and /h/ (*hobbit*). Notice that when articulating these consonants, air flows uninterruptedly until you run out of air or move on to the next sound.

Some consonants are pronounced with complete obstruction followed by narrowing of the vocal tract. These are **affricates**, combining a stop and a fricative phase. Contrastive affricates in English include voiceless /tʃ/ (*chin*) and voiced /dʒ/ (*jinn*). If you pronounce both consonants slowly, you will notice the tip of the tongue making complete contact with the **palato-alveolar** region, and then lowering slightly. This creates a narrowing through which air flows turbulently.

Nasals are pronounced with complete obstruction in the oral tract and opening of the nasal tract, which permits air to flow through the nose. The opening of the nasal tract is accomplished by lowering the uvula (we'll come back to this point in Section 4.1.3). Pronounce the sound [n]: halfway through, pinch your nose while maintaining the oral tract closure. Pinching your nose stops airflow, which shows the sound is nasal. English contrasts three nasals: /m n ŋ/ (as in su*m*, su*n*, su*ng*); /ŋ/ only occurs word-finally (as in wi*ng*) and word-medially (as in hu*ng*er).

Approximants are pronounced with hardly any constriction, allowing air to flow relatively unobstructed (almost but not quite as much as for a vowel). English has four contrastive approximants /j w ɹ l/: as in the minimal set *y*ou, *w*oo, *r*oo and *l*oo (if you are wondering, *roo* is used informally in Australian English to refer to a kangaroo; and *loo* refers to the bathroom in British English). /j w ɹ/ are **central approximants** since air flows through the center of the mouth. On the other hand, [l] is a **lateral approximant** (or lateral for short) since it involves an obstruction in the middle of the vocal tract and an opening in one or both sides of the tongue. Pronounce an [l] and then draw air in; you will feel one or both sides of the tongue cooling, which shows that the air flows freely in that area.

Stops, fricatives and affricates are **obstruents**, that is, they involve a significant constriction in the vocal tract. Obstruents tend to be voiceless; in fact, if a language has voiced obstruents, it usually has voiceless obstruents as well, but not the other way around. For example, there are natlangs that have /p t k/, and natlangs that contrast /p t k/ with their voiced counterparts /b d g/; but there are almost no languages that have /b d g/ exclusively. Nasals, approximants and laterals are **sonorants**; they permit airflow to flow relatively unimpeded. Sonorants tend to be voiced. If a language has voiceless sonorants, it will have voiced sonorants as well, but not the other way around. Thus, there are natlangs that have /m n/, and natlangs that contrast both /m n/ and their voiceless counterparts /m̥ n̥/; but there are no natlangs that have /m̥ n̥/ exclusively. These are important generalizations to consider when deciding which contrastive consonants to include (or exclude) in your conlang.

English has twenty-four contrastive consonants, as shown in Table 4.1. Note that **manner of articulation** is rendered in rows. When two consonants

Table 4.1 Contrastive consonants in English

	Bilabial	Labio-dental	(Inter)dental	Alveolar	Post-alveolar	Palatal	Velar	Glottal
Stop	p b			t d			k g	
Fricative		f v	θ ð	s z	ʃ ʒ			h
Affricate					tʃ dʒ			
Nasal	m			n			ŋ	
Approximant	(w)			ɹ		j	(w)	
Lateral				l				

share a cell, the one to the left is voiceless, and the one to the right is voiced. Columns indicate place of articulation, which we cover in Section 4.1.3. Obstruents are indicated with shading.

> **Your Turn**
>
> How many more consonants than vowels does English have?

Natlangs can contrast a few additional manners, including **taps** and **trills**. **Taps** are pronounced with a fast contact ('tapping') of one articulator against another, creating a very brief obstruction. Taps occur contrastively in Spanish, as in *mo*r*a* 'blackberry' or *ce*r*a* 'wax.' This sound, transcribed [ɾ], occurs non-contrastively in American English and other dialects as a variant of /t d/ in words like *ci*t*y* or *play*d*ough*.

Trills involve a series of fast contacts of one articulator against another, with brief openings in between. Spanish is well known for its contrastive trill in the **alveolar** region – transcribed /r/ – in words like *tierra* 'land' or *risa* 'laugh.' Scottish English and other English dialects pronounce 'r' as a trill rather than as an approximant. Klingon, Esperanto, Dothraki, Kēlen and Quenya have contrastive trills. Taps and trills don't involve a significant constriction in the vocal tract and thus are considered sonorant.

Sibilants and **rhotics** are not manners of articulation but refer to specific groups of sounds with shared articulatory and perceptual characteristics. Sibilants are fricatives and affricates that sound like 's,' and rhotics are r-like sounds (regardless of their specific manner of articulation). Sibilants are obstruents, and rhotics are sonorant.

> **DID YOU KNOW?**
>
> There is a famous *Avatar* scene where Neytiri is grilling Jake Sully about the names of body parts in Na'vi. For 'eye' [naɾi], Jake pronounces 'r' as an approximant [ɹ], as in English, rather than as a tap, which bothers Neytiri immensely.
>
> I like this scene because it features a Na'vi sound perceived by a non-native Na'vi speaker through the prism of his first language (English). Both [ɾ] and [ɹ] are rhotics, but they have different manners of articulation. While taps are frequent in natlangs, approximant 'r' is very rare. It occurs in about 5 percent of natlangs, although it is also found in another natlang spoken by millions: Chinese.

4.1.3 Place of Articulation

Let's now consider the locations of consonant constriction in the vocal tract. The most common **places of articulation** are shown with numbered arrows in Figure 4.2; most of them are found in English, as we'll see next. In this figure, note that the uvula is shown in two different positions: lowered (in grey) for nasal sounds, and raised against the pharynx wall (marked in dashed lines) for oral sounds, which forces air to go through the oral cavity.

Numbered arrows (1, 2) in Figure 4.2 comprise **labial** consonants, that is, pronounced with a constriction at the lips. **Bilabial** consonants involve both lips, while in **labiodentals** the lower lip moves toward the upper teeth. In English, /p b m/ are bilabial and /f v/ are labiodental. Two bilabial consonants of note in the world's languages are [ʙ], a voiced bilabial trill (which many children use to convey the sound of cars or trucks) and the voiceless bilabial fricative [ɸ], which sounds very similar to [f] but is pronounced by drawing both lips close. The latter is contrastive in Kēlen.

Numbered arrows (3–6) in Figure 4.2 involve **coronal** consonants, that is, pronounced with a constriction involving the tip or blade of the tongue. **Interdentals** are pronounced with the tip of the tongue between the teeth.

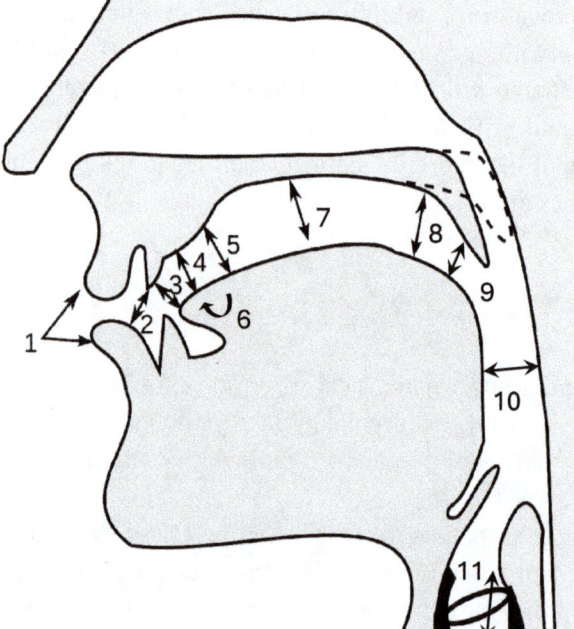

Labial consonants
1. Bilabial
2. Labiodental

Coronal consonants
3. (Inter)dental
4. Alveolar
5. Post-alveolar
6. Retroflex

Dorsal consonants
7. Palatal
8. Velar
9. Uvular

Radical consonants
10. Pharyngeal

Laryngeal consonants
11. Glottal

Figure 4.2 Main places of articulation. Adapted from a diagram from Tavin. https://commons.wikimedia.org/wiki/File:PlaceOfArticulation.svg
Licensed under the Creative Commons Attribution 3.0 Unported license.

If the tongue tip is behind the upper teeth, the consonant is considered **dental**. In English, /ð θ/ are classified as dental but are variably pronounced as interdental; do you pronounce them as dental or interdental in words such as *thought* or *these*? In Spanish, 't, d' are dental; they are often transcribed as /t̪ d̪/ (the IPA diacritic [̪], which resembles a tooth, indicates that a consonant is dental). /θ/ in North-Central Spain is interdental. These three phonemes contrast in some Spanish dialects, as shown in (1). Dothraki contrasts five dental consonants: /d̪ t̪ θ n̪ l̪/.

(1) Dentals and interdentals in North-Central Peninsular Spanish
    a. *ten*   /t̪en/   'have (imperative)'
    b. *den*   /d̪en/   'they give (present subjunctive)'
    c. *zen*   /θen/   'zen'

Alveolars are pronounced with the tongue tip toward the alveolar ridge (the small, curved area between your upper teeth and the hard palate). Six consonants in English are alveolar: /t d s z l ɹ/. How do you pronounce the middle consonant in *pizza* or *mozzarella*? It is very likely that you pronounce it as an alveolar voiceless affricate, transcribed [ts]. In English, [ts] occurs in a few Italian borrowings, but this sound is used contrastively in about a fifth of natlangs, and in conlangs such as Na'vi and Esperanto.

Although /ɹ/ can be classified as alveolar in English, for many speakers it is **retroflex**, that is, pronounced by curling the tongue tip backwards. Hindi and other languages have several contrastive retroflex consonants, including the voiced and voiceless retroflex stops /ɖ ʈ/ (2). Klingon has two retroflex consonants: /ɖ/ (romanized as 'D') and voiceless fricative /ʂ/ (romanized as 'S').

(2) Hindi: retroflex consonants (http://phonetics.ucla.edu/vowels/chapter12/hindi.html)
    a. /ɖal/   'lentil'   /ɖal/   'branch'
    b. /ʈal/   'rhythm'   /ʈal/   'postpone'

Post-alveolars (aka **palato-alveolars** or **alveo-palatals**) involve the movement of the tongue tip towards the area between the alveolar ridge and the hard palate. English has both voiced and voiceless palato-alveolar fricatives (/ʃ/ in *assure*; /ʒ/ in *azure*) and affricates (/tʃ/ in *chain*, /dʒ/ in *gem*). Ithkuil has six palato-alveolar consonants: /ʃ ʒ tʃ dʒ/ (as in English) and /tʃʰ tʃ'/, which we discuss in Section 4.4.

Numbered arrows 7–9 in Figure 4.2 encompass **dorsal** consonants, that is, consonants involving a constriction made by the back (or dorsum) of the tongue. **Palatals** are pronounced with the tongue body toward the hard palate. English has only one contrastive palatal, /j/ as in *yellow* or *yeet*.

However, some speakers pronounce the middle consonant of *million* as a voiced palatal lateral [ʎ] in fast speech, and the middle consonant of *onion* as the voiced palatal nasal [ɲ]. [ʎ] is contrastive in Italian; it is found in words like *foglie* 'leaves' and *aglio* 'garlic,' while /ɲ/ is contrastive in French (*agneau* 'lamb') and Spanish (*año* 'year'). Palatals are well represented in conlangs. For example, Ithkuil has both /j/ and its voiceless counterpart /ç/, and Kēlen contrasts /c ç ʎ ɲ/.

In **velars**, the tongue body rises toward the soft palate (velum). English has three contrastive velars /k g ŋ/, as in *rack*, *rag* and *rang*. Many languages, including Scotts Gaelic and German, have a voiceless velar fricative /x/. This sound is found in English words borrowed from German, as in *Bach* or *Mach*. If you are an *Outlander* fan, you might have heard it in the pronunciation of the Scottish word *Sassenach* [sasənax], meaning 'English person.' Many conlangs contrast velar consonants. For example, Dothraki has /k g x/, and Klingon contrasts /x/ (romanized as 'H'), /ŋ/ (romanized as 'ng') and the voiced velar fricative /ɣ/ (romanized as 'gh').

It's time now to address /w/, which was enclosed within parentheses at both the bilabial and velar regions in Table 4.1. The reason is that /w/ is **labio-velar**, that is, it involves simultaneous constrictions at the lips and the velum. Despite its double constriction, /w/ is one of the most frequent consonants in the world's languages.

Dorsal consonants also include **uvulars**, which are pronounced with the tongue body toward the uvula. English lacks uvulars, but many other languages have them, including French (which has a voiced uvular fricative /ʁ/ in words like *roche* [ʁɔʃ] 'rock' and *rêve* [ʁɛv] 'dream') and Hebrew (which has a voiceless uvular fricative /χ/ in words like /laχ/ 'for you (feminine)'). Uvular stops are found in several natlangs, including K'ekchi, which has the voiceless uvular stop /q/, as in /qa/ 'our.' Several well-known conlangs have uvulars consonants, including Klingon, which has /q/ (romanized as 'q') and the voiceless uvular affricate /qχ/ (romanized as 'Q').

Figure 4.2 also includes **radical** and **laryngeal** consonants, pronounced with a constriction involving the root of the tongue or the larynx, respectively. **Pharyngeal** consonants are pronounced with the root of the tongue moving toward the pharynx. Pharyngeals are rare in natlangs, but they occur in some dialects of Arabic, for example.

Glottal (aka laryngeal) consonants are pronounced with a constriction in the larynx. /h/ is a voiceless glottal fricative; in English, it tends to be pronounced as voiced [ɦ] after a vowel; compare *heinous* [h] and *bohemian* [ɦ]. The glottal stop [ʔ], pronounced with a complete closure of the vocal folds, occurs non-contrastively in some English dialects in words like *uh-oh* or *kitten*. In Klingon /ʔ/ (romanized as ') is contrastive; both /h ʔ/ are contrastive in Na'vi and Ithkuil.

Spanish has a velar voiceless fricative /x/ in words like *hoja* 'leaf.' However, this phoneme has several pronunciation variants or **allophones** depending on the dialect. Thus, /x/ is velar [x] in countries such as Mexico and Argentina, laryngeal [h] in Cuba and Puerto Rico, and uvular [χ] in Northern Peninsular Spanish. Examples of the dialectal allophonic pronunciations of /x/ in Spanish are given in (3).

(3) Allophonic realization of /x/ in Spanish

Word			Mexico, Argentina	Caribbean	North-Central Spain
a.	*hoja* 'leaf'	/oxa/	[oxa]	[oha]	[oχa]
b.	*genio* 'genie'	/xenio/	[xenio]	[henio]	[χenio]
c.	*hobbit* 'hobbit'	/xobit/	[xobit]	[hobit]	[χobit]

Figure 4.3 reproduces the consonant chart of the IPA. Note that this chart (also available at the front of the book) includes symbols for pulmonic consonants (consonants pronounced with air coming out of the lungs; non-pulmonic consonants are covered in Section 4.4). Figure 4.3 does not distinguish between dentals and interdentals and includes a manner of articulation we have not yet discussed, **lateral fricatives**. Lateral fricatives are pronounced with a central narrowing and lateral opening simultaneously. Lateral fricatives are attested in Diné (Navajo) and Welsh, as well as in the conlang Láadan.

Figure 4.4 shows additional IPA symbols for pulmonic consonants not listed in the main IPA consonant chart, including [w] and **epiglottal** consonants (pronounced with a constriction of the epiglottis). You can refer to the sources listed at the end of this chapter to listen to these sounds.

Labial and coronal consonants, which are articulated toward the front of the mouth, tend to sound brighter, while dorsal (except for palatals) and radical consonants are often perceived as darker. We come back to this point in Section 4.4.

4.2 Consonant Inventories

Languages vary in their **consonant inventories**, that is, the set of consonants that are contrastive. On average, natlangs have 22 contrastive consonants, but they range from a minimum of 6 (as in Rotokas) to a maximum of 122 (as in !Xóõ). Small consonantal inventories have 6–14 consonants; they occur in 16% of natlangs, including Pirahã and Ainu. Relatively small consonantal inventories with 15–18 consonants are attested in 22% of natlangs, including Finnish and Tagalog. Average inventories encompass 19–25 consonants; they are found in 36% of natlangs, including English

CONSONANTS (PULMONIC)

	Bilabial	Labiodental	Dental	Alveolar	Postalveolar	Retroflex	Palatal	Velar	Uvular	Pharyngeal	Glottal
Plosive	p b			t d		ʈ ɖ	c ɟ	k ɡ	q ɢ		ʔ
Nasal	m	ɱ		n		ɳ	ɲ	ŋ	ɴ		
Trill	ʙ			r					ʀ		
Tap or Flap		ⱱ		ɾ		ɽ					
Fricative	ɸ β	f v	θ ð	s z	ʃ ʒ	ʂ ʐ	ç ʝ	x ɣ	χ ʁ	ħ ʕ	h ɦ
Lateral fricative				ɬ ɮ							
Approximant		ʋ		ɹ		ɻ	j	ɰ			
Lateral approximant				l		ɭ	ʎ	ʟ			

Symbols to the right in a cell are voiced, to the left are voiceless. Shaded areas denote articulations judged impossible.

Figure 4.3 Main pulmonic consonants. www.internationalphoneticassociation.org/content/ipa-chart, available under a Creative Commons Attribution-Sharealike 3.0 Unported License. Copyright © 2018 International Phonetic Association.

4.3 Other Dimensions of Contrast

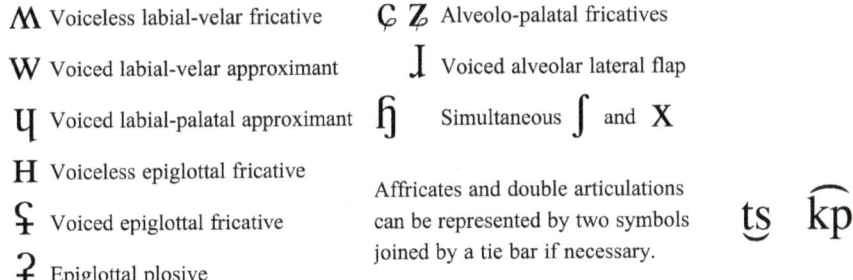

Figure 4.4 Additional pulmonic consonants. www.internationalphoneticassociation.org/content/ipa-chart, available under a Creative Commons Attribution-Sharealike 3.0 Unported License. Copyright © 2018 International Phonetic Association.

and Spanish. About 17% of natlangs feature moderately large consonant inventories with 26–33 consonants, as in Berber or Swahili. Last but not least, large inventories with 34 or more consonants are attested in 10% of natlangs; !Xóõ and Saami fall in to this category.

Conlangs also vary in how many contrastive consonants they have. Conlangs with small consonantal inventories include Toki Pona, with 9, and Láadan, with 13. Average consonant inventories occur in Na'vi (20), Klingon (21), Dothraki and Esperanto (23), while Ithkuil has a large inventory featuring 45 contrastive consonants.

Unlike for vowels, consonant inventories take into consideration both basic consonantal contrasts (voicing, place, manner) and not so basic ones, which we discuss next. The number of contrastive consonants in a natlang bears no correlation to the number of contrastive vowels. Most often, natlangs have three to four times as many consonants as vowels, as in Spanish or Turkish. However, other patterns are attested; for example, Andoke has 10 consonants and 9 vowels, and Abkhaz has 58 consonants but only 2 vowels.

4.3 Other Dimensions of Contrast

In addition to voicing, place and manner of articulation, consonants can contrast in duration, **secondary articulation**, non-modal phonation and **airstream mechanism**, as we see next.

4.3.1 Duration

Consonants can contrast in duration; **long consonants** (also referred to as **geminates**) are 1.5 to 3 times as long as short consonants. Examples from Hindi and Taba are given in (4, 5). As you remember from Chapter 3, the IPA diacritic [ː] after a sound indicates that it is long.

(4) Geminates in Hindi (Ohala 1999)
　　　a. /bətʃa/　'save'　　　/bətʃːa/　'child'
　　　b. /pəka/　'cook (v.)'　/pəkːa/　'firm'

(5) Geminates in Taba (Bowden & Hajek 1999)
　　　a. /lo/　'inside'　/lːo/　'blood'
　　　b. /kut/　'louse'　/kːu/　'tail'

Natlangs might have durational contrasts for all consonants, or only for some. Table 4.2 lists the fourteen most frequent geminate consonants according to the PHOIBLE database; each is attested in at least 1 percent of natlangs. Geminate consonants are not as frequent in natlangs as contrastive long vowels. As is the case for vowels, all natlangs have short consonants, and some contrast them with long consonants, but there are no natlangs that have only long consonants.

Some well-known conlangs have contrastive long consonants, including Quenya (/pː tː kː mː nː sː lː rː/) and Kēlen (/mː nː ɲː ŋː lː rː/). Dothraki has a contrast in duration as well: an example of a minimal pair is 'jeli' [dʒeli] 'lemon' vs. 'jelli' [dʒelːi] 'cheese' (Peterson 2014:19).

4.3.2 Secondary Articulation

Consonants can have a **secondary articulation** in addition to their main place of articulation; secondary articulations always involve an approximant-like lip or tongue gesture. Consider, for example, how you pronounce /k/ in *cool* and *key*. In *cool*, /k/ is pronounced with a lip rounding gesture, anticipating that the following vowel is rounded, that is, it is labialized. In *key*, /k/ is pronounced with some fronting of the tongue, that is, **palatalization**, anticipating the high front vowel that follows.

Table 4.2 Most common geminates in natlangs (based on Moran & McCloy 2019)

Geminate	%	Geminate	%
mː	3	gː	2
nː	3	tː	2
kː	3	rː	2
lː	3	jː	2
sː	2	ʃː	2
pː	2	fː	2
bː	2	dː	1

4.3 Other Dimensions of Contrast

Labialization (aka lip rounding), transcribed [ʷ], is the most widely occurring secondary articulation across languages. It tends to be common with velar and uvular obstruents. Labialization is not contrastive in English, but it is in Classical Latin (which had /k/ and /kʷ/) and Kwuakw'ala, which contrasts /q/ and /qʷ/ (as in /qesa/ 'coiling,' /qʷesa/ 'peeling' (Ladefoged & Maddieson 1996:356).

Palatalization, transcribed [ʲ], is also a common secondary articulation. Examples from Russian are given below (to listen to these examples, go to the UCLA Phonetics Lab Data website: http://phonetics.ucla.edu/appendix/languages/russian/russian.html).

(6) Palatalization in Russian (Ladefoged & Maddieson 1996:364)
 a. /mal/ 'little' /mʲal/ 'crumple'
 b. /nos/ 'nose' /nʲos/ 'he carried'

Velarization, transcribed [ˠ], is a secondary articulation that involves raising the back of the tongue toward the velum. In American English /l/ is often velarized, particularly syllable-finally, as in *bull* or *mall*. Contrastive velarization is rare in natlangs, but one example is found in Marshallese (7); note that velarized 'l' is commonly transcribed as [ɫ].

(7) Velarization in Marshallese (Ladefoged & Maddieson 1996:362–363)
 a. /ɫaɫ/ 'knock' /laɫ/ 'earth'
 b. /matʲ/ 'eye' /mˠatʲ/ 'eel, worm'

Finally, **pharyngealization**, transcribed [ˤ], is a secondary articulation involving the retraction of the tongue root toward the pharynx. Contrastive pharyngealization is quite rare, although it occurs in several Arabic dialects.

Table 4.3 lists the most frequent contrastive consonants with secondary articulations in natlangs according to the PHOIBLE database; all involve labialization or palatalization. Velarized or pharyngealized contrastive consonants are rare; for example, /lˠ/ is attested in only twelve natlangs, and /sˤ/ in ten (i.e., both occur in fewer than 1 percent of languages). Note that one of the consonants in Table 4.3 /kʷ'/ is non-pulmonic; we address non-pulmonic consonants in the next section.

4.3.3 Phonation Type

As for vowels, the action of the vocal folds (**phonation**) can also create contrasts beyond voiced and voiceless. The main phonation options used contrastively for consonants are **aspiration**, **creaky voice** (**glottalization**) and **breathy voice**.

Aspiration occurs when the vocal folds are close to each other enough for air to flow through the larynx with some turbulence. If this occurs after

Table 4.3 Frequent consonants with secondary articulations (based on Moran & McCloy 2019)

Consonant	%	Consonant	%
/kʷ/	12	/kʷʼ/	3
/gʷ/	6	/gʲ/	3
/ŋʷ/	4	/xʷ/	3
/kʲ/	3	/mʲ/	2
/tʲ/	3	/lʲ/	2

a consonant is released, it results in a 'puff' of air that makes the release more salient. To experience how this works, place your hand (or a tissue) in front of your lips and pronounce the word *pie*. Right after [p], you will feel air hitting your hand (or moving the tissue away from you). This is because /p/ is aspirated in this word. Now, do the same for the word *spy*. This time you won't feel a burst of air, since the /p/ in this word is not aspirated. The same applies for /t/ in *tat* vs. *stat*, and for /k/ in *cool* vs. *school*.

Aspiration is transcribed with the diacritic [ʰ] (thus, *pit* would be transcribed [pʰɪt]). In English, aspiration is not contrastive; /p t k tʃ/ are aspirated word-initially and in stressed syllables when not preceded by [s]; otherwise, they are unaspirated. Aspiration is, however, contrastive in many natlangs, including Hindi, as exemplified in (8). Note that stops without aspiration are referred to as plain or unaspirated.

(8) Aspiration in Hindi (http://phonetics.ucla.edu/vowels/chapter12/hindi.html)
  a. /pal/   'take care of'   /pʰal/   'knife blade'
  b. /kal/   'era'   /kʰal/   'skin'

The most common contrastive aspirated consonants in natlangs are /kʰ/ and /pʰ/, each occurring in 20 percent of natlangs, followed by /tʰ/ (12 percent of languages). As in English, voiceless stops in Klingon are aspirated, but not contrastively. However, Ithkuil contrasts plain and aspirated stops: /p t k q/, /pʰ tʰ kʰ qʰ/.

Creaky voice (glottalization) (transcribed [̰], as you probably remember from Chapter 3) involves tense vocal folds, which results in a constriction and reduced airflow. In English, creaky voice is not contrastive. It is often associated with young women, although men and older women also use it. Contrastive creaky voiced consonants are rare in natlangs; the most common are /j̰ w̰ m̰ b̰ n̰/, all occurring in 1 percent of natlangs. Languages with contrastive creaky consonants include Kambaata and Fula.

Breathy voice involves loose vocal fold vibration and higher airflow than with voicing. It is transcribed [̤] as we saw in the previous chapter. The most frequent breathy voiced consonant is [m̤], occurring in 1 percent of natlangs. Breathy voice is contrastive in Hindi, as shown in (9).

(9)   Breathy voice in Hindi (from http://phonetics.ucla.edu/vowels/chapter12/hindi.html)
    a. [bal]   'hair'   [b̤al]   'forehead'
    b. [gal]   'cheek'   [g̤al]   'confusion'

4.3.4 Airstream Mechanism

All spoken natlangs have **pulmonic** consonants, but some also have **non-pulmonic** consonants involving other sources of airflow (**airstream mechanism**). These can be **glottalic** or **velaric**, in which the larynx or the velum respectively trap the air within the vocal tract before releasing it forcefully.

For all airstream mechanisms, we consider the direction in which the air flows when pronouncing speech sounds: **egressive** (out of the mouth) or **ingressive** (into the mouth). All pulmonic sounds we have described so far are egressive. Ingressive pulmonic sounds are rare in natlangs, but ingressive airflow can be used for specific communication purposes (i.e., paralinguistically). Examples are often found in interjections, as in the gasping interjection *huh!* in English, its equivalent *¡ah!* in Spanish, and the words *ja* 'yes' and *nei* 'no' in Norwegian. There is no IPA symbol to indicate ingressive airflow, but following Catford (2001) we transcribe it with a downward arrow [↓]; thus, *huh!* would be transcribed [hə↓].

Non-pulmonic consonants comprise **ejectives**, **implosives** and **clicks**. Ejectives and implosives are pronounced with glottalic initiation since they involve the release of air constricted by the larynx. Ejectives are egressive, and implosives ingressive. Clicks have velaric initiation, since they involve the release of air constricted by the velum (in addition to another constriction in the vocal tract); they are ingressive. We will consider each in turn.

Ejectives are pronounced with a closure of the vocal folds, followed by an obstruction in the vocal tract. The larynx rises and compresses the air in the vocal tract in a small cavity; when the articulators come apart, the release is very forceful. Contrastive ejectives occur in about 18 percent of natlangs. They are transcribed with an apostrophe to the right of the consonant; thus, /p' t' k'/ are voiceless bilabial, alveolar and velar stop ejectives, respectively. Natlangs with contrastive ejectives include Lakhota and K'ekchi; examples of the latter are given in (10).

(10) K'ekchi ejectives (http://phonetics.ucla.edu/appendix/languages/ketchi/ketchi.html)
 a. [ka]   'grindstone'   [k'a]   'bitter'
 b. [qa]   'our'   [q'a]   'bridge'

English lacks contrastive ejectives, but they occur in some English dialects, including Edinburgh Scottish English, as allophones of word-final stops, particularly /k/.

Ejectives are always voiceless (otherwise the larynx isn't able to close and compress air). They are often velar or uvular, since the further back in the mouth the constriction, the smaller the area where air is compressed, leading to a forceful release. Most ejectives are stops, probably because it is easier to compress air in the oral cavity with a full oral constriction. However, ejective fricatives and affricates are also attested in natlangs, including Tlingit, where the word for 'crab' is /s'aaw/, and Chulupí, where 'milk' is /ts'oʔs/.

Implosives are pronounced with the lowering of the larynx and a closure in the vocal tract; this has the effect of increasing the space in the oral tract. When the oral constriction is released, air flows into the vocal tract, lowering pressure and facilitating voicing. Implosives occur in about 10 percent of natlangs. Implosive consonants are transcribed with a rightward hook on the top: thus, /ɓ ɗ ɠ/ are voiced bilabial, alveolar and velar implosives, respectively. Implosives favor places of articulation in the front of the mouth, probably since vocal fold vibration is sustained more easily when there is a large oral tract cavity. Implosives are usually voiced, but voiceless implosives are attested, as in Owerri Igbo (11); note that /í/ indicates that the vowel has high tone.

(11) Implosives in Owerri Igbo (http://phonetics.ucla.edu/vowels/chapter12/igbo.html)
 a. /íba/   'to get rich'
 b. /íɓa/   'to dance'
 c. /íɓ̥a/   'to gather'

Although English lacks contrastive implosives, these can occur as emphatic allophones of voiced bilabial stops, as in *absolutely billions and billions*. Implosive bilabials are attested in some rural dialects of Western American English as well. Eddington and Turner (2017) refer to this pronunciation as 'the cowboy B.'

Clicks are pronounced by trapping air between the velum or the uvula and another articulator further to the front of the mouth. When the front constriction is released, air moves into the mouth, producing a popping sound. In spite of being perceptually salient, clicks occur in less than 2 percent of natlangs, including Xhosa and Dahalo. However, clicks are used in many natlangs to express affective meaning such as irritation, impatience and disappointment, to address babies or animals, and even to convey appreciation or logical meaning (often 'yes' or 'no').

English uses several clicks in this manner. For example, when you throw somebody a kiss (particularly to babies or children), you are pronouncing a bilabial click [ʘ]. This bilabial click is pronounced by bringing your lips together while making a closure at the velum. The air compressed between lips and velum sounds very loud when the constrictions are released.

Another click used paralinguistically in English is dental [ǀ], used to express disapproval, irritation or disappointment (it is commonly written 'tut-tut' or 'tsk-tsk'). To pronounce it, the tip of the tongue makes full contact with the alveolar ridge, and at the same time the back of the tongue makes a closure at the velum. The release of the air compressed between both regions is quite loud.

Two other clicks you might know relate to horses: to imitate the sound a horse's hoofs make on a hard surface ('clip-clop') you compress the air between the alveolar and velar areas of the vocal tract, then release it forcefully. Its IPA symbol is [!]. Finally, when riders want a horse to move ('tchick!'), they place the tip of the tongue on one side of the alveolar ridge, while making a concomitant closure at the velum. The resulting sound is a lateral alveolar click [ǁ].

Note that paralinguistic uses of clicks vary across natlangs; the dental click [ǀ] expressing irritation in English means 'no' in Hebrew and in some Arabic dialects – while in the San'ani dialect of Arabic in North Yemen, it means 'yes.'

Palato-alveolar clicks are also attested. They are pronounced with a closure at the velum and another one in the palato-alveolar region of the mouth. They are transcribed [ǂ] in IPA. They occur in Nama and other languages.

The most common clicks are dental, and the least frequent bilabial. Contrastive clicks can be voiced, voiceless and even nasal; this is conveyed in IPA via an **accompaniment**, that is, an IPA consonant that precedes the click symbol to clarify its pronunciation. Thus, /kǀ/ stands for a voiceless dental click, /gǀ/ for a voiced dental click and /ŋǀ/ for a nasal dental one.

Figure 4.5 reproduces the IPA symbols for non-pulmonic consonants (this chart is also found at the front of the book). Note that voiced implosives can also be palatal and uvular. None of the best-known conlangs have contrastive implosives or clicks; but contrastive ejectives are attested in Na'vi (/p' t' k'/, romanized as 'px,' 'tx' and 'kx,' respectively) and Ithkuil /p' t' k' q'/.

CONSONANTS (NON-PULMONIC)

Clicks	Voiced implosives	Ejectives
ʘ Bilabial	ɓ Bilabial	ʼ Examples:
ǀ Dental	ɗ Dental/alveolar	pʼ Bilabial
ǃ (Post)alveolar	ʄ Palatal	tʼ Dental/alveolar
ǂ Palatoalveolar	ɠ Velar	kʼ Velar
ǁ Alveolar lateral	ʛ Uvular	sʼ Alveolar fricative

Figure 4.5 Non-pulmonic consonants. www.internationalphoneticassociation.org/content/ipa-chart, available under a Creative Commons Attribution-Sharealike 3.0 Unported License. Copyright © 2018 International Phonetic Association.

4.4 Conlanging Tips

As we have seen, all natlangs have contrastive short, pulmonic consonants involving various constrictions (manners of articulation) in different parts of the vocal tract (place of articulation). Some natlangs also have consonants that contrast in duration, secondary articulation, non-modal phonation and/or airstream mechanism. All possibilities of consonant articulation are summarized in Figure 4.6. Note that our discussion of consonantal contrasts is not exhaustive; to explore additional options, check the resources listed at the end of the chapter.

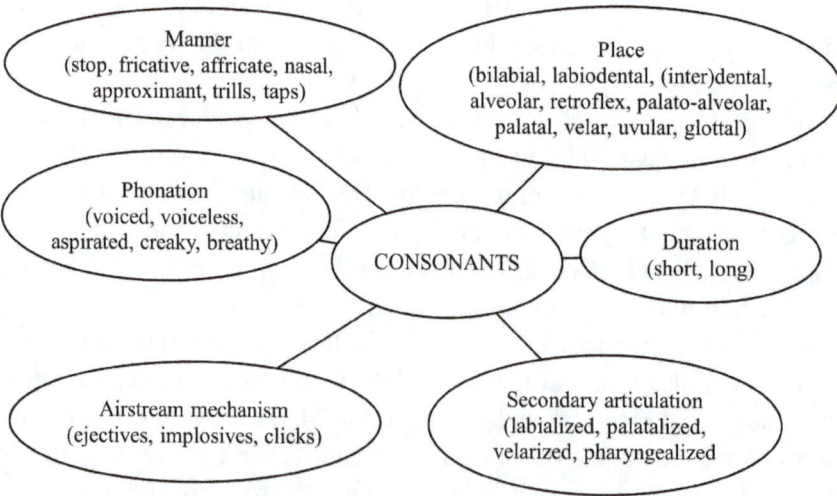

Figure 4.6 Possible consonant contrasts.

It is important to make sure the consonant inventory of your conlang is different from that of English and other natlangs. It might exclude consonants occurring in English, such as voiced fricatives, or include some from other natlangs, such as voiceless nasals or ejectives. Considering relative consonant frequency in natlangs might help you decide which consonants to include. Depending on your conlanging goals and personal preference, you might choose more frequent or rare consonants.

Table 4.4 lists consonants that occur in at least 20 percent of natlangs according to the PHOIBLE database. Cells are shaded if a consonant is attested in at least 50 percent of natlangs. Note that the most frequent manners of articulation are stops, nasals and approximants, and the most frequent places are bilabial, alveolar and velar. Non-pulmonic, long and creaky and breathy consonants are relatively uncommon and thus not included.

The decision of how many consonants (or vowels) to include in your conlang might have an impact on how long words will be. Dixon (2016) argues that the more phonemes a language has, the more words it can have of a particular length. For example, a language with a relatively small inventory of 12 consonants and 3 vowels will have up to 36 monosyllabic words with a consonant-vowel (CV) structure (12 x 3), and up to 1,296 CVCV words (36 x 36). On the other hand, a language with a large inventory of 45 consonants and 16 vowels can have up to 720 CV words (45 x 16) and 518,400 CVCV words (720 x 720). Thus, a language with many phonemes can have many short words; and a language with few phonemes will have many long words. According to Dixon, the ideal phonological system lies between these extremes.

Indeed, many well-known conlangs have 'ideal' phonological systems since they have an average number of contrastive consonants and vowels. Thus, Dothraki has 23 consonants and 4 vowels; Klingon 21 consonants and 5 vowels; Na'vi 20 consonants and 7 vowels; and Esperanto 23 consonants and 5 vowels. Toki Pona has a smaller inventory (9 consonants and 5 vowels), but its lexicon is restricted to 120 words, and words tend to be on the shorter side. Láadan has a small consonantal inventory (13) and a large vowel inventory (10); its total number of contrastive phonemes (23) is close to that of some of the conlangs mentioned above. At the other end, Ithkuil has a very large inventory featuring 45 consonants and 13 vowels; we would expect it to have many short words.

As you build your consonantal inventory, it is important to consider that consonantal inventories tend to involve sets of consonants. For example, it is more common for languages to have sets of stops or alveolar consonants rather than just one of each. Your consonantal inventory does not have to be perfectly symmetrical, however; historical change and language contact can impact consonant patterning. For example, Arabic has /b/ but not /p/.

Table 4.4 Most frequent consonants in natlangs (based on Moran & McCloy 2019)

	Bilabial	Labio-dental	(Inter)dental	Alveolar	Post-alveolar	Palatal	Velar	Glottal
Stop (plain)	p 86% b 63%		t̪ 23%	t 68% d 46%			k 90% g 57%	ʔ 37%
Stop (aspirated)	pʰ 20%						kʰ 20%	
Fricative		f 44% v 27%		s 67% z 30%	ʃ 37%			h 56%
Affricate				ts 22%	tʃ 40% dʒ 27%			
Nasal	m 96%			n 78%		ɲ 42%	ŋ 63%	
Approx.	(w) 82%			l 68%		j 90%	(w) 82%	
Tap				ɾ 26%				
Trill				r 44%				

In addition to consonant frequency, you can consider **phono-aesthetics**, that is, the association of certain sounds with characteristics such as beauty or roughness. We mentioned in Chapter 3 that certain vowels sound 'brighter' and others 'darker'; similar phono-aesthetic effects can be achieved with consonants too. For example, sonorant consonants tend to sound more melodic, and stops and affricates choppier. Obstruents pronounced in the back of the vocal tract, particularly dorsal ones, often evoke roughness and force, as do ejectives. On the other hand, consonants pronounced toward the front of the mouth tend to sound brighter. Phono-aesthetic considerations are not necessarily universal: they are often tied to personal preferences and cultural associations.

Perhaps your conlang favors front or back consonants, or obstruents or sonorants depending on the effect you want to convey. Perhaps it combines both for balance. In any case, if you are not sure how many consonantal contrasts your conlang will have, you can start with a few and add more later. If you do so, remember to update your consonant chart and any words you have created for consistency. Finally, make sure you can pronounce all the consonants of your conlang as best as you can!

4.5 Conlanging Practice: Consonants

A. Which consonants do you think could evoke the following effects?
- Smallness
- Cuteness
- Ugliness
- Raspiness
- Secrecy
- Elegance

B. As shown in Tables 4.5 and 4.6, Toki Pona and Láadan have small consonantal inventories. Which conlang has more unusual consonantal contrasts (refer to Table 4.3)?

Table 4.5 Toki Pona consonant inventory (based on Lang 2014:16)

	Bilabial	Alveolar	Palatal	Velar
Stop	p	t		k
Fricative		s		
Nasal	m	n		
Approximant	(w)		j	(w)
Lateral approximant		l		

Table 4.6 Láadan consonant inventory (based on Elgin 2020:15)

	Bilabial	Dental	Alveolar	Post-alveolar	Velar	Glottal
Stop	b		d			
Fricative		θ		ʃ ʒ		h
Nasal	m		n			
Approximant	(w)		ɹ		j	(w)
Lateral approximant			l			
Lateral fricative			ɬ			

C. Tables 4.7–4.9 show different consonantal inventories found in the Ur languages. Taking into consideration your answers to 1.7, which of these inventories could be a better fit for the Aqua, Gem, Grass and Fog languages? Devise an additional inventory for the fourth language.

Table 4.7 Ur inventory I

	Bilabial	Alveolar	Velar	Uvular
Stop	p	t	k	q
Fricative		s	x	χ
Nasal	m	n		ɴ
Trill	ʙ	r		
Lateral		l		ʟ

Table 4.8 Ur inventory II

	Bilabial	Alveolar	Velar	Glottal
Stop	p b	t d	k g	ʔ
Fricative		s z		h ɦ
Nasal		ŋ̊ n		
Trill	m̥ m	r̥ r		
Lateral		l̥ l		

D. We saw in Section 3.10 that the Moon language has 12 contrastive vowels (4 oral, including /i/; 4 nasal, 4 long). The Moon language has 26 contrastive consonants, including /m f s/ as shown in Chapter 3, as well as some non-pulmonic and uvular consonants.

4.6 Consonants in the Salt Language

Table 4.9 Ur Inventory III

	Bilabial	Alveolar	Post-alveolar	Palatal	Velar
Stop (plain)	p b	t d		c ɟ	k g
Stop (aspirated)	pʰ	tʰ		cʰ	kʰ
Ejective stops	p'	t'		c'	k'
Fricative	ɸ	s	ʃ		x
Affricate		ts	tʃ		
Nasal	m	n		ɲ	
Approximant				j	
Tap		ɾ			

- Choose 23 additional consonants (including uvular and non-pulmonic ones). Remember that consonants tend to occur in sets!
- Chart all consonants. Non-pulmonic consonants can be incorporated in additional rows (as in Table 4.9) or in a separate chart.
- Are any consonants connected to phono-aesthetics or/and any aspect of the fictional world? (review your answers to Section 3.10 for consistency; fill in cultural or historical details as needed).
- Provide minimal pairs showcasing the contrastive consonants; take into consideration the contrastive vowels from Section 3.10. Remember to indicate the meaning of each word!

4.6 Consonants in the Salt Language

As you probably remember from the previous chapter, the Salt language has nine contrastive vowels /i e æ ɨ ə a ɑ o u/. For the consonant inventory, my main goals were making it larger than average, and including some typologically unusual consonants, mostly for fun.

As you see in Table 4.10, there are twenty-nine contrastive consonants in the Salt language. From the minimal pairs provided in example (9) in Chapter 3, I needed to include /m n t s k/. Beginning with these consonants already provides sets of nasals (/m n/) and stops /t k/. It also means that consonants contrast at least in three places of articulation (bilabials, alveolar and velar). To make the consonant inventory more interesting, I decided to include both palatal and uvular consonants. I also made the decision to include a set of fricatives, and to incorporate laterals and trills at various places of articulation.

Table 4.10 Contrastive consonants in the Salt language

	Bilabial	Alveolar	Palatal	Velar	Uvular
Stops	p b	t d	c ɟ	k g	q ɢ
Fricatives	ɸ	s z	ç j	x ɣ	χ ʁ
Nasals	m	n	ɲ	ŋ	ɴ
Trills	ʙ		r		
Laterals		l	ʎ	ʟ	

The resulting consonant inventory includes voiceless and voiced obstruents and voiced nasals at five places of articulation. Trills can be bilabial and alveolar; and laterals alveolar, palatal or velar. The consonantal inventory includes consonants at the front and back regions of the vocal tract, and includes some frequent consonants, and some rarer ones.

Because the consonant inventory is quite large, I'm only including a selection of minimal pairs below; I will continue to develop the lexicon in the following chapters. Note that some words are nouns, some verbs, and there is a word for 'thank you.' 'Muq' [muq] is the name the Salt People give to their language and their community. The word /num/ 'to go' was introduced in Chapter 3.

(12) Minimal sets in muq

/m n ɲ/   /num/   'to go'
          /mum/   'thank you, it's appreciated'
          /ɲum/   'stone'
/s z/   /zeza/   'to talk'
          /seza/   'to look'
/c k q/   /muq/   '(our) people; the muq; our language'
          /muk/   'money, payment'
          /muc/   'to stop'
/ç x/   /ɸuç/   'night'
          /ɸux/   'fish'

As you add words to your conlang, it helps to organize them in a database. I use Excel since sorting is helpful and you can also easily copy-paste IPA symbols in it. Right now, the Salt lexicon in excel includes three columns: one for the IPA transcription of each word, another for its English translation, and a third for its word type (which we consider in detail in Chapter 6). Table 4.11 shows the muq lexicon database at this point. The following chapters explore additional information that can be added to your lexicon database.

Table 4.11 Muq lexicon so far

IPA	Translation	Word type
/kost/	'to understand'	Verb
/kust/	'salt, life force'	Noun
/mum/	'thank you, it's appreciated'	Interjection
/muc/	'to stop'	Verb
/muk/	'money, payment'	Noun
/muq/	'(our) people; the muq; our language'	Noun
/nem/	'below'	Adverb
/num/	'to go'	Verb
/ɲum/	'stone'	Noun
/ɸuç/	'night'	Noun
/ɸux/	'fish'	Noun
/seza/	'to look'	Verb
/zeza/	'to talk'	Verb

4.7 Guide to Developing Your Conlang Consonants

- What type of sound effect (if any) would you like your conlang to convey?
- Will your consonant inventory lean towards uniqueness or simplicity?
- List the basic consonant contrasts (place, manner, voicing) in your conlang compatible with your answers above (take into consideration any consonants you included in your answers in Section 3.12).
- List any non-pulmonic consonants.
- List any contrasts in consonant duration, secondary articulation, or phonation.
- Are any consonants associated to specific phono-aesthetic effects?
- Chart all consonants using IPA symbols. If your inventory has unusual consonantal patterns, indicate why this is the case. Non-pulmonic consonants can be charted separately, or you can add rows to the main consonant chart.
- Is your consonant inventory small, average or large? How is your choice connected to other aspects of the conlang or the fictional world?
- Provide minimal pairs/sets illustrating your consonant contrasts. You can use some of the words you created in 3.12 if relevant. Remember to

render your conlang words in IPA (within slanted bars / /) and to indicate their translation within quotation marks. Make sure all vowels are consistent with your answers in 3.12.
- What is the conlang name? (Make sure it has consonants and vowels from the conlang inventory!)

To Learn More

The Interactive Sagittal Section website by Daniel Currie Hall (http://smu-facweb.smu.ca/~s0949176/sammy/) is a great resource for visualizing different consonant articulations. The Sounds of Speech website provides animations, videos and audio for the sounds of English, Spanish and German: https://soundsofspeech.uiowa.edu/. For interactive clickable IPA charts, see the resources listed at the end of Chapter 3.

For more information on consonants in natlangs, see Catford (2001), Maddieson (1984) and Ladefoged and Maddieson (1996). Maddieson (2013c) in the *World Atlas of Language Structures* (WALS) online is a highly recommended overview of consonantal inventories. Other WALS chapters are good sources for exploring other aspects related to consonant typology.

The PHOIBLE database (Moran & MCcloy 2019) lists information on consonant (and vowel) frequency in over 2,000 natlangs and includes consonantal inventories for you to browse.

For bilabial implosives in American English, see Eddington and Turner (2017). Robert Eklund's page on ingressive phonation and speech has a wealth of information on ingressive sounds in natlangs and animal communication, including sound files and acoustic displays: http://ingressivespeech.info/. Also recommended is Eklund (2008).

Clicks feature prominently in the movie *The Gods Must be Crazy* (1980; Jamie Uys), for the San language in Botswana, and more recently in *Black Panther* (2018; Ryan Coogler), set in the fictional country of 'Wakanda' and featuring Xhosa. A famous song featuring Xhosa clicks is the 'Click song' (Qongqothwane) sung by Miriam Makeba, which you can find in YouTube. To learn more about the paralinguistic use of clicks, see Gil (2013) in WALS online.

Many of the examples introduced in this chapter are from the UCLA Phonetics Lab Data (http://phonetics.ucla.edu/). Other sources mentioned in this chapter are listed in the reference section at the end of this book.

5 From Sounds to Syllables

Once you have selected the vowels and consonants in your conlang, you need to consider how they combine into syllables; this is the focus of this chapter. Syllables and the basics of syllabification are covered in Sections 5.1 and 5.2. Sections 5.3 and 5.4 address how languages organize syllable margins and nuclei respectively. Section 5.5 covers **phonotactics**, that is, how languages restrict how sounds combine. The remaining sections focus on conlanging: Section 5.6 offers some practice on syllabification, Section 5.7 describes the syllable structure and the phonotactics of the Salt language, and Section 5.8 provides a set of guided questions for you to work out the syllable structure of your conlang. The chapter closes with a list of sources to explore further.

Key Words

Coda (syllable-final consonant)
Complex onset/coda/nucleus
Falling sonority
Monosyllabic
Nucleus
Onset (syllable-initial consonant)
Phonotactics
Polysyllabic
Rhyme
Rising sonority
Simple onset/coda/nucleus
Sonority
Sonority scale
Syllabic consonant
Syllabification
Syllable
Closed syllable
Open syllable
Syllable margin
Vowel hiatus

5.1 What Are Syllables?

Consonants and vowels are combined into **syllables**, defined as a group of sounds pronounced and perceived as a speech unit. Syllables are intermediate speech units between sounds and words (Table 5.1). Syllables have psychological reality; native speakers of a language typically agree on how many syllables a word has. For example, native speakers of English agree that *earth* and *breeze* have one syllable, *earthquake* and *typhoon* two, and *tornado* and *hurricane* three. They also agree that [pi] is a possible syllable in English, unlike [pti]. Words with only one syllable, like *dead*, are **monosyllabic**; words with more than one syllable, like *alive* or *heptapod*, are **polysyllabic**.

The loudest, most prominent sound in a syllable is the **nucleus** (or syllable peak). In most languages, the syllable nucleus is always a vowel. Most often, syllable nuclei are preceded and/or followed by consonants, as in *pea* [pi], or *moon* [mun]. Sometimes, however, syllables only have a nucleus, as in *a* or *oh*.

Syllable margins are the outermost segments of syllables: **onsets** or **syllable-initial** consonants precede the nucleus, and **codas** or **syllable-final** consonants follow it. Syllables without codas are **open**, and those with codas are **closed**. In addition, the **rhyme** is the combination of the nucleus and the coda. Table 5.2 exemplifies the structure of the syllable for the monosyllabic words *moon* and *dead*.

Table 5.1 Syllables: between sounds and words

Words	[dɛd] 'dead'	[əlaiv] 'alive'	[hɛptəpɑd] 'heptapod'
Syllables	[dɛd]	[ə] [laiv]	[hɛp] [tə] [pɑd]
Sounds	[d] [ɛ] [d]	[ə] [l] [ai] [v]	[h] [ɛ] [p] [t] [ə] [p] [ɑ] [d]

Table 5.2 Simple syllable units

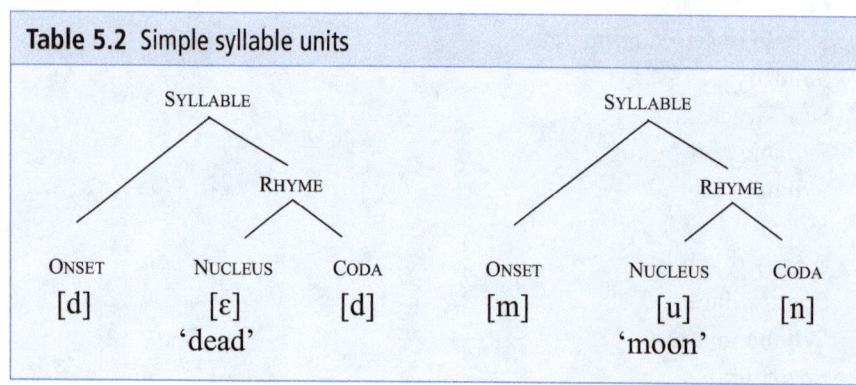

Onsets, codas and nuclei can be **simple** if they comprise one sound, and **complex** if they involve more than one. For example, *breeze* [bɹiz] has a complex onset, and *wind* [wɪnd] has a complex coda. Simple nuclei have only one vowel sound (or monophthong) as in *breeze* and *wind*. Complex nuclei consisting of two vowel sounds are diphthongs, and those with three are triphthongs. Examples of English words with complex nuclei include *eye* [aɪ] and *new* [nju]. Examples of triphthongs in Spanish are *buey* 'ox' and *guay* 'cool.' Table 5.3 exemplifies the syllable structure for the words *breeze*, which has a complex onset, and *kind*, which has both a complex nucleus and a complex coda.

Table 5.3 Complex syllable units

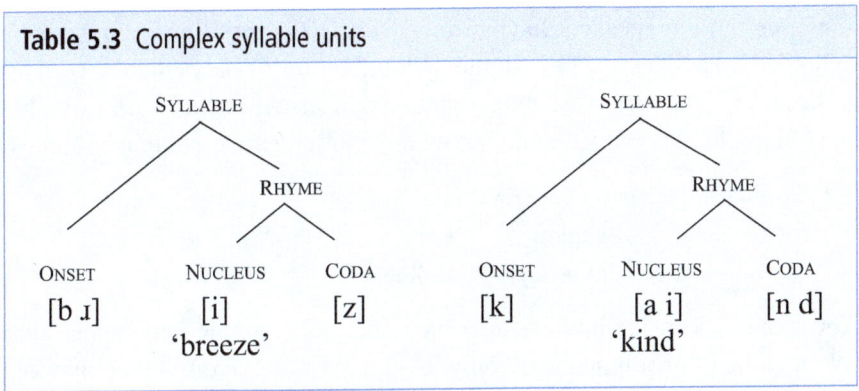

All natlangs have onsets and nuclei; but not all have codas. Languages also vary in the amount of complexity they allow for both nuclei and syllable margins. For example, English allows up to three consonants in onsets (as in *spray*) and up to four in codas (as in *worlds*). In Spanish, on the other hand, only two consonants are allowed in onset or coda. The maximum number of consonants allowed in complex syllable margins in natlangs is six, as in Sipakapense (Barrett 1999:22), although this is quite rare.

> **Your Turn**
>
> Consider the following monosyllabic words from Láadan (from Elgin et al. 2020). Identify their nuclei, onsets and codas. Are they simple or complex?
>
> [ɪb]   'crime'   [nɛm]   'pearl'   [do]   'to be strong'

5.2 Syllabification

Syllabification is the process of grouping sounds into syllables. In monosyllabic words, syllabification is straightforward; the vowel is the nucleus, any consonants to the left comprise the onset and any consonants to the right are the coda (Tables 5.2, 5.3).

5 From Sounds to Syllables

> **Your Turn**
>
> The sentences *If you must*, *As you wish* and *We duel at dawn* are composed of monosyllables.
> - Transcribe all words in these sentences in IPA.
> - Draw their syllable structure, as shown in Tables 5.2 and 5.3.
> - Which of these words have complex nuclei? Which have complex syllable margins?

Syllabification can be more challenging in polysyllabic words. In some natlangs, native speakers have strong, consistent intuitions about where syllable boundaries are placed and syllabification of polysyllabic words is quite straightforward. This is the case in Spanish, as shown in (1). Note that we follow IPA conventions and use a dot [.] to indicate a syllable boundary.

(1) Syllabification in Spanish (I)
    a. *luna*   [lu.na]   'moon'
    b. *satélite*   [sa.te.li.te]   'satellite'

The examples in (1) involve open syllables with simple syllabi margins. Word-initial consonants can only be onsets; and consonants between vowels are syllabified as onsets as well. The syllabification of intervocalic consonants as onsets applies cross-linguistically; thus, in English, *easy* is syllabified [i.zɪ], and *planet* [plæ.nət].

> **Your Turn**
>
> Syllabify the following Láadan words (from Elgin et al. 2020)
>
> [uhud] 'nuisance' [uhudɛmɪd] 'tick' (insect; 'nuisance creature')
> [lalɛn] 'guitar' [lalɪlom] 'sound of rain in the roof'

Natlangs differ in how they syllabify adjacent word-medial consonants. Consider, for example, the disyllabic Spanish words in (2).

(2) Syllabification in Spanish (II)
    a. *soplo*   [so.plo]   'puff'
    b. *cofre*   [ko.fre]   'coffer'
    c. *verso*   [ber.so]   'verse'
    d. *este*   [es.te]   'this; East'

The word-medial consonants [pl], [fr] in (2a, b) syllabify as the complex onset of the second syllable. The reason is that Spanish words can begin with the sequences [pl] (as in *plata* [pla.ta] 'silver; money') and [fr] (as in *fresa* [fre.sa] 'strawberry; posh'). However, the medial consonants [ɾs] and [st] in (2c, d) are split between the first and second syllables. The reason is that Spanish lacks words beginning with 'rs' or 'st'; thus, neither [ɾs] or [st] can be complex onsets in Spanish.

Like Spanish, English has words beginning with 'pl' (*platypus, plausible*) and 'fr' (*frothy, friend*), and lacks words beginning with 'rs.' However, English does have words beginning in 'st,' as in *stunned* or *story*. Thus, the sequence [st] is syllabified word-medially as a complex onset in English (*tasty* [te.stɪ]), unlike in Spanish. This is the reason why an 'e' tends to be added word-initially in Spanish in English borrowings beginning with 'st,' as in *estrés* (from English *stress*).

Word-final consonants are codas; this is the case of [lk] in *silk* [sɪlk] or [st] in *zest* [zest]. Word-medial consonants that cannot be syllabified as onsets are also codas. For example, in *silky*, [l] cannot be part of a complex onset with [k], since there are no English words that begin with [lk]. Thus, [l] is syllabified as coda of the first syllable: [sɪl.ki].

> ### Your Turn
>
> Are the underlined consonants below onsets or codas?
>
> a<u>nv</u>il hu<u>sk</u>y di<u>mp</u>le e<u>n</u>tropy o<u>bsc</u>ure o<u>rb</u>it i<u>nt</u>erstellar

Natlangs vary in how they syllabify adjacent vowels in a word. Two adjacent vowels pronounced in the same syllable make a diphthong (as in *eye* [aɪ], *boy* [bɔɪ]); if they are pronounced in different syllables, they are in **hiatus** (as in *near* or *Liam*, both of which are pronounced as two syllables). Three adjacent vowels in a syllable comprise a triphthong. Triphthongs are more common in British English than American English; some words where they can be heard include *fire* and *higher*, when pronounced as one syllable.

> ### Your Turn
>
> Check your conlang lexicon. Select a few words and draw their syllable structure, taking as a model Tables 5.1, 5.2.

5.3 The Typology of Syllable Margins

Depending on the complexity of the syllable margin, natlangs can be classified as having simple, moderately complex or complex syllable structure. Languages with simple syllable structure have no codas. About 13 percent of natlangs fall into this category. The syllable structure of these languages is represented as CV (if onsets are always required, as in Sénoufo or Fijian) or (C)V (if onsets are optional, as in Hawaiian or Yoruba). Note that the V stands for the vowel nucleus, regardless of its complexity.

Languages with moderately complex syllables have one consonant in coda and up to two in onset, with the second onset consonant being a liquid or a glide. About 57 percent of natlangs are of this type, including Turkish and Cherokee.

Natlangs with complex syllable structures have more complex onset structures or two or more consonants in coda. Examples include English, Tuareg, and Georgian. The latter has one of the most complex syllable structures attested in natlangs, with up to seven consonants in the onset. Examples of English words with complex onset and coda structures are given in (3).

(3) English: complex syllable structure
    a. Three-consonant onset: 'spray' [spɹeɪ] 'splat' [splæt]
    b. Four-consonant coda: 'texts' [tɛksts] 'sixths' [sɪksθs]

Note that if a language has complex codas, it also has simple ones, and if a language has complex onsets, it also has simple ones. Usually, codas are more restricted than onsets in languages. Sometimes coda consonants are restricted to specific sets, such as sonorants, voiceless stops, or coronal consonants, for example.

5.3.1 Syllable Margins in Conlangs

Láadan, Toki Pona and Dothraki have moderately complex syllable structure. Toki Pona and Láadan syllables are maximally (C)V(C). Láadan allows different coda consonants (as in [lom] 'song' or [nɪθ] 'frost'; Elgin et al. 2020). In Toki Pona, only /n/ can be coda (4). Dothraki syllables are maximally (C)(C)V(C); the second consonant of complex onsets is always a liquid (5).

(4) Toki Pona syllables (from Lang 2014)
    a. *ale* [a.le] 'all' *pimeja* [pi.me.ja] 'black'
    b. *wan* [wan] 'one' *pan* [pan] 'pasta, bread'

(5) Dothraki syllables (from Peterson 2014)
    a. *jahak* [dʒa.hak] 'braid' *nesikh* [ne.six] 'knowledge'
    b. *vroz* [vroz] 'slow' *hrazef* [hra.zef] 'horse'

Klingon, Esperanto and Na'vi have complex syllable structures. Klingon requires a simple onset in all syllables; complex codas are possible but rare, as in [tarɣ] 'targ (a type of animal).' Esperanto has up to three consonants in onset (6a), and up to two in codas (6b).

(6)   Esperanto syllables (from van Oostendorp 1999)
      a. *knabo*   [kna.bo]   'boy'   *skribi*   [skri.bi]   'to write'
      b. *sort*   [sort]   'fate'   *post*   [post]   'after'

Na'vi has up to two consonants in onset and one coda consonant. Codas are restricted to ejectives, stops, nasals and liquids. Complex onsets always begin with /f s ts/; the second consonant can be /p t k p' t' k' m n ŋ ɾ l w j/. Examples of Na'vi words with complex onsets are given in (7).

(7)   Na'vi syllables (from Müller 2024)
      a. *fngap*   [fŋap]   'metal'
      b. *tsmi*   [tsmi]   'nectar'

> **Your Turn**
>
> - Are onsets obligatory in your conlang? How many consonants are allowed in onset?
> - Are codas permitted? If so, what is the maximum number of consonants in coda?
> - Based on your previous answers, what type of syllable structure does your conlang have?

5.4 The Typology of Nuclei

In addition to thinking through the number and type of consonants allowed as syllable margins in your conlang, you need to decide whether adjacent vowels occur, and if so, whether they are syllabified as nuclei of the same or different syllables. Many natlangs allow complex nuclei but often restrict them in some ways. Natlangs might favor diphthongs with **falling sonority** (i.e., beginning with a more open vowel; *I* [ai̯], *ouch* [aut̯ʃ]), or with **rising sonority** (i.e., ending with a more open vowel, as in *guapo* [gu̯a.po] 'handsome' in Spanish). Note that the IPA diacritic [̯] is placed below the least open vowel(s) in a complex nucleus.

Some natlangs do not permit complex nuclei or show a general preference for vowels in hiatus. Languages that permit hiatus have optional onsets; languages with obligatory onsets cannot have vowels in hiatus.

We mentioned earlier in the chapter that syllable nuclei are usually vowels. In fact, sometimes consonants act as syllable nuclei; they are **syllabic consonants** and occur in 11 percent of natlangs, including Slovak, Swahili and English. Syllabic consonants can be nasals (as in Swahili), liquids (as in Slovak) or both (as in English), as shown in (8). Note that syllabic consonants are transcribed in IPA with the diacritic [̩].

(8) Word-final syllabic consonants in English
    a. [m̩]   rhythm   prism
    b. [n̩]   human   kitten
    c. [ŋ̍]   wagon   taken
    d. [l̩]   castle   bagel
    e. [ɹ̩]   rover   sister

> **Your Turn**
>
> Does your name have a syllabic consonant? Some examples of proper names that have syllabic consonants word-finally are *Marvin*, *Kendall* and *Roger*. One example of a proper name with a syllabic consonant word-medially is *Guerna*.

A few natlangs have syllabic obstruents, but this is rare since the syllable nucleus is the most open position in the syllable, so consonants with less constriction make better nuclei. One example is Tashlhiyt Berber, exemplified in (9).

(9) Syllabic consonants in Tashlhiyt Berber (Ridouane 2014:217)
    a. [tṣ.kr̩]   'she did'
    b. [tb̩.dg̩]   'it was wet'

Syllabic consonants are present in English but are rare in the world's languages. Thus, if you are interested in incorporating them in your conlang, you might decide to have them in a smaller or larger set of consonants.

5.4.1 Syllable Nuclei in Conlangs

Láadan, Toki Pona and Dothraki lack complex nuclei, and Esperanto, Klingon and Quenya allow them. So does Na'vi, although these are restricted to the falling diphthongs [au̯] [ai̯] [ɛu̯] [ɛi̯] (10a, b). Other adjacent vowels are in hiatus (10c). Na'vi also has syllabic consonants ('pseudo-vowels') [l̩ r̩], romanized as 'll' and 'rr' respectively (11).

(10) Adjacent vowels in Na'vi (from Müller 2024)
    a. *'aw*   [ʔau̯]   'one'   *wew*   [wɛu̯]   'cold'
    b. *meyp*   [mɛi̯p]   'weak'   *way*   [wai̯]   '(ancient) song'
    c. *leioae*   [lɛ.i.o.ˈa.ɛ]   'respect'

(11) Syllabic consonants in Na'vi (from Müller 2024)
    a. *trr*   [tr̩]   'day'
    b. *kxll*   [k'l̩]   'charge, running attack'

> **Your Turn**
>
> - Does your conlang have diphthongs? If so, are they restricted?
> - Are there triphthongs?
> - Are there syllabic consonants? If so, which consonant types can be syllabic?

5.5 Phonotactics

Languages differ regarding which sounds occur next to each other, that is, in their **phonotactics**. Phonotactics often depends on **sonority** considerations. Sonority refers primarily to the relative openness of the vocal tract. The more open a sound, the more sonorous it is. Conversely, the more obstructed the sound, the less sonorous it is. Highly sonorous sounds are louder and can be prolonged; this makes them more salient perceptually. Highly sonorous sounds also tend to be voiced.

Sounds can be ranked according to their sonority in a **sonority scale** (12). Vowels are the most sonorous sounds, and voiceless stops the least. Note that decreasing sonority involves increased obstruction. For example, low vowels are more sonorous than mid vowels since the former are more open; and fricatives are more sonorous than stops since the latter are more obstructed.

(12)

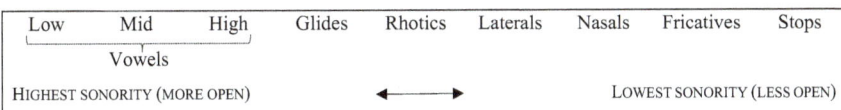

Low	Mid	High	Glides	Rhotics	Laterals	Nasals	Fricatives	Stops
	Vowels							
HIGHEST SONORITY (MORE OPEN)			←	→			LOWEST SONORITY (LESS OPEN)	

Sonority is relevant for syllable phonotactics in two ways. First, it explains why vowels are typically the syllable nuclei: vowels are the most open sounds and therefore ideal sonority peaks, while, on the other hand, consonants are more obstructed and thus tend to occur as syllable margins. Second, sonority underlies the typical location of sounds within the onset, nucleus and coda. The syllable is organized around the sonority peak (typically a vowel); sonority tends to increase toward the nucleus and decrease toward the coda, as exemplified in (13). Note that the onset comprises a stop followed by a rhotic, resulting in increasing sonority toward the nucleus; and the coda is formed of a fricative followed by a stop, involving decreasing sonority toward the end of the syllable. Other words following this pattern include *plant* and *friends*.

(13)   [tɹʌst]

Note that the following words are impossible in English: *rtust, *lpatn, *friedsn. The reason is that their onset clusters have decreasing sonority, and/or their coda clusters have increasing sonority.

Similarly, in triphthongs the middle vowel is the most open: sonority increases toward the middle vowel and decreases toward the end, as exemplified in (14) for the word *guai* 'trouble' in Italian. Note that the middle vowel is low and thus more sonorous than the surrounding high vowels.

(14)   [g u̯ a i̯]

If your conlang allows complex onsets, usually the first consonant will be of lower sonority than the second. If it allows complex codas, the first consonant will have higher sonority than the one following it. And if your conlang allows triphthongs, usually the middle vowel will be the most open. However, there are exceptions; in English, for example, /s ʃ/ can precede stops in onset clusters (*spray, skunk*). /s/ can also follow stops in coda, as in *prints, maps*. Crosslinguistically, sibilant fricatives tend to be exceptional in this respect.

> ### Your Turn
>
> Draw sonority diagrams for the following Na'vi words (from Müller 2024):
>
> *meyp*   [mɛi̯p]   'weak'
> *fngap*   [fŋap]   'metal'

Phonotactics also might involve restrictions of certain sounds in certain syllable positions. We've already mentioned earlier in the chapter that some natlangs only allow rising or falling diphthongs. Consonants can be restricted as well. For example, in English /h/ can only occur in onset (*here, home*) and /ŋ/ in coda (*sing, rang*); in Spanish, /tʃ/ and /ɲ/ are found in onset only (*chicle* [tʃi.kle] 'chewing gum,' *año* [a.ɲo] 'year'). Sometimes, sounds are restricted to specific onsets or codas in the word. For example, in English [ʒ] only occurs as an onset word-medially (as in *treasure*), except for *genre* and in borrowings from other languages. A similar case is found in Spanish, where [ɾ] is found only as an onset word-medially (as in *caro* 'expensive'). Other languages allow consonants only with certain places or manners of articulation in onset or coda.

Specific consonant combinations might be disallowed in syllable margins; for example, in some languages complex codas are required to have identical phonation or place of articulation. The reason for these restrictions is often articulatory; it is easier to maintain the position of the articulators and the same configuration of the larynx across sounds sharing the same syllable position.

> **Your Turn**
>
> - If there are complex onsets in your conlang, does sonority increase toward the nucleus?
> - If there are complex codas, does sonority decrease toward the end of the word?
> - If your conlang has triphthongs, is the middle vowel the most open?
> - Are there any consonants that can exclusively occur in onset or coda?

5.6 Conlanging Practice: Syllabification in the Ur Languages

A. The following are words from one of the languages spoken in Ur. Find examples of monophthongs, diphthongs and triphthongs. For diphthongs and triphthongs, indicate if they have **falling or rising** sonority.

[ao̯]	'flower'	[xrin]	'water'	[nez]	'air'
[li̯ae̯]	'seaweed'	[roi̯.mi]	'boy'	[xai̯r.za.li]	'to live'

B. Now find examples of complex codas and complex onsets:

[nerz]	'moon'	[tla.ni]	'girl'	[oz.nelt]	'fire'
[u.xro]	'to see'	[kru.xur]	'to die'	[znoi̯]	'ocean'

C. Considering the words above, choose the correct syllabification of the following words:

[az.ni] / [a.zni] 'heart'
[pi.tlo] / [pit.lo] 'tomorrow'

5.7 Syllables in the Salt Language

As we saw in previous chapters, muq has nine contrastive vowels /i e æ ə a ɑ o u/ and twenty-nine consonants /p t c k q b d ɟ g ɢ m n ɲ ŋ N ʙ r ɸ s z ç j x ɣ χ ʁ l ʎ ʟ/. From the lexicon so far (Section 4.6), syllables can have codas (stops, as in [muk] 'money, payment,' or fricatives, as in [ɸuç] 'night').

The Salt language has three diphthongs: [ei] [ou] [əɨ]; all begin with a mid vowel and have falling sonority. In addition, the vowels in each diphthong share the same advancement (front, back and central, respectively) (15a). Other adjacent vowels are nuclei of separate syllables (15b).

(15) Adjacent vowels in muq
    a. Diphthongs: [χei]   'tree'   [χou]   'light'
    b. Hiatus: [ɣi.ɑm]   'to rest'   [ʁo.eŋ]   'greetings'

Complex onsets are formed with stops followed by an alveolar trill or lateral (16). All consonants can be codas (17). Complex codas of up to two consonants are allowed for nasal + fricative, fricative + stop, and nasal + stop sequences (18).

(16) Complex onsets in muq
    a. Voiced stop + alveolar trill: [brei]   'pale, faint'
    b. Voiceless stop + alveolar trill: [tri.za]   'floor'
    c. Voiced stop + alveolar lateral: [gli.mæ]   'sea snail'
    d. Voiceless stop + alveolar lateral: [tlouq]   'large stone, rock'

(17) Simple codas in muq
    a. Coda laterals: [θoʟ]   'child'
    b. Coda nasals: [zim]   'friend'
    c. Coda stops: [muq]   'the muq; our people; our language'
    d. Coda fricatives: [ɸuç]   'night, death'

(18) Complex codas in muq
    a. Nasal+ fricative: [ʎens]   'shore'
    b. Fricative+ stop: [kust]   'salt, life force'
    c. Nasal+ stop: [ʟumt]   'snow, cold'

The Salt language has complex syllable structure. Most words are one or two syllables long. Examples of disyllabic words with varied syllabic structures are given in (19).

(19) Syllabification in muq
    a. CV. CV   [ze.za]   'to talk'
    b. CCV.CV   [gli.mæ]   'sea snail'
    c. CV. CVC   [ɲa.çen]   'mountain'
    d. CVC. CV   [sæm.ʎu]   'archer'
    e. CVC. CVC   [qæn.qən]   'to work'
    f. CVC. CVCC   [tət.penk]   'to gather, to collect'

5.8 Guide to Developing Your Conlang Syllable Structure

- List all contrastive vowels in your conlang (in IPA).
- List all contrastive consonants (in IPA).
- Are onsets obligatory or optional?
- Are there complex onsets? What is the maximum number of consonants in onset? Are there restrictions as to how they combine?
- Are codas allowed? If so, can all consonants be codas?
- Can codas be complex? If so, are there any restrictions as to how they combine?
- Based on your answers above, what syllable structure does you conlang have?
- Are diphthongs allowed? If so, are they restricted to specific vowel combinations?
- Are vowels allowed to be adjacent nuclei of different syllables (i.e., hiatus)?
- Are there triphthongs?
- Are there syllabic consonants? Which consonants can be syllabic?
- Provide examples of words with different syllable structures. If any structure is not possible, indicate N/A. If other syllable structures are attested, add them to the list and provide examples.

CV	CVC	CCV	CVCC
CCVC	CCVCC	CCCV	CCCVC

- Syllabify (or revise the syllabification) of all words in your conlang lexicon taking into consideration your answers above.

To Learn More

The discussion of syllable structure in this chapter follows Maddieson (2013d). For a detailed account of English syllable structure and phonotactics, see chapter 6 in Yavaş (2020); pages 68–71 provide many examples of syllabic consonants in English. For Spanish syllabification, see chapter 5 in Hualde (2005). Chapter 4 in Gordon (2016) offers a detailed account of syllables and syllabification in natlangs. The Tashlhiyt Berber examples are from Ridouane (2014). Other sources mentioned in this chapter are included in the list of references at the end of this book.

6 Stress and Tone

Once you have worked out the syllable structure of your conlang, you need to decide whether it will have stress or tone. Sections 6.1 and 6.2 discuss stress and the types of stress systems attested in languages. Sections 6.3 and 6.4 focus on tone, and Section 6.5 previews intonation. Section 6.6 exemplifies stress and tone in conlangs, and Section 6.7 provides conlanging practice on both. Section 6.8 describes the stress system of the Salt language, and Section 6.9 includes a list of guided questions to facilitate the incorporation of stress or tone in your conlang. As usual, the chapter ends with a list of sources to explore further.

Key Words

Clitics
Demarcative property
Intonation
   Uptalk
Stress
   Primary stress (main stress)
   Secondary stress
   Stress clash
   Stress lapse
Stress systems
   Fixed stress
   Lexical stress
   Morphological stress
   Weight-sensitive (quantity-sensitive) stress
      Heavy syllables
      Light syllables
Tonal language
   Complex tonal language
   Pitch accent language
   Simple tonal language

Tone
    Contour tone
        Rising vs. falling tone
    Level tone

6.1 What Is Stress?

Stress refers to relative syllable prominence. Consider, for example, the word *centaur*; the first syllable is more prominent than the second. On the other hand, in the word *mirage* the second syllable is more prominent than the first. Prominent syllables are stressed, and those that are not prominent are unstressed.

What exactly makes a syllable 'prominent'? It depends on the language: prominent syllables might involve higher amplitude (i.e., they are 'louder'), longer duration and/or a change in pitch (i.e., the rate in which vocal folds vibrate). Russian and Thai are natlangs where stressed syllables have higher amplitude and increased duration, respectively, while in Spanish stressed syllables tend to have higher pitch. In English, stressed syllables tend to be longer and involve pitch changes. Stressed syllables might also have more fully articulated segments than unstressed syllables.

In stress languages, nouns, verbs and other content words have at least one prominent syllable, that is, a syllable with **primary** or **main stress**. Examples for English are given in (1). Following IPA conventions, main stress is indicated with the superior vertical stroke diacritic ['] before the stressed syllable. Monosyllabic content words are stressed in English, but this is not always the case in natlangs.

(1)　　Main stress in English
　　　a. Nouns:　　　book　　['bʊk]　　mirage　　[mɪ.'ɹɑʒ]
　　　b. Verbs:　　　seem　　['sim]　　escape　　[ɛ.'skeɪp]
　　　c. Adjectives:　blue　　['blu]　　pinkish　　['pɪŋ.kɪʃ]
　　　d. Adverbs:　　well　　['wɛl]　　fondly　　['fɑnd.lɪ]

In longer words, there might be additional prominent syllables; these have **secondary stress**. Syllables with secondary stress have less prominence than those with primary stress (but more than unstressed syllables). Examples of secondary stress in English are given in (2); the diacritic for secondary stress in IPA is the inferior vertical stroke [ˌ] placed before the syllable.

(2)　　Secondary stress in English
　　　a. secondary　　['sɛ.kn̩ˌdɛ.ɹɪ]
　　　b. universe　　　['ju.nɪˌvɛɹs]

In some natlangs, main and secondary stress might fall on (or close to) opposite word edges. This occurs in Saynáwa: the final syllable in a word has main stress, and the initial or second syllable has secondary stress (3). In other natlangs, secondary stress occurs in alternating syllables, as in Huariapano (4). Stress alternation conveys a rhythmical quality to the word and avoids **stress clash** (i.e., having adjacent stressed syllables) and **stress lapse** (i.e., having adjacent unstressed syllables).

(3) Stress in Saynáwa (from Couto 2010: 141, 146, 181)
    a. [ˌbuʃ.ˈkaʔ] 'head'
    b. [i.ˌkə.ne.ˈβĩʔ] 'castanet'
    c. [ma.ˌpo.tə.ˈɾe.peʔ] 'nape'

(4) Stress in Huariapano (from Parker 1998:7, 8)
    a. [mi.ˌβom.bi.ˈra.ma] 'you plural'
    b. [ˌjo.mɯ.ˌraj.βan.ˈşi.ki] 'they hunted'

> **DID YOU KNOW?**
>
> Natlangs vary in their tolerance for stress clash. Sometimes adjacent stressed syllables are permitted; but other times, one of the syllables loses prominence, or results in stress shifting to another syllable. In English, for example, the word *sixteen* has main stress on the last syllable when pronounced in isolation: [sɪkˈstin]. However, when it precedes a word with initial stress, the stress in *sixteen* shifts to the first syllable: thus, *sixteen candles* is pronounced [ˈsɪk.stin ˈkæn.d|z], and *sixteen tons* [ˈsɪk.stin ˈtɑnz].

Not all natlangs have secondary stress. Spanish is a case in point; lexical words have only one stressed syllable (5a, b) except for adverbs ending in *-mente* (a suffix akin to English *-ly* in words such as *smartly* or *pathetically*; 5c, d). The fact that Spanish adverbs ending in *-mente* have secondary stress is a historical quirk; these adverbs originated from combining adjectives in Latin with the lexical word *mente*, which meant 'in the manner of.' Eventually, *-mente* became a suffix in Spanish but, remarkably, it kept its initial prominence. As we saw previously, the diacritic [̪] indicates a dental sound, and [̯] is used for the least open vowel in a diphthong. In addition, the diacritic [˕] indicates that a sound has less constriction; in (5b, c) it indicates that the consonant is approximant.

(5) Spanish stress
   a. *secundario*   [se.kuṇ.ˈda.ɾi̯o]   'secondary'
   b. *universe*   [u.ni.ˈβer.so]   'universe'
   c. *suavemente*   [ˈsu̯a.βe.ˌmeṇ.te]   'softly'
   d. *malamente*   [ˈma.la.ˌmeṇ.te]   'badly'

> **Your Turn**
>
> Which syllables are stressed in the words below?
>
> conlang invent universe wizard challenge

Functional words such as prepositions or conjunctions tend to be unstressed (6). However, they can be stressed if emphasized, as in the bolded examples in: *I saw the unicorn **in** the forest, not next to it*, or in *I saw **her** buying a cauldron, not him*.

(6) Grammatical words in English
   a. Pronouns: him   [hɪm]   her   [hɜɹ]
   b. Articles: a, an   [ə], [ən]   my   [mai̯]
   c. Prepositions: in   [ɪn]   with   [wɪθ]
   d. Conjunctions: and   [ənd]   while   [wai̯l]

Stress languages differ regarding where main stress is located and whether they allow secondary stress; we explore various options next.

6.2 Stress Typology

There are four main types of **stress systems: lexical, morphological, fixed** and **weight-sensitive.** Natlangs tend to favor one of these systems, although sometimes different stress systems coexist in a language.

6.2.1 Lexical Stress

Some natlangs have **lexical stress systems**, since the location of the stressed syllable in a word is unpredictable. Examples include Ukrainian (7) and Spanish (8). In Spanish, words can be stressed on the final, penultimate or antepenultimate syllable. This is sometimes referred to as a 'three-syllable window' for stress. Stress occurs beyond these three syllables only in verbs that have attached pronouns (**clitics**) (8d, e). Note that Spanish orthography does not always indicate where stress falls.

(7) Stress in Ukrainian (from Pompino-Marschall et al. 2017:354)
    a. [ˈku.rɪ]   'chicken' (plural)   [kuˈrɪ]   'to smoke'
    b. [dɔˈrɔ.ɦa]   'road'   [dɔ.rɔˈɦa]   'dear'

(8) Stress in Spanish
    a. *límite*   [ˈli.mi.te]   '(the) limit'
    b. *limite*   [liˈmi.te]   '(s/he) limits (subjunctive)'
    c. *limité*   [li.miˈte]   '(I) limited'
    d. *invéntatelo*   [imˈbeṉ.ta.te.lo]   'invent it yourself'
    e. *cántamela*   [ˈkaṉ.ta.me.la]   'sing it for me'

6.2.2 Morphological Stress

In **morphological stress**, stress is on different syllables in different types of words. This occurs in English, where verbs tend to be stressed on the last syllable (*to en_chant_, to sa_shey_*), and nouns on the penultimate (*_an_gel, _cen_taur*) or antepenultimate (*_fic_tional, _u_niverse*). The addition of certain suffixes can make stress shift; compare *_u_niverse* vs. *uni_ver_sal*.

Languages with morphological stress can have minimal pairs where stress is contrastive; examples in English include *coral*, *(to) corral* and *insight*, *(to) incite*.

6.2.3 Fixed Stress

In natlangs with **fixed stress**, stress predictably falls on the same syllable. About half of stress natlangs have this pattern. Crosslinguistically, stress tends to gravitate to certain syllables. In fact, most natlangs with fixed stress have main stress on the first syllable (Finnish, Comanche), the last (French, Berber) or the penultimate (Hawaiian, Quechua). Less commonly, natlangs with fixed stress have it on the second syllable (Dakota, Mapudungun) or the antepenultimate (Greek, Plains Cree).

Overall, natlangs favor stressed syllables at or close to the edges of the word. This is known as the **demarcative property** of stress, and it is considered to help in language acquisition and language processing.

6.2.4 Quantity-Sensitive Stress

If a language has **weight-sensitive (quantity-sensitive) stress**, stress depends on syllable structure, particularly the rhyme (as you remember, this syllable unit comprises the nucleus and the coda, if present). In quantity-sensitive languages, syllables are **heavy** if they have a long vowel, a diphthong and/or a coda consonant, and **light** if they don't. Heavy syllables attract stress, unlike light syllables.

One example of a language with quantity-sensitive stress is Latin. Latin has antepenultimate stress by default (9a, b). However, when the penultimate syllable has a long vowel or a coda, the syllable counts as heavy and attracts stress (9c, d).

(9) Quantity-sensitive stress in Latin
    a. *vetulus* ['ve.tu.lus] 'old'
    b. *ōrāculum* [oː.'raː.ku.lum] 'oracle'
    c. *purpurātus* [puɾ.pu.'raː.tus] 'dressed in purple'
    d. *salsāmentum* [sal.saː'men.tum] 'brine, salted fish'

Another example of a natlang with quantity-sensitive stress is Capanahua, where stress is initial if the second syllable is light (10a). But if the second syllable has a coda, it counts as heavy and attracts stress (10b).

(10) Capanahua stress (from Loos 1969)
    a. ['ho.no] 'wild pig' ['tsis.ti] 'ashes'
    b. [hi.'sis] 'ant' [ma.'pop] 'clay'

Natlangs with quantity-sensitive stress vary regarding which syllables count as heavy. In some it is syllables with long vowels (as in Estonian), in others syllables with coda consonants (as in Dutch) and in others, both (as in Latin). In addition, some natlangs treat only certain coda consonants as heavy. For example, in Mam only glottal stop codas make syllables heavy, and in Inga, which has default penultimate stress, only sonorant codas do (11).

(11) Inga stress (from Goedemans & van der Hulst 2013c)
    a. [kam.'ku.na] 'you (plural)'
    b. ['kan.tʃis] 'seven'
    c. [ja.'war] 'blood'

If your conlang has codas, long vowels and/or diphthongs, you might consider quantity-sensitive stress. Note that languages might have weight-sensitive stress for primary stress, for secondary stress, or both.

> **Your Turn**
>
> Sindarin has quantity-sensitive stress as in Latin: the first syllable of a disyllabic word is stressed, and in longer words, stress falls on the penultimate if heavy, otherwise on the antepenultimate. Heavy syllables have either a long vowel, a diphthong or a complex coda (Salo 2004:23, 24). Based on this, indicate the stressed syllable in the following Sindarin words.

lembas	[lɛm.bɑs]	'journey-bread'
dúnadan	[duː.nɑ.dɑn]	'man of the west'
angerthas	[aŋ.ger.θɑs]	'long rune-row'
annúnaid	[ɑ.nːuː.na̯id]	'Westron language'

6.3 What Is Tone?

As we've seen before, pitch can be a cue to stress, together with duration and amplitude. A second use of pitch is to use it contrastively in words; this is known as **tone**. If you are not familiar with **tonal languages**, it might seem daunting to incorporate tone in your conlang. But the basics of tonal systems are not hard; and there are advantages of making your conlang tonal. In addition, scholars estimate that 40 percent to 60 percent of natlangs are tonal; thus, tonal languages are almost as common as stress languages – maybe even more.

In some natlangs all syllables have tones (as in Thai or Mandarin Chinese). In others, only certain syllables carry it (as in Ainu and certain varieties of Basque). The latter are often referred to as **pitch accent languages**. We will focus mostly on tonal languages of the first type.

If a tone is mostly flat within the syllable, it is considered a **level tone**. High, low and mid tones are the most common level tones. If there is a pitch movement within the syllable (e.g., a rise or fall), it is considered a **contour tone**.

Tonal languages can be **simple** or **complex**. Simple tonal languages have a two-way contrast between High (H) and low (L) tones. Navajo and Igbo fall in this group; examples from Igbo are given in (12). Note that high tone is transcribed with an acute accent [´], and low tone with a grave accent [`] over the vowel.

(12)   Tone in Igbo (Hyman 2018: 699; Hayes 2009:291–292)
     a. H H   [ákwá]   'crying'
     b. H L   [ákwà]   'cloth'
     c. L H   [àkwá]   'egg'
     d. L L   [àkwà]   'bed'

(listen at https://linguistics.ucla.edu/people/hayes/IP/Sound/IbgoAkpaHH_LH_HL_LL.wav)

Complex tonal languages include additional contrasts. This is the case in Thai, which has high, mid and low tones, as shown in (13). Note that the mid tone is transcribed with a macron [¯]. Simple tonal languages are more common in natlangs than complex tonal languages.

(13)　　Level tones in Thai (from Kalaya Tingsabadh & Abramson 1999:149)
　　　　a. High　[kʰá:]　'to engage in trade'
　　　　b. Mid　　[kʰā:]　'to get stuck'
　　　　c. Low　　[kʰà:]　'galangal (a kind of spice)'

Natlangs can distinguish up to five tonal levels: high, mid, low, extra low and extra high. One example of a natlang with all these distinctions is Gimira (Bench), shown in (14). Extra low and extra high tones are transcribed with double grave [ˋˋ] and double acute accents [ˊˊ], respectively.

(14)　　Level tones in Gimira (from Villupillai 2012:81 and references therein)
　　　　a. Extra high　[kȁr]　'clear'
　　　　b. High　　　　[kári]　'inset; banana leaf'
　　　　c. Mid　　　　　[kār]　'to circle'
　　　　d. Low　　　　　[kàr]　'wasp'
　　　　e. Extra low　　[kȁr]　'loincloth'

The most common contour tones are **rising**, involving a rise from low to high tone, and **falling**, with a fall from high to low. Examples from Thai are given in (15); rising and falling tones are transcribed with wedge [ˇ] and circumflex diacritics [ˆ], respectively.

(15)　　Contour tones in Thai (from Kalaya Tingsabadh & Abramson 1999:149)
　　　　a. Rising　　[kʰǎ:]　'leg'
　　　　b. Falling　[kʰâ:]　'I'

Table 6.1 lists the most frequent tones in natlangs according to the PHOIBLE database (Moran & McCloy 2019). Note that the IPA transcribes tones in two ways: with accent diacritic marks on the vowel (as shown in examples 12–15), and with tonal letters following or preceding the syllable. Tonal letters involve the use of a vertical stroke connected to a preceding line which signals tonal height and tonal movement, if relevant. Tonal letters are iconic; for level tones the five possible heights within a speaker's pitch range (from extra high to extra low) are conveyed as [˥ ˦ ˧ ˨ ˩]. For contour tones, the beginning and end points of the line convey specific tonal movements. For example, a rising tone is represented as [˩˥], and a falling tone as [˥˩]. Although tonal diacritics and tone letters are equivalent, it is worth pointing out that tonal diacritics are often used to transcribe languages with level tones, and tonal letters are favored for languages with contour tones.

As shown in Table 6.1, the most frequent tones in natlangs are high and low, followed by mid. Other tonal distinctions are rarer. Contour tones other than rising and falling are attested, but since they occur in 1 percent or less of natlangs they are not included here.

Table 6.1 Most frequent tones in natlangs (based on Moran & McCloy 2019)

	Tone	Diacritic	Tone letter	Frequency %
Level	Extra high	[á̋]	˥	3
	High	[á]	˦	18
	Mid	[ā]	˧	10
	Low	[à]	˨	18
	Extra low	[ȁ]	˩	2
Contour	Rising	[ǎ]	˦˥	2
	Falling	[â]	˥˦	2

6.4 Tone, Segments and Syllable Structure

Tonal languages tend to have somewhat larger segmental inventories than non-tonal languages. Specifically, complex tonal natlangs have on average 26 contrastive consonants, simple tonal languages 23, and non-tonal languages 22. In addition, complex tonal natlangs have on average 7 contrastive vowels, compared to 6 in simple tonal languages and 5–6 in non-tonal languages. Complex tonal languages also tend to have moderately complex syllable structures, and non-tonal languages complex syllable structures (simple tonal languages can go either way).

Contour tones tend to occur in syllables that have long vowels and/or coda sonorants since they involve two tonal targets and take longer to be pronounced. Tone can be conveyed through sonorants, but not obstruents, explaining why contour tones are more likely to be realized in syllables with sonorant codas. An additional restriction found in some natlangs is that contour tones are often limited to word-final syllables, a position that tends to be lengthened.

The discussion in this chapter so far implies that languages are either stress-based or tonal; most natlangs are in fact like this. But tone and stress can co-occur. For example, in Zapotec and Trique, only stressed syllables may bear tonal contrasts, while in some dialects of Mixtec, stress depends on the specific tones of a syllable.

Incorporating tone in your conlang will certainly help to distinguish it from English, Spanish and other major Indo-European languages. Having a complex tonal system allows you to increase the number of possible contrastive words in the lexicon. This is a particularly good strategy to consider if your conlang has relatively short words and/or has a small segmental inventory. Dixon (2016) notes that if you have a segmental inventory with 5 contrastive vowels and 20 contrastive consonants, you can have 100 different CV words (5 x 20), and up to 10,000 possible CV.CV words (100 x 100). With two tones per word, the possibilities double. At least with two-syllable words, you would get a similar number of possible contrastive words with lexical stress. But as we have seen, tonal languages can have up to ten different tones, and these might be different in various syllables of the word, which greatly increases the possibilities of expanding the lexicon.

6.5 Intonation

Intonation is the use of pitch beyond the word level to encode discourse meaning. All languages, regardless of whether they have stress or tone, have intonation. Intonation has many possible functions: one of them is to distinguish among sentence types such as statements or questions. Usually, statements have final falling intonation, and yes–no questions have final rising intonation (16). Note that ↘ conveys falling intonation and ↗ rising intonation in IPA.

(16)   English intonation
      a. Dark matter cannot be seen directly. ↘
      b. Dark matter cannot be seen directly? ↗

The 'standard' way to convey neutral statements in English is with falling final intonation. However, there is a growing trend for younger people in the USA, Australia and other English-speaking countries to end statements with rising intonation; this is known as **uptalk**. Uptalk used to be more common in young women, but recent studies show that men and older women also use it. In fact, you might use uptalk when you answer a question or order a drink at your favorite coffee shop!

Intonation is typically not described in conlangs; a similar intonation to that of English is often assumed. We will return to the role of intonation in Chapter 11, in connection to syntax.

6.6 Stress and Tone in Conlangs

Toki Pona and Esperanto have fixed stress. Toki Pona has initial stress: [ˈwa.lo] 'white,' [ˈpi.me.ja] 'black.' Esperanto has penultimate stress: [ˈba.tu] 'beat,' [fa.mi.ˈli.o] 'family.' Na'vi has lexical stress (17a, b); secondary stress can occur in polysyllabic words (17c).

(17)　Na'vi stress (from Müller 2024)
　　　a. *túte*　　　　　['tu.te]　　　　　　'person'
　　　b. *tuté*　　　　　[tu.'te]　　　　　　'female person'
　　　c. *meoauniaea*　　[ˌmɛ.o.a.u.ni.a.'ɛ.a]　'harmony'

Quenya, Sindarin and Dothraki have quantity-sensitive stress. Stress in Sindarin and Quenya is like that of Latin: stress falls on the penultimate syllable if heavy, otherwise on the antepenultimate. Heavy syllables have either a long vowel, a diphthong or a complex coda (Salo 2004:23, 24; Fauskanger 2002:58–62).

In Dothraki, a closed final syllable attracts stress (18a). If the final syllable is open but the penultimate has a coda, the penultimate is stressed (18b). Otherwise, stress falls on the initial syllable (18c).

(18)　Dothraki stress　　　　　　　　　(from Peterson 2015)
　　　a. Final stress:　　　　*eyel*　　　　[e.'jel]　　　'rain'
　　　b. Penultimate stress:　*zhavorsa*　　[ʒa.'vor.sa]　'dragon'
　　　c. Initial stress:　　　*ataki*　　　　['a.ta.ki]　　'first'

Klingon stress is both morphological and quantity-sensitive. In verbs, stress falls on the root. Verbal suffixes with coda [ʔ] (romanized ⟨'⟩) are also stressed unless immediately adjacent to the stressed root. In nouns, stress falls on the final syllable if there are no suffixes; otherwise on the syllable before the suffix (Okrand 1985:17).

Láadan has a simple tonal system. The word *Láadan* is pronounced [lá.à.dàn]. Orthographically, Láadan indicates high tone with an acute accent but leaves low tone unmarked (Elgin et al. 2020:16). Ithkuil has a complex tonal system featuring three level tones (low, mid, high) and four contour tones: rising, falling, rising-falling and falling-rising. Ithkuil also has stress; each word in this conlang has a tone, pronounced from the stressed syllable until the end of the word. The mid-tone is neutral and occurs in unstressed syllables at the beginning of a word. Stress in Ithkuil usually falls on the penultimate syllable, but it is affected by morphology.

6.7 Conlanging Practice: Stress and Tone in the Ur Languages

A. Consider the words from the following Ur language introduced in Section 5.6.

[roi̯.mi]　'boy'　　[tla.ni]　'girl'　　[oz.nelt]　'fire'
[u.xro]　'to see'　[kru.xur]　'to die'　[xai̯r.za.li]　'to live'

Indicate how the following stress patterns would apply to the words above:

- Final stress
- Initial stress
- Stress the first syllable of verbs; stress the last syllable of nouns.
- Stress the last syllable if it has a coda; otherwise stress the penultimate.

B. The four main languages in Ur are related; its linguistic ancestor, Ancient Urish, was a tonal language with three level tones and four contour tones.
- List the tones of Ancient Urish.
- Using IPA, transcribe seven CV words in Ancient Urish (ideally having identical sounds) that contrast tonally only. Don't forget to indicate the meaning of each word.

6.8 Stress in the Salt Language

As indicated in Section 5.7, muq allows certain complex codas but lacks complex onsets. It doesn't have long vowels, but it has the diphthongs [ei] [ou] [əi]. The muq language has quantity-sensitive stress. Stress falls on the first syllable unless the second syllable has a diphthong or a complex coda. Monosyllabic content words are always stressed. Examples are given in Table 6.2.

Table 6.2 Muq stress			
Monosyllabic words		Disyllabic words	
[ˈθə]	'one, single'	[ˈze.za]	'to talk'
[ˈlou]	'sky'	[ˈɣi.ɑm]	'to rest'
[ˈθoʟ]	'child'	[ka.ˈzei̯]	'eyes'
[ˈzei̯]	'flower'	[tət.ˈpenk]	'to gather, to collect'
[ˈkust]	'salt, life force'	[sa.ˈlenj]	'to live, to be alive'

While working on possible stress patterns, I needed to include words illustrating quantity sensitivity; in particular, [sa.ˈlenj] 'to leave' and [ka.ˈzei̯] 'eyes.' My lexicon was lacking disyllabic words with complex codas at the end of the word and words with final diphthongs. Thus, working out the stress pattern helped me build my lexicon to some extent.

I'm a fan of secondary stress, so muq has it in words of three or more syllables. Since the muq lexicon so far includes only monosyllabic and disyllabic words, I could (i) create longer words right now or (ii) wait to develop morphology, since usually morphology involves affixes that make words longer. I decided to create compounds, which gives me the opportunity to increase the lexicon using words I already have.

Let's begin with compounds combining two monosyllabic words. The first word will keep its stress (19a, b) unless the second has a complex coda or a diphthong (19c). This avoids stress clash and is consistent with the general stress pattern of muq.

(19) Stress in muq compounds combining monosyllabic words
   a. [ˈmuq]   +   [ˈçem]   [ˈmuq.çem]   'our island; the Muq homeland'
      muq   island
   b. [ˈχei̯] +   [ˈzei̯]   [χei̯.ˈzei̯] 'blossom, tree flower'
      tree   flower
   c. [ˈzei̯] +   [ˈχei̯]   [zei̯.ˈχei̯] 'flowering tree'
      flower   tree

Next, let's go over compounds combining disyllabic words. When both combined words have light syllables, the main stress falls on the initial syllable of the compound; the third syllable will have secondary stress (19a, b). When both combined words have a heavy final syllable, the main stress falls on the second syllable, and secondary stress on the fourth syllable (20c). This is consistent with the general stress pattern of muq and achieves rhythmicity.

(20) Stress in muq compounds combining disyllabic words (I)
   a. [ˈɲo.xe]   +   [ˈɴi.ʟa]   [ˈɲo.xe.ˌɴi.ʟa]   'to feast, to celebrate'
      to eat   to drink
   b. [ˈŋa.xen] +   [ˈji.ʟu]   [ˈŋa.xen.ˌji.ʟu]   'to party'
      to dance   to sing
   c. [sa.ˈlenj] +   [ka.ˈzei̯] [sa.ˈlenj.ka.ˌzei̯] 'beautiful'
      to live   eyes

Let's consider one last case. Certain compounds might result in stress shift to avoid stress clash or lapse. For example, when a compound combines a word with a heavy final syllable and a word with initial stress, the stress from the heavy syllable shifts left to avoid stress clash (21). Since the second syllable is now unstressed, it is pronounced as a monophthong (the second vowel, which was less open, is no longer pronounced, making the syllable light).

(21) Stress shift in muq compounds (III)
      [ka.ˈzei̯] +   [ˈkust]   [ˈka.ze.ˌkust]   'tear'
      eyes   salt

6.9 Guide to Developing Stress and Tone in Your Conlang

1. Will your language have stress or tone?
2. If your conlang has stress, will it be fixed, lexical, morphological or weight-sensitive stress?
   - For lexical stress, provide minimal pairs that differ in stress.
   - For fixed stress, indicate the default stress location.
   - For morphological stress, indicate how stress is assigned for nouns, verbs and other relevant word classes.
   - For weight-sensitive stress, indicate whether long vowels, diphthongs and/or coda consonants make a syllable heavy. Also indicate the default location of stress for light syllables.
   - If your lexicon includes words with three or more syllables, indicate if these words have secondary stress.
3. If your conlang is tonal, will it have a simple or complex tonal system?
   - How many level tones will it have?
   - How many contour tones?
   - Will contour tones be restricted to specific syllables/syllable structures?
4. Provide examples of how stress/tone works. You can use words from previous challenges. For stress, make sure that you include polysyllabic words. Remember to use IPA conventions and to indicate the meaning of each word.
5. Update your conlang database, including diacritics for tone or stress as needed.

To Learn More

A classic introduction to tone and tonal languages is Yip (2002). The distinction between simple and complex tonal languages is from Maddieson (2013e) in the *World Atlas of Language Structures Online* (WALS). The discussion of the benefits of tonal languages is based on Dixon (2016) and Hyman (2018); the latter is also the main source on Igbo for this chapter, together with Hayes (2009). Zhang (2002) is a great source for learning more on tonal restrictions.

Chapters 14–17 in WALS (Goedemans & van der Hulst 2013a–d) explore aspects of stress in languages. Chapter 17 focuses on patterns of secondary stress, which we leave mostly unexplored here. Chapter 6 in Gordon (2016) provides a detailed overview of stress typology. To browse stress patterns in over 700 natlangs, see the stress typology database Stresstyp2 at http://st2.ullet.net/.

For uptalk see Richart and Arvanite (2014) and Warren (2016). Additional sources mentioned in this chapter are listed in the references section at the end of the book.

7 The Lexicon

This chapter explores vocabulary building in conlanging. It is the first of three chapters focusing on morphology, that is, the study of words and their meaningful building blocks. This chapter introduces the lexicon and discusses how languages encode concepts into words. It also highlights strategies you can use to increase the number of words in your conlang.

Section 7.1 introduces the lexicon and word categories attested in natlangs. Section 7.2 focuses on content words (such as nouns and verbs), while Section 7.3 discusses function words (such as articles or pronouns). Section 7.4 previews possible strategies to develop the lexicon. The final sections provide practice in lexicon building (Section 7.5), discuss aspects of the muq lexicon (Section 7.6) and provide a set of guided questions to expand your conlang vocabulary (Section 7.7). The chapter closes with a list of references to explore.

Key Words

Affixation
  Affix
  Prefix
  Suffix
Antonym
Blends
Content/Lexical words
  Adjective
    Color terms
      Basic
      Secondary
  Adverb
    Degree
    Linking
    Manner
    Sentence
    Space
    Time

    Interjection
        Cognitive
        Conative
        Expressive
        Phatic
    Noun
        Abstract
        Common
        Concrete
        Count
        Mass
        Proper
    Verb
        Action
        Cognition
        Emotion
        Factive
        Motion
        Position
        Process
        Utterance
Derivational morphology
Endocentric compounds
Exocentric compounds
Function/Grammatical words
    Adposition
    Auxiliary verb (AUX)
    Conjunction
    Determiner
    Modal verbs
    Postposition
    Preposition
    Pronoun
        Demonstrative
        Interrogative
        Personal
        Possessive
        Relative
Lexicon
    Closed class
    Open class
    Subclasses

Lexicon building approaches
  Building block approach
  Corpus list approach
    Fantasy Frequency Wordlist
    Leipzig–Jakarta word list
    Swadesh list
  Dictionary approach
  Fictional text approach
  Lexicon-generator approach
  Proto-language approach
Roots

7.1 What Is the Lexicon?

The **lexicon** refers to the set of words in a language: its **nouns** (such as *vampire* or *universe*), **verbs** (*to dash, to experience*) and **adjectives** (*worldly, haphazard*), among others. Natlangs have thousands of words in their lexicons, but not all speakers of a language share all of them. Speakers' 'mental' dictionaries will differ somewhat, depending on the dialect and the speaker's previous linguistic experience, which is mediated by their age, occupation and hobbies, among other factors.

How many words does a language have? The 2022 edition of the Oxford English Dictionary lists over 600,000 words for English. Of these, many were common in earlier stages of the language but are no longer in use. A native speaker of English will have fewer words in their mental lexicon – perhaps between 20,000 and 50,000. Dixon (2016:172) estimates that languages have 5,000–10,000 words on average. This does not mean you need to come up with that many words in your conlang though! In fact, many conlangs are designed to have fewer words: Toki Pona has a core of 120 words; Esperanto began with over 900; and Láadan and Loglan started with 1,000. The number of words in your conlang will depend on your goals and time constraints. A reasonable goal is to aim for 100–200 at first.

This chapter provides ideas on how to develop the vocabulary of your conlang, focusing on **lexical** or **content words**. Content words refer to objects, ideas, properties, actions and states, and comprise most of the words in any given language. Because ideas, culture and technology change, the number of content words is large and is usually in flux; that is, content words are **open classes**. New words become part of the lexicon via compounding (*burner phone, to zoom bomb*); borrowing from other languages (*skunk* from Wampanoag; *mahi-mahi* from Hawaiian) or other creative means. Content words can also become dated (a fate common to most slang eventually, including words such as *groovy* or *fly*) or fall out of use completely when their referent is no longer in use (examples include *walkman, rolodex* and *zip disk*).

> **DID YOU KNOW?**
>
> It is unusual for natlangs to borrow words from conlangs – but there are exceptions. Some involve the names of specific conlangs (Klingon, Esperanto, Toki Pona) and the names of fictional worlds and beings, such as 'Mordor' or 'hobbit.' Other conlang borrowings in English include *mithril* [mi.θril] from Sindarin, meaning 'true silver' (from *mith* 'gray' and *ril* 'brilliance') and the insult *petaQ* [pɛ.tɑqχ] (from Klingon, meaning 'weirdo' or 'contemptible person'), used often in social media. In some parts of the United States, the word *silflay* from Lapine, the rabbit language of *Watership Down*, is also used with the meaning 'to eat' (in Lapine it means 'to feed above ground').

The lexicon also includes **grammatical** or **functional words**, which indicate a relationship between words in a phrase or **sentence**. Unlike content words, function words are few (i.e., they are **closed classes**) and tend to remain stable across time. It is much more unusual for natlangs to develop new function words or to borrow them from other languages. For example, although various gender-neutral **pronouns** have been proposed in English recently (among them *e, thon, hesh, tey, zie, ey* and *ve*), none of them has yet caught on (although this might change). In fact, most speakers prefer to use the pronoun *they*, which has been part of the language for a long time, to refer to a non-binary person.

Table 7.1 lists the most common word categories in natlangs and provides some examples from English. The following sections explore these categories in more detail.

Table 7.1 List of word categories

Content words		Function words	
Nouns	seaweed, dune	Determiner/article	the, a(n)
Verbs	to bewitch, to dance	Pronouns	they, them, their, theirs
Adjectives	intergalactic, magical	Auxiliary verbs	will, have
Adverbs	honestly, well	Adpositions	on, about, from
Interjections	ouch, uh-oh	Conjunctions	and, or, because, despite

> **Your Turn**
>
> - Can you think of relatively new words in English or another language? Why do you think these words have become part of the language?
> - What word types are represented in your conlang lexicon so far?

7.2 Content Words

Word categories differ according to their meaning, how they combine with other words, and their grammatical characteristics and/or functions. For example, **nouns** usually refer to people, objects and ideas. They might combine with articles (*the astronaut, a meteor*), and they can take plural endings (*astronauts, astronautas*). The characteristics that define word categories are variable across languages, however. For example, nouns in Finnish and Quechua cannot combine with articles since these languages don't have them; and not all natlangs have plural nouns (Pirahã and Mapudungun are examples). In fact, not all natlangs share the same word classes, except for nouns, verbs and interjections.

7.2.1 Nouns

Take a moment to examine the words you've created in your conlang. Chances are that most (or all) are nouns; and that most refer to people or objects. No judgment! Most of my muq words so far are **concrete nouns**, that is, nouns that refer to material, tangible objects. Several refer to objects relevant to the fictional world, including 'mountain,' 'island' or 'salt' (of course). Some refer to people, encompassing general terms ('the muq people,' 'human being,' 'child') and a few family relationships ('mother,' 'father,' 'parents').

From this cursory approximation, you might notice some lexical gaps. For example, muq does not yet have words referring to family relationships such as siblings or marriage/partnership. You might want to make a note (perhaps in the database itself) about any gaps you notice and come back to them later. Alternatively, you can take a mini break from this chapter and fill in some of these gaps now.

Another gap in the Salt conlang so far is the absence of **abstract nouns**, which refer to intangible ideas or concepts such as 'evil,' 'sadness' or 'patience.' Abstract ideas and concepts can be connected to culturally important notions and vary across languages. For example, in Portuguese *saudades* conveys melancholic longing or yearning. In addition, a language might not convey certain abstract words if the idea referred to is considered obvious. For example, the extinct Australian language Dyirbal lacked nouns or adjectives to indicate honesty, since it was a cultural assumption that everyone in the tribe was honest (Dixon 2016:186).

> **Your Turn**
>
> Consider abstract nouns that you might want to encode in your conlang. Think of whether the fictional group is isolated or well-connected; and any cultural aspects that are assumed, favored or unappreciated in the fictional world. For example, self-sufficient people living in isolation might lack a word for 'war,' 'peace' or even 'trade'; some fictional cultures might particularly favor friendship, loyalty, bravery or sensitivity.

In addition to denoting different types of referents, abstract and concrete nouns might have different grammatical properties in a language. If this is the case, they will form different **subclasses**. Nouns in a language might belong to various groups conveying different meanings and associated with specific grammatical properties. Beyond abstract and concrete nouns, other common noun subclasses are **proper** vs. **common** nouns and **count** vs. **mass** nouns.

Proper nouns identify individual people, places and organizations, whereas **common nouns** describe people, objects, places or concepts more generally. Because they have such specific referents, proper nouns do not typically co-occur with **determiners** or other modifiers (*the Liam, *a Tanzania). Note that capitalization or other orthographic conventions might convey this difference in writing in some languages, including English, but not in others. In German, for example, all nouns are capitalized regardless of whether they are common or proper. Even in English, some proper nouns are not capitalized: *bell hooks, danah boyd, will.i.am*. More importantly, proper and common nouns might have different morphology in languages. Note that although you might not (yet) need proper nouns referring to people in your conlang, you will need them for the geographical features in your fictional map.

Languages also tend to have **count nouns** and **mass nouns**. While count nouns can be counted (*unicorn, meteor*), mass nouns cannot (*fog, sand*). While you can have two meteors and many unicorns, you cannot have two fogs or two sands. Note that languages differ in the types of nouns considered mass or count as well as their grammatical properties.

> **Conlanging Tip**
>
> If your conlang has noun subclasses (proper/common nouns; count/mass nouns), you can indicate it in your lexicon database, perhaps under a 'subclass' column.

7.2.2 Verbs

Like nouns, **verbs** are attested in all conlangs. Verbs describe events (*to happen*), actions (*to dance*), emotions (*to love, to weep*), processes (*to grow*) and states (*to be*). They are typically marked for tense (when an action occurs in time: past, tense, future) and aspect (the perspective on an event: e.g., completed, in progress). Verbs might also carry agreement and/or indicate negation or other functions, as we will see in Chapter 9.

Table 7.2 lists various types of verbs distinguished according to their meaning. **Action verbs** describe events that do not necessarily affect another person. **Process verbs** convey situations that change over time, and action-process verbs refer to actions that influence somebody or something. **Factives** are used to describe actions that result in new existence; and states describe situations where there is no action or change. **Motion, position, emotion** and **utterance verbs** are quite self-explanatory. **Cognition verbs** involve an experiencing entity; sensation verbs express concepts related to the senses; and manipulation verbs depict actions involving force (physical or not) to make someone do something. These verb types can form subclasses; for example, utterance verbs tend to be irregular in many languages. Even if your conlang lacks verb subclasses, the list in Table 7.2 might be useful as you build your lexicon.

Table 7.2 Some verb types and meanings

Actions	dance, eat	States	be, have	Emotion	love, fear
Processes	grow, die	Motion	come, go	Sensation	feel, hear
Action-processes	break, kill	Position	sit, stand	Manipulation	cause, let
Factives	make, create	Cognition	know, forget	Utterance	say, sing

DID YOU KNOW?

The alien conlang Kēlen by Silvya Sotomayor has nouns, but not verbs. Instead, Kēlen has four relationals: *la* [la], *ñi* [ɲi], *se* [se] and *pa* [pa]. Existence relational *la* expresses a static state, a location, or equivalence. Change relational *ñi* expresses coming into existence or change in state or location. Transactional relational *se* conveys transactions such as giving and receiving, in addition to the sensing and experiencing of mental states. Finally, relational *pa* expresses a passive meaning.

7.2.3 Adjectives

Adjectives specify qualities or attributes, including size (*tiny*), shape (*wide*), color (*purple*) and value (*excellent*). Adjectives can also refer to temperature (*warm*), age (*ancient*) and other characteristics.

Adjectives modify nouns, as in <u>*heavy*</u> *cauldron*, <u>*young*</u> *wizard* and <u>*black*</u> *unicorn*. Typically, adjectives can have comparative and superlative forms. For example, in English the comparatives of *small* and *excellent* are *smaller* and *more excellent*, and their superlative forms *smallest* and *most excellent*.

All natlangs can express qualities, but not all natlangs have a class of adjectives. Among these are Hausa, which expresses qualities with nouns, and Ainu, which expresses them with verbs. In natlangs with adjectives, some have a limited (closed) set. For example, Toqabaqita has only the adjective *kali/kasi* 'small' (*kaala* in the plural). Another example is Igbo, which has only eight adjectives. Natlangs with a closed class of adjectives usually encode size, age, value and/or color. Other properties, including speed (*fast, slow*), temperature (*hot, cold*) and physical characteristics (*hard, soft*), tend to be expressed in these languages with nouns or verbs.

Some adjectives can be organized into pairs of **antonyms** conveying opposite meanings: fast vs. slow, good vs. bad, and so on. If your conlang has adjectives, you can consider these and other antonym pairs and consider adding additional degrees later (such as *excellent* and *awful* for value).

> **DID YOU KNOW?**
>
> The adjective *tween*, referring to a person between approximately nine and twelve years old, was coined by J. R. R. Tolkien in *Lord of the Rings* to describe the rough time hobbits hit when entering their second decade, before full adulthood.

Table 7.3 provides some possible adjective meanings and might be a good place to start when including adjectives in your conlang. Adjectives related to size, age, value and color are listed first since they tend to be more common cross-linguistically. Note that some adjectives listed apply to humans in English (*old, young, tween*) or might be restricted to describing specific objects; but this is by no means universal. Note also that color adjectives are discussed in more detail below. Even if your conlang lacks adjectives, this table might give you ideas of properties that could be expressed using nouns or verbs.

Table 7.3 Some adjective types and meanings

Property	Some possible meanings
Size	tiny, small, regular, large, immense, tall, short
Age	new, young, tween, adolescent, middle-aged, old, ancient
Value	great, excellent, good, average, bad, awful
Color	dark, light, black, white, red, yellow, blue, green
Position	high, low, far, distant, close
Speed	inert, slow, brisk, fast
Physical characteristics	soft, hard, deep, shallow, wide, narrow, thick, thin, beautiful, ugly
Human character	kind, evil, humble, arrogant, brave, cowardly, happy, unhappy

Your Turn

Will your conlang have adjectives?

- If adjectives comprise a limited set, list them and add them to your database.
- If adjectives are an open class, include at least ten, ideally related to the fictional world.

7.2.3.1 Color Terms

As we mentioned in Chapter 2, human beings appear to perceive color similarly, but not all natlangs convey the same colors in the lexicon or divide the color spectrum in the same way. As you develop your conlang, you might want to consider the relative importance of vision and colors in the fictional world and decide how many colors will have their own terms. Before doing so, it is useful to briefly describe how colors are expressed in natlangs.

One important distinction typically made is between **color terms** that are **basic** or **secondary** (non-basic). **Basic color terms** cannot be described as a variety of another color in the language, while **secondary color terms** can. Thus, *white*, *pink* and *blue* are primary color terms in English, while *off-white*, *magenta* and *turquoise* are secondary color terms because they refer to shades of white, pink and blue, respectively. Basic color terms are usually abstract and morphologically simple. On the other hand, secondary color terms might primarily refer to objects (*turquoise*, *gold*), can be limited in application (e.g., *blond* refers to hair and wood color), and are often derived morphologically. For example, the **suffix** *-ish* is used in English to refer to shades close in hue to a basic color term: *yellowish*, *reddish*; and compounding can be used to denotes shades of basic colors: *off-white*, *millennial pink*.

Natlangs distinguish two–twelve basic color terms. In natlangs with two basic color terms, as in Bassa, one encompasses 'light' colors (white, red and yellow) and the other 'dark' colors (such as black, green and blue). In natlangs with three basic color terms, as in Axininca Campa, a distinction is usually made among white, red-yellow and black-blue-green; and in natlangs with four basic color terms, as in Tifal, there is a distinction among either white, red, yellow and black-blue-green or among white, black, red-yellow and blue-green. In natlangs with five basic colors, as in Mikasuki, either red and yellow are differentiated, or green from black-blue.

Intriguingly, natlangs distinguishing fewer than five basic color terms tend to cluster in the tropics. Languages spoken by communities that are more technically developed and that manipulate and create color appear to have a larger number of color terms. English and Spanish fall in this category, distinguishing eleven basic color terms (white, black, yellow, red, green, blue, brown, pink, grey, purple and orange). Note that *orange* in English and the Spanish equivalent *naranja* are considered basic color terms since it is not clear whether their primary referent nowadays is the color or the fruit. This is also the case for *rosa* 'pink' in Spanish, which refers to a color and to the rose flower. Hungarian and Italian among other languages hold the record for distinguishing the highest number of basic color terms; Hungarian has basic terms for both dark red and light red, and Italian for light blue and dark blue (*azurro* [a.'tsu.ro] and *blu* ['blu], respectively).

A fascinating aspect in color systems in the world's languages is the treatment of 'cool' and 'warm' primary colors. For 'cool' primary colors, some natlangs distinguish lexically between blue and green (as English and Spanish); but most often, natlangs have just one word for both (sometimes translated as *grue*), as in Mikasuki. On the other hand, most natlangs distinguish between the 'warm' colors yellow and red. Just a few natlangs have a common term for both (rellow?), as in Central Tarahumara.

If a language has basic color terms, it might also have non-basic ones, but not the other way around. For example, in English we have the secondary color terms *beige* and *chartreuse* (borrowed from French) and we use terms such as *ivory* or *silver* to describe colors (via metaphoric extension from nouns). We can also combine basic color terms with other referents to convey specific hues, as in *jade green*, *baby blue* or *merlot red*. Some recent secondary color terms coined in English include *singularity black* and *vantablack*, which arose in the context of paint and pigments, and refer to the blackest black.

7.2.3.2 Color Terms in Conlanging

Toki Pona has five color adjectives: *pimeja* [pi.me.ja] 'black, dark,' *walo* [wa.lo] 'white, pale,' *loje* [lo.je] 'red,' *jelo* [je.lo] 'yellow' and *laso* [la.so] 'blue, green.' These words can be combined to refer to other colors: for example, *laso loje* is 'reddish blue' and *loje laso* is 'bluish red.' Both translate as 'purple' (Lang 2014:51).

Klingon expresses color through verbs (1). Orange and red are encoded as one term, and green, blue and yellow as another. Klingon lacks a term for 'purple,' apparently because the Klingons cannot process its wavelength.

(1) Klingon color terms (from Okrand 1985)
    a. *chIS* [tʃɪṣ] 'be white'
    b. *qIj* [qɪdʒ] 'be black'
    c. *Doq* [ɖoq] 'be red, orange'
    d. *SuD* [ṣuɖ] 'be yellow, blue, green'
    e. *Wov* [wow] 'be light, bright'
    f. *Hurgh* [xurɣ] 'be dark'

Láadan and Na'vi distinguish nine color terms each. In Na'vi they are all adjectives, but in Láadan they function as both adjectives and verbs (2, 3). Note that all Láadan color terms begin with [l].

(2) Na'vi color adjectives (from Müller 2024)
    a. *teyr* ['teir̩] 'white'   f. *neyn* ['nei̯n] 'light, white-shaded'
    b. *layon* [la.'jon] 'black'   g. *vawm* ['vawm] 'deep dark, brown'
    c. *rim* ['rim] 'yellow'   h. *ean* ['ɛ.an] 'green, blue'
    d. *tun* ['tun], ['tʊn] 'red, orange'   i. *ngul* ['ŋul] 'gray, drab'
    e. *'om* ['ʔom] 'violet, purple, magenta'

(3) Láadan color adjectives/verbs (from Elgin et al. 2020)
    a. *líithi* [lí.ɪ.θɪ] '(to be) white'
    b. *líithin* [lí.ɪ.θɪn] '(to be) gray'
    c. *laya* [la.ja] '(to be) red'
    d. *leyan* [lɛ.jan] '(to be) brown'
    e. *leyi* [lɛ.jɪ] '(to be) blue'
    f. *liyen* [lɪ.jɛn] '(to be) green'
    g. *léli* [lé.lɪ] '(to be) yellow'
    h. *layun* [la.jun] '(to be) orange'
    i. *loyo* [lo.jo] '(to be) black'
    j. *lula* [lu.la] '(to be) purple'

> **Your Turn**
>
> - Which conlang color system described above do you find most interesting, and why?
> - Which basic color terms will your conlang include? How will they be expressed?
> - Will your conlang have secondary color terms? If so, provide examples.
> - To what extent will the color system in your conlang be connected to the fictional world?

7.2.4 Adverbs

Adverbs can modify other lexical categories except for nouns. They can modify adjectives, as in *extremely blue*; verbs, as in *speak gently*; and other adverbs, as in *tremendously fast*. Adverbs can also modify sentences, as in *Obviously, this is a great chapter*.

Not all natlangs have adverbs; Ainu, for example, lacks them. Languages with adverbs might have different **subclasses**, including adverbs referring to **space** or **time** (*here, now*), **manner** (*sweetly, harshly*) and **sentence** adverbs (*frankly, supposedly*). Manner adverbs tend to be an open class of words, unlike other adverb types. Sentence adverbs tend to occur only in written European languages. In addition, sometimes languages have adverbs referring to **degree** (such as *almost* or *extremely*) or **linking** ideas (such as *thus* or *similarly*).

Table 7.4 provides a list of possible adverb meanings; it might be a good place to start if you are including adverbs in your conlang. We will explore adverbs further in Chapter 15.

Table 7.4 Examples of adverb types and meanings

Property	Possible meanings conveyed
Time	now, soon, late, later, never, always, yesterday, tomorrow, tonight
Space	here, there, above, below, close, far, downriver, north, outside, nearby
Degree	too, very, just, almost, really, slightly, barely, extremely, completely, highly
Linking	however, therefore, consequently, thus, hence, so, still, indeed, similarly
Sentence	obviously, evidently, apparently, reportedly, presumably, visibly, definitely, honestly, maybe, perhaps, unfortunately, probably
Manner	well, badly, slowly, cheerfully, clumsily, repeatedly, distractedly, sweetly

Many of the adverbs listed in Table 7.4 end in *-ly*, a suffix deriving adverbs from adjectives in English. In some languages, manner adverbs and adjectives have the same form, as in Swedish. This also occurs in English in some cases; for example, *fast* can be used both as an adjective (*This is a fast car*) and an adverb (*This car runs fast*).

7.2.4.1 Adverbs in Conlanging

One conlang that features adverbs of different types is Klingon; examples are given in (4).

(4)   Adverbs in Klingon (Okrand 1985:56)
   a. Setting   *not*   [not]   'never'
   b. Manner   *batlh* [bɑtɬ]   'with honor, in an honored fashion'
   c. Linking   *vaj*   [vɑdʒ]   'thus, in that case, so, accordingly, yet'
   d. Sentence *chaq*   [tʃɑq]   'perhaps'
   e. Degree   *neH*   [nɛx]   'only, merely, just'

> **Your Turn**
>
> - Does your conlang have adverbs? If so, of which type (e.g., spatial, temporal)?
> - Do adverbs have the same form as adjectives, or do they derive from other words?

7.2.5 Interjections

Interjections (such as *alas!*, *bah* or *ouch*) are lexical classes that express a range of meanings, including emotion. They seemingly occur in all natlangs. They differ from other word classes in various ways. First, interjections form complete utterances, unlike other word classes. Second, they can include sounds that are not present in the phonological inventory of the language. For example, in English the interjection of disgust *ugh* ends in a velar fricative; *tut tut* involves dental clicks; and *hmm*, conveying pondering, can be pronounced with a voiceless nasal. Third, interjections can deviate from the syllabic structure and phonotactics of the language. For example, *shh!* and *psst!* lack vowels, and *psst!* has a [ps] onset cluster.

Interjections can have different functions. **Expressive** interjections such as *yippee* or *yuck!* express emotion or the speaker's mood. **Cognitive** interjections convey the thoughts or state of knowledge of the speaker (*hmm*, *aha*). **Conative** interjections are used to address another person; these include *psst!* to get someone's attention and *shh!* to request that somebody be quiet. Finally, **phatic interjections** provide communicative cues (*eh?, uh-huh*); this subgroup includes greetings (*hi, bye*).

As with other word classes, natlangs vary in the interjections they use. For example, in Spanish *¡ay!* [ˈai̯] expresses sudden pain and *¡guau!* [ˈguau̯] conveys amazement. Interjections might also vary across dialect and speakers. For example, *vale* 'ok' is used to indicate agreement or understanding in Spain, unlike in other Spanish-speaking countries. In addition, some natlangs have unique interjections. For example, in Italian *bo!* [bo] indicates 'I don't know'; in Éwé, *ehẽ!* means 'I now remember!' (Ameka 1992:113).

You might want to include interjections or equivalent formulaic expressions in your conlang to convey greetings, goodbyes, thanks and apologies; ideally, they will be tailored to the fictional world. For example, it might be crucial in the fictional world to use polite interjections; or perhaps expressions meaning 'thank you' or 'please' might come across as too formal or inappropriate. Some possible meanings conveyed by interjections are included in Table 7.5.

Table 7.5 Some interjection types and meanings

Expressive (emotion/reaction)		Cognitive (state of knowledge)	
Happiness	*yippee!*	hesitation	*hmm*
Sadness	*aww*	confusion/thinking	*um*
surprise	*oh!*	suspicion	*hmm*
amazement	*wow!*	triumphant discovery	*eureka!*
disgust	*ugh, yuck!*	not knowing	*bo!* (Italian)
pain	*ouch!*	remembering	*ehẽ!* (Éwé)
Conative (to address people)		Phatic (communicative cues)	
to listen closely	*psst!*	greetings	*hi, bye*
be quiet	*shh!*	information request	*eh?*
warning	*uh-uh*	understanding	*uh-huh, ok*
to get someone's attention	*hey!, ahem*	misunderstanding	*huh?*
		to thank	*thanks*
		apologies	*sorry*
		other	*yes, no*

7 The Lexicon

7.2.5.1 Interjections in Conlanging

Salo (2004:153) lists four interjections in Sindarin: *A!* [a] 'O' (to address a person directly), *Alae!* [a.lae] 'ah' (to express deep emotion); *Elo!* [e.lo] 'Oh, wow' (to express wonder, admiration or delight) and *Nae!* [nae] 'Alas!' (to express sadness).

Okrand (1985:57) lists several interjections and expressions in Klingon; some examples are given in (5). Some, like (5e), can come across as rude to non-Klingons.

(5) Klingon interjections (from Okrand 1985:57, 58)
    a. *lu', luq*   [luʔ], [luq]   'yes, ok, I will'
    b. *ghobe'*   [ɣo.bɛʔ]   'no' (response to a question)
    c. *Qo'*   [qχoʔ]   'no, I won't, I refuse'
    d. *toH*   [tox]   'well, so, aha'
    e. *nuqneH*   [nuq.nex]   'What do you want?' (greeting)

> **Your Turn**
>
> Consider a few interjections or expressions for greetings, saying thank you, etc., in your conlang, and add them to your lexicon database.

7.3 Grammatical Words

Grammatical or function words encompass pronouns, determiners, adpositions, **conjunctions** and auxiliary verbs. They do not occur in all natlangs; when they do, they are closed word classes. This section briefly introduces grammatical words; they will be discussed in more detail in later chapters.

7.3.1 Pronouns

Pronouns are words referring to or standing for nouns and noun phrases. For example, in English, *he*, *she* and *it* replace or refer to a singular noun or noun phrase – masculine, feminine or inanimate, respectively, as shown in (6).

(6) English pronouns (I)
    a. <u>Imanol</u> is my brother.   = <u>He</u>
    b. <u>The kid with the green hair</u> lives upstairs.   = <u>She</u>
    c. <u>The book with snakes on the cover</u> was a present. = <u>It</u>

There are five main different types of pronouns. **Personal pronouns** refer to a person or thing (*you*, *it*). **Possessive pronouns** indicate possession (*yours*, *theirs*). **Demonstrative pronouns** indicate the relative location of the referent: *this*, *that*. We'll explore personal, possessive and demonstrative pronouns in more detail in Chapter 15.

Interrogative pronouns are used in questions (7). Finally, **relative pronouns** connect parts of sentences (8). We will return to interrogative pronouns in Chapter 11, and to relative pronouns in Chapter 13.

(7) Interrogative pronouns in English
 a. <u>What</u> would you like to read?
 b. <u>Who</u> is Jane dating now?

(8) Relative pronouns in English
 a. Kiana sold the car <u>that</u> she won in the sweepstakes.
 b. The singer, <u>who</u> I once met, died of cancer a few years back.

7.3.2 Determiners

Determiners are words that specify or quantify a noun phrase. They are also referred to as 'articles.' Determiners specify some aspect of the noun, including whether it is definite (*the boat*) or indefinite (*a boat*). As with pronouns, there is variability in whether determiners specify number, gender and case.

7.3.3 Adpositions

Adpositions are relatively common in natlangs; they are called **prepositions** if they precede the noun, and **postpositions** if they follow it. English has several prepositions, such as *in*, *on* or *at*. One example of a natlang with postpositions is Japanese. We'll explore adpositions in more detail in Chapter 10.

7.3.4 Conjunctions

Conjunctions are words linking sentences or parts of sentences; examples in English are given in (9). We examine conjunctions in more detail in Chapter 13.

(9) Conjunctions in English
 a. Mariel wants to travel to Mars, <u>but</u> I don't.
 b. <u>If</u> I buy a new space suit, I'll let you know.

7.3.5 Auxiliary Verbs

Auxiliary verbs (abbreviated Aux) differ from lexical verbs in several respects: they modify a lexical verb (as in: <u>have</u> eaten, <u>will</u> drive) and cannot appear in isolation (unless there is a clear discourse context, as in: *Will you date him? I <u>won't</u>*). They also tend to be shorter than lexical verbs. Typical auxiliary verbs in natlangs are *be*, *do* and *have*. These verbs can function lexically in isolation (*I am here*; *She has a migraine*) but act as supporting verbs next to a lexical verb. **Modal verbs** are a subtype of auxiliary verb expressing speaker attitudes or evaluation. Examples of modal verbs in English include *will, would, should* and *could*. Auxiliary verbs are explored further in Chapter 9.

> **Your Turn**
>
> Which types of grammatical words will you consider including in your conlang?

7.4 Developing the Lexicon

As noted earlier, only nouns, verbs and interjections are universal. This does not mean that languages lacking adverbs or adjectives are missing out; languages can recruit other word categories to convey any meaning that needs to be expressed.

Even when sharing word categories, not all languages encode meaning in the same way. You have probably realized this if you are multilingual or if you are learning another language. For example, in Spanish, the noun *dentera* [deṇ.'te.ɾa] indicates a (usually extremely) unpleasant feeling produced by tasting certain foods, hearing certain shrill noises or touching certain objects. In English, an equivalent noun does not exist, but you can convey the same meaning using the verbs or expressions *to shiver, to cringe* or *to set one's teeth on edge*. If you know several languages, you can probably think of other examples.

It is important to keep these considerations in mind when developing your conlang lexicon. This chapter has previewed possible meanings conveyed by word classes, but much of the **lexicon building** will depend on both your goals, preferences and characteristics (physical, technical, cultural and/or ideological) of the fictional world. There are different strategies you can use to develop the lexicon. The remainder of this section will focus on six: (i) the **dictionary approach,** (ii) the **corpus list approach,** (iii) the lexicon-generator approach, (iv) the **proto-language approach,** (v) the **building block approach** and (vi) the **fictional text approach.**

7.4.1 The Dictionary Approach

The **dictionary approach** to lexicon building consists of borrowing words from natlangs. The conlanger flips through (or, perhaps more plausibly now, scrolls down) natlang dictionaries and selects various words; their sound structure will need to be changed or adapted to the conlang phonology, and ideally the meaning will be changed or tweaked as well.

This approach is more commonly used for conlangs devised for international or cross-cultural communication, which are often based on combining different languages. Thus, in Esperanto the central parts of words (i.e., the **roots**) were chosen according to their relative frequency in Indo-European languages. This means that most words in Esperanto originated from Latin, including *patro* 'father' and *domo* 'house.'

7.4.2 The Corpus List Approach

Some conlangers draw part of the lexicon from lists of words compiled in various corpora. This is known as the **corpus list approach**. Probably the best-known corpus is the **Swadesh list**, which comprises 100–200 words considered 'universal' or at the very least frequent across languages. Linguist Morris Swadesh composed this list according to his intuition about which words are basic in different languages.

A more recent, more objective word list along these lines is the **Leipzig–Jakarta** word list, compiled by Tadmor (2009). It is based on a corpus of forty-one languages in Haspelmath and Tadmor (2009). This list includes 100 basic words considered to occur in all or most human societies. These words are neither compounds nor loans and have been part of the lexicon for a long time (see Section 7.4.5.1). The top 50 words in the Leipzig–Jakarta word list are given in Table 7.6 (some of these words are tied in the ranking).

The words in the Leipzig–Jakarta list are mostly nouns. They refer to nature elements ('fire,' 'water,' 'root'), body parts ('nose,' 'mouth'), basic verbs ('to go,' 'to come'), pronouns ('you,' 'I/me') and animals found wherever humans live ('louse,' 'fly'). It also includes products of human culture common in present-day societies ('house'), and some adjectives and adverbs ('bitter,' 'far,' 'yesterday').

Another word list that might serve as inspiration is Mark Rosenfelder's **Fantasy Frequency Wordlist** (2013). This list includes the 1,500 most frequent words in a corpus of over 1.1 million words from sci-fi and fantasy stories in English available online. Many of the words in the top 50 are grammatical words such as 'the', 'and' and 'of,' which of course not all languages share. Others include common verbs such as 'be', 'have' and 'know' that are probably handy to include in all if not most conlangs.

> ### Your Turn
>
> Examine the lexical meanings of the first half of the Leipzig–Jakarta list in Table 7.6. Which of these meanings are present in your conlang? Which ones would you like to include? Are there any words that might not be a good fit in the fictional world (e.g., if the fictional beings have no hair, they might lack a word for it).

Table 7.6 Words 1–50 in the Leipzig–Jakarta list (Tadmor 2009)

1–10	11–20	21–30	31–40	41–50
fire	to come	night	hair	yesterday
nose	breast	ear	big	to drink
to go	rain	neck	one	black
water	I/me	far	who?	navel
mouth	name	to do/make	3SG pronoun	to stand
tongue	louse	house	to hit/beat	to bite
blood	wing	stone/rock	leg/foot	back
bone	flesh/meat	bitter	horn	wind
you (SG)	arm/hand	to say	this	smoke
root	fly	tooth	fish	what

7.4.3 The Lexicon-Generator Approach

The **lexicon-generator approach** consists of generating random words according to the phonological pattern of the conlang. This can be accomplished by using a lexicon generator such as Rosenfelder's GEN. Simply stated, the conlanger specifies the sounds and syllable patterns in the conlang and indicates the relative frequency of monosyllabic words in the vocabulary. The word generator then lists a set of words that you can use or modify. If you follow this approach, you still need to assign meaning to the words you select.

> **Your Turn**
>
> Use Rosenfelder's GEN lexicon generator (www.zompist.com/gen.html) and generate a list of words compatible with your conlang phonology. Add any you like to your database, ideally matching them with lexical meanings you have identified but not assigned yet. Note that you can click 'generate' several times or/and change some of the settings to see additional potential words. Rosenfelder (2012:254–259) provides more information about how GEN works.

7.4.4 The Proto-Language Approach

Another way to generate words is the **proto-language approach**. This approach involves making up a proto-conlang (ancient version of the conlang) first, and then applying sound rules to derive the vocabulary of your present-day fictional language. Conlangers who favor this approach include J. R. R. Tolkien and David Peterson. While naturalistic, this approach requires an understanding of historical linguistics and of the most frequently occurring phonological changes. If you would like to explore this approach further, see chapter 3 in Peterson (2015). We examine some aspects of linguistic change in Chapter 16.

7.4.5 The Building Block Approach

The **building block approach** consists of inventing words as you need them, taking into consideration the characteristics of the fictional world and the phonological structure of the conlang. You can also use **derivational morphology** to create new words out of existing ones, for example, combining already existing words (compounding) or adding specific affixes (affixation). We examine each in turn.

7.4.5.1 Compounding

As mentioned in Chapter 1, compounds are words (most often lexical) created by combining two or more words. In English, compounds can be written as one word, with a hyphen, or as two connected words (10). Compounds written as one single unit have been part of the English language the longest.

(10) English compounds
	a. Nouns:	firefly	zero-sum	dark matter
	b. Adjectives:	bittersweet	happy-go-lucky	millennial pink
	c. Verbs:	to overbook	to color-code	to zoom bomb
	d. Adverbs:	elsewhere	self-consciously	sometimes

Nouns, verbs and adjectives have a particular affinity for compounding. Often, compounds involve the combination of two words (*spaceship*; *butterfly*), but more can be joined (*happy-go-lucky*; *off the record*). One of my favorite compounds in Spanish is *correveidile* 'gossip (a person)' formed out of four words: *corre* 'runs,' *ve* 'sees,' *y* 'and' and *dile* 'tell him/her.'

Compounds tend to be language specific. For example, *butterfly* is a compound in English, but its corresponding translation in Spanish (*mariposa*) is not. On the other hand, the Spanish word *paraguas* is a compound (*para* 'to stop' + *aguas* 'waters'), but its English equivalent 'umbrella' is not. It is important to keep this in mind as you build your lexicon, particularly if uniqueness is your goal.

In English, the lexical category of a compound is determined by that of the word furthest to the right; but in other natlangs it is the other way around. Compounds might have the same referent as the main word in the compound, as in *escape room* (a room from which you need to escape) or *space exploration* (the exploration of space) (the fancy term for these is **endocentric compounds**). But the beauty of compounds is that they do not have to convey such a transparent meaning. For example, a *killjoy* is a person who 'kills the joy of others' (rather than a type of joy that kills), and a *turtleneck* is a type of sweater (not the neck of a turtle). These compounds are known as **exocentric**. Both endocentric and exocentric compounds are great resources for building the lexicon.

> **Your Turn**
>
> Consider the Láadan compounds below (from Elguin 2020). Are they endocentric or exocentric?
>
> | | | | |
> |---|---|---|---|
> | *lalilom* | [la.lɪ.lom] | 'sound of rain on the roof' | from [la.lɪ] 'rain' + [lom] 'song' |
> | *lalidáan* | [la.lɪ.dá.an] | 'poem' | from [la.lɪ] 'rain' + [dá.an] 'word' |
> | *ahana* | [a.ha.na] | 'chocolate' | from [a] 'love' + [ana] 'food' |
> | *adama* | [a.da.ma] | 'tickle' | from [a.da] 'laugh' + [da.ma] 'touch' |
> | *Láadan* | [lá.a.dán] | 'Láadan' | from [lá.a] 'perception' + [dán] 'language' |

In compounding, the sounds of one or more of the involved words can be modified. Some compounds are shortened, as in *sci-fi* from *science fiction*. Others are **blends**, merging the beginning of one word and the end of another. Recent English blends are given below (11d also involves shortening).

(11)   English blends
a. picture + cell   *pixel*
b. botulinum + toxin   *botox*
c. gym + inspiration   *gymspiration*
d. fake + Instagram   *finsta*

Blending is common in English but not in other European languages. Other natlangs who make use of blending include Japanese and Hebrew. Examples of Hebrew blends include *prígurt* 'fruit yogurt,' from *prí* 'fruit' and *yógurt* 'yogurt,' and *sukrazít* 'saccharin,' from *sukár* 'sugar' and *razít* 'you (feminine singular) lost weight' (Bat-El 1996).

7.4 Developing the Lexicon

> **Your Turn**
>
> - Does your conlang lexicon include compounds? Which word category are they?
> - Come up with at least five compounds in your conlang. Indicate whether the rightmost or leftmost word in the compound determines the lexical category of the resulting word.
> - Which of the compounds in your conlang so far are endocentric (have a transparent meaning) and which are exocentric (have an opaque meaning)?

7.4.5.2 Affixation

Another way to create new words is via **affixation**, that is, the addition of **affixes** to a root. **Affixes** are morphemes that modify the meaning of the root; the most common types are **suffixes** (which follow the root) and **prefixes** (which precede it). We will here focus on meaning-modifying prefixes and suffixes; other affix types are covered in Chapter 8.

English *-ly* and Spanish *-mente* are examples of suffixes that turn adjectives into adverbs, while *-ful* and *-able* in English derive adjectives from nouns and verbs respectively (*colorful* from *color*; *beautiful* from *beauty*; *breakable* from *to break*; *replaceable* from *to replace*).

One example of a prefix used productively in English is *re-* 'again,' which derives verbs from other verbs (*rewrite, recreate, regenerate*), as we saw in Chapter 1. Another example is *un-* 'not,' which derives adjectives from other adjectives (*uncool, uncertain, unclear*). Unlike the suffixes *-ly, -ful* or *-able*, these prefixes do not change the lexical category of the word.

Affixation is a great resource in lexicon building, particularly since new words can be created out of already existing ones. For example, from the verb *to create* we can derive the verb *to recreate*, the noun *creation* and the adjective *creative*. From these, we can further derive the adverb *creatively* and the noun *recreation*.

Another way to derive words is by extending their lexical category without using overt affixes. For example, in English the verbs *to host, to mail* and *to parent* derive from the nouns *host, mail* and *parent*, respectively.

> **Your Turn**
>
> Will your conlang use affixation to create new words? Which categories will be involved?

7.4.6 The Fictional Text Approach

In Chapter 2, we indicated that composing a short text can be a great tool in conlanging. Consider, for example, the text in (12), an origin myth of the |ɛt people, a fictional alpaca herding community (as you remember, [|] indicates a dental click in IPA). This fable-like myth explains the geography and tribal organization of the |ɛt people.

> (12) |ɛt creation myth (courtesy of Carolina Macchi and Juli Chicherelli)
> Two siblings walked to the lake to collect water, discussing which was more important: cleverness or kindness? Along the shore was a herd of alpaca, drinking from the water. Both siblings wanted an alpaca, to have wool and a way to carry heavy things. The clever elder made a harness of rope, while the kind younger offered a handful of grain. Seeing that both methods worked, the siblings agreed to part ways to seek their own fortunes. The elder went to the west, and his footsteps became the River of the Head. The younger went to the east, and his footsteps became the River of the Heart. This is why our people live at the mouths of two separate rivers but remain one people.

In addition to helping to flesh out the |ɛt fictional world, the text in (13) can help identify words that should be added to the lexicon. These include essential verbs ('to carry,' 'to become'), nouns related to the environment ('river,' 'grain,' 'alpaca,' 'wool'), important cultural ideals ('cleverness,' 'kindness') and kinship terms ('sibling,' and possibly 'elder,' 'younger' as well). Throughout this book we use the building block and fictional text approaches as the main bases for developing our conlang lexicon; they can be supplemented by others discussed above, as you see fit.

7.5 Conlanging Practice: The Lexicon in Ur Languages

- Which of the Ur languages, in your opinion, is more likely to lack adjectives and adverbs?
- One Ur language has a closed set of six adjectives to refer to size, age and value. Indicate which language this is, and why you think that it falls into this category.
- Which Ur language has the richest basic color system, and which has the simplest? Make sure to connect your answer to aspects of the fictional world and to your answers above.
- Pick one Ur language and come up with expressive, conative, cognitive and phatic interjections. Try to ground them on cultural aspects of the fictional world.

7.6 The Muq Lexicon

In Chapters 3–6 we introduced some Salt nouns and verbs. As the next step to develop the muq lexicon, (13) reproduces the fictional text for the Salt language introduced in Chapter 2, with all lexical words and expressions underlined. Underneath each lexical word we indicate its word category (noun, adjective, verb, adverb). If you prefer you can use color-coding or a different formatting to identify different lexical words easily. Note that repeated lexical words are marked with discontinuous underlining.

(13) Muq fictional text with lexical words underlined

A long time ago [ADVERB] the world [NOUN] slept [VERB]; there was [VERB] darkness [NOUN]. The wind [NOUN] was silent [ADJECTIVE] and the ocean [NOUN] whispered [VERB] with sadness [NOUN]. Then [ADVERB] the mountain [NOUN] screamed [VERB] and spewed [VERB] out fire [NOUN], and the island [NOUN] burned [VERB]. It burned and burned for many days [NOUN]. When it stopped [VERB] burning, the island had changed [VERB]. The ocean soothed [VERB] the burning land [NOUN] and gave [VERB] it some of its life force [NOUN]. The life force from the ocean destroyed [VERB] the darkness [NOUN]; and dawn [NOUN] returned [VERB]. This is how life on our island started again [VERB] (awakened).

Table 7.7 groups the underlined words from (13) according to their lexical category. Some words are not yet translated; this is indicated with a question mark (?). Some words and expressions from the text above won't translate literally in muq. For example, 'a long time ago' will correspond to one word (the closest equivalent in English would be 'once' or 'long ago'). It is also expected that there will be changes in your fictional text as you continue conlanging; you might decide or will have to rephrase parts of the text as you think through the lexicon, morphology and syntax of your conlang. For example, in English *many* is an adjective, but in muq, it will be conveyed morphologically, as we will see in Chapter 8.

The fictional text for the Salt language lists only three adjectives. In the remainder of this section, I elaborate this part of the lexicon. Adjectives in this conlang are an open class; examples related to size, temperature and value are given in Table 7.8.

Adjectives and adverbs can be derived from abstract nouns via the addition of the prefix [-ə], as exemplified in Table 7.9. Note that while stress is initial in the abstract nouns listed in this table, it falls on the second syllable on the derived adjectives, since the second syllable in these cases has a diphthong or a complex coda.

Table 7.7 Lexicon from fictional text in Salt language

	Nouns		Verbs		Adjectives
[ˈi.xi]	'world'	[ˈxaɸ]	'to sleep'	[ˈseʁ]	'silent, quiet'
[ˈyeç]	'darkness'	[ˈxi.ma]	'to whisper'		
[ˈlu.ma]	'wind'	[ˈlam.xɑ]	'to stop burning'		
[ˈlei.za]	'sadness'	[ˈmeq]	'to return, to come back'		
[ˈlei]	'ocean, sea'	[ˈχe.ʁɑ]	'to break, to destroy'		
[ˈŋa.çen]	'mountain'	[ˈnei]	'to give'	[ˈŋou]	'later, then'
[ˈʁouq]	'fire'	[ˈou.na]	'to begin, to start'	?	'once, long ago'
[ˈçem]	'island'	[ˈɸiθ]	'to soothe'	?	'again'
[ˈŋuç]	'day'	[ˈmei]	'to be'		
[ˈsi.an]	'life, life force'	[ˈʁɑ.Li]	'to scream, to yell'		Adverbs
[ˈmis.tə]	'dawn'	[ˈtɑʁ]	'to thrust, to spew'		
[ˈmuq.çem]	'our island'	[ˈçis]	'to burn'		
?	'land'	[ou.ˈsei]	'to change, to transform'		

Table 7.8 Salt language: adjectives

Size		Temperature		Value	
[ˈzan.ze]	'small'	[ˈʟumt]	'cold'	[ˈɸe.xa]	'bad'
[ˈməp.qi]	'average'	[ˈçei]	'lukewarm'	[ˈmi.pik]	'average'
[ˈtip.ʙek]	'large'	[ʙu.na]	'hot'	[ˈsa.ɟit]	'good'

Table 7.9 Adjectives derived from abstract nouns in Salt language

Abstract nouns		Derived adjectives and adverbs	
[ˈlei.za]	'sadness, longing'	[ə.ˈlei.za]	'sad, with longing; sadly'
[ˈʎasq]	'friendliness'	[ə.ˈʎasq]	'friendly, in a friendly manner'
[ˈʎei.xa]	'faith, hope'	[ə.ˈʎei.xa]	'faithful, hopeful; faithfully, hopefully'

Table 7.10 Color terms in muq

[ˈʟər]	'black'	[ˈχa.el]	'blue'
[ˈqa.e]	'white'	[ˈɸæd]	'green'
[ˈmi.na]	'gray'	[ˈçe.mi]	'pale pink'
[ˈtid]	'yellow'	[ˈɴou̯.mə]	'saturated pink'
[ˈlei̯r]	'orange'	[ˈʎa.le]	'violet'
[ˈɢu.na]	'red'	[ˈkəi̯.ni]	'brown'

The Salt language has twelve basic color adjectives (Table 7.10); these include terms for light pink and saturated pink. Salt harvested in the muq island is a pale pink color, and I thought that splitting 'pink' into two basic color terms would make the conlang unique and better connected to the fictional world.

Some of the lexicon in the Salt language is derived via compounding; the word to the right of the compound typically indicates the main semantic meaning. One example from Table 7.7 is [ˈmuq.çem] 'our island, the muq island.' Additional compounds introduced in Chapter 6 include [zei̯.ˈχei̯] 'flowering tree' and [χei̯.ˈzei̯] 'tree flower' (from [ˈχei̯] 'tree,' [ˈzei̯] 'flower'). We will see more examples of muq compounds in Chapter 15.

7.7 Guide to Developing Your Conlang Lexicon

1. Go back to the fictional text you drafted in Chapter 2. Revise it (if needed), and indicate which lexical words need to be incorporated in your lexicon.
2. Think of additional concepts related to the fictional world that you might want to incorporate. Organize them according to word type. You can make a note of lexical gaps (such as kinship or abstract nouns) and return to them later.
3. For nouns, consider if your conlang distinguishes **subclasses** (concrete/abstract; proper/common; mass/non-count).
4. Incorporate verbs of motion, action, position, emotion, etc.
5. Decide whether your lexicon will have adjectives and/or adverbs.
6. If your conlang includes adjectives, indicate whether they form an open or closed class. Common adjective distinctions relate to size, value, age and color. Consider including adjectives for categories such as position and speed as well.
7. Indicate any adverbs conveying time, space, degree, manner. Indicate whether they are derived from other word categories (such as adjectives).
8. Work out the color system, taking into consideration the characteristics of the fictional world. Indicate if colors are conveyed via adjectives or other word classes.
9. Consider including some interjections.
10. Update your conlang lexicon database, adding columns for lexical categories and subclasses if present.
11. Create some compounds based on the words you have devised so far. These can be identified in your database in a separate column if needed.
12. Make sure that your lexicon is written using IPA conventions. Double check that any new words are syllabified consistently and include stress/tone diacritics. Include the corresponding English translation in a different column.
13. Make sure that your lexicon exemplifies (i) all contrastive vowels; (ii) all contrastive consonants; (iii) all possible syllable structures and (iv) all types of stress/tone in the conlang.
14. Indicate the specific strategies that you used so far to build the lexicon (word lists you are drawing from, word generator used, modification of words from other languages, etc.).

To Learn More

This chapter draws from chapter 6 in Velupillai (2012) and chapter 4 in Payne (2006). For an introduction to color terms, see Kay and Maffi (2013). Amika (1992) and Goddard (2014) are accessible introductions to interjections in natlangs.

For the Leipzig–Jakarta list, see Tadmor (2009). For the Fantasy Frequency Wordlist, see Rosenfelder (2013:34–45). Rosenfelder (2013:46–47) reproduces the Swadesh list organized by word and semantic class. Rosenfelder's Gen generation is available at http://zompist.com/gen.html; information on how to use it is found in Rosenfelder (2012:254–259).

To learn more about Kēlen, see Sylvia Sotomayor's 'An Introduction to Kēlen' webpage (www.terjemar.net/kelen/kelen.php). Lapine borrowings in English are discussed in Murray (1985). The information on Hebrew blends is from Bat-El (1996). Finally, if you are a Tolkien fan, you might enjoy the account of his time working at the Oxford English Dictionary by Gilliver et al. (2006).

8 The Morphology of Nouns

In the previous chapter we introduced different strategies that you can use to develop your conlang lexicon. Some of them (compounding, blending, affixation) involve derivational morphology. This chapter and the next focus on inflectional morphology, which languages use to convey grammatical meaning. Section 8.1 previews inflectional morphology and introduces affixes beyond suffixes and prefixes; Section 8.2 introduces glossing, a set of conventions used to indicate word structure and meaning; and Section 8.3 focuses on ways in which natlangs vary morphologically. Sections 8.4–8.6 focus on nominal morphology, in particular the expression of number, gender and case. Section 8.7 provides practice exercises in the topics covered in this chapter, and Section 8.8 outlines the basics of nominal morphology in muq. Section 8.9 is a set of guided questions you can use to develop the nominal morphology of your conlang. The chapter ends with a list of resources to explore further.

Key Words

Allomorphs
Case
  Ablative (ABL)
  Absolutive (ABS)
  Accusative (ACC)
  Allative (ALL)
  Aversive (AVR) / Evitative (EVIT)
  Benefactive (BEN)
  Comitative (COM)
  Dative (DAT)
  Ergative (ERG)
  Genitive (GEN)
  Instrumental (INST)
  Locative (LOC)
  Malefactive (MAL)
  Nominative (NOM)

Partitive (PTV)
  Vocative (VOC)
Circumfix
Degree of exponence
  Cumulative (fusional)
  Separative (agglutinative)
Degree of flexion
  Flexive
  Non-flexive
Degree of fusion
  Concatenative
  Non-linear (non-concatenative)
Degree of synthesis
  Analytic (periphrastic)
  Polysynthetic
  Synthetic
Gender
  Feminine (F)
  Masculine (M)
  Neutral (N)
  Animate (AN)
  Inanimate (INAN)
Glossing
Infix
Inflectional morphology
Nominalizer (NMZ)
Noun classes
Number
  Associate plural ('group plural') (ASC.PL)
  Collective plural ('general plural') (COL.PL)
  Dual (DU)
  Paucal (PAU)
  Plural (PL)
  Singular/Singulative (SG)
  Superplural (PL.PL)
  Trial (TRI)
Propositional/postpositional phrase (PP)
Reduplication
Stem change

8 The Morphology of Nouns

8.1 Inflectional Morphology

Morphology focuses on how words are put together. In Chapter 7 we introduced derivational morphology (including affixation and compounding) as a way to create new words. Derivational morphology is primarily lexical since it changes the meaning and/or word class of a word. For example, *universe* is a noun, and *universal*, with the addition of the suffix *-al*, is an adjective; the meanings of both words are related, but not identical. In this and the next chapter we focus on **inflectional morphology**, a way to use affixation to express grammatical meaning. In inflectional morphology, the core meaning of the word does not change; and neither does its word class.

Let's consider some examples. In English, the noun *planet* is singular; to refer to more than one planet, we add the suffix *-s*: *planets*. Although it now conveys the plural, the core meaning of the inflected word has not changed. The same suffix *-s* can be added to other English nouns to indicate plurality, as in *oceans* or *cauldrons*. Some nouns have irregular plurals, as in *foot/feet* and *ox/oxen*. This irregularity is related to historical changes in the language, as we will see later.

Adjectives in English cannot be pluralized; but they can take the comparative suffix *-(e)r* and the superlative *-(e)st*: for example, *cool, cooler, coolest*. The meaning of the three words is the same; but *cooler* implies a higher degree, and *coolest*, the highest. Not all adjectives form the comparative and superlative morphologically in English. Adjectives which are three or more syllables long, such as *original* or *sycophantic*, tend to form them syntactically (*more original, most sycophantic*). Some adjectives express comparative and superlative in either way; for example, the comparative of *thick* can be *thicker* or *more thick*.

Verbs in English also convey certain grammatical meanings morphologically. For example, the past tense is indicated with the suffix *-(e)d* (as in *she walked* or *it traveled*). Some verbs have irregular past forms, including the verbs *to go* (*went*) and *to think* (*thought*).

This chapter focuses on the main aspects of inflectional morphology for nouns and nominal elements; Chapter 9 focuses on the inflectional morphology of verbs. Before we proceed, however, it is important to clarify that morphemes have two sides: they have a meaning or function, and a corresponding pronunciation (shape). Morpheme meaning can be semantic (*planet, freedom*), or grammatical (plural, comparative, superlative). Forms with the same shape but dissimilar meanings correspond to different morphemes. For example, the third person singular present tense suffix *-s* in *she walks* or *it travels* has the same pronunciation as the plural suffix *-s* (*planets, cakes*). However, these are different morphemes since they convey different meanings.

8.1 Inflectional Morphology

Another important consideration is that suffixes and prefixes are not the only affix types attested in languages. Other affixes, including **infixes** and **circumfixes**, are also possible. Infixes are affixes placed within the root. In English, two examples of infixes are *-iz(z)-* used in hip-hop slang (1), and *-ma-*, a favorite of Homer Simpson in *The Simpsons* show (2). Note that *-iz(z)-* is placed after the first consonant of the word, and *-ma-* before the last two syllables in words with four or more syllables.

(1)   Hip-hop *-iz(z)-* infix (Yu 2007; Another Bad Creation's 'Playground')
  a. 'house'   *h-iz-ouse*
  b. 'park'   *p-izz-ark*
  c. 'ahead'   *ah-iz-ead*
  d. 'dark'   *d-izz-ark*

(2)   Homeric *-ma-* infix (Yu 2004)
  a. 'saxophone'   *saxo-ma-phone*
  b. 'education'   *edu-ma-cation*
  c. 'pantomime'   *panto-ma-mime*
  d. 'macadamia'   *maca-ma-damia*

The English infixes in (1, 2) are paralinguistic since they convey playfulness and ironic pseudo-sophistication respectively. One example of a grammatical infix occurs in Tagalog, where *-um-*, placed after the first consonant of the verb, conveys the infinitive.

(3)   Tagalog infinitive infix (Schachter & Otanes 1972)
  a. *sulat*   'writing'   *s-um-ulat*   'to write'
  b. *kain*   'eating'   *k-um-ain*   'to eat'
  c. *tawa*   'laughing'   *t-um-awa*   'to laugh'

Circumfixes are affixes that surround roots. One example of a derivational circumfix in Dutch is given in (4): *ge- ... -te* conveys 'a collection of items.' An example of an inflectional circumfix in German is shown in (5): *ge- ... -t* indicates the verb is in the past participle.

(4)   Dutch derivational circumfix (Booij 2016, Marušič 2023)
  a. *berg*   'mountain'   *ge-berg-te*   'mountain range'
  b. *boom*   'tree'   *ge-boom-te*   'woodland'
  c. *steen*   'stone, rock'   *ge-steen-te*   'rocks'

(5)   German past participle circumfix (Zingler 2022:60)
  a. *spielen*   'to play'   *ge-spiel-t*   '(to have/be) played'
  b. *googeln*   'to google' *ge-googel-t*   '(to have/be) googled'

8.2 Glossing

You might have noticed the use of the hyphen – to separate morphemes in this and previous chapters. This is a convention in **glossing**, that is, a set of guidelines used to identify the meaning and structure of morphemes and words consistently across languages. Glossing is an important tool in conlanging since it allows you to clearly indicate which part of the word corresponds to which meaning or function. This section introduces the essentials of glossing; additional conventions and examples are provided in later chapters.

The main goal of glossing is to provide a one-to-one correspondence between morphemes and their meaning or function. For example, consider the Spanish phrase *el unicornio azul*, which translates in English as 'The blue unicorn.' A simple word-by-word gloss of this phrase is shown in (6). Note that each word in the phrase is vertically aligned to the left of its translation in English (tabs can be used to ensure proper alignment). The full translation of the phrase is given to the right of the example, although it can also follow the gloss, as we see later.

(6)   Glossing (I)
        el   unicornio   azul   'The blue unicorn'
        the   unicorn   blue

Now consider *unicornios azules* 'blue unicorns.' The plural suffixes in Spanish are segmentable, so we indicate this with hyphens in the example and its gloss (7). The glosses for **plural** and **singular** are PL and SG, respectively. Note that glosses for inflectional morphemes are given in upper case, typically small caps.

(7)   Glossing (II): using hyphens
        unicornio-s   azul-es   'blue unicorns'
        unicorn-PL   blue-PL

When a morpheme encompasses various meanings and these cannot be segmented, we indicate this with a dot instead of a hyphen. This is shown in (8) for the determiner *los* 'the (PL)'; its singular form in Spanish is *el*, as shown in (6).

(8)   Glossing (III): using dots
        los   unicornio-s   azul-es   'the blue unicorns'
        the.PL   unicorn-PL   blue-PL

However, a dot is not needed when the combined meanings involve person and number, as shown in (9) for Spanish.

(9) Glossing (III): no dots needed if morpheme combines person and number
yo 'I' tú 'you (singular)'
1SG 2SG

We will see more examples of glossing for natlangs and conlangs throughout the book. A list of all glossing conventions used in this book is provided at the front. You can also check the reference section at the end of this chapter for additional information and resources on glossing.

8.3 Morphological Typology

Before diving into nominal morphology, it is useful to have a general sense of how words can be put together in languages. Languages vary widely regarding how much grammatical information is conveyed in a word (8.3.1), the types of inflectional morphemes used (8.3.2) and how variable morphemes are (8.3.3).

8.3.1 How Much Grammatical Information Is Conveyed in a Word?

Natlangs differ in their **degree of synthesis**, that is, how many morphemes a word holds (Table 8.1). **Analytic** (or **periphrastic**) languages have one morpheme per word; examples include Chinese and Toki Pona. **Synthetic** languages have more than one morpheme per word, but only one root per word (except in compounds). Examples are English, Spanish and most well-known conlangs, including Esperanto and Klingon. **Polysynthetic** languages have several morphemes per word, including multiple roots. One polysynthetic natlang is Alutor; as shown in (10), in this language one single word expresses the English sentence 'I am making a son dry a skin,' encompassing eleven morphemes, three of which are roots (indicated in bold). You already know that SG stands for singular and 1 for first person; we will go over other morpheme glosses in this and the next chapter.

Notice that the gloss in this example is four lines long; the first line conveys the pronunciation; the second breaks down each morpheme in Alutor, the third line indicates the meaning or function of each morpheme; and the fourth line provides an English translation. Here and throughout, glosses include separate lines for pronunciation and morphological structure when provided in the source.

(10) Polysynthesis in Alutor (from Gerdts 1998:87)
[gə.mːə.ta.kːa.nːal.gən.ku.wːa.ta.və.kːən]

gəmmə t-	akka- n-	nalgə- n-	kuww- at-	avə-	kk-	ən
1.ABS 1SG.S	son CAUS	skin CAUS	dry SUFFIX	SUFFIX	PRS	1SG.S

'I am making a son dry a skin/skins.'

Table 8.1 Degree of synthesis: how many morphemes/roots per word?

Analytic	Synthetic	Polysynthetic
One morpheme per word	Multiple morphemes per word One root per word	Multiple morphemes per word Multiple roots per word

Languages also vary in how many meanings a morpheme encodes (**degree of exponence**) (Table 8.2). In **separative (agglutinative)** languages each morpheme tends to convey exactly one meaning, as in Swahili (11) or Láadan. On the other hand, in **cumulative** languages one morpheme can encode several meanings at once. For example, in Spanish, in the verb *pisé* [pi.'se] 'I stepped,' the suffix [-e] encodes four meanings: first person, singular, past tense and indicative.

(11) Swahili: separative morphology (Almasi et al. 2014:44, 48)

	a. *ni-*	*li-*	*cheza*	'I played.'
	1SG	past	play	
	b. *m-*	*ta-*	*cheka*	'You (plural) will laugh.'
	2PL	future	laugh	

Table 8.2 Degree of exponence: how many meanings per morpheme?

Separative	Cumulative
One meaning per morpheme	Multiple meanings per morpheme

8.3.2 What Types of Affixes Are Used?

Languages vary in the types of affixes they allow (this is called **degree of fusion**; Table 8.3). In **isolating** languages like Chinese or Toki Pona, morphemes stand alone and are not bound to other roots. In **concatenative** languages, like English or Dothraki, suffixes, prefixes, infixes and/or circumfixes are added to the root. Finally, in **non-concatenative** languages, **non-linear** affixes are allowed. For example, in Arabic and other Semitic languages roots are often triconsonantal; affixation can be achieved by interleaving vowels (and sometimes other consonants) around the consonants of the root. One example from Hebrew is given in (12). We will see additional examples of non-linear morphology later.

(12)   Modern Hebrew (Bickel & Nichols 2007:182 and refs. therein)
   a. Root: g-d-r   'to enclose'
   b. Past: gadar   'he enclosed'
   c. Future/Imperative: gdor   'enclose it!'

Table 8.3 Degree of fusion: what types of affixes are allowed?

Isolating	Concatenative	Non-concatenative
Morphemes stand alone	Affixes attached to the root (suffixes, prefixes, infixes, circumfixes)	Non-linear morphemes attached to the root

8.3.3 How Variable Are Morphemes?

Finally, languages vary in whether morphemes have variable or invariant shapes; this is referred to as **degree of flexion** (Table 8.4). **Non-flexive** languages tend to have invariant morphemes; Láadan is one example. In contrast, **flexive** languages have variant morpheme forms (**allomorphs**). Examples include English, German and Sindarin. For example, the English plural suffix has three allomorphs [-s] [-z] [-əz], depending on whether the last root sound is voiceless (*planets*), voiced (*unicorns*) or a sibilant (*universes*).

Table 8.4 Degree of flexion: how variable are morphemes?

Non-flexive	Flexive
Morphemes are invariant	Morphemes have multiple forms (i.e., allomorphs)

Languages combine degrees of fusion, synthesis, exponence, and flexion to different extents. Most languages are flexive-concatenative as in Latin. In any case, it is important to note that pure types for these morphological characteristics are few and far between.

8.4 Number

Let's consider now how languages convey **number** distinctions in nouns and other nominal words such as pronouns, determiners and adjectives. Most commonly, natlangs distinguish between singular and plural (8.4.1), but other number distinctions are also attested (8.4.2, 8.4.3). Section 8.4.4 provides examples of morphological number in conlanging.

8.4.1 Singular and Plural

Number is a grammatical category that indicates how many entities or items are referred to. Most natlangs convey number, but they do so in different ways. In some languages, number is conveyed via articles or plural words, as in Hawaiian (13).

(13) Number in Hawaiian (adapted from Elbert and Pukui 1979: 159)
 [ʔelua   aʔu   mau   iʔa]   'my two fish'
 two   my   PL   fish

Natlangs that distinguish **singular** and **plural** morphologically can do so in different ways. Most often, nouns are singular by default, and affixes convey the plural. Examples include Spanish and English, as we saw earlier. In some natlangs, nouns are plural by default; a **singulative** affix is added to indicate that a noun is singular (SG). Examples for Southern Barasano are given in (14). In other natlangs, nouns are always marked for number, as in Swahili (15).

(14) Southern Barasano singulative (Payne 2006:149–150 and refs. therein)
 a. *kahe*   'eyes'   *kahe-a*   'eye'
    eye.PL   eye-SG
 b. *biti*   'beads'   *biti-a*   'bead'
    bead.PL   bead-SG

(15) Number in Swahili (Almasi et al. 2014:58)
 a. *m-toto*   'child'   *wa-toto*   'children'
    SG-child   PL-child
 b. *m-tu*   'person'   *wa-tu*   'people'
    SG-person   PL-person

About 50 percent of natlangs with morphological plurals encode them with suffixes, while 10 percent use prefixes (as in Swahili). Natlangs can also express number using non-linear affixes, including **reduplication** or **stem changes**. Reduplication involves doubling the root or part of it; full reduplication conveys plurality in Indonesian (16). **Stem changes** refer to modifying a segmental or suprasegmental characteristic of the root; in English, some irregular plurals are formed by changing the stem vowel, as in *man/men, woman/women* and *goose/geese*. In Piipaash, plurality is conveyed by lengthening the final vowel: *humar* 'child,' *humaːr* 'children' (Gordon 1986: 29). Tone can also be used to express number. For example, in Ngiti, singular nouns have low tone on the last syllable and mid (or no tone) on the penultimate, while plural nouns have high tone on both the penultimate and final syllables (17).

(16) Indonesian plural reduplication (Sneddon 1996:16–17)
    a. *rumah*   'house'   *rumah-rumah*   'house'
    b. *perubahan*   'change'   *perubahan-perubahan*   'change'

(17) Ngiti (Kutsch Lojenga 1994:135)
    a. *màlàjikà*   'angel'   *màlàjíká*   'angels'
    b. *màlimò*   'teacher'   *màlímó*   'teachers'

Finally, not all natlangs express number grammatically. One example is Pirahã, where number is interpreted according to context. Thus, the sentence in (18) can be translated as 'The Pirahã people are afraid of evil spirits,' 'The Pirahã people are afraid of an evil spirit,' 'A Pirahã is afraid of evil spirits' and 'A Pirahã is afraid of an evil spirit.'

(18) Pirahã: No number (Velupillai 2012:160; Everett 2005:623)
    Hiatíihi   *hi*   *kaoáibogi*   *bai-aagá*
    Pirahã   3   evil.spirit   fear-be

8.4.2 Beyond Singular and Plural: Dual, Trial and Paucal

Singular and plural are not the only number distinctions attested in natlangs. For example, Lavukaleve also has a **dual** ('only two'), as shown in (19). Note that uninflected nouns are singular by default; the gloss for dual is DU.

(19) Lavukaleve number (Terril 1999:97)
    a. *funfun*   'firefly'
        firefly.SG
    b. *funfun-il*   'two fireflies'
        firefly-DU
    c. *funfun-aul*   'fireflies'
        firefly-PL

A few languages have a **trial** ('only three'), including Larike, which distinguishes singular, dual, trial and plural pronouns (20). The gloss for trial is TRI.

(20) Larike number (Laidig & Laidig 1990:90)
    a. *ane*   'you (singular)'   *irua*   'you two'
        2SG   2DU
    b. *iridu*   'you three'   *imi*   'you many (more than 3)'
        2TRI   2PL

Paucal number ('a few'), glossed as PAU, is more common. For example, in Biak, demonstratives have singular, dual, paucal and plural forms (21); note that nouns don't carry number affixes.

(21)   Biak (Dalrymple & Mofu 2013:45)
    a. *rum*   *ine*   'this house'
        house   this.SG
    b. *rum*   *suine*   'these two houses'
        house   this.DU
    c. *rum*   *skoine*   'these few houses'
        house   this.PAU
    d. *rum*   *nane*   'these houses'
        house   this.PL

In conlanging, morphological number can be connected to specific characteristics of the fictional world, for example an emphasis on couples or triads. Note, however, that the dual and paucal imply distinguishing between singular and plural, and a trial assumes a dual distinction as well.

8.4.3   Superplural, Collective and Associate Plural

Rarer number distinctions are also attested, including the **superplural** 'a lot of, heaps of,' which we will gloss as PL.PL. One example occurs in Barngarla (22).

(22)   Barngarla superplural (Zuckerman 2020:227–228)
    a. *wárraidya*   'emu'   *mina*   'eye'
        emu.SG   eye.SG
    b. *wárraidyal-bili*   'two emus'   *mínal-bili*   'two eyes'
        emu-DU   eye-DU
    c. *wárraidya-rri*   'emus'   *mína-rri*   'eyes'
        emu-PL   eye-PL
    d. *wárraidya-*   'lots of emus'   *mína-ilyarranha*   'lots of eyes'
        ilyarranha
        emu-PL.PL   eye-PL.PL

The associate plural refers to a group consisting of the referent and those associated with them (most typically family, friends and/or members of a common group). Associate plurals are most often employed with nouns referring to humans, particularly with proper names and kinship terms. One example from Hawai'i Creole English is given in (23); associate plural is glossed ASC.PL.

(23)   Hawai'i Creole English associative plural (from Velupillai 2012:164)
a. *John-dem*   'John and them/John and those associated
   John-ASC.PL   with him'
b. *ma   faðe-dem*   'My father and them/my father and his
   my   father-ASC.PL associates'

Finally, the **collective (general plural)** indicates that the items or individuals referred to form a group. Some examples in English are *people* (compare with singular *person* and plural *persons*) and *cattle* (cf. with singular *cow* and plural *cows*). The collective plural is glossed COL.PL; we will see examples of its use in conlanging in the following section.

8.4.4 Number in Conlanging

Toki Pona and Klingon don't distinguish number morphologically, although Klingon has optional plural affixes (see 8.5.1). Esperanto and Dothraki distinguish singular and plural nouns. Examples from Esperanto are given below; note that the suffix *-o* is a **nominalizer**, that is, an affix that turns the root into a noun; it is glossed NMZ.

(24)   Esperanto number (from lernu.net)
a. *telefon-o*   [te.le.fo.no]   'a telephone'
   telephone-NMZ
b. *telefon-o-j*   [te.le.fo.noi̯]   'telephones'
   telephone-NMZ-PL

Na'vi has prefixes for dual, trial and plural (Müller 2024:18). In Láadan, nouns are not marked for number, but pronouns have different forms for singular, paucal and plural (25).

(25)   Láadan number in pronouns (Elgin et al. 2020:315)
a. *Le*   [lɛ]   'I'
   1SG
b. *le-zh*   [lɛʒ]   'Us few (2–5 of us)'
   1PAU
c. *le-n*   [lɛn]   'Us many (more than 5)'
   1PL

Sindarin has a complex number system with different patterns and irregularities. Some nouns are plural by default and take a singulative suffix; for example, *glam* [glam] 'orcs,' *glam-og* [gla.mog] 'orc'; *filig* [fi.lig] 'small birds,' *filig-od* [fi.li.god] 'small bird' (Salo 2004:98). Sindarin also has the collective plural suffix *-ath* [aθ] (26).

(26) Sindarin collective plural (from Salo 2004:98, 99)
    a. *perian*   [pe.ri.an]   'halfling (hobbit)'
        halfling.SG
    b. *periann-ath*   [pe.ri.a.nːaθ]   '(all) halflings'
        halfling-COL.PL
    c. *el-in*   [e.lin]   'stars'
        star-PL
    d. *elen-ath*   [e.le.naθ]   'all the stars of heaven'
        star-COL.PL

8.5 Gender

Gender is a way to categorize **noun classes** grammatically. About 44 percent of natlangs have grammatical gender. Most commonly, languages have a two-way contrast between **feminine** and **masculine** (glossed M and F respectively), as in Spanish (27). A contrast of three or more genders is less frequent. One example is German, which differentiates masculine, feminine and **neuter** (glossed N). Gender in German is observed in articles and pronouns (28) as well as adjectives and plural nominal suffixes (not shown). A three-way gender distinction is also found in English, but only in pronouns: cf. feminine *she, her, hers*, masculine *he, him, his*, and inanimate *it, its*. In addition, the gender neutral or non-binary pronouns *they, them, theirs* are gaining ground.

(27) Gender in Spanish
    a. *Él,*   *el*   *bruj-o*   *malvad-o*
        He   the.SG.M   wizard-M   wicked-M
        'Him, the wicked wizard'
    b. *Ella,*   *la*   *bruj-a*   *malvad-a*
        She   the.SG.F   wizard-F   wicked-F
        'Her, the wicked witch'

(28) Gender in German
    a. *Der*   *Elf*   'The elf'   *Er*   'he'
        the.SG.M   elf   3SG.M
    b. *Die*   *Fee*   'The fairy'   *Sie*   'she'
        the.SG.F   fairy   3SG.F
    c. *Das*   *Ungeheuer*   'The monster'   *Es*   'it'
        the.SG.N   monster   3SG.N

Gender and number can be conveyed via separate affixes (as in Spanish), or can be bundled within the same affix, as in Italian (29).

(29) Italian gender and number
    a. *la*   *ragazz-a*   *le*   *ragazz-e*
        the.SG.F   child-F.SG   the.PL.F   child-F.PL
        'the girl'   'the girls'
    b. *il*   *ragazz-o*   *i*   *ragazz-i*
        the.SG.M   child-M.SG   the.PL.M   child-M.PL
        'the boy'   'the boys'

There is usually a semantic basis to gender distinctions, most often connected to biological sex. For example, in Tamil, female humans and deities are referred to with feminine nouns, and male humans and deities with masculine nouns. However, this connection is often idiosyncratic. For example, in Spanish and French masculine nouns can denote male entities (*el chico, le garçon* 'the boy') as well as non-gendered objects or concepts (*el libro, le livre* 'the book'). Similarly, feminine nouns can denote female entities (*la chica, la fille* 'the girl') and non-gendered objects or concepts (*la mesa, la table* 'the table'). Which objects or concepts are feminine or masculine depends on the language. For example, in Spanish the noun 'plastic' is masculine (*el plástico*), but in Italian, it is feminine (*la plastica*).

> **DID YOU KNOW?**
>
> In many languages where case is based on biological sex, the masculine is often considered generic or default, which raises questions on inclusivity. For example, singular *they* in English is increasingly used as a gender-neutral pronoun. Although some people feel strongly about this use of 'they,' it has been around since the sixteenth century, and it is even attested in Shakespeare's writings. A growing awareness of non-binarity and gender fluidity also leads to non-traditional uses of 'he' or 'she.' Gender neutral/inclusive pronouns have also been proposed, such as *zie, sie* or *ey* (and instead of *he/she*).
>
> The linguistic encoding of gender is being challenged in other languages as well. For example, the Argentinian youth is championing the replacement of default masculine determiners and pronouns *el, los* and *ellos* by the innovative gender neutral *le, les* and *elles*, respectively, and the nominal masculine suffix *-o* by the gender-neutral suffix *-e*: *todes elles* instead of *todos ellos* 'all of them.'

Around 75 percent of natlangs with gender are sex-based, at least to some extent; the rest are based on animacy, humanness or rationality. For example, Bantu and Algonquian languages differentiate **animates**, glossed

AN (humans and animals) from **inanimates**, glossed INAN (everything else). Fula/Fulfulde distinguishes human and non-human gender, and Tamil makes a distinction between rational (humans) vs. non-rational (inanimates and non-human animates, including children); rational nouns distinguish masculine and feminine.

Shape, size and function can also be used in gender systems. For example, Supyire has different genders for humans, big things, small things, collectives and liquids; and Kisi distinguishes animates, inanimates, liquids and collective plants and grains. More complex systems are found in Nigerian Fula dialects, which have up to twenty different genders.

As with biological sex, the association between animacy, size, shape and function varies from language to language. For example, in the Sepik region in New Guinea, small or round objects are feminine, and big or long ones are masculine, while in Tiwi, small objects and animals are masculine, and large ones are feminine. Often, cultural, historical, and mythological associations are behind exceptional or non-transparent gender assignment in languages. This makes gender interesting for conlanging, as we see next.

8.5.1 Gender in Conlanging

Esperanto nouns are either masculine or inclusive; the suffix *-in* [-in] conveys feminine gender (30). Some Esperanto speakers advocate for a masculine suffix *-iĉ* [-itʃ].

(30)   Esperanto gender (from lernu.net)
  a. *knab-o*   [kna.bo] 'boy'   *knab-in-o*   [kna.bi.no] 'girl'
     child-NMZ   child-F-NMZ
  b. *best-o*   [be.sto] 'an animal' *best-in-o*   [be.sti.no] 'a female
     animal-NMZ   animal-F-NMZ   animal'

Esperanto third person singular pronouns are *li* [li] for masculine, *ŝi* [ʃi] for feminine and *ĝi* [dʒi] for neuter. Some speakers propose a gender-neutral singular pronoun *ri* [ri]. *ili* [i.li] 'they' is gender-neutral (Harlow 1995).

Ido, which originated from reformed Esperanto, is gender neutral but can encode masculine and feminine morphologically in cases of ambiguity; so does Na'vi. Ido also has four singular third person pronouns: *il* [il] (M), *el* [el] (F), *ol* [ol] (N), and pan-gender *lu* [lu], which can refer to either gender depending on context (de Beaufront 2004:25).

Láadan nouns are feminine by default: *with* [wıθ] 'person, woman,' *hu* [hu] '(female) ruler.' Masculine nouns are formed with the suffix *-id* [ıd]: *with-id* [wı.θıd] 'man,' *hu-hid* [hu.hıd] 'masculine ruler' (Elgin et al. 2020).

In Dothraki, Klingon and High Valyrian, gender is not sex-based. Dothraki distinguishes between animate vs. inanimate, although what counts as either is specific to Dothraki. Thus, animate nouns include *rizh* 'son' and *khaleen* 'elder woman,' but also *ashefa* 'river' and *nhare* 'head.' Examples of inanimate nouns are *rhiko* 'stirrup' and *ize* 'poison,' but also *zhavvorsa* 'dragon' and *hrazef* 'horse.' Only animate nouns and any modifying adjectives take plural suffixes: *rizh-i* 'sons,' *ashefa-si* 'rivers' (Peterson 2014:53–55).

Klingon distinguishes three **noun classes**: (i) living beings with the innate capability to learn language; (ii) body parts and (iii) all other nouns. These noun classes carry distinct plural suffixes: *-pu'* [puʔ], *-Du'* [ɖuʔ] and *-mey* [meɪ], respectively (Okrand 1985:22, 23).

High Valyrian has a complex gender system based on semantics and phonology. Four genders are distinguished: (i) solar, (ii) lunar, (iii) terrestrial and (iv) aquatic. Nouns related to humans and animals are usually lunar or solar; most diurnal animals are solar, and most nocturnal animals, lunar. In addition, most solar nouns end in [s] and most lunar ones end in a vowel. Foods and plants tend to be terrestrial; and liquids and liquid bodies are aquatic. Most terrestrial nouns end in [n], and most aquatic ones in [r]. As in many natlangs, gender in High Valyrian has several exceptions.

> **Your Turn**
>
> Which gender system previewed above do you find more appealing, and why?

8.6 Case

Case is used in many natlangs to indicate the role of nominal elements in sentences. English used to have a full case system until the eleventh century. Nowadays, case occurs mostly in personal pronouns, which vary depending on whether they are subjects (*I, they*) or direct objects in a sentence (*me, them*). Compare pronoun use in the sentences *I saw them* vs. *They saw me*, for example.

Case assigned to subjects and direct objects in this way is referred to as **nominative** (NOM) and **accusative** (ACC) respectively. Some English speakers make a similar distinction in the use of the interrogative pronoun *who/whom* in sentences such as *Who saw you?* vs. *Whom did you see?* However, the use of the accusative in the second case tends to be rare and/

or formal. Beyond expressing nominative and accusative in certain pronouns, English nouns are marked with the suffix -*s* to indicate ownership, both in nouns (*Bill's guitar, Annie's shawl*) and pronouns (*The song is theirs*). This is an example of the **genitive** (GEN) case.

Case allows for concise expression of grammatical functions and is conducive to flexibility in word order. Consider, for example, the Latin sentences in (31); all have the same translation despite their different word orders. Because the subject is marked with the nominative suffix -*us*, and the direct object with accusative -*m*, there is no possible confusion regarding who loves who(m). In contrast, in English the subject most often precedes the verb, and the direct object follows it; 'Emilio loves Sophia' and 'Sophia loves Emilio' do not mean the same thing.

(31) Latin case: 'Emilio loves Sophia'
    a. *Aemili-us*   *Sophia-m*   *ama-t.*
        Emilio-NOM   Sophia-ACC   to.love-3SG
    b. *Sophia-m*   *Aemili-us*   *ama-t*
        Sophia-ACC   Emilio-NOM   to.love-3SG

About 62 percent of natlangs express case, although there is variation regarding the number of cases and their specific meanings. The minimum number of cases in natlangs is two; the maximum is twenty-one, as in Hungarian (Kayardild follows closely with twenty). Languages have small systems if they contrast two or three cases, as in English. Average case systems contrast four or five cases, as in Icelandic, which distinguishes nominative, accusative, genitive and **dative** (DAT), indicating the indirect object (the recipient of an action) (32). Note that the accusative form is the default in Icelandic since it carries no morphological marking.

(32) Icelandic case (Thráinsson 1994:153, cited in Iggesen 2013a)
     hest-ur   *hest*   *hest-s*   *hest-i*
     horse-NOM   horse.ACC   horse-GEN   horse-DAT

Latin and Basque have larger case systems. Latin has the four cases of Icelandic, in addition to the **vocative** (VOC) (used to address a person or thing directly) and the **ablative** (ABL), used for nouns that are objects of prepositions. Latin nouns are inflected according to number (S, PL), gender (first, second, third, fourth or fifth declension), and case. Examples for the words *puella* 'girl' (belonging to the feminine gender or 'first declension') and *hortus* 'garden' (belonging to the masculine gender or 'second declension') are given in (33).

(33) Latin case: *puella* 'girl', *hortus* 'garden'

	SG	PL	SG	PL
NOM	puell-a	puella-e	hort-us	hort-i
VOC	puell-a	puella-e	hort-e	hort-i
ACC	puella-m	puella-s	hort-um	hort-os
GEN	puella-e	puell-arum	hort-i	hort-orum
DAT	puella-e	puell-is	hort-o	hort-is
ABL	puell-a	puell-is	hort-o	hort-is

Basque has fifteen cases. Instead of nominative and accusative, Basque distinguishes **ergative** (ERG) (subjects of transitive sentences, i.e., those having a direct object) and **absolutive** (ABS) (subjects of intransitive sentences as well as direct objects). This is shown in (34). In (34a, c) 'the witches' is subject of a transitive sentence and takes the plural ergative suffix *-ek*. In (34b), however, 'the witches' is the subject of an intransitive sentence and carries the plural absolutive suffix *-ak*, as do the direct object 'unicorns' in (34a, c). Note that as in Latin, Basque cases have different forms in singular and plural.

(34) Ergative and absolutive case in Basque
    a. *Sorgin-ek*   *unikornio-ak*   *nahi*   *dituzte.*
       witch-ERG.PL   unicorn-ABS.PL   want   AUX
       'The witches want unicorns.'
    b. *Sorgin-ak*   *doaz.*
       witch-ABS.PL   go.3PL
       'The witches go.'
    c. *Sorgin-ek*   *unikornio-ak*   *ikusi*   *dituzte.*
       witch-ERG.PL   unicorn-ABS.PL   see   AUX
       'The witches have seen the unicorns.'

Additional cases in Basque include the **benefactive** (BEN) for the beneficiary or receiver of the action; the **comitative** (COM), indicating accompaniment; the locative (LOC), conveying location; the **allative** (ALL), expressing destination; and the **instrumental** (INST), indicating devices used to perform an action. Examples are given in (35).

(35) Benefactive, comitative, allative and instrumental cases in Basque
    a. *Sorgin-ak*   *lore-ak*   *nahi*   *ditu*   *unikornio-arentsat.*
       witch-ERG.SG   flower-ABS.PL   want   auxiliary   unicorn-BEN.SG
       'The witch wants flowers for the unicorn.'
    b. *Sorgin-a*   *unikornio-arekin*   *baso-ra*   *doa.*
       witch-ABS.SG   unicorn-COM.SG   forest-ALL.SG   go.3SG
       'The witch goes to the forest with the unicorn.'
    c. *Sorgin-a*   *oin-ez*   *baso-ra*   *doa.*
       witch-ABS.SG   foot-INST   forest-ALL.SG   go.3SG
       'The witch goes to the forest on foot.'

Two additional cases that might be of interest for conlangers include the **evitative** (EVIT) or **aversive** (AVR), expressing a person or thing avoided or feared, and the **malefactive** (MAL), indicating a person or thing harmed by the action. One example of the evitative is given in (36); note that PST indicates past tense.

(36) Aversive case in Djabugai (Dixon 2002)
      djama-lan   ŋawu   yarrnga-nj.   'I was afraid of the snake'.
      snake-EVIT   1SG   be afraid-PST

Case is most often expressed with suffixes in natlangs, although prefixes (as in Zapotec or Berber), tone (as in Maasai) or stem changes (as in Nuer) are also attested. Blake (2001) proposed that there is a case hierarchy in languages (37).

(37) Case hierarchy (adapted from Blake 2001:156)
      NOM > ACC > GEN > DAT > LOC > ABL/INST > other

Languages with any given case to the right of the hierarchy tend to have all the cases to their left.

8.6.1 Case in Conlanging

Esperanto has a small case system with a nominative default and an accusative suffix *-n*: *pomo* 'apple.NOM,' *pomo-n* 'apple-ACC.' This suffix appears to be in the process of being lost. The disappearance of case is common in the historical development of many natlangs (including English and Romance languages).

Dothraki has an average case system. It distinguishes nominative, accusative, genitive, allative (motion toward a place) and ablative (motion away from a place). Na'vi has ergative, accusative (for direct objects), intransitive (for intransitive subjects), dative, genitive and topical (which indicates the main topic in the sentence). The three-way difference between ergative, accusative and intransitive is rare typologically.

High Valyrian, Quenya and Láadan have large case systems. High Valyrian and Quenya have eight cases, and Láadan twenty-one (among them four beneficiary cases and five genitive ones, including a **partitive**, used to indicate that something is part of something else; 38, 39).

(38) Láadan beneficiary cases (Elgin et al. 2020:293, 294)
      a. *-da*   [dɑ]   voluntarily
      b. *-daá*   [dɑ.á]   accidentally
      c. *-dáa*   [dá.ɑ]   obligatorily, as by duty
      d. *-dá*   [dá]   by force, against somebody's will

(39) Láadan genitive cases (from Elgin et al. 2020:293, 294)
    a. *-tha* [θɑ] by birth
    b. *-thi* [θɪ] by chance
    c. *-tho* [θo] by other (purchase, gift, law, etc.)
    d. *-the* [θɛ] for unknown or unacknowledged reasons
    e. *-thu* [θu] partitive (false possessive)

Ithkuil might hold the record for the largest number of cases in a conlang, with ninety-six. A revised version of this conlang from 2023, New Ithkuil, pares them down to sixty-eight.

8.7 Conlanging Practice: Number, Gender and Case in Deep Aqua

A. The Aqua language of Ur has different dialects. One of them is Deep Aqua, which expresses number via prefixes. The singular prefix is /ma-/. Indicate the forms for the dual, paucal and plural prefixes, and write and gloss the number forms for the nouns /silan/ 'seaweed' and /ori/ 'sun' in Table 8.5. The singular has been done for you.

Table 8.5 Deep Aqua number

	/silan/ 'seaweed'		/ori/ 'sun'	
singular [ma-]	/ma-silan/ SG-waterfall	'one seaweed'	/ma-ori/ SG-sun	'one sun'
dual				
paucal				
plural				

B. Deep Aqua differentiates between animate (humans, animals, spirits, seaweed) and inanimate (everything else). Gender is conveyed via definite articles, glossed as DEF and which, unlike in English, always follow the noun.
- The singular definite article is /ko/ for animates, and /ato/ for inanimates. Indicate which are the definite article forms for dual, paucal and plural definite articles, for animate and inanimate nouns.
- Exemplify nominal phrases involving definite articles and the nouns below. Remember to include the right number prefix on the noun, to place the determiner after the noun, and to use relevant glosses.

The singular forms for all examples are given in (40). Remember that INAN refers to inanimate gender; AN is the gloss for animate gender.

Nouns	/silan/	'seaweed'	(AN)	/ori/	'sun'	(AN)
	/fode/	'stone'	(INAN)	/ler/	'hand'	(INAN)

(40) Deep Aqua: singular noun examples
    a. /ma-silan ko/   'the seaweed'   c. /ma-fode ato/   'the stone'
       SG-seaweed DEF.AN   SG-stone DEF.INAN
    b. /ma-ori ko/   'the sun'   d. /ma-ler ato/   'the hand'
       SG-sun DEF.AN   SG-ghost DEF.INAN

C. Deep Aqua has five cases (NOM, ACC, DAT, GEN, BEN). The nominative is the default; all other cases are expressed via suffixes on the noun. The accusative suffix is [-le]. Indicate the suffix forms for dative, genitive and benefactive.
- Exemplify how the case system works for the singular and plural forms of /silan/ 'seaweed,' /ori/ 'sun' and /ler/ 'hand.' Don't forget to include number prefixes and to use glosses. The singular nominative and accusative for /silan/ 'seaweed' is given in (41).

(41) Deep Aqua: Singular nominative and accusative for /silan/ 'seaweed'
    a. /ma-silan/   [ma.si.lan]   'seaweed (NOM)'
       SG-seaweed.NOM
    b. /ma-silan-le/   [ma.si.lan.le]   'seaweed (ACC)'
       SG-seaweed-ACC

- Deep Aqua does not allow adjacent vowels or consonants. Indicate any phonological modification needed to ensure that the preferred syllable structure is maintained when nouns are inflected for number, gender, and case. For example, a possible modification for 'sun' in the nominative singular (/ma-ori/) is to delete the prefix vowel: [mo.ri].

8.8 Nominal Morphology in Muq

Adjectives in muq precede the nouns they modify. There are definite and indefinite articles; when present, they follow the noun. There are three number suffixes: [-xa] SG; [-je] PAU and [-na] PL, which articles, adjectives and nouns take (42). The exception is abstract nouns, which are not marked for number, as we will see in (43).

(42) Number in muq
 a. ['zei-xa] '(a) flower' ['kust-xa] 'salt' ['ɴiq-xa] 'ugly (SG)'
   flower-SG   salt-SG   ugly-SG
 b. ['zei-je] '(a few) ['kust-je] 'some salt' ['ɴiq-je] 'ugly (PAU)'
   flower-PAU flowers' salt-PAU   ugly-PAU
 c. ['zei-na] '(many) ['kust-na] 'much salt' ['ɴiq-na] 'ugly (PL)'
   flower-PL flowers' salt-PL   ugly-PL

The Salt language lacks case but distinguishes animate and inanimate gender. Humans, animals and spirits are animate; anything else is inanimate, except the words for 'life, life force' ['si.an] and 'salt' ['kust], considered animate since they are mythologically connected with the origin of life. Gender is conveyed through the definite articles [ɬi] for animates, and [ko] for inanimates; both are always specified for number. When a determiner occurs, number is not expressed on the accompanying noun or adjective (43).

(43) Determiners in muq: number and gender
 a. ['zei ko-xa] 'the flower' ['kust ɬi-xa] 'the salt'
   flower DEF.INAN-SG   salt DEF.AN-SG
 b. ['zei ko-je] 'the few flowers' ['kust ɬi-je] 'the bit of salt'
   flower DEF.INAN-PAU   salt DEF.AN-PAU
 c. ['zei ko-na] 'the flowers' ['kust ɬi-na] 'the lot of salt'
   flower DEF.INAN-PL   salt DEF.AN-PL

Let's now begin glossing the morphology of the nouns, adjectives and determiners in our fictional text. It is useful to first outline the order in which these categories occur in the Salt language and the morphemes that express number and gender, as in Table 8.6.

Table 8.6 Outline of nominal morphology in Salt language

Adjective			Noun			Determiner			
Root	number suffix		Root	number suffix		Root		number suffix	
	[-xa]	SG		[-xa]	SG	[ɬi]	AN	[-xa]	SG
	[-je]	PAU		[-je]	PAU	[ko]	INAN	[-je]	PAU
	[-na]	PL		[-na]	PL			[-na]	PL

Table 8.7 illustrates the glosses and translations of nominal elements in the muq fictional text (with some slight rephrasing compared to Section 7.6). Note that there is only one adjective ('silent'). I will come back to the translation of 'burning' in a later chapter; discontinuous underlining indicates this word is still not translated. There are two abstract nouns: 'darkness,' and 'sadness'; these lack number suffixes.

There are two examples of the plural: 'many days', and '(much) fire'; and of a paucal ('some of its life force,' rendered here as 'some life force' to better reflect the way this is rendered in muq). All other nouns and adjectives are singular. Nouns without a determiner are marked for number (unless they are abstract); if they have a determiner, the number is marked on the determiner, but not on the noun. Except for 'life force,' which is animate, all other nouns in the fictional text are inanimate.

Note that I've used a table for easier gloss alignment. For each line of text, the corresponding translation of nominal elements is given, followed by its specific gloss. I have chosen not to include glosses for derivational morphemes, but you can choose to do so when glossing and translating your own fictional text.

Table 8.7 Fictional text: nominal morphology translation and gloss

A long time ago	the world ['i.xi ko-xa] world DEF.INAN-SG	slept; there was		darkness. ['ɣeç] darkness
The wind was ['ɫu.ma ko-xa] wind DEF.INAN-SG	silent ['seʁ-xa] silent-SG	and the ocean ['ɫei ko-xa] ocean DEF.INAN-SG	whispered with	sadness. ['ɫei.za] sadness
Then the mountain screamed and spewed ['ɲa.çen ko-xa] mountain DEF.INAN-SG		much fire, ['ʁouq-na] fire-PL	and	the island burned. [çem ko-xa] island DEF.INAN-SG
It burned and burned for		many days. ['ŋuç-na] day-PL		
When it stopped burning	the island [çem ko-xa] island DEF.INAN-SG		had changed.	
The ocean ['ɫei ko-xa] ocean DEF.INAN-SG	soothed	the burning land and gave it ['muq.çem ko-xa] land DEF.INAN-SG		some life force. ['si.an-je] life.force-PAU
The life force from ['si.an ɬi-xa] life.force-SG	the ocean destroyed ['ɫei ko-xa] ocean DEF.INAN-SG	the darkness and ['ɣeç ko-xa] darkness DEF.INAN-SG	dawn returned ['mis.tə-xa] dawn-SG	
This is how	life on ['si.an-xa] life-SG	our island ['muq.çem-xa] land-SG	awakened.	

Note that there are a few pronouns in the text ('it,' 'this'); we will address them in Chapter 15.

8.9 Guide to Developing Nominal Morphology

- What degree of fusion will your conlang have? (isolating, concatenative, non-linear)
- Will your conlang have analytic, synthetic, or polysynthetic morphology?
- Will your conlang have cumulative or separative morphology?
- Will your conlang express number morphologically? In which nominal category (nouns, pronouns, adjectives, determiners)?
- If so, will there be a number default?
- Indicate how many numbers will be distinguished (e.g., singular, dual, trial, paucal), and whether they will be conveyed with concatenative or non-concatenative affixes.
- Will your conlang have morphological gender? If so, will it be based on sex or animacy?
- How many gender distinctions will be encoded?
- Which word types will carry gender (nouns, determiners, pronouns, adjectives)?
- Will gender be conveyed separately from number (as in Spanish) or together (as in Italian)?
- Will your conlang have case? If so, how many cases will it have?
- Indicate which cases will be expressed, and whether there is an unmarked default.
- What type of affix will convey case?
- If your conlang expresses number, gender and/or case with separate affixes of the same type (e.g., suffix, prefix), indicate the relative order among them.
- Provide glossed examples of how number, gender and case are expressed in your conlang (if relevant).
- Provide a translation for the geographical features of your fictional map. Take into consideration the nominal morphology in your conlang in addition to the relative order among adjectives, determiners and nouns in the noun phrase (if relevant). Remember to add any new words to your conlang database!

> **Conlanging Tip**
>
> To keep track of the affixes in your conlang, it is a good idea to list them in a separate tab in excel (or a similar database).

To Learn More

This chapter draws from chapter 5 in Velupillai (2012) as well as from Bickel and Nichols (2007, 2013a, b). The information on glossing follows the Leipzig Glossing Rules (Comrie et al. 2008). Wikipedia has a detailed list of glosses, available at https://en.wikipedia.org/wiki/List_of_glossing_abbreviations.

For a fun book about irregularities in the English language, see Okrent (2021). More information on infixes can be found in Yu (2004, 2006); for circumfixes, see Zingler (2022) and Marušič (2023). For number, see chapters 33–35 in WALS online in addition to Corbett (2000).

For an introduction to gender see Corbett (2013a, b). An informative and entertaining discussion on this topic is found in chapter 8 of Deutscher (2010); see Aikhenvald (2016) for a book-length study. A good source for non-binary singular *they* in English is Konnelly et al. (2023). The discussion of case is based largely on Iggesen (2013a, b); see also Blake (2001). To learn more about pronouns and gender in conlangs, see Zottola (2023). The Esperanto examples in this chapter come from lernu!, a website promoting the learning of Esperanto: www.lernu.net.

9 The Morphology of Verbs

This chapter focuses on verbal morphology, in particular, agreement and so-called TAM, that is, tense, aspect and mood. As we saw in Chapter 7, there are two types of verbs: lexical and auxiliary. Both are relevant in this chapter, because tense, aspect, mood and agreement can be expressed on either.

The structure of verbs in languages that use inflection tends to be the most complex part of the morphology, particularly since verbal agreement (Section 9.1) and tense (Section 9.2) tend to be expressed morphologically. Sections 9.3 and 9.4 focus on aspect and mood respectively. Section 9.5 provides conlanging practice on the verbal morphology of one of the Ur languages, and Section 9.6 describes the verbal morphology of muq. Section 9.7 provides a set of guided questions to develop the verbal morphology of your conlang; the chapter ends with a list of sources to explore this topic further.

Key Words

Agent (A)
Aspect
  Completive (CMPL)
  Contemplative (CONTEM)
  Continuative (CONT)
  Habitual (HAB)
  Imperfective (IMPF)
  Inchoative (inceptive) (INCH)
  Iterative (ITER)
  Perfective (PFV)
  Progressive (PROG)
  Semelfactive (SEM)
  Strong perfective (STRONG.PFV)
Clitic
Degrees of remoteness

Ditransitive
Modality
  Assumptive (ASSUM)
  Deductive (DED)
  Dubitative (DUB)
  Speculative (SPECL)
Mood
  Indicative
  Irrealis (IRR)
  Realis (REAL)
  Subjunctive
Morpho-phonology
Patient (P)
Person marking
Tense
  Future (FUT)
    Distant future (DIST.FUT)
    Near future (REC.FUT)
    Remote future (REM.FUT)
  Hesternal (HEST)
  Hodiernal (HOD)
  Non-future (NFUT)
  Non-past (NPST)
  Past (PST)
    Distant past (DIST.PST)
    Recent past (REC.PST)
    Remote past (REM.PST)
  Present (PRS)
Tense, aspect and mood (TAM)
Transitive
Verbal agreement

9.1 Verbal Agreement

One grammatical function associated with verbs is **verbal agreement**, that is, the marking of person, number and/or gender on the verb. In most cases, verbal agreement involves **person marking**. English expresses agreement for the verb *to be* in the **present tense** (singular: *am, are, is*; plural: *are*), as well as with the use of the third person singular suffix *-s* in the present tense (*it crawls*; cf. *they crawl*). Spanish has verbal agreement for person and number in all tenses (1); note that the glosses 1, 2 and 3 denote first, second and third person, respectively, and PRS the present tense.

(1) Spanish verbal agreement (present tense)
    a. *viaj-o*   'I travel'   *viaj-amos*   'we travel'
        travel-1SG.PRS   travel-1PL.PRS
    b. *viaj-as*   'you (SG) travel'   *viaj-áis*   'you all travel' (*Spain*)
        travel-2SG.PRS   travel-2PL.PRS
    c. *viaj-a*   's/he travels'   *viaj-an*   'they travel'
        travel-3SG.PRS   travel-3PL.PRS

Person marking occurs in 88 percent of natlangs. English and Spanish have so-called 'subject agreement', where the verb agrees with the subject of the sentence. This type of agreement is attested in 19 percent of languages. Other natlangs have direct object agreement, as in Yawa (2). The gloss P ('**patient**') indicates agreement with the object.

(2) Verbal agreement in Yawa (from Siewierska 2013a)
    Dorpinus   *po*   *Marianna*   *r-anepata*
    Dorpinus   ERG.3SG.M   Marianna   3SG.F.P-hit
    'Dorpinus is/was hitting Marianne.'

Only 6 percent of natlangs have object verbal agreement; other examples include Warao and Indonesian. A much more common pattern occurring in 51 percent of natlangs is to have both subject and object agreement, as in Tawala (3) and Basque (4). Note that the gloss A ('agent') indicates verbal agreement with the subject of **transitive** verbs, that is, verbs that have a direct object. Unlike in the examples in (1–3), verbal agreement in Basque is conveyed by the auxiliary verb.

(3) Verbal agreement in Tawala (Ezard 1997: 99)
    kedewa   *kamkam*   *i-uni-hi*   'A dog killed the chickens'
    dog   chicken   3SG.A-kill-3PL.P

(4) Verbal agreement in Basque: transitive sentences
    a. *txori*   *bat*   *ikusi*   *du-t*   'I have seen one bird'
        bird   one   see   have.3SG.P-1SG.A
    b. *bi*   *txori*   *ikusi*   *ditu-t*   'I have seen two birds'
        two   bird   see   have.3PL.P-1SG.A

In Basque, when the sentence is **ditransitive**, that it, it has both a direct and an indirect object, the auxiliary verb includes agreement with the indirect object as well (5). Note that the gloss IND (indirect) indicates indirect object agreement.

(5) Verbal agreement in Basque: ditransitive sentences
   a. *txori* *bat* *eman* *di-o-t* 'I have given her/him one bird'
      bird   one   give   have.3SG.P-3SG.IND-1SG.A
   b. *txori* *bat* *eman* *di-e-t* 'I have given them one bird'
      bird   one   give   have.3SG.P-3PL.IND-1SG.A

Natlangs with both subject and object agreement vary in the linear order between both. Subject and object agreement can also be expressed in one single affix, as in Klingon, as we show in the next section. Verbal agreement is usually conveyed via affixes, but another option is to use **clitics**, that is, units that can attach to different words and sometimes are pronounced as separate words. One example is found in Spanish, where clitics *los* 'them' and *se* 'to him/her/them' can appear as separate words before the verb (6a) or be attached to the lexical verb (6b).

(6) Clitics in Spanish
   a. *Se*   *los*   *est-á*   *llevando.*
      3.DAT   3PL.ACC   be-3SG.PRS   taking
      '(She/he) is taking them to her/him/them.'
   b. *Est-á*   *llevando-se-los.*
      be-3SG.PRS   taking-3.DAT-3PL.ACC
      '(S/he) is taking them to her/him/them.'

Verbal agreement can also involve gender, as we saw for Yawa (2). This is also the case in Arabic, as shown in (7). Note that gender agreement is expressed in the singular and plural forms of the imperative, but not in the dual.

(7) Arabic person agreement (Adam Gaiser, p.c.)
   a. [kul]   'eat (2SG.M)'   [ku.luː]   'eat (2PL.M)'
   b. [ku.li]   'eat (2SG.F)'   [kul.na]   'eat (2PL.F)'
   c. [ku.laː] 'eat (2DU)'

In some natlangs, including Spanish and Basque, verbal agreement is obligatory. In others, including Macushi, verbal agreement is needed only if the subject or object is not overtly expressed via a noun or pronoun in the sentence.

9.1.1 Verbal Agreement in Conlanging

Esperanto, Na'vi and Toki Pona lack verbal agreement. Láadan indicates plural subject agreement with the prefix *me-* [mɛ]; for example, '(s/he) works' is [hal], and '(they) work' [mɛ.hal] (Elgin et al. 2020:22).

Dothraki and Sindarin have subject verbal agreement suffixes for person and number. In Sindarin, these are *-n* '1SG', *-m* '1PL' and *-r* '3PL'; the third person singular is unmarked (8). Suffixes for second person singular/plural are not found in published materials for this conlang (Salo 2004:111).

(8) Sindarin verbal agreement (from Salo 2004:113)
    a. *naro-n*   [na.ron] 'I tell'   *nara-m*   [na.ram] 'we tell'
        to.tell-1SG   to.tell-1PL
    b. *nara*   [na.ra] 's/he/it tells'   *nara-r*   [na.rar] 'they tell'
        to.tell.3SG   to.tell-3PL

Klingon has subject and object verbal agreement, encoded via prefixes that fuse both; examples are given in (9).

(9) Klingon person marking (from Okrand 1985:33, 34)
    a. *qa-legh*   [qɑ.lɛɣ]   'I see you'
        1SG.A.2SG.P-to.see
    b. *cho-legh*   [tʃo.lɛɣ]   'you see me'
        2SG.A.1SG.P-to.see
    c. *vI-legh*   [vɪ. lɛɣ]   'I see them'
        1SG.A.3.P-to.see
    d. *Da-legh*   [ɖɑ. lɛɣ]   'you see them'
        2SG.A.3.P-to.see

9.2 Tense

Tense refers to the point in time of an event. All languages have the means to express differences among **past**, present and **future**. Tense differences can be expressed lexically with temporal adverbs such as *yesterday* or expressions such as *last night*. Tense can also be conveyed morphologically or syntactically. In English, lexical expression for tense is possible (10a); syntactic expression occurs in the **future** (10b), and morphological expression in the **past** and **present** (for third person singular only) (10c).

(10) Tense in English
    a. Lexical expression: I dance <u>tomorrow</u>.
    b. Syntactic expression: I <u>will</u> dance.
    c. Morphological expression: He danc<u>ed</u>, She danc<u>es</u>.

Some natlangs express tense lexically; examples include Dyirbal and Juǀ'hoan. In natlangs that express tense grammatically, two or more tenses are distinguished. In binary tense systems, a distinction is made between **past** and **non-past** tense, as in Harar Oromo (11), or between future and **non-future**, as in Kolyma Yukaghir (12). Note that 'past' is glossed PST, 'non-past' NPST; and 'future' FUT.

(11) Tense in Harar Oromo (adapted from Owens 1985:83)
    a. *inːii*   *magaláa*   *deːm-e*
       3SG.M   market   to.go-PST
       'He went to the market.'
    b. *inːii*   *magaláa*   *deːm-a*
       3SG.M   market   to.go-NPST
       'He is going/will go to the market.'

(12) Tense in Kolyma Yukaghir (adapted from Maslova 2003:168)
    a. *terikiedie*   *iŋd'et*   *modo-j*
       old.woman   sew.3SG   to.sit-NFUT.3SG
       'The old woman is/was sitting and sewing.'
    b. *met*   *qaninere*   *kel-te-je*
       1SG   one.day   to.come-FUT-1SG
       'I will come one day.'

Languages that indicate a three-way distinction among past, present and future grammatically are the most frequent crosslinguistically, as in English (10). A language expressing three tenses syntactically is Fijian (13).

(13) Tense in Fijian (adapted from Dixon 2016:86)
    a. *au*   *na*   *lako*   'I will go'
       1SG   FUT   go
    b. *au*   *aa*   *lako*   'I went'
       1SG   PST   go
    c. *Au*   *lako*   'I am going'
       1SG   go.PRS

In addition, about a quarter of natlangs have more complex tense systems with multiple past or future tenses. This is referred to as **degrees of remoteness**. For example, in some dialects of Spanish, including my own, there is a distinction between past events that happened earlier in the day and those that occurred the day before or earlier (14).

(14) Degrees of remoteness in the past: Spanish
    a. *He*   *ido*   *a*   *la*   *playa.*
       have.1SG   gone   to   the   beach
       'I went to the beach (today).'
    b. *Fui*   *a*   *la*   *playa.*
       go.1SG.PST   to   the   beach
       'I went to the beach (before today).'

Some natlangs distinguish three degrees of remoteness in the past. One example is Matsés, which distinguishes **recent past** (up to one month before), **distant past** (from one month before to the time of the speaker's childhood) and **remote past** (a time during the speaker's infancy or before their birth). Examples are given in (15); recent, distant and remote past are glossed as REC.PST, DIST.PST and REM.PS, respectively.

(15) Degrees of past remoteness: Matsés (adapted from Fleck 2003:395, 402; Fleck 2007:598)
    a. *ninitʃokid-n*   *ak-ak*
       shaman-ERG   kill-REC.PST.INFR.EV
       'A shaman (must have) killed him.'
    b. *mibi*   *nid-onda-k*
       2SG.ABS   go-DIST.PST.DIR.EV-1/2
       'You went long ago.'
    c. *poʃtó*   *kues-denne-mbi*
       woolly.monkey.ABS   kill-REM.PST.DIR.EV-1A
       'I used to kill woolly monkeys (when young).'

About 1 percent of natlangs have four to six remoteness distinctions in the past. One example is Yagua, which distinguishes recent, distant and remote past, like Matsés, but also **hodiernal (HOD)** past ('earlier today') and **hesternal (HEST)** past ('yesterday') (16).

(16) Degrees of past remoteness: Yagua (from Payne & Payne 1990:386–388)
    a. HOD.PST   within a few hours   *-jásiy*
    b. HEST.PST   one day before   *-jay*
    c. REC.PST   several weeks ago   *-siy*
    d. DIST.PST   several months ago   *-tíy*
    e. REM.PST   several years ago   *-jada ~ -janu* (dialectal variant)

Yaminahua holds the record for the number of possible degrees of remoteness in the past (six) and also for the number of degrees of remoteness overall (nine), since it distinguishes **near future, distant future** and **remote future** (glossed as REC.FUT, DIST.FUT and REM.FUT, respectively). The suffixes that express these distinctions are given in (17). Note that Yaminahua has two distant past tenses, glossed as DIST.PST1 and DIST.PST2 below.

(17) Degrees of remoteness: Yaminahua (from Faust & Loos 2002, Neely 2019)
    a. HOD.PST   last night ('immediate past')   *-wa*
    b. HEST.PST   yesterday   *-waiyabia*
    c. REC.PST   a few days/weeks back   *-ita*
    d. DIST.PST1 many weeks/months before   *-yabia*
    e. DIST.PST2 6–9 months to 1–2 years before *-ti*
    f. REM.PST   several years ago   *-di*
    g. REC.FUT   in one or a few days   *-waidaka*
    h. DIST.FUT   weeks or months from now   *-nũpukui*
    i. REM.FUT   months or years from now   *-daka*

You might have noticed that what counts as recent, distant or remote past differs from language to language. Indeed, tense cut-off points within the 'past' or 'future' are tied to cultural (or mythical) conceptions of time. They are often connected to recurring cycles (day/night; seasons; years) or common phases (childhood, adulthood). Generally, degrees of remoteness closer to the time of the utterance tend to be more precise and cover shorter time periods, while those further away in time lack a specific cut-off point and cover a larger time span. In addition, natlangs express more tense distinctions in the past than in the future (Dixon 2016:87).

9.2.1 Tense in Conlangs

In Klingon and Toki Pona, tense is expressed lexically (via adverbials) or understood by context. Esperanto and Dothraki distinguish present, past and future morphologically. In Dothraki, present and past are expressed with suffixes, and the future with a prefix. Esperanto present, past and future suffixes are *-as*, *-is* and *-os*, respectively (18).

(18) Tense in Esperanto (from Harlow 1995)
    a. *am-is*   'loved'
       love-PST
    b. *am-as*   'love(s)'
       love-PRS
    c. *am-os*   'will love'
       love-FUT

Láadan and Na'vi distinguish two degrees of remoteness in the past and two in the future. In Na'vi, tense is optionally expressed via infixes (Annis 2024); in Láadan, with auxiliary verbs (19).

(19) Tense auxiliaries in Láadan (from Elgin et al. 2020:312)

a.	Present:	*ril*	[rɪl]	'present time, now'	PRS
b.	Past:	*eril*	[ɛ.rɪl]	'past'	REC.PST
		eríli	[ɛ.rí.lɪ]	'far past, long ago'	REM.PST
c.	Future:	*aril*	[a.rɪl]	'far future'	REC.FUT
		aríli	[a.rí.lɪ]	'far future, long ahead'	REM.FUT

9.3 Aspect

Aspect refers to how an action extends over time: how long it lasted, how often it occurs and whether it is viewed as completed. Consider, for example, the sentences in (20): they have different tenses, but they all refer to an event in progress, that is, the **progressive aspect** (PROG). In English, the progressive is indicated with the auxiliary verb *to be* and the *-ing* suffix on the main verb.

(20) Progressive aspect in English
    a. Present: You are piloting a spaceship.
    b. Past: You were piloting a spaceship.
    c. Future: You will be piloting a spaceship.

English also expresses the **perfective aspect** (PFV), indicating an event viewed as completed. In the past tense, the perfective is conveyed by the suffix *-ed*, and in the future, with the auxiliary verbs *will have* followed by a verb in the participle form. Examples are shown in (21).

(21) Perfective aspect in English
    a. Past: Andrea danced with Sofía.
    b. Future: Andrea will have danced with Sofía.

Some natlangs have perfective aspects conveying specific nuances. For example, the **strong perfective** emphasizes the completion of an event and/or the event completely affecting an object. One example from Rama is given in (22); note that the **strong perfective** verbal suffix (glossed STRONG.PFV) precedes the past suffix.

(22) Strong perfective aspect in Rama (from Grinevald 1988:154)
    yaing   kwiik   alauk-atkul-u   'He burned his hand completely.'
    his   hand   burn-STRONG.PFV-PST

A common aspect in natlangs is the **imperfect** (glossed IMPF), used to indicate ongoing and habitual actions. Spanish has perfective, progressive and imperfect aspects, as shown in (23). Note that (23c) implies that the action was completed, unlike (23a, b).

(23) Aspect in Spanish
    a. *Bill*   *est-aba*   *toc-ando*   *la*   *guitarra.*
       Bill   to.be-3SG.PST   to.play-PROG the   guitar
      'Bill was playing guitar.'
    b. *Bill*   *toc-aba*   *la*   *guitarra.*
       Bill   to.play-PST.IMPF   the   guitar
      'Bill used to play guitar.'
    c. *Bill*   *toc-ó*   *la*   *guitarra.*
       Bill   to.play-3SG.PST.PFV the   guitar
      'Bill played the guitar.'

Perfective, imperfective and progressive are the most common aspects expressed grammatically in natlangs; all focus on whether the action is viewed as completed. But other aspectual distinctions are attested, including whether an action is beginning (**inchoative**, or **inceptive**, glossed INCH), in the middle (**continuative**, glossed CONT), or ending (**completive**, glossed CMPL). The **contemplative aspect** (CONTEM) expresses actions that have been considered by the speaker but have not taken place yet. These four distinctions focus on the specific phase of an event. They can be lexically conveyed in English, as shown in (24).

(24) Lexical occurrence of phase of an event in English
   a. Inchoative (INCH):   I began to sing.
   b. Continuative (CONT):   I continued to sing.
   c. Completive (CMPL):   I stopped singing.
   d. Contemplative (CONTEM): I'm thinking of singing; I would sing.

Aspect can also refer to the frequency of occurrence of the event: often (**habitual**, glossed HAB), only once (**semelfactive**, glossed SEM) or repeatedly (**iterative**, glossed ITER). Examples of lexical expressions conveying these distinctions in English are given in (25).

(25) Lexical expression of frequency of occurrence of an event in English
   a. Semelfactive (SEM): I once sang.
   b. Iterative (ITER):   I sang repeatedly.
   c. Habitual HAB):   I often sang.

Tense and aspect tend to be expressed morphologically with suffixes or prefixes, although other options are attested, including tonal changes. Tense and aspect can be expressed with different affixes, or with fused affixes, as in Spanish, as shown in (26).

(26) Spanish perfective and imperfective aspect
   a. *Annie*   *bail-aba.*   'Annie used to dance.'
      Annie   dance-3SG.PST.IMPF
   b. *Annie*   *bail-ó.*   'Annie danced.'
      Annie   dance-3SG.PST.PFV

9.3.1 Aspect in Conlanging

Toki Pona and Dothraki lack grammatical aspect. Navi' has perfective and imperfective infixes. Klingon distinguishes four aspectual suffixes: (i) perfective, (ii) perfective plus intent (glossed here as PFV.INT), (iii) progressive and (iv) progressive plus a definite ending point (glossed here as PROG.DEF) (27).

(27) Klingon aspect (adapted from Okrand 1985:40–42)
    a. *lu-HoH-pu'*   [lu.xox.puʔ]   'They have killed him/her.' (accidentally)
       3PL.A.3SG.P-kill-PFV
    b. *lu-HoH-ta'*   [lu.xox.taʔ]   'They have killed him/her.' (on purpose)
       3PL.A.3SG.P-kill-PFV.INT
    c. *nu-ghoS-taH* [nu.ɣoʂ.taʔ]   'It is approaching us.'
       3SG.A.1PL.P-approach-PROG
    d. *chol-lI'*   [tʃo.lɪʔ]   'It is getting closer.'
       come.near-PROG.DEF

Láadan has five aspectual prefixes: (i) continuative *ná-* [ná-]; (ii) inchoative *na-* [nɑ-]; (iii) iterative *ne-* [nɛ-]; (iv) perfective *no-* [no-] and (v), completive *nó-* [nó-]. Aspectual prefixes follow the plural agreement prefix *me-* [mɛ-] (Elgin et al. 2020:209–210, 295).

> **Your Turn**
>
> Which of these aspectual systems do you find most interesting, and why?

9.4 Mood and Modality

Modality conveys the degree of confidence a speaker has about a situation, and **mood** whether they believe the situation is real. Boye (2016) indicates that both are important in language since otherwise we would not be able to distinguish between knowledge or belief, or among certain, uncertain and possible facts, which would impact our chance of survival.

A common mood distinction in natlangs is that between **realis** (glossed REAL), which expresses the speaker's certainty regarding the reality of the situation, and the **irrealis** (glossed IRR), which makes no claims about it. The latter is used in many languages to convey that an event is uncertain, desired or hypothetical. One example is Spanish, where the realis mood is conveyed by the **indicative** and the irrealis by the **subjunctive**. Consider the examples below:

(28) Mood in Spanish
    a. *Busc-o   a una líder   que sabe   dothraki.*
       search-1SG.PRS P a   leader who know.3SG.PRS.REAL Dothraki
       'I'm looking for a female leader who knows Dothraki.' (I know she exists)
    b. *Busc-o   a una líder que   sepa   dothraki.*
       search-1SG.PRS.RL P a   leader who   know.3SG.PRS.IRR Dothraki
       'I'm looking for a female leader who knows Dothraki.' (I don't know if she exists)

In the first sentence, the verb *sabe* 'knows' is in the indicative form, since the speaker knows the female leader searched for exists. In the second sentence, *sepa* is in the subjunctive form, since the speaker is not sure whether the leader looked for exists.

> **Your Turn**
>
> Unlike Spanish, English does not distinguish between realis and irrealis grammatically. How would you convey the Spanish sentences above in English maintaining the same nuances in meaning?

English expresses modality with the modal auxiliary verbs *may*, *must* and *will*. Consider the examples in (29) which differ in the degree of certainty conveyed: (29a) indicates a likely conclusion, (29b) the only possible conclusion and (29c) a reasonable conclusion. The use of 'may' indicates the least degree of certainty; and the use of 'must' the most. The use of 'will' indicates an inference or assumption by the speaker. These modalities are termed **speculative** (SPECL), **deductive** (DED), and **assumptive** (ASSUM), respectively. An additional distinction is the **dubitative** modality (DUB), exemplified in Tauya (30); note that the gloss DEC indicates the sentence is a statement (we'll explore this in detail in Chapter 11).

(29) Modality in English
    a. Binti *may* have survived.
    b. Binti *must* have survived.
    c. Binti *will* have survived.

(30) Dubitative modality in Tauya (McDonald 1990:208–209)
    ʔeira   mene-a-rafo-ʔa   'Maybe he's there'
    There   stay-3SG-DUB-DEC

Degree of certainty can also be expressed lexically via so-called epistemic adjectives, adverbs and even verbs, as exemplified below for English.

(31) Lexical modality in English
    a. I *know* it is a meteorite.   I *doubt* it is a meteorite.
    b. I am *certain* it is a meteorite.   I am *unsure* it is a meteorite.
    c. It is *definitely* a meteorite.   *Perhaps* it is a meteorite.

Finally, mood and modality can occur together; for example, in the Wardaman sentence in (32), the particle *yilama* 'maybe' expresses modality, and the verbal prefix [ya-] the irrealis mood.

(32) Wardaman (Merlan 1994:299)
   yilama   ya-yinyja   ma-yinyja   wurrugu   ngarlg-ba
   maybe   IRR.3SG-go   HAB.3SG-go   3N.SG.DAT   call-PCL
   'Maybe he'll go, he always goes to call them.'

9.4.1 Mood and Modality in Conlanging

In Láadan, the auxiliary verb *rilrili* [rıl.rı.lı] 'hypothetical, would, might, let's suppose' is used to convey hypothetical events and thus can be considered to be an irrealis auxiliary verb; the auxiliary verb *wil* [wıl] is used to express an option or a wish (Elgin et al. 2020:190, 312). Na'vi expresses the irrealis with the subjunctive and the adverb *nirangal* [nı.'ɾa.ŋal]; the latter expresses an unachievable wish. Na'vi also has modal auxiliaries, including *zene* ['zɛ.nɛ] 'must' and *tsun* ['tsun] 'can' (Annis 2024:50). In Klingon, 'qualification' suffixes express modality; examples are given in (33).

(33) Modality in Klingon (from Okrand 1985:40)
   a. *baH-chu'*   [bɑx.tʃuʔ]   'S/he fired (the torpedo) perfectly.'
      fire.a.torpedo-clearly
   b. *chIm-bej*   [tʃɪm.bɛj]   'It is undoubtedly empty.'
      be.empty-certainly
   c. *chIm-law'*   [tʃɪm.lɑwʔ]   'It appears to be empty.'
      be.empty-seemingly

9.5 Conlanging Practice: Tense, Aspect and Mood in the Moon Language

The Moon language (whose vowels and consonants were introduced in Chapters 3 and 4 respectively) has complex TAM morphology, making it an excellent case study for this chapter. The Moon language distinguishes five different tenses, two aspects and two moods. Tense and aspect are expressed via prefixes on the main verb, and mood via suffixes (Table 9.1).

Table 9.1 TAM in Moon

Tense prefixes		Aspect prefixes	
Recent past (up to one month ago)	[si-]	Perfective	[fım-]
Remote past		Imperfective	
Present		Mood suffixes	
Near future (up to one month from now)		Realis	
Remote future		Irrealis	

1. List all tense and aspect prefixes (two are already done for you, as shown in Table 9.1)
2. Decide on the relative order between tense and aspect prefixes.
3. List the mood suffixes for realis and irrealis.
4. The verb 'to dance around' is [fɪs] in the Moon language. Translate the following realis sentences.
   a. 'danced around (recently)'
   b. 'danced around (a long time ago)'
   c. 'was dancing around (recently)'
   d. 'was dancing around (a long time ago)'
   e. 'dances around'
   f. 'will dance around (soon)'
   g. 'will dance around (next year)'
5. Now provide translations for the irrealis (hypothetical) sentences below.
   a. 'maybe danced around (recently)'
   b. 'maybe danced around (a long time ago)'
   c. 'maybe was dancing around (recently)'
   d. 'maybe was dancing around (a long time ago)'
   e. 'maybe dances around'
   f. 'maybe will dance around (soon)'
   g. 'maybe will dance around (next year)'

9.6 Verb Morphology in Muq

The Salt language lacks verbal agreement. It has five tenses (present, recent past, remote past, near future and remote future) and two aspects (perfective and imperfective). The recent past refers to past events within the speaker's lifetime, and the remote past, to events beyond it. The near future refers to events or situations expected or imagined within the speaker's lifetime, and the remote future beyond it. Tense distinctions are indicated via suffixes except for the present tense (34).

(34) Salt language tense suffixes
   a. /-æ/   REC.PST
   b. /-i/   REM.PST
   c. /-a/   REC.FUT
   d. /-u/   REM.FUT

Perfective and imperfective are expressed with the suffixes /-s/ and /-m/, respectively. Aspectual suffixes precede tense suffixes in the main verb. Examples of perfective and imperfective verbal forms are given in (35, 36) for the verb [ˈχe.ʁa] 'to break.'

9.6 Verb Morphology in Muq

(35) Perfective aspect in muq
- a. REM.PST ['χe.ʁa.si] 'broke (long ago)'
- b. REC.PST ['χe.ʁa.sæ] 'broke'
- c. PRS ['χe.ʁas] 'breaks'
- d. REC.FUT ['χe.ʁa.sɑ] 'will break'
- e. REM.FUT ['χe.ʁa.su] 'will break (one day)'

(36) Imperfective aspect in muq
- a. REM.PST ['χe.ʁa.mi] 'was breaking (long ago)'
- b. REC.PST ['χe.ʁa.mæ] 'was breaking'
- c. PRS ['χe.ʁam] 'is breaking'
- d. REC.FUT ['χe.ʁa.mɑ] 'will be breaking'
- e. REM.FUT ['χe.ʁa.mu] 'will be breaking (one day)'

Let's now work on translating and glossing the verbal morphology of the fictional text introduced in Chapter 2. Before we do so, it is a good idea to chart the verbal morphology of muq for easy reference (Table 9.2).

Table 9.2 Outline of verbal morphology in muq

	Aspect		Tense			
Verb root	IMPF	-m	Past	REC.PST	-æ	REM.PST -i
	PFV	-s	Future	REC.FUT	-ɑ	REM.FUT -u
			Present			–

All verbs in the fictional text in Table 9.3 refer to the remote past, and thus end in /-i/, with the exception of 'is' in the last sentence, in the present and thus without a tense suffix. The verbs in the first two sentences focus on states or actions in progress, so they need the suffix /-m/. All other verbs refer to completed actions and carry the perfective suffix /-s/. Note that 'stopped burning' is translated as one word; the verb 'to return,' untranslated in Chapter 7, is ['meq].

After adding affixes, we need to check that the result is still compatible with the phonological structure of the conlang. One issue arises in the verb ['çis-s-i] 'burned (a long time ago),' since the perfective suffix /-s/ is added to a verb that also ends in /s/. Various 'repairs' or possible solutions to this issue are given in (37). One is to delete one 's' (probably the one corresponding to the verb root, since coda consonants tend to be deleted more often than onsets) (37a). A second solution is to insert a vowel between both 's' sounds; the mid central vowel [ə] is a good choice since it is the muq vowel that approximates the neutral position of the tongue most closely (37b) (if the conlang does not have central mid vowels, other good options are mid

Table 9.3 Fictional text: verbal morphology

A long time ago the world <u>slept</u>		there <u>was</u> darkness.	
	['xaɸ-m-i]		['mei-m-i]
	sleep-IMPF-REM.PST		be-IMPF-REM.PST

The wind <u>was</u> silent and the ocean		<u>whispered</u> with sadness.	
	['mei-m-i]		['xi.ma-m-i]
	be-IMPF-REM.PST		whisper-IMPF-REM.PST

Then the mountain <u>screamed</u> and	<u>spewed</u> much fire,	and the island <u>burned</u>.
['ʁɑ.ʟi-s-i]	['tɑʁ-s-i]	['çis-s-i]
scream-PFV-REM.PST	spew-PFV-REM.PST	burn-PFV-REM.PST

It <u>burned</u>	and <u>burned</u> for many days.
['çis-s-i]	['çis-s-i]
burn-PFV-REM.PST	burn-PFV-REM.PST

When it <u>stopped burning</u> the island		<u>had transformed</u>.
['ɬam.xɑ-s-i]		['ou.sei-s-i]
dry.up-PFV-REM.PST		transform-PFV-REM.PST

The ocean <u>soothed</u>	the burning land and <u>gave</u> it some life force.
['ɸiθ-s-i]	['nei-s-i]
soothe-PFV-REM.PST	give-PFV-REM.PST

The life force from the ocean <u>destroyed</u> the darkness	and dawn <u>returned</u>
['χe.ʁɑ-s-i]	['meq.ze-s-i]
destroy-PFV-REM.PST	return-PFV-REM.PST

This <u>is</u> how life on	our island <u>awakened</u>.
['mei-s]	['ou.na-s-i]
be-PFV	awaken-PFV-REM.PST

front or even high front vowels). A third solution is to combine both 's' sounds into a long [sː] (37c).

(37)   Possible repairs for ['çis-s-i] 'burned (a long time ago)'
      a. Deletion of 's'   ['çi.si]
      b. Insertion of a vowel   ['çi.sə.si]
      c. Lengthening of 's' (gemination) ['çi.sːi]

I have decided to go with combining both 's' sounds into a long one, which means that the phonology of muq needs to be revised, since now geminate consonants are possible. However, these are not contrastive geminates; they can only occur at morpheme boundaries when two adjacent identical consonants occur next to each other. This is an example of **morpho-phonology**: phonological patterns that arise when morphemes are put together in words.

9.7 Guide to Developing Verbal Morphology

- Does your conlang include verbal agreement?
    - If so, will it involve the subject, the object, or both?
    - If so, will it provide information on person, number and/or gender?
- Does your conlang express tense morphologically or syntactically?
    - If morphologically, list all tense aspects and whether they modify the main or auxiliary verb.
    - If syntactically, indicate which auxiliary verbs convey tense.
    - If lexically, indicate which words refer to time adverbs/expressions (e.g., today, yesterday, last night).
- Are there degrees of remoteness in the past or future? If so, indicate the cut-off point for each, ideally relating them to the fictional world.
- Does your conlang convey aspect morphologically or syntactically?
    - If morphologically, list all affixes and whether they modify the main or auxiliary verb.
    - If syntactically, indicate if the aspectual auxiliary verb precedes or follows the main verb.
- Does aspect relate to event completion (perfective, strong perfective, progressive, imperfective)?
- Does aspect relate to the phase of the event (inceptive, continuative, completive, contemplative)?
- Does aspect relate to frequency of the event (semelfactive, iterative, habitual)?
- Does your conlang encode mood/ modality?
    - If morphologically, list the affix(es) and whether they modify the main or auxiliary verb.
    - If syntactically, indicate the auxiliary verbs conveying mood/modality.
- Does your conlang convey realis/irrealis, and/or deductive/assumptive/speculative modality?
- If your conlang expresses verbal agreement, tense, aspect and/or mood with similar affix types, indicate their relative order.

To Learn More

The discussion of verbal agreement in this chapter draws from Velupillai (2012) and Siewierska (2013a, b). For tense, a classic source is Comrie (1985). Dahl and Velupillai (2013a, b) are good introductions to present and future tense in natlangs. For degrees of remoteness, see Botne (2012), Martin (2010) and Valenzuela and Castro Soares de Oliveira (2021). A classic monograph on aspect is Comrie (1976); Dahl and Velupillai (2013c, d) are also recommended.

For a short introduction to mood and modality see van de Auwera and Ammann (2013). Book-length treatments on this topic include Palmer (2001) and Nuyts and van der Auwera (2016). Boye (2016), cited in this chapter, is one of the articles in this edited volume. Other sources mentioned in this chapter are listed in the reference section at the end of the book.

10 Word Order

So far, you have created dozens of words in your conlang and devised the morphology of nouns and verbs. But a list of words, however extensive, does not constitute a language: words form larger units, including sentences and paragraphs.

This is the first of four chapters covering how sentences are structured, that is, syntax. This chapter focuses on constituents (i.e., groups of words with a function in a sentence) and how they are organized into simple sentences. Later chapters explore sentence types (Chapter 11), negation and source of information (Chapter 12) and complex sentences (Chapter 13).

We begin by introducing some syntax basics, including the distinction between clauses and sentences (Section 10.1) and the main constituents in a sentence (Section 10.2). Section 10.3 previews sentence structure, and Section 10.4 covers word order options. In Section 10.5 we discuss how the order between verb and direct object tends to correlate with other linguistic characteristics, and in Section 10.6 we examine morphological and syntactic strategies conducive to word order flexibility. Examples of word order in conlangs are given in Section 10.7. Practice exercises are included in Section 10.8; and Section 10.9 describes the basic sentence structure in the Salt language. Finally, Section 10.10 outlines various steps you can follow to design the basic structure of sentences in your conlang.

Key Words

Clause
Constituency tests
  'Does/did so' substitution (for VPs)
  Pronoun substitution (for NPs)
  'There/then/thus' substitution (for PPs)
  'So' substitution (for APs)
Constituent (phrase)
  Adjective phrase (AP)
  Adverbial phrase (AdvP)
  Noun phrase (NP)

    Prepositional phrase (PP)
    Verb phrase (VP)
Direct object
Focus (FOC)
Intransitive
Predicate
Questionable (?)
Sentence
    Simple
    Complex
Subject
Topic (TOP)
Ungrammatical (*)
Utterance
Word order
    Fixed word order
        Head-initial languages
        Head-final languages
    Flexible word order

10.1 Utterances, Sentences and Clauses

What is a **sentence**, exactly? Consider the examples below: they include a statement (1a), a question (1b) and a command (1c). Statements express facts, opinions, wishes, and so on; questions are typically used to request information; and commands are employed to give orders or demand specific actions or behaviors. All are sentences, since they are **utterances** that include a verb ('is,' 'does have' and 'turn', respectively). On the other hand, the **utterances** in (2) lack verbs and thus they are not sentences.

(1)   English sentences
       a. The dragon isn't blind.
       b. What toppings does the pizza have?
       c. Turn now!

(2)   Non-sentential utterances in English
       a. Ouch!
       b. Yes?
       c. No way!

The sentences in (1) are **simple** since they consist of one **clause** – that is, they only have one main lexical verb. But sentences can also be **complex**, that is, have more than one clause. Examples of complex sentences are given in (3); each has two lexical verbs (underlined) and thus two clauses (indicated with angle brackets). This chapter focuses on simple sentences; complex sentences are discussed in Chapter 13.

(3)   Complex sentences in English
      a. < What toppings does the pizza have > and < how much does it cost >?
      b. < Turn now>, or < face the consequences >!

> **Your Turn**
>
> Are the following utterances sentences? If so, are they simple or complex?
>
> a. The usual suspects.
> b. Wow! A meteor shower!
> c. Have you ever seen a liger?
> d. You can borrow my convertible. Psych!
> e. I think that *Interstellar* is the best movie ever.

10.2 Constituents

Sentences are formed of smaller **constituents** or **phrases**, that is, word groupings with a specific function. Two constituent types attested in all natlangs are **noun phrases (NPs)** and **verb phrases (VPs)**, centered around nouns and verbs, respectively. Other common constituents are **prepositional/ postpositional phrases (PPs)**, **adjective phrases (AP)** and **adverbial phrases (AdvP)**. These are centered around prepositions/postpositions, adjectives, and adverbs, respectively. We consider each constituent type next.

10.2.1 NPs

Noun phrases (NPs) revolve around a noun (often referred to as 'head noun') or pronoun. Minimally they include one noun or pronoun (4). In English and other languages, they can also be formed of a noun and a determiner, as in (5).

(4)   Simple NPs in English
      a. Narineh   Xhosa   Amazonia   exoplanets
      b. She   it   them   you

(5)   NPs with determiners in English
      a. My daughter   The garden
      b. Many galaxies   These unicorns

We know that the phrases in (5) are NPs because (i) they are centered around a head noun, and (ii) they can be substituted by a pronoun. Thus, *she* can substitute *my daughter*; *it* can stand for *the garden*, and *they* for *many galaxies* and *these unicorns*. **Pronoun substitution** serves as a **constituency test** for NPs; other **constituency tests** can be used to ascertain that other phrase types (such as VPs or PPs) are constituents, as we will see later.

In English and other languages, NPs can also include modifying adjectives or possessive modifiers, as in (6). Note that the phrases in (6a, b) are still centered around a noun and can be substituted by a pronoun, thus fulfilling the NP constituency test. NPs can include more complex modifiers, as we will see later.

(6) NPs with adjectival and possessive modifiers
    a. My <u>lovely</u> daughter   ('she') <u>Fiona's</u> garden   ('it')
    b. Many <u>distant</u> galaxies   ('they') These <u>moody</u> unicorns   ('they')

10.2.2 VPs

As mentioned earlier, **verb phrases** (VPs) are centered around a verb. They minimally include a lexical verb (7a) but can comprise additional elements (7b, c). We know these examples are all VPs because (i) they are centered around a lexical verb ('reads'), and (ii) the whole phrase can be replaced by the expression 'does so.' **'Does so' substitution** (with its variants 'did so' in the past; and 'will do so' in the future) is a constituency test used to ascertain that a phrase is indeed a VP.

(7) VPs in English
    a. Reads
    b. Reads a lot of books
    c. Reads a lot of books obsessively

The VP is usually referred to as the **predicate**. Sentences usually include an overt **subject** (typically the NP referred to by the predicate). Whether subjects are obligatory or not varies across natlangs; in English they are (but see below), unlike in Spanish, for example. The sentences in (8) are broken down into subjects and predicates.

(8) English subjects and predicates

Subject	Predicate
a. The moody unicorn	ran off.
b. Adela	will read a lot of books.
c. This ice cream	has delicious toppings.
d.	Walk away!

Sentences (8b, c) are transitive, since they have **direct objects,** that is, constituents, most often NPs that receive the action of the verb (here 'a lot of books' and 'delicious toppings,' respectively). On the other hand, (8a, d) are **intransitive** since they lack a direct object. Note that all examples in (8) have an overt subject except for (8d), which is a command. Commands typically address a second person and lack an overt subject unless they are emphatic (cf. (8d) with *You walk away!*).

10.2.3 Other Constituent Types: PPs, APs, AdvPs

Let's now turn to other constituent types. **Prepositional phrases (PPs)** are centered on a preposition or postposition, and usually introduce a NP, as exemplified in (9) for English (NPs are indicated with square brackets here). When denoting location or direction, PPs can be substituted by the adverb *there* (9a); when referring to time, PPs can be replaced with the adverb *then* (9b). Other PPs can be substituted with the adverb *thus,* as in (9c). PPs can modify nouns (as in 'tea with a hint of lemon'), and verbs (as in 'arrives on time').

(9)   PPs in English
      a. into [Mordor]   across [pale hills]   beyond [distant galaxies]
      b. on [time]   during [the year]   at [that precise moment]
      c. without [shame]   with [a hint of lemon]

Another common constituent is the **adjective phrase (AP)**. Minimally, APs consist of one adjective (10a), although they can also include a modifying adverb (10b), a modifying adjective (10c) or a modifying noun (10d); nouns that modify adjectives act as adjectives. APs in English can be substituted by the adverb *so*. **'So' substitution** can be used as a constituency test for APs. APs generally modify nouns (as in *pink clouds*) and verbs (as in *is blind*).

(10)   APs in English
      a. blue   pink
      b. intensely blue   insanely pink
      c. cerulean blue   millennial pink
      d. midnight blue   bubblegum pink

Finally, **adverbial phrases (AdvPs)** are phrases centered around adverbs. AdvPs can encompass one single adverb (11a) or one adverb modified by another (11b). Adverbs can modify adjectives (12a), VPs (12b) and sentences (12c).

(11)   AdvPs in English (I)
      a. unusually   weekly
      b. very unusually   almost weekly

(12)   English AdvPs (II)
   a. The ocean is insanely blue.
   b. One simply walks into Mordor.
   c. Usually I have coffee in the morning.

10.2.4   Constituents within Constituents

Constituents are often nested within other constituents, very much like Matryoshka dolls. For example, consider the following NP:

(13)   An unusually large meteor from outer space.

The constituent structure of this phrase is shown in (14). The head noun is 'meteor' (underlined); and the whole phrase can be substituted with the pronoun *it*, confirming this is a NP; the beginning and end of the NP are indicated with curly brackets. 'Meteor' is modified by a determiner ('an'), and also by an AP ('unusually large') and a PP ('from outer space'), both enclosed within square brackets. Additional constituent nesting is observed within the AP (which includes the modifying AdvP 'unusually') and within the PP (which comprises the NP 'outer space'). These further embedded constituents are enclosed within parentheses.

(14)   Constituent nesting
   {An [(unusually)$_{AdvP}$ large]$_{AP}$ meteor [from (outer space)$_{NP}$]$_{PP}$}$_{NP}$

Languages differ regarding the specific order in which elements occur within phrases. For example, in English determiners and adjectives precede the nouns they modify, while in Spanish, adjectives tend to follow nouns (15).

(15)   NPs in Spanish
   {*Un   meteorito   [(extraordinariamente)$_{AdvP}$ grande]$_{AP}$}$_{NP}$
   a   meteorite   unusually   large
   'An extraordinarily large meteorite'

When building the sentence structure of your conlang, you should consider which constituents it can have, based on the lexical categories in its lexicon and how words are organized within constituents. We explore different possibilities to organize sentence elements in the following sections.

10.3   Basic Sentence Structure

As mentioned earlier, sentences are composed of a subject and a predicate, and predicates can be transitive or intransitive depending on whether they have or lack a direct object. In most natlangs, there are consistent patterns regarding the ordering of constituents in sentences. Basic **word order** considers the relative ordering between the main verb (V), the subject (S) and the direct object (O) in neutral transitive statements, as in (16). In English statements, the subject precedes the verb; the direct object, if present, follows it. Thus, the preferred word order in English statements is SVO. This is also the case for Spanish, as illustrated in (17).

(16) English: SVO word order
    a. Neityri throws arrows.
        S   V   O
    b. Julia eats seaweed.
        S   V   O

(17) Spanish: SVO word order
    a. *Adam*   *dispar-a*   *flecha-s.*
       Adam   throw-3SG.PRS.REAL   arrow-PL
       'Adam throws arrows.'
    b. *Adela*   *com-e*   *galleta-s.*
       Adela   eat-3SG.PRS.REAL   cookies-PL
       'Adela eats cookies.'

There are six possible combinations of subject (S), verb (V) and direct object (O): SVO, SOV, VSO, VOS, OSV and OVS. In English, VOS, VSO and OVS word orders are **ungrammatical** (i.e., not considered acceptable or comprehensible by native speakers) in statements, as exemplified in (18) (ungrammatical sentences are indicated with an asterisk *). SOV and OSV are possible for some speakers in specific contexts, including poetry, a genre that allows a degree of syntactic flexibility. Examples are given in (19); a question mark (?) indicates the sentence is **questionable** (i.e., not considered grammatical in all contexts and/or by all native speakers). Direct objects are indicated in square brackets.

(18) Ungrammatical word orders in English
    a. VOS   *Threw [an arrow] Neytiri.
    b. VSO   *Threw Neytiri [an arrow].
    c. OVS   *[An arrow] threw Neytiri.

(19) Questionable word order in English statements
    a. SOV   ? Neytiri [an arrow] threw.
    b. OSV   ? [An arrow] Neytiri threw.

In English, OSV word order can also occur in emphatic statements focusing on the direct object, as in 'Murder, she wrote' or 'Clowns, he hates.' OSV is also a possible word order when emphasizing a message or reporting what someone said verbatim (20a, b) and in questions (20c).

(20) OSV in English
   a. [Plenty of people support her], the documentary showed.
   b. [There might be a tornado watch], officials said.
   c. [Which movie] did you watch?

10.4 Word Order Typology

SVO word order occurs in 35 percent of natlangs, including English, Spanish, Mandarin Chinese and Swahili; even more frequent is SOV word order, attested in 41 percent of natlangs, including Japanese (21).

(21) Japanese: SOV (Payne 2006:194)
Taro	ga	[inu	o]	mita
Taro	NOM	dog	ACC	saw

   'Taru saw a dog.'

VSO word order occurs in 7% of natlangs, including Hawaiian (22). Other word orders are even rarer: VOS occurs in 2% of languages, including Malagasy (23); OVS in about 1%, as in Urarina (24); and OSV is attested only in a handful of natlangs, including Warao (25).

(22) Hawaiian: VSO (from Lyovin et al. 2017:292)
ua-ka:kau	ka-wahine	[i-ka-puke]
PFV-write	DEF-woman	ACC-DEF-book

   'The woman wrote the book.'

(23) Malagasy: VOS (from Bennett 1986:25)
Mijery	[ny	lehilahy]	ny	vehivavy
see	the	man	the	woman

   'The woman sees the man.'

(24) Urarina: OVS (Olawsky 2006:144)
[enejtɕu]	kwára-a	kateá
monkey	see-3SG.A	aan

   'The man saw the monkey.'

(25) Warao: OSV (Romero-Figueroa 1985:107)
Erike	[hube]	abun-ae
Enrique	snake	bite-PST

   'A snake bit Enrique.'

Note that the three most frequently attested word orders have the subject before the object. This suggests a general preference in natlangs for the subject to be expressed before the object.

10.5 Head-Initial and Head-Final Languages

> **Your Turn**
>
> - Which word order would work better for an auxlang?
> - Which word order(s) could be a good fit for an alien language?

It is important to note that sometimes different word orders coexist in statements in a natlang. For example, Syrian Arabic allows both SVO and VSO. Sometimes, different word orders occur in different syntactic structures. For example, in Dutch SVO occurs in main clauses and SOV in dependent clauses (26). In addition, emphasizing different elements of the sentence might result in alternative word order, as we saw in (20) for English.

(26)   Dutch word order and syntactic structure (Antje Muntendam, p.c.)
     a. SVO: Ken   lees-t   [boek-en].
                  Ken   read-3SG.PRS book-PL
                  'Ken reads books.'
     b. SOV: Ik   denk   [dat   Ken   boek-en lees-t]
                  I   think that   Ken book-PL read.3SG.PRS
                  'I think that Ken reads books.'

10.5 Head-Initial and Head-Final Languages

Word order – in particular, the relative ordering between verb and direct object – tends to pattern with other syntactic characteristics. For example, VO languages tend to have prepositions (as in English or Spanish), while OV languages favor postpositions (as in Basque and Japanese). In addition, auxiliaries tend to precede lexical verb in VO languages, while in OV languages auxiliaries follow them. The latter pattern is exemplified in (27, 28).

(27)   Basque: lexical verb precedes auxiliary verb
     Neska   dantzatu-ko   da.   'The girl will dance'
     girl.DEF   dance-FUT   3SG.PRS

(28)   Japanese: lexical verb precedes auxiliary verb (Payne 2006: 196)
     taro   ga   [inu   o]   miru   bekida   'Taru should see a dog'
     Taro   NOM   dog   ACC   see   should

Another pattern connected to word order is that in VO languages nouns tend to precede relative clauses that modify them, as in English (29), while in OV languages it is the other way around, with relative clauses preceding the noun they modify (30, 31). Relative clauses are enclosed within angle brackets; we'll explore them further in Chapter 13.

(29) English: noun precedes relative clause
 a. Taru saw [the dog < that ate the meat >].
 b. The girl <who is pretty> will dance.

(30) Japanese: noun follows relative clause (Payne 2006:196)

taro	ga	[<	niku	o	tabeta>	inu	o]	mita
Taro	NOM		meat	ACC	ate	dog	ACC	saw

'Taro saw the dog that ate the meat.'

(31) Basque: noun follows relative clause

< polita	den >	neska	dantzatu-ko	da.
pretty	is.who	girl	dance-FUT	3SG.PRS

'The girl who is pretty will dance.'

Because of these patterns, OV languages are considered to be **head final** and VO languages **head initial**. Other characteristics, such as the ordering between nouns and adjectives, do not clearly pattern with different word orders. Of course, the patterns noted above are tendencies, and not all natlangs conform to them.

> ### Your Turn
>
> To what extent would the head-initial/head-final distinction be relevant for an alien conlang?

10.6 Flexible Word Order

About 14 percent of natlangs use **flexible word order**; they usually rely on adpositions, case and/or verbal agreement to avoid ambiguity between subject and direct object.

10.6.1 Adpositions

As you know, adpositions encompass postpositions and prepositions, which come after and before the NP they introduce, respectively. Natlangs tend to have either postpositions or prepositions, but some languages have both (including Mandarin Chinese). Adpositions allow flexibility in word order; this is shown below for Hebrew, where the preposition *et* indicates direct object (32).

(32)　Hebrew: post-positions and flexible word order (from Deutscher 2005:32)
    a. SVO:　ha-liviatan　bala?　　[et　　Yonah].
    　　　　　DEF-whale　swallowed　ACC　　Jonah
    　　　　　'The whale swallowed Jonah.'
    b. OVS:　[et　　　　ha-liviatan]　bala?　　　Yonah.
    　　　　　ACC　　　　DEF-whale　　swallowed　Jonah
    　　　　　'Jonah swallowed the whale.'

10.6.2 Case

Case also allows flexibility in word order, particularly when it is used to distinguish between subjects and direct objects, as in Latin (Section 8.6). Another example is Ukrainian; although the preferred word order in this language is SVO, word order is flexible since nominative and accusative case suffixes (*-a* and *-u* respectively) help disambiguate between subject and direct object. This is shown in (33) for the sentence 'Halia brings (the) water.' Note that *Halia* is 'Halia' (a woman's name, in the nominative), *vodu* is '(the) water' (in the accusative) and *nese* is the verb 'brings.'

(33)　Ukrainian case and word order (Robert Romanchuk, p.c., after Deutscher 2005:33)
    a. Hali-a　nese　　vod-u.
    b. Hali-a　vod-u　nese.
    c. Nese　　vod-u　Hali-a.
    d. Nese　　Hali-a　vod-u.
    e. Vod-u　Hali-a　nese.
    f. Vod-u　nese　　Hali-a.

It is important to note that even if a language has flexible word order, some word orders might be more frequent and/or might be connected to specific registers or genres. Thus, in the example above, (33a) (SVO) is neutral, (33e) (OSV) is possible but quite rare, and (33d) (VSO) is typical of folksongs (indeed, there is a famous Ukrainian folk song that begins with this line). In addition, certain word orders in Ukrainian and other languages with flexible word order are associated with specific pragmatic uses, such as emphasis. For example, some languages distinguish between **topic** (what the sentence is about) and **focus** (i.e., the new information conveyed). In Ukrainian and Russian, the topic is sentence initial, while the focus is sentence final (Comrie 1990:345). Example (34) provides more information on the use of each of the word orders exemplified in (33) for Ukrainian, including which constituent is emphasized, when relevant.

(34)   Ukrainian word order in context (Robert Romanchuk, p.c.)
a. Hali-a   nese   vod-u.   Ordinary narrative: 'Halia brings water.'
('water' is the new information)
b. Hali-a   vod-u   nese.   'Halia brings (the) water'
(the verb is the new information; we might expect 'but' to follow)
c. Nese   vod-u   Hali-a.   'It's Halia who brings the water'
(Halia is the new information)
d. Nese   Hali-a   vod-u.   Order found in folksong or proverbial narrative
e. Vod-u   Hali-a   nese.   Possible but unusual word order
f. Vod-u   nese   Hali-a.   'Halia brings the water (... and Ivanko, the bread and salt). (Halia is the new information)

10.6.3 Verbal Agreement

Verbal agreement is also conducive to flexible word order. One example is Alqosh Aramaic. In (35a, b), the word order differs, and the words for 'girl' and 'boy' are neither marked for case nor accompanied by an adposition. Verbal agreement, however, ensures that (35a) is interpreted with 'the girl' as subject, and (35b) with 'the girl' as object.

(35)   Alqosh Aramaic: agreement and word order (from Deutscher 2005:33, 34)
a. ɛ   braːta   kemxaz-yaː-le   [brona]
   that   girl   saw-3SG.F-3SG.M   boy
   'The girl saw the boy.'
b. [ɛ   braːta]   kemxaːz-eː-la   brona
   that   girl   saw-3SG.M-3SG.F   boy
   'The boy saw the girl.'

10.7 Word Order in Conlanging

Both Esperanto and Na'vi have case and flexible word order. In Esperanto, word order is free, but the topic of the sentence tends to come first (Harlow 1995). As we saw in Chapter 8, the suffix *-n* indicates the direct object (36); its diminishing use might result in word order becoming more fixed (Gledhill 2020).

(36)   Esperanto: word order and case
[ˈmul.taj   ˈho.moj   paˈro.las   e.speˈran.ton]
multa-j   *homo-j*   *parol-as*   *Esperanto-n.*
many-PL   people-PL   speak-PRS   Esperanto-ACC
'Many people speak Esperanto.'

Na'vi allows free word order, but emphasized constituents tend to appear sentence-finally. As we saw in Chapter 8, Na'vi has a case system that includes nominative, ergative and absolutive (referred to in Na'vi sources as 'subjective,' 'agentive' and 'patientive,' respectively).

Dothraki, High Valyrian and Klingon have **fixed word order**. Dothraki and High Valyrian are SVO and SOV, respectively; both have case, as shown in Chapter 9. Klingon has OVS word order (37) and verbal agreement, as we saw in Chapter 9. The examples below lack overt verbal agreement prefixes since they involve third person singular subjects and objects.

(37) Klingon: OVS word order and verbal agreement (Okrand 1985:59–60)

a. [puq lɛɣ jɑs̪]   'The officer sees the child.'
   puq legh yaS
   child sees officer

b. [jɑs̪ lɛɣ puq]   'The child sees the officer.'
   yaS legh puq
   officer sees child

Teonaht has an OSV word order, and Láadan and Sindarin are VSO. We'll see examples of Láadan sentences in the following chapter.

10.8 Conlanging Practice: Word Order in the Ur Languages

A. Exemplify all possible word orders among subject, verb and object for the sentence 'The hatching dragon eats pink moss' in one of the Ur languages.

[sgoton]   'hatching.dragon'
[miliʃ]   'eat.3SG.PR'
[nosto]   'pink.moss'

B. The Fog language is head final.
- Indicate which word orders are more likely to occur in Fog.
- What will be the most likely order between main and auxiliary verb?
- Will Fog be more likely to have postpositions or prepositions?

10.9 Word Order in Muq

Muq has the preferred word order VOS; it is a head-initial language. It has neither case nor verbal agreement. Examples of word order in sentences from the fictional text introduced in Chapter 2 are given in (38, 39).

(38) Fictional text: intransitive sentence
['ɕis-s-i   ɕem ko-xa]
burn-PFV-REM.PST   island DEF.INAN-SG
'The island burned.'

(39) Fictional text: transitive sentence
['ɸiθ-s-i   'muq.ɕem   ko-xa   'ɬei   ko-xa]
soothe-PFV-REM.PST land   DEF.INAN-SG   ocean   DEF.INAN-SG
'The ocean soothed the land.'

The focus particle [na] is placed in front of a constituent to emphasize it. Example (40) provides an example of a sentence emphasizing the object; this is akin to the passive in English. (41) provides an example of a sentence emphasizing the subject.

(40) Emphasized statements in Salt language
['χe.ʁa.mi   na   'ɣeɕ   ko.xa   'kust   ɬi.xa]
 χeʁa-m-i   na   'ɣeɕ   ko-xa   'kust   ɬi-xa
 break-IMPF-REM.PST FOC darkness   DET.INAN-SG   salt   DET.ANIM-SG
'The darkness was broken by the salt'

(41) ['χe.ʁa.mi   'ɣeɕ   ko.xa   na   'kust   ɬi.xa]
 χeʁa-m-i   'ɣeɕ   ko-xa   na   'kust   ɬi-xa
 break-IMPF-REM.PST darkness   DET.INAN-SG   FOC   salt   DET.ANIM-SG
'The salt caused the darkness to break (to be destroyed)'

10.10 Developing Sentence Structure

- Indicate the structure of NPs in your conlang. Specifically:
    a. Do determiners precede or follow the head noun in the NP?
    b. Do adjectives precede or follow the head noun in the NP? Do they precede or follow determiners?
    c. Provide examples.
- Indicate the structure of VPs in your conlang. Specifically:
    a. Does the object precede or follow the verb?
    b. What is the order between main and auxiliary verb?
    c. Provide examples.
- Work out the basic sentence structure of your conlang:
    a. Does your conlang show a preference for SOV, SVO, OVS, OSV, VOS or VSO?
    b. Is word order fixed or (relatively) flexible?

c. Does your conlang make use of case, verbal agreement and/or adpositions?
d. Provide glossed examples of neutral statements in your conlang. Make sure that you use or revise the nominal and verbal morphology you worked out in Chapters 8 and 9.

- If your conlang has adverbs or/and adpositions, provide examples of AdvP and PPs.
- To what extent is your conlang head-final or head-initial? (Compare the relative order between verb and direct object, main and auxiliary verb, and whether there are prepositions and postpositions.)

To Learn More

The discussion of word order in this chapter draws from Dryer (2013a, b); for more information on case, see Comrie (2013). Several recordings and videos of the Ukrainian folksong 'Halia brings water' ('Несе Галя воду') referred to in Section 10.6 can be found online; see, for example, https://youtu.be/g596K8QOTyE. For discussion and examples of flexible word order in Russian, see Chapter 6 in Bailyn (2012). Other sources mentioned are listed in the reference section at the end of this book.

11 Statements, Questions and Commands

The previous chapter introduced the basics of sentence structure, including sentence constituents and word order. This chapter examines ways in which languages express three basic sentence types: statements, questions and commands (Sections 11.1–11.3). Section 11.4 provides practice in constructing these sentence types in a fictional language; and Section 11.5 describes statements, questions and commands in muq. Finally, Section 11.6 provides guided questions to help you design these types of sentences in your conlang.

Key Words

Commands (imperatives)
  Direct
  Familiar (informal) (FAM)
  Indirect
    Polite (formal) (POL)
    Do-support
    Evidential (EV)
    Hortative (HORT)
    Imperative (IMP)
    Near imperative (PRS.IMP)
Distant imperative (FUT.IMP)
Interrogative (INT)
Interrogative word (or phrase)
  Interrogative adverb
  Interrogative affix
  Interrogative determiner/adjective
  Interrogative particle
  Interrogative pronoun
  Interrogative quantifier
  Interrogative verb (or verb phrase)
Inversion
Narrative (NAR)

Questions
   Content questions
   Fronting
   In situ
   Echo questions
   Polar questions
   Intonation
      Falling (↘)
      Rising (↗)
Statement (declarative) (DEC)
Tags
   A-not-A construction
   Do-support
   Inversion

11.1 Statements

Statements or **declaratives** are the most common sentence type in languages. They are used to describe, assert, report, complain, brag, predict and promise, among other functions. They tend to have final **falling intonation**, as we saw in Section 6.5. Neutral transitive **statements** show us what the basic word order in a language is like, as you know from the preceding chapter. In English and most other natlangs, statements lack special morphology or syntax, unlike **questions** or **commands**. But several languages, including Korean and Capanahua, indicate that a sentence is **declarative** with an affix or particle. Examples are given in in (1, 2); the gloss DEC stands for declarative.

(1)   Korean statements (Kim et al. 2023 :59)
       yeppeu-da   '(She) is pretty.'
       is.pretty-DEC

(2)   Capanahua statements (adapted from Loos & Loos 1998:40)
       joxo   *ta*   *ke:n-ai*   'I want the white one.'
       white   DEC want-PRS

11.1.1 Statements in Conlanging

In Esperanto, Dothraki, Na'vi and Klingon, statements are not marked with specific morphology or syntax. In Toki Pona, statements and questions with third person subjects include the particle *li* between subject and predicate (3).

(3) Toki Pona statements and questions (from Lang 2014 :27, 33)
    a. [jan so.na li ku.te]

jan	sona	li	kute.
person	know	PARTICLE	to.listen

'A person of knowledge listens.'

    b. [ka.la wa.wa li mo.ku e se.me]

kala	wawa	li	moku	e	seme?
fish	strong	PARTICLE	eat	ACC	what

'What does a shark eat?'

In Láadan all sentences begin with a speech act particle indicating whether the sentence is a statement, question or command, a warning or a promise. These particles are obligatory, aside from declarative *bíi* [bí.i], which is optional. Speech act particles can be modified with affixes to clarify emotion or intent. For example, in (4b) the suffix *-de* clarifies that the sentence is 'said in **narrative**' (glossed below as NAR), and in (4c) *-li* indicates that the sentence is 'said with love' (glossed LOV). EV stands for **evidential**, which we will address in Chapter 12.

(4) Láadan statements (adapted from Elgin et al. 2020: 29; 47, 243)
    a. [bí.ɪ a.ɹɪl dɪ lɛ lá.a.dan wa]

Bíi	aril	di	le	Láadan	wa.
DEC	FUT	speak	1SG	Láadan	EV

'I will speak Laadan.'

    b. [bí.ɪ.dɛ ɛ.ɹɪl nɛ.lo.lá.ad wiθ mɛ.nɛ.dɛ.bɛ ʃa.laθ wa.a]

Bíi-de	eril	ne-loláad	with	menedebe	shala-th	waa.
DEC-NAR	PST	ITER-feel	woman	to.be.many	grief.with. reason-ACC	EV

'Once there were many women who felt grief, for good reasons.' (said in narrative)

    c. [bí.ɪ.lɪ bɹɛ a.ɹɪl θá.a ɹa á.wɪ.θɛ.ho.o ɛ.bɹɛ a.ɹɪl mí.ɪ lɛ]

Bíi-li	bre	aril	tháa	ra	áwithe-hóo	ébre	aril	míi	le!
DEC-LOV	if	FUT	thrive	NEG	baby-FOC	then	FUT	be.amazed	I

'If this baby doesn't do well, I'll be very surprised.' (said with love)

11.2 Questions

Questions are used to request information. There are two main types: **polar questions** (aka 'partial' or 'yes–no' questions) and **content questions** (aka 'total questions'). The main difference between the two is that the former expect a yes or no answer, unlike the latter. Thus, if somebody asks you 'Do you want to see an asteroid? (a polar question), you can answer 'yes' or 'no' (or 'maybe'). The same answer to a content question such as 'What do you want?' would be very strange. We explore both types of questions next.

11.2.1 Polar Questions

Polar questions are most often expressed with **interrogative particles**; this strategy is attested in 61 percent of natlangs. One example is French, where the particle *est-ce que* (historically arising from the combination of the *est* 'is,' *ce* 'this' and *que* 'that' *that*) introduces yes–no questions (5b). Interrogative particles are most frequent sentence-finally, as shown in (6) for formal polar questions in Japanese.

(5) French polar questions: interrogative particle
    a. *Timothée   est   beau.*   'Timothée is handsome.'
       Timothée   is   handsome
    b. *Est-ce que Timothée   est   beau?*   'Is Timothée handsome?'
       INT   Timothée is   handsome

(6) Japanese polar questions (McGloin 2014:188)
    biiru   o   nomimasu   ka   'Do you drink beer?'
    beer   ACC drink   INT

Polar interrogative particles also occur frequently in the second position in a sentence, as in Cherokee and Shipibo-Konibo. Other positions are attested but less common. Some languages have interrogative particles in various positions in the sentence, as in San Carlos Apache (7).

(7) San Carlos Apache questions (adapted from Rice & De Reuse 2017:728)
    a. *yaʔ   Fiinigisyú   dínyāā*
       INT   Phoenix.to   2SG.SUBJ.started.to.go
       'Are you going to Phoenix?'
    b. *Fiinigisyú   dínyāā   né*
       Phoenix.to   2SG.SUBJ.started.to.go   INT
       'Are you going to Phoenix?'

Polar questions can also be conveyed with **interrogative affixes**, as in Scots Gaelic or Capanahua, exemplified in (8). As shown in (2), Capanahua statements involve a declarative particle. However, all questions are marked morphologically with the clitic [-n], attached to the evidential particle *qui*, which expresses certainty (this **particle** is glossed as EV below) (8).

(8) Capanahua polar questions (adapted from Loos & Loos 1998:25)
    nea   miːn   bake   ki-n   'Is this your son?'
    this   your   son   EV-INT

Polar questions can also be conveyed intonationally, typically with final rising intonation, as we saw in Section 6.5. It has been proposed that the rising intonation is connected to questions since it conveys uncertainty and hesitation, unlike falling intonation, which indicates certainty and assurance. In some languages, including Coast Tsimshian and Gujarati, final rising intonation is the only way to indicate a polar question. In others, including English, French and Japanese, it's one of several possible ways to do so. Examples for English and French are given below (as you probably remember, **rising intonation** is indicated with an upward pointing arrow ↗ in IPA and falling intonation with the downward pointing arrow ↘).

(9) English: intonation in statements and polar questions
   a. He has been admitted to the space program. ↘
   b. He has been admitted to the space program? ↗

(10) French: rising intonation in polar questions
   a. *Timothée   est   beau.*   ↘   'Timothée is handsome.'
      Timothée   is   handsome
   b. *Timothée   est   beau?*   ↗   'Is Timothée handsome?'
      Timothée   is   handsome

Very rarely, polar questions have final falling intonation and statements rising intonation; natlangs with this pattern include Fanti and Grebo.

> **Your Turn**
>
> - Do statements always have final falling intonation in English?
> - Many well-known conlangs do not discuss intonation for speech acts (e.g., statements/questions). What could be the reason for this?

Let's now preview other less common ways to express polar questions in natlangs. **Tags** are words, phrases or clauses used with **interrogative** intent; they are usually sentence-final and signal a biased question. Examples for English and German are given in (11, 12) below.

(11) English tag questions
   a. You like lollipops, right?
   b. You don't like lollipops, do you?

(12) Polar tags in German (König & Siemund 2007: 297)
   Er   ist   sehr   reich,   nicht   wahr?
   3SG.M   is   very   rich   not   true
   'He is very rich, isn't he?'

Inversion, or a change in word order, is common in Indo-European languages; it usually involves moving the verb to the front of the sentence, as shown in (13) for French and English.

(13) Inversion in polar questions in French and English
  a. *Il*   *est*   *beau.*   'He is handsome'.
    He   be.3SG.PRS   handsome
  b. *Est-il*   *beau?*   'Is he handsome?'
    be.3SG.PRS-he   handsome

In English sentences with verbs other than 'to be,' polar questions involve the addition of *do* sentence-initially (14). This type of strategy, termed **do-support**, is rare in natlangs.

(14) English 'do-support' in polar questions
  a. You want to escape.   Do you want to escape?
  b. You will want to escape.   Will you want to escape?

The **A-not-A construction** involves stating the verb twice, separated by negation. One example from Beijing Mandarin is shown in (15).

(15) Beijing Mandarin: A-not-A questions (Li & Thompson 1990:828)
   Tā   *chī-bu-chī*   *píngguǒ?*   'Does s/he eat apples?'
   3SG   eat-not-eat   apple

Natlangs might favor one single polar question strategy or use several in different contexts. For example, Beijing Mandarin allows rising final intonation and the interrogative particles *ma* and *ne* as polar question strategies in addition to the A-not-A strategy. In English, final rising intonation usually occurs with inversion or do support, while tags are used in non-neutral questions. And in French, inversion is typically used in formal registers, interrogative intonation in informal contexts, and the particle *est-ce que* in either.

> **Your Turn**
>
> Which polar question strategy described above would be a better fit for an alien language?

11.2.2 Polar Questions in Conlanging

Klingon conveys polar questions via the interrogative verbal suffix *-'a'* [-ʔaʔ] (16). Esperanto, Dothraki and Láadan have sentence-initial polar question particles. Examples from Dothraki and Láadan are given in (17, 18).

(16) Polar questions in Klingon (from Okrand 1985:44)
   a. *cho-legh-'a'*   [tʃo.lɛɣ.ʔaʔ]   'Do you see me?'
     2SG.A.1SG.P-see-INT
   b. *yaj-'a'*   [jadʒ.ʔaʔ]   'Does s/he understand?'
     understand.3.A-INT

(17) Dothraki polar questions (from Peterson 2014:40)
[haʃ jer do.θra.e tʃek]

Hash	yer	dothrae	chek?
INT	you	ride.2SG	well

'How are you?' (literally: 'do you ride well?')

(18) Láadan polar questions (from Elgin et al. 2020:27)
[bá.a a.ɹɪl hɑl nɛ]

Báa	aril	hal	ne?
INT	FUT	work	you

'Will you work?'

Toki Pona forms polar questions with the sentence-final tag *anu seme* ('or what?') and the A-not-A strategy (19).

(19) Toki Pona polar questions (Lang 2014 :31, 38)
  a. [si.na pu a.nu se.me]

sina	pu		anu	seme?
you	interacting.with.the.official.Toki.Pona.book		or	what

  'Have you touched the official Toki Pona book?'
  b. [si.na so.na a.la so.na e to.ki in.li]

sina	sona	ala	sona	e	toki Inli?
you	know	not	know	ACC	English

  'Do you know English?'

Na'vi has multiple strategies to convey polar questions. Two of them are the particle *srak(e)* (which can be initial or final) and the structure *ftxey ... fuke* ('choose ... or not') (20).

(20) Na'vi polar questions (Annis 2024:53)
  a.

['sɾa.kɛ	ŋa	'za.ʔu]		'Are you coming?'
srake	nga	za'u?		
INT	you	come		

  b.

[ft'ej	ŋa	'za.ʔu	fu.kɛ]	'Are you coming or not?'
ftxey	nga	za'u	fu.'ke	
choose	you	come	or.not	

11.2.3 Content Questions

Content questions might have a specific or preferred intonation. Unlike polar questions, they always include an **interrogative word (or phrase)** that clarifies whether the question refers to a place ('where'), person ('who'), object ('what', 'which'), reason ('why') or manner ('how'). In English, interrogative words tend to occur sentence-initially; since most begin with *wh*, they are often referred to as wh-questions (21).

(21)   English content questions
     a. How is the Mars mission coming along?
     b. Where can I find good Vietnamese food?
     c. Which planet do you think we'll explore next?

Placing interrogative words sentence-initially is attested in over 29 percent of languages, including English, Spanish and Urarina among others. This is commonly referred to as **fronting**. In some languages, interrogative words may be left in place (**in situ**), most often to request repetition of the information conveyed or to express surprise or shock. These questions are sometimes referred to as **echo questions**; examples from English and Spanish are given in (22). In other natlangs, the interrogative phrase is always in situ, as in Mandarin Chinese, or it might be left in place or move to the front of the sentence, as in Swahili, exemplified in (23).

(22)   English and Spanish echo questions
     a. *¿Binti vive dónde?*
        Binti lives where?
     b. *¿Okwu es amigo de quién?*
        Okwu is friends with who(m)?

(23)   Swahili content questions (adapted from König & Siemund 2007:301)
     a. *a-li-fika   lini?*
        3SG-PST-arrive   when
        'When did s/he arrive?'
     b. *kwa   nini   tʃakula   ki-me-tʃelewa?*
        for   what   food   3SG-PERF-late
        'Why is the food late?'

The placement of **interrogative pronouns** and **adverbs** tends to pattern with certain word orders. Thus, VSO languages tend to have fronted interrogative words, and SOV languages in-situ questions. There is no strong tendency regarding interrogative words in SVO languages.

In some natlangs content questions have both interrogative particles or affixes and interrogative words or phrases, as in Capanahua (24). This is also the case in West Greenlandic, but note where the interrogative suffix also encodes subject agreement (25).

(24)   Capanahua content questions (adapted from Loos & Loos 1998:40)
        jahuemeha   mi-n   keːn-ai-n
        which   you-ERG   want-PRS-INT
        'Which one do you want?'

(25)   West Greenlandic content questions (Dixon 2016:49)
        su-mik   neri-vit?   What did he eat?'
        what-INSTR   eat-INT.2SG

11.2.3.1 Interrogative Words and Phrases

What type of words can be interrogative? English has **interrogative pronouns** (*who(m), what*); **interrogative adverbs** (*where, when, how, why*); and the **interrogative determiner/adjective** *which*. Natlangs might have one or more of these interrogative word types. Table 11.1 lists interrogative words in English, Spanish and Basque.

Table 11.1 Interrogative words in English, Spanish and Basque

	English	Spanish	Basque
Pronouns	who(m)	quién	nor (absolutive), nork (ergative)
	what	qué	zer
Adjectives	which	cuál	zein
	where	dónde	non (locative)
		(a)dónde	nora (allative)
Adverbs	when	cuándo	noiz
	why	por qué	zergaitik
	how	cómo	nola

The comparison of the interrogative words in Table 11.1 reveals some interesting points. First, sometimes an interrogative word in one language corresponds to an interrogative phrase in another: 'why' is the phrase *por qué* in Spanish. Second, one single interrogative word in one language might correspond to several distinct ones in another. For example, 'where' corresponds to *non* and *nora* in Basque depending on whether the meaning is locative or allative; and 'who' corresponds to *nor* and *nork* depending on whether the pronoun is absolutive or ergative. Examples of these interrogative words in Basque are given below.

(26) Basque content questions
  a. *Nora*   *zoaz?*   'Where are you going?'
     where.ALL   go.2SG
  b. *Non*   *zaude?*   'Where are you?'
     where.LOC   be.2SG
  c. *Nor*   *da*   *hau?*   'Who is this?'
     who.ABS   is   this
  d. *Nork*   *du*   *liburu-a?*   'Who has the book?'
     who.ERG   has   book-DEF

Finally, interrogative words in a language might share phonological characteristics. While in English most interrogative words in English begin with 'wh' /w/, in Spanish most begin with /k/; and in Basque, they tend to begin with 'n' or 'z' (/s/).

Natlangs might have **interrogative quantifiers** (such as *combien* 'how many' in French) and ordinal numbers (such as *monesko* 'many-th' in Finnish). More rarely, natlangs have **interrogative verbs**, corresponding to meanings such as 'be what,' 'what happened,' 'be how,' 'go where' or 'say what.' These verbs occur in interrogative sentences lacking overt interrogative marking. One example from Lavukaleve is given below.

(27) Interrogative verbs in Lavukaleve (Terrill 1999 :413)
      me-kalem   *vasia-m*   'Where is your (pl) father?'
      2PL-father(M)   be.where-SG.M

Interrogative verbs are different from similar verbs used in other sentence types. For example, while the verb *yahmi* in Chickasaw means 'to do,' the interrogative verb *katihmi* means 'to do what' (28).

(28) Interrogative verbs in Chickasaw (adapted from Munro 2012:275)
      a. *Hat:ak-at*   *yahm-aʔtʃi*.   'The man is going to do it.'
         person-NOM   do-IMPF
      b. *Hat:ak-at*   *katihm-aʔtʃi?*   'What is the man going to do?'
         person-NOM   do.what-IMPF

In Urarina, the interrogative verbs [ɲatahaa] and [ɲaaohwaa] mean 'be how much' (Olawsky 2006:259). Other interrogative words in Urarina are formed with the word [dʒa] 'what, who' combined with other morphemes (29).

(29) Urarina interrogative pronouns (Olawsky 2006:814)
      a. [dʒa]   'what/who'
      b. [dʒa-rihi]   'which'
         who-be.like
      c. [dʒ-u]   'where'
         what-LOC

Finally, in some natlangs interrogative pronouns are identical to indefinite pronouns. This is the case in Jaminjung, where *nanggayin* means both 'who' and 'somebody' (Schultze-Berndt 2000:45).

11.2.3.2 Content Questions in Conlangs

In Esperanto, content questions tend to have final rising intonation. Interrogative words are sentence-initial and do not involve inversion. They all begin with /k/; examples include *kiu* 'who, which,' *kio* 'what' and *kiel* 'how.' Dothraki content questions are similarly non-inverted and involve sentence-initial interrogative words based on the interrogative pronoun *fin* 'which, who': *fini* 'what,' *kifinosi* 'how,' *kifindirgi* 'why' (Peterson 2014:100).

All Láadan questions involve the sentence-initial particle *báa*, which can be modified to encode speaker intent (30). Interrogative words are based on the indefinite pronoun *be* 'someone' suffixed with [-báa]; case markers are added as needed.

(30) Láadan content questions (from Elgin et al. 2020:75, 239)
    a. [bá.a ɛ.ɹɪl ʃá.ad nɛ bɛ.bá.a.dɛ]

Báa	*eril*	*sháad*	*ne*	*bebáa-de?*
INT	PST	come	you	what-ABL

    'Where did you come from?'
    b. [bá.a.da a.ɹɪl dɛn bɛ.bá.a lɛθ]

Báa-da	*aril*	*den*	*bebáa*	*leth?*
INT-jokingly	FUT	help	who	1SG.ACC

    'Who will help me? (I ask in jest)'

In Klingon, interrogative pronouns stay in situ, as exemplified in (31a, b) for *'Iv* [ʔɪv] 'who' (remember that word order in Klingon is OVS). Interrogative quantifier *'ar* [ʔar] 'how many, how much' follows the noun it refers to (31c). Interrogative adverbs are sentence-initial (31d).

(31) Klingon content questions (from Okrand 1985:69, 70)
    a.
yaS	*legh*	*'Iv*	[jaʂ	lɛɣ	ʔɪv]
officer	see.3A	who			

    'Who sees the officer?'
    b.
'Iv	*legh*	*yaS*	[ʔɪv	lɛɣ	jaʂ]
who	see.3A	officer			

    'Who does the officer see?'
    c.
nIn	*'ar*	*wI-ghaj*	[nɪn	ʔar	wɪ.ɣadʒ]
fuel	how.much	2PL.A.3SG.P-have			

    'How much fuel do we have?'
    d.
chay'	*haw'-pu'*	*yaS*	[tʃaj?	xaw?.pu?	jaʂ]
how	flee.3A-PFV	officer			

    'How did the officer flee?'

In Toki Pona, content questions are in situ (32). Interrogative pronoun *seme* 'what, which, how' can be combined with other words to form additional interrogative words (32d).

(32) Toki Pona content questions (from Lang 2014:31, 33, 124)
    a. [se.me li sin]

seme	*li*	*sin?*
what	PARTICLE	new

    'What is new?'

b. [jan se.me li to.ki]

jan	seme	li	toki?
person	what	INT	speak

'Which person is speaking?'

c. [ka.la wa.wa li mo.ku e se.me]

kala	wawa	li	moku	e	seme?
fish	strong	INT	eat	ACC	what

'What does a shark eat?'

d. [to.mo te.lo li lon se.me]

tomo	telo	li	lon	seme?
room	water	INT	at	what

'Where is the washroom?'

In Na'vi, interrogative words are formed with the affix *pe* [pɛ], which can be a suffix or a prefix. For example, 'who?' is *pesu* or *tupe*; and 'why?' *pelun* or *lumpe*. Interrogative words can appear in various positions in the sentence (Müller 2024:63)

> **Your Turn**
>
> Which way of forming content questions discussed above do you find the most interesting?

11.3 Commands

Commands are typically employed to issue orders and requests, entreat or ask for advice, issue warnings or convey instructions and wishes. Like statements and questions, commands are found in all languages. Commands tend to involve forceful intonation, particularly if conveying orders or earnest requests. They can be **direct** (as in *Open the window!*) or **indirect** (as in *Could you open the window?*). Direct commands often have specific morphological or syntactic characteristics commonly referred to as the **imperative** (IMP).

Commands tend to be directed to one or more second person addressee(s); however, they might also involve the speaker ('Let us go'). Section 11.3.1 focuses on commands involving second person addressees, while Section 11.3.2 discusses commands involving the speaker. Section 11.3.3 provides examples of commands in conlanging.

11.3.1 Imperatives

Some natlangs convey commands syntactically, as in English, where the second person pronoun is omitted and the lexical verb placed sentence-initially (33a–f). If present, the second person pronoun adds emphasis (33g). Indirect commands can be conveyed with questions (33h, i), often preceded by modal auxiliaries, and sometimes with statements as well (33 j).

(33) English commands
    a. Command: Give me your phone!
    b. Entreaty: Run, you fools!
    c. Advice: Do apply again!
    d. Warning: Be careful!
    e. Instructions: First cross the bridge.
    f. Wishes: Have a great day!
    g. Emphatic: You go to bed now!
    h. Request: Could you start running now?
    i. Disguised request Isn't it cold in here?
    (hoping that addressee closes the window):
    j. Polite request: Thank you for turning off your phone.

Around 78 percent of natlangs express commands morphologically; examples include Spanish, Limbu and Acholi. In Limbu, there is only one imperative suffix (34), while in Acholi it differs according to number (35).

(34) Limbu imperatives (adapted from König & Siemund 2007:304)
    a. *ips-ɛʔ* 'Sleep!'
       sleep-IMP
    b. *ips-ettʃ-ɛʔ* 'Sleep (you two)!'
       sleep-2DU-IMP
    c. *ips-amː-ɛʔ* 'Sleep (all of you)!'
       sleep-2PL-IMP

(35) Acholi imperative (adapted from König & Siemund 2007:305)
    a. *lok-i* 'Turn!'
       turn-2SG.IMP
    b. *lok-wuʔ* 'Turn (plural)!'
       turn-2PL.IMP

The Acholi pattern is very common in the world's languages; more rarely, the singular imperative is marked, unlike the plural imperative, as in Italian or Icelandic. In a few languages, including Latvian and Apurina, the plural imperative is marked, unlike the singular imperative.

Imperatives might vary according to gender. For example, in various Arabic dialects the singular imperative differs depending on the gender of the addressee, unlike the plural imperative (Section 9.1). In Tashlhiyt, plural imperatives distinguish gender, unlike singular ones; this pattern is very rare in natlangs. Also rare is to have various imperative affixes depending on the speaker's sex. For example, in Biloxi, the imperative suffixes *-ta*, *-di*, indicated male speaker to male or female addressee(s), respectively; the suffix *-te* indicated female speaker to male addressee(s). In addition, the lack of an overt imperative suffix conveyed female speaker to female addressee, or male/female speaker to child (36).

(36)   Biloxi imperatives and gender (Velupillai 2012:360).
    a. *umaki-di*   'Bathe!'   (male speaker to male addressee)
       bathe-IMP.M/F
    b. *toho-te*   'Lie down!'   (female speaker to male addressee)
       lie.down-IMP.F/M

Imperatives can encode politeness or degree of formality, as in Peninsular Spanish, where commands are expressed differently depending on whether the speaker is familiar with the addressee or wants to convey politeness or respect (37). Note that the gloss FAM stands for **familiar/informal**, and POL for **polite/formal**.

(37)   Peninsular Spanish imperatives and politeness
    a. *¡Gir-a*   *ahora!*   'Turn now!' (singular, informal)
       turn-2SG.IMP.FAM   now
    b. *¡Gir-e*   *ahora!*   'Turn now!' (singular, formal)
       turn-2SG.IMP.POL   now
    c. *¡Gir-ad*   *ahora!*   'Turn now!' (plural, informal)
       turn-2PL.IMP.FAM   now
    d. *¡Gir-en*   *ahora!*   'Turn now!' (plural, formal)
       turn-2PL.IMP.POL   now

Some natlangs distinguish between **near** vs. **distant imperatives**; sometimes the latter is considered more polite. Examples include Tucano and Jarawara (38). Note that the near imperative is glossed as PRS.IMP, and the distant imperative as FUT.IMP.

(38)   Jarawara near and distant imperative (from Dixon 2016:50, 51)
    a. *kaba-hi* 'eat (it) here and now!'
       eat-PRS.IMP
    b. *kaba-jahi* 'eat (it) later/in some other place'
       eat-FUT.IMP

Natlangs also vary in their expression of indirect commands; these could be conveyed with questions or statements (as in English), the future tense (as in Hebrew) or the irrealis mood (as in Hungarian). In German they involve the expression *jetzt aber* 'but now' followed by an infinitive.

> **Your Turn**
>
> Which of the imperative options in this section do you consider more interesting, and why?

11.3.2 Hortatives

The **hortative** (HORT) is an imperative that involves both the speaker and the addressee. In English, hortatives are expressed syntactically using the expression *let's/let (us)* before the main verb: *Let's dance, Let's go out*. Some natlangs express hortatives morphologically, as in French (39). In Spanish, the hortative is conveyed with irrealis suffixes (40).

(39) French imperatives and hortatives (from König & Siemund 2007:314)
  a. *Chant-ez!*   'Sing!' (plural)
     sing-IMP.PL
  b. *Chant-ons!*   'Let's sing'
     sing-HORT

(40) Peninsular Spanish imperatives and hortatives
  a. *¡Cant-ad*   *ahora!*   'Sing now (plural, informal)'
     sing-IMP.PL.FAM   now
  b. *¡Cant-emos*   *ahora!*   'Let's sing now'
     sing-1PL.PRS.IRR   now

11.3.3 Commands in Conlanging

In Esperanto, the suffix *-u* conveys both imperative and hortative (41); in Sindarin, the imperative is formed with the suffix *-o* (42).

(41) Commands in Esperanto
  a. *lern-u*   *Esperanto-n!*   'Learn Esperanto!'
     learn-IMP   Esperanto-ACC
  b. *ni*   *lern-u!*   'Let us learn!'
     we   learn-IMP

(42) Commands in Sindarin (from Salo 2004:121, 207)
  a. *edr-o!*   'Open!'
     open-IMP
  b. *ped-o*   *mellon*   *a*   *minn-o.*
     say-IMP   friend   and   enter-IMP
     'Say friend/Let a friend speak and enter.'

Klingon has imperative prefixes. In intransitive verbs, imperative prefixes differ according to whether the addressee is singular or plural (43). In transitive verbs, imperative prefixes vary depending on the object person and number (44).

(43) Klingon: intransitive imperatives (Okrand 1985:34)
    a. *yi-Qong*   [jɪ.qχoŋ]
         IMP.SG-sleep
         'Sleep!' (singular)
    b. *pe-Qong*   [pɛ.qχoŋ]
         IMP.PL-sleep
         'Sleep!' (plural)

(44) Klingon: intransitive imperatives (Okrand 1985:34)
    a. *HI-qIp*   [xɪ.qɪp]
         IMP.1SG.P-hit
         'Hit me!'
    b. *gho-qIp*   [ɣo.qɪp]
         'Hit us!'
         IMP.1PL.P-hit

Dothraki formal imperatives involve the suffix *-i* in verbs ending in consonants, with no overt marking otherwise. Informal imperatives are formed with the suffix *-(a)s* (Peterson 2014:52–53).

Toki Pona and Láadan convey imperatives syntactically. In Toki Pona, *o* is used to express requests and commands (45). In Láadan, *bóo* [bó.o] is used for requests or polite commands, and *bó* [bó] for commands directed at small children (46). Both particles can take suffixes indicating specific emotion or intent, including *-d* 'said in anger' or *-li* [lɪ] 'said in love' (Elgin et al. 2020:299–305).

(45) Toki Pona commands (Lang 2014:42)
     [o ku.te e ma.ma si.na]
     o   *kute*   *e*   *mama*   *sina.*   'Obey your parents'
     IMP   to.obey   ACC   parent   you

(46) Láadan imperatives (Elgin et al. 2020:53, 240)
    a. [bó.o a.ɹɪl ɛ.dɛ.θɪ]
        Bóo   *aril*   *edethi*
        IMP.POL   FUT   share
        'Please share with me/ Would you share with me?'
    b. [bó.o mɛ.wam nɛθ. ɛ.ɹɪl dɪ lub]
        '*Bó*   *me-wam*   *ne-zh!*'   *eril*   *di*   *lub.*
        IMP   PL-be.still   you-PAU   PST   say   hen
        'You just stay where you are'! Said the hen (to her chicks).'

11.4 Conlanging Practice: Speech Acts in Deep Aqua

Deep Aqua, introduced in Chapter 8, has SVO word order and little verbal inflection (although as you know its nominal morphology is somewhat complex). Deep Aqua distinguishes statements, questions and commands by means of obligatory sentence-final particles. All questions are conveyed with the same interrogative particle; content questions have interrogative words at the beginning of the sentence. Statements are indicated with the particle [sim].

a. Indicate the sentence-final particle that signals a question.
b. Indicate the sentence-final particle that signals commands.
c. Consider the following mini-lexicon:
   [disr]   'you'
   [zi. 'ze]   'to be crazy, to act crazy'
   [dal]   'why'
   [sim]   DEC
d. Translate and gloss the following sentences (the first sentence is done for you):
   1. 'You are crazy.'   [disr   zi. 'ze   sim]
                           2SG   to.be.crazy   DEC
   2. 'Are you crazy?'
   3. 'Why are you acting crazy?'
   4. 'Act crazy!'

11.5 Speech Acts in Muq

Statements are unmarked in the Salt language. Polar questions are formed with the clitic [zos] (which derives historically from *zoqs*, the first person present progressive of the verb 'to ask'). In neutral polar questions, *zos* occurs sentence-initially or is attached to the end of the main verb (47).

(47) a. [zos 'χe.ʁa.si   'ɣeç   ko.xa   'si.an   łi-xa]
        zos 'χeʁa-s-i   'ɣeç   ko-xa   'sian   łi-xa
        INT break-PFV- REM.PST   darkness   DET.INAN-SG   life.force   DEF.AN-SG
     b. ['χe.ʁa.si.zos   'ɣeç   ko.xa   'si.an   łi-xa]
        'χe.ʁa-s-i-zos   'ɣeç   ko-xa   'si.an   łi-xa
        break-PFV-REM.PST-INT   darkness   DET.INAN-SG   life.force   DEF.AN-SG
     'Did the life force destroy the darkness?'

Interrogative words are based on the particle *zos* (48). All are stressed on the first syllable. Content questions are formed by placing the interrogative word at the beginning of the sentence; otherwise, the word order stays the same as in statements (VOS) (49).

(48) Interrogative words in muq
['zi.ʁos]   'who?'   ['zi.os]   'what?'
['ze.os]   'which?' ['a.zos]   'when?'
['ei.zos]   'where'? ['i.zos]   'why?'
['ʁa.zos]   'how?'   ['ɬi.zos] 'what for?'
['Ba.zos]   'how much/ many?'

(49) Content questions in muq
a. ['zi.ʁos 'mis.tɨn.mæ]
ziʁos   'mis.tɨn-m-æ
who   travel-PFV-REC.PST
'Who traveled? (recently)'
b. ['ei.zos 'mis.tɨn.mæ 'sæm.ʎu ɬi-xa]
eizos   'mis.tɨn-m-æ archer   DET.AN
where   travel-PFV-REC.PST
'Where did the archer travel? (recently)'

Direct commands have near and distant forms, conveyed by the particles [ei] and [ou], respectively (50).

(50) Near and distant commands in muq
a. [ei   'χe.ʁa]   'Break (it) now!'
   IMP   break
b. [ou   'χe.ʁa]   'Break (it) later!'
   FUT.IMP   Break

The fictional muq text only exemplifies statements; some examples were given in Section 10.9.

11.6 Guide to Developing Statements, Questions and Commands

- How are statements conveyed in your conlang (morphologically, syntactically, intonationally)?
  - If statements are expressed via declarative particles, what is their position in the sentence?
  - If statements are conveyed morphologically, which affix type is involved? Indicate the relative order of this and other affixes (if relevant).
  - Indicate whether statements have falling or rising final intonation.

- How are polar questions conveyed (morphologically, syntactically, intonationally)?
  - If polar questions are expressed syntactically, indicate which is the interrogative particle, and where it is positioned in the sentence.
  - If polar questions are indicated morphologically, indicate the affix type, and the specific position it occupies in the verb.
  - Specify whether polar questions have falling or rising final intonation.
  - If there are different ways to convey polar questions, explain whether some options are used in some contexts (such as in formal/informal speech).
- How are content questions conveyed?
  - Indicate the interrogative words corresponding to 'who, what, where, when, how' and 'why.' Remember to add these words to your lexicon database.
  - Are there additional interrogative words in your conlang? If so, remember to add them to your lexicon database.
- How will your conlang express commands?
- Indicate whether your conlang distinguishes polite and regular commands, or/and near and distant commands.
- Are there hortatives in your conlang? If so, how are they expressed?

To Learn More

For more information on polar questions in natlangs, see Dryer (2013c, d); for content questions, see Dryer (2013e). If you are interested in learning more about interrogative verbs, see Hagège (2008) and Munro (2012). For commands, see Aikhenvald (2010) and van der Auwera and Lejeune (2013a).

For Dothraki, in addition to Peterson (2014), I consulted the Dothraki–English dictionary available at https://docs.dothraki.org/Dothraki.pdf.

Other sources mentioned in this chapter are listed in the reference section at the end of this book.

12 Negation and Evidentials

This chapter focuses on how languages express negation and source of information (so-called evidentials). While all natlangs have ways to express negation (Section 12.1), evidentials are optional; however, they can be used to great effect in conlanging, as we will see in Section 12.2. Sections 12.3 and 12.4 provide conlanging practice, and Section 12.5 describes how negation and evidentials are conveyed in muq. Finally, Section 12.6 provides a guided set of questions to help you develop these aspects in your conlang.

Key Words

Double negatives
Evidentials (EV)
   Direct evidentials (DIR.EV)
      Auditory evidential (AUD.EV)
      Non-visual evidential (NONVIS.EV)
      Visual evidential (VIS.EV)
   Indirect (reported) evidentials (INDIR.EV)
      Assumed evidential (ASSUM.EV)
      Inferential evidential (INFR.EV)
      Quotative evidential (QUOT.EV)
Negation (NEG)
Negative affixes
Negative imperatives
   Prohibitives (PROH)
   Prohibitives for commands (PROH.POL)
   Prohibitives for requests (PROH.FAM)
Negative particles
Rarer negation strategies
   Negative auxiliaries

12 Negation and Evidentials

12.1 Negation

All natlangs express **negation** (NEG) to negate constituents (1a) or sentences (1b–d). Negation can also be expressed via negative pronouns or adverbs (1e, f).

(1) English: examples of negation
    a. Constituent: *No* dragons appeared.
    b. Statement: Binti did *not* die.
    c. Question: *Didn't* Lyra save her friends?
    d. Command: *Don't* use the ring!
    e. Negative pronouns: My mistress' eyes are *nothing* like the sun.
    f. Negative adverbs: Betty *never* gives up.

In the remainder of this section, we mostly focus on sentential negation for statements and questions (Sections 12.1.1–12.1.3), while Section 12.1.4 addresses negation in commands. Section 12.1.5 provides examples of negation in conlanging.

12.1.1 Negative Particles

Negative particles occur in 43 percent of natlangs, including English, Spanish, Basque and French. They can be placed in different locations in the sentence, most often at the beginning, at the end, or before or after the main verb or auxiliary verb. In English a negative particle occurs after the (first) auxiliary or modal verb (2a–c). If there is no auxiliary/modal verb, the negative particle occurs after the verb (2d).

(2) Negative particles in English
    a. Tristan has <u>not</u> failed.
    b. Lamia will <u>not</u> kill Yvaine.
    c. Yvaine would <u>not</u> have walked to the wall.
    d. Princess Una is <u>not</u> free.

In Spanish, negative particles immediately precede the modal or auxiliary verb (3b). When there are no auxiliaries or modal verbs, the negative particle precedes the main verb (3a, c, d). A difference between English and Spanish involves **double negatives**: Spanish requires double negation with words such as *nada* 'nothing' or *nadie* 'nobody,' while double negatives in English tend to convey emphasis (and are frowned upon in 'standard' English use; cf. *I don't want anything* with *I don't want nothing*).

(3) Negative particles in Spanish
    a. *La princesa Una no es libre.* 'Princess Una is not free.'
        the princess Una not be.3SG.PRS free

b. *Tristan   no   ha   fall-ado.*   'Tristan has not failed.'
   Tristan   not   have.3SG.PRS   fail-PART

c. *Lamia no   mat-ará   a   Yvaine.*   'Lamia won't kill Yvaine.'
   Lamia not kill-FUT   ACC   Yvaine

d. *No   quier-o   nada.*   'I don't want anything.'
   not   want-1SG.PRS   nothing

In Basque, negative statements are formed with the sentence-initial negative particle *ez* 'not' and inversion of the auxiliary verb (if present) from the end of the sentence to the second position (4b). If no auxiliary verb is present, the main verb is inverted (4d).

(4) Negative statements in Basque
   a. *sagar bat   hartu du-t.*   'I have taken one apple.'
      apple one   take have.PRS-1SG
   b. *ez   du-t   sagar bat   hartu.*   'I have not taken one apple.'
      NEG   have.PRS-1SG   apple one   take
   c. *nire   sagarra   da.*   'It is my apple.'
      my   apple   be.3SG.PRS
   d. *ez   da   nire   sagarra.*   'It is not my apple.'
      NEG   be.3SG.PRS   my   apple

Less commonly, negative particles occur sentence-finally, as in Kresh (5).

(5) Negative statements in Kresh (Dryer 2013h)
   Kôkó   ãmbá   gõkó   'dĩ.   'Koko did not hit Goko.'
   Koko   hit.3SG.M   Goko   NEG

In some natlangs negative particles can occupy different positions in the sentence, as in Eipo, where they can either precede or follow the verb (6).

(6) Negative statements in Eipo (Dryer 2013h)
   a. *... gum   dib-nu-n.*
          NEG   eat-FUT-1SG
      'I will not eat'
   b. *na   ton   maral-ya-ne-lam   gum.*
      1SG   and   wound-come-1SG-2SG.PRES   NEG
      'It is not that you come to wound me'

French has two ways to negate statements. In informal speech, the negative particle *pas* is used after the main verb (7a). However, in formal speech, the (auxiliary) verb is also preceded by the negative particle *ne* (often pronounced [n]) (7b).

(7) Negative statements in French
    a. *Tristan mange pas.*   'Tristan does not eat (informal).'
       Tristan eat.3SG NEG
    b. *Tristan ne mange pas.*   'Tristan does not eat (formal).'
       Tristan NEG eat.3SG NEG

> **DID YOU KNOW?**
>
> In Early French, negation was conveyed via the particle *ne*. The word *pas* 'step' was used in emphatic negative statements involving verbs of movement; *Il ne marche pas* meant 'He does not walk a (single) step.' Eventually, *pas* was extended to other verbs and became the preferred way to negate all verbs. We'll explore this change further in Chapter 16.

12.1.2 Negative Affixes

Negative affixes occur in 34 percent of natlangs; in most cases they are suffixes, as shown for Shawã and Jarawara in (8, 9). In Jarawara, negative suffixes differ depending on the gender of the subject.

(8) Negative statements in Shawã (from Souza 2012:81)
    daua   *da-a-ba*   'The man did not die'
    non.Indian.ABS   die-PST-NEG

(9) Negative statements in Jarawara (Dixon 2016:130)
    a. *Mee ati Jane wato-ra*
       3PL voice Jane understand-NEG.F
       'Jane (a woman) can't understand what they are saying (their voices)'
    b. *Mee ati Okomobi wato-re*
       3PL voice Okomobi understand-NEG.M
       'Okomobi (a man) can't understand what they are saying (their voices)'

Negative affixes other than suffixes are rare. Negative prefixes are found in Kolyma Yukaghir (10) and negative circumfixes in Izii (11).

(10) Negative statements in Kolyma Yukaghir (adapted from Dryer 2013g)
    met numøg-ge el-jaqa-te-je   'I will not reach the house'
    1SG house-LOC NEG-achieve-FUT-1SG

(11) Negative statements in Izi (Dryer 2013g)
    ó tó-òmé-dú ré   'He does not do well.'
    3SG NEG-do-NEG well

Some natlangs allow both syntactic and morphological strategies to express negation. For example, in Rama, negative statements can be formed with a negative particle (12a) or with a negative suffix (12b). Note that the gloss TNS stands for tense.

(12) Negative statements in Rama (adapted from Dryer 2013h)
    a. *nki:kna-lut   uut   aa   kain-i*   'The men don't make a dory.'
       man-PL   dory NEG make-TNS
    b. *i-ik-ta:ma*   'He did not arrive.'
       3-arrive-NEG

12.1.3 Other Negation Strategies

Rare negation strategies include **negative auxiliaries**, tonal changes and differences in word order. Negative auxiliaries occur in 4 percent of natlangs, including Thai, Finnish and Northern Saami. The difference between negative particles and negative auxiliaries is morphological: negative auxiliary verbs are inflected morphologically, unlike negative particles. Consider the example from Finnish below: while in (13a) the main verb is inflected for person and number, in (13b) the negative auxiliary verb carries inflection, while the main verb is in the participle form (PART).

(13) Negative statements in Finnish (from Miestamo 2007:295)
    a. *laula-n*   'I sing'
       sing-1SG
    b. *e-n*   *laula*   'I do not sing.'
       NEG-1SG sing.PART

In about 6 percent of natlangs it's hard to tease apart whether a negative word is a particle or an auxiliary verb. For example, in Maori, both the verb and the negative word are uninflected, and thus the negative word is ambiguous between a particle and an auxiliary (in the Maori glosses below, INCL stands for inclusive, and T/A for tense/aspect).

(14) Negative particle/auxiliary in Maori (adapted from Bauer 1993:140)
    ka:hore   *ta:tou*   *e*   *haere*   *ana*   *a:po:po:*
    NEG   1PL.INCL T/A move T/A tomorrow
    'We are not going tomorrow.'

Rarer still is indicating negation via other means, including tone (as in Ewondo and Oromo), stem changes (Tamashek) or word order changes (as in Lokaa, where affirmative statements are SVO, but negative ones are typically SOV).

> **Your Turn**
>
> - Which negation strategy discussed above do you think is more interesting, and why?
> - Which strategy could work well for (a) an alien conlang, (b) an auxlang devised for international communication?

12.1.4 Negative Imperatives

In English, **negative imperatives** use a similar negation strategy as statements (the auxiliary verb *do* followed by *not*, as in 'Do not throw a burrito at me'). In some natlangs, negative imperatives are expressed with dedicated **prohibitive** (i.e., negative imperative) particles or affixes. Examples include Hawaiian and Lezgian (Caucasian: Dagestan) (15, 16). Note that prohibitives are glossed PROH.

(15) Hawaiian prohibitive (adapted from Elbert & Kawena 1979: 61)
  a. *e*   *hele*   *ʔoe!*   'Go!' (strong command)
     IMP   go   you
  b. *mai*   *uwe:*   *ʔoe*   'Don't cry!'
     PROH   cry   you

(16) Lezgian prohibitive (adapted from König & Siemund 2007:311)
  a. *wuna*   *badʒiʃlamiʃ-a,*   *buba*   'Forgive me, father!'
     you.ERG forgive-IMP   father
  b. *wa-z*   *kitʃ'e*   *ʒe-mir* 'Don't be afraid!'
     you.DAT afraid   be-PROH

Other languages might not have dedicated prohibitive morphology or syntax, but nonetheless express positive and negative imperatives in different ways. For example, in Peninsular Spanish positive commands involve imperative suffixes, at least in informal speech, as shown in Section 11.3.1. However, negative commands involve irrealis suffixes in addition to the particle *no* (17).

(17) Peninsular Spanish: informal prohibitives and imperatives
  a. ¡*No*   *gir-es*   *ahora!*
     NEG   turn-2SG.IRR   now
     'Do not turn now (singular, informal)'
  b. ¡*No*   *gir-e*   *ahora!*
     NEG   turn-3SG.PRS.IRR   now
     'Do not turn now (singular, formal)'

12.1.5 Negative Statements and Imperatives in Conlanging

Esperanto, Toki Pona, Láadan and Na'vi have negative particles. In Esperanto, negative sentences involve the preverbal negative particle *ne*; this particle is omitted when there is another negative word in the sentence (Harlow 1995, Kellerman Reed 2003). In Na'vi, the preverbal particle *ke* appears in negative statements and questions (18a, b). Double negatives occur with negative pronouns and adverbs, as seen in (18a). Prohibitives are formed with the particle *rä'ä* [ɾæ.'ʔæ] (18c). When *rä'ä* follows the verb, the prohibitive conveys special emphasis.

12.1 Negation

(18) Negation in Na'vi (from Annis 2024:52–54)

a. [ˈkɛ.ʔu kɛ   lu   ŋaj]   'Nothing is true'
   ke'u   ke   lu   ngay
   nothing NEG be   true

b. [ŋal   kɛ   tsɛ.ʔa t'ɛ.pɪt   sɾak] 'Do you not see the fire?'
   nga-l   ke   tse'a   txep-it   srak?
   you-ERG NEG see   fire-ABS INT

c. [ɾæ.ˈʔæ ˈha.haw]   'Don't sleep'
   rä'ä   hahaw
   PROH   sleep

In Toki Pona and Láadan, negative particles are placed after the verb in statements and imperatives (19, 20). In Toki Pona, *ala* can follow another word to negate it. As shown in Chapter 11, imperatives in both conlangs involve sentence-initial particles.

(19) Negation in Toki Pona (Lang 2014:28, 30, 41)

a. [mi mo.ku a.la e so.we.li]
   mi   moku ala e   soweli   'I don't eat animals.'
   1SG   eat   NEG ACC animal

b. [jan a.la li i.ke]
   jan   ala li   ike   'Nobody is bad.'
   person NEG AUX bad

c. [o to.ki a.la o pa.li]
   o   toki   ala o   pali.   'Don't speak. Take action.'
   IMP speak NOT IMP to.do

(20) Negation in Láadan (Elgin et al. 2020:23, 25, 68)

a. [bí.ɪ hɑl ɹɑ ɛ.ʒɑ wɑ]
   Bíi   hal   ra   ezha   wa
   DEC   work NEG   snake EV
   'The snake doesn't work'

b. [bí.ɪ ɛ.ɹɪl wí.ɪ ɹɑ mɪd wɑ]
   Bíi   eril   wíi   ra   mid   wa.
   DEC   PST   to.be.alive NEG   creature EV
   'The creature was not alive.'

c. [bó.o dɑ.mɑ ɹɑ nɛ θom lɛ.θoθ]
   Bóo   dama   ra   ne   thom   le-tho-th
   IMP.POL   touch NEG   you   pillow 1-POSS-ACC
   'Please don't touch my pillow.'

Klingon has negative suffixes. The general negation suffix is *-be'* [-bɛʔ], which immediately follows the word or constituent negated. In negative statements, this suffix is attached to the verb (21a). It is a so-called rover morpheme, since it can be placed in different positions leading to different sentence meanings (21b, c). Negative commands are formed with the prohibitive suffix *-Qo'* in addition to imperative prefixes (21d).

(21)   Negation in Klingon (Okrand 1985:46)
    a. *jI-SaH-be'*   [jɪ.ʂɑx.bɛʔ]
        1SG.A-care-NEG
        'I don't care'
    b. *cho-HoH-vIp-be'*   [tʃo.xox.vɪp.bɛʔ]
        2SG.A.1.SG.P-kill-afraid-NEG
        'You are not afraid to kill me'
    c. *cho-HoH-be'-vIp*   [tʃo.xox. bɛʔ.vɪp]
        2SG.A.1.SG.P-kill-NEG-afraid
        'You are afraid to not kill me'
    d. *yI-ja'-Qo'*   [jɪ.dʒɑʔ.qχoʔ]
        IMP.3.SG-tell-PROH
        'Don't tell him/her!'

In Dothraki, negative statements are formed with the preverbal negative particle *vo(s)* (Peterson 2014:42). Verbs in negative statements carry specific negative suffixes (22a). Negative imperatives are formed with the particle *vo(s)* and the informal or formal imperative suffix for **requests** or **commands**, respectively (Peterson 2014:52–53). These are glossed below as PROH.FAM and PROH.POL (22b, c).

(22)   Negation in Dothraki (Peterson 2014:46, 53)
    a. [mo.ɾi vos as.ti]
        Mori   *vos*   *ast-i.*
        3SG.NOM   NEG   say-3PL.NEG
        'They don't say.'
    b. [vos as.to]
        Vos   *ast-o!*
        NEG   speak-PROH.POL
        'Don't speak!'
    c. [vo li.wos haz hɾa.zef]
        Vo   *liw-os*   *haz*   *hrazef*
        NEG   tie-PROH.FAM   that   horse
        'Don't tie that horse down.'

> **Your Turn**
>
> Which negation strategy in this section do you consider most interesting, and why?

12.2 Evidentials

All natlangs can express the source of the information. English does so lexically, via adverbs (23a, b), expressions (23c, d), or complex sentences (23e, f). About 57 percent of natlangs have morphological or syntactic ways to express the source of information, that is, **evidentials (EV)**. The main types of evidentials are **direct evidentials**, conveying that evidence was gathered through the senses (typically visually or auditorily); and **indirect** or **reported evidentials**, for information obtained indirectly. Most commonly languages have indirect evidentials; only 17 percent of natlangs have both direct and indirect evidentials.

(23) English: source of information (I)
    a. <u>Apparently</u>, Mrs. Coulter stole the knife.
    b. There are <u>reportedly</u> 100 billion galaxies in the universe.
    c. I saw a black unicorn <u>with my own eyes</u>.
    d. The concert will be cancelled; <u>I heard it through the grapevine</u>.
    e. <u>It is rumored that</u> the launch will take place next Sunday.
    f. <u>I read that</u> there are many unexplained flying objects.

For example, Turkish has two past tense suffixes, a direct evidential indicating direct witnessing of an event (glossed DIR.EV) and an indirect evidential conveying indirect evidence (glossed INDIR.EV) (24).

(24) Turkish evidentials (adapted from de Haan 2013a)
    a. *Ahmet gel-di.*   'Ahmet came.' (witnessed by the speaker)
       Ahmet come-PST.DIR.EV
    b. *Ahmet gel-miş.*   'Ahmet came.' (not witnessed by the speaker)
       Ahmet come-PST.INDIR.EV

Natlangs might have more than one direct or indirect evidential. For example, in Tuyuca, there are two types of direct evidentials: **visual (VIS.EV)** and **non-visual (NONVIS.EV)** (25).

(25) Tuyuca direct evidentials (from Barnes 1984:257)
    a. *apé-wi*   'He played.' (I saw it)
       play.3SG.M.PST-VIS.EV
    b. *apé-ti*   'He played.' (I heard it)
       play.3SG.M.PST-NONVIS.EV

When a language has only one direct evidential, it usually conveys visual evidence, as in Fasu (26). But other options exist; for example, Koasati has a direct **auditory evidential (AUD.EV)** (27).

(26) Fasu visual evidential (de Haan 2013a)
   a-pe-re   '[I see] it coming.'
   VIS.EV-come-VIS.EV

(27) Koasati auditory evidential (Kimball 1985:79)
   nipó-k   aksóhka-ha   'It sounds like the meat is charring.'
   meat-SUBJ   char-AUD.EV

Natlangs can also have a variety of indirect evidentials. **Inferential evidentials** (INFR.EV) are used when the speaker infers information based on physical evidence. **Quotatives** or second-hand **evidentials** (QUOT.EV) are employed when the information was overheard or conveyed by someone else (these are also known as hearsay or reportative evidentials). **Assumed evidentials** (ASSUM.EV) convey information inferred based on general knowledge, logical reasoning or assumption. Tuyuca differentiates these three indirect evidentials (28).

(28) Tuyuca indirect evidentials (from Barnes 1984:257)
   a. *apé-yi*
      play.3SG.M.PST-INFR.EV
      'He played.' (I have seen evidence, such as distinctive prints on a field.)
   b. *apé-yigi*
      play.3SG.M.PST-QUOT.EV
      'He played.' (Somebody told me.)
   c. *apé-hiyi*
      play.3SG.M.PST-ASSUM.EV
      'He played.' (It is reasonable to assume it.)

Evidentials are mostly expressed via verbal morphemes or clitics (clitics are grammatical words that can attach to verbs and other categories). One example of the latter is found in Takelma (29).

(29) Evidential clitics in Takelma (adapted from de Haan 2013b)
   gane:-ihi?   'Now, it is said.'
   now-QUOT.EV

Evidential particles tend to encode indirect evidentials, as in Estonian (30). In Spanish, the particle *dizque* (which historically arose from *decir* 'to say' and *que* 'that') is used to convey second-hand information, as exemplified below for Colombian Spanish (31) (the equivalent *diz que* is used in Brazilian Portuguese).

(30) Estonian evidentials (from Dixon 2016:91)
   a. *Elsa   on   ilus*   'Elsa is beautiful (I know it)'
      Elsa   is.DIR.EV   beautiful
   b. *Elsa   olevat   ilus*   'Elsa is beautiful (they say)'
      Elsa   is.QUOT.EV beautiful

(31) Colombian Spanish evidentials (from Travis 2006)
    Y   es-o,   dizque   es   peligros-o   ¿no?
    and   that-SG.M   QUOT.EV   be.3SG.PRS   dangerous-SG.M   no
    'And it, it is said to be dangerous, isn't it?

In some natlangs evidentials are expressed via auxiliary verbs, as in Dutch, where the modal verb 'moet' is used as an indirect evidential (32).

(32) Dutch evidentials (from de Haan 2013a)
    Het   moet   een   goede   film   zijn.
    It   INDIR.EV   a   good   film   be
    'It is said to be a good film / It appears to be a good film.'

Evidential distinctions tend to be more extensive in the past tense than in the present, and they are usually absent in the future tense. For example, in Tuyuca there are five evidential distinctions in the past, four in the present (the quotative evidential is not expressed in the present), and none in the future. In addition, evidential distinctions tend to be more common in statements than in questions. One example is Shipibo-Konibo, which has four evidential suffixes in statements (direct *-ra*, inferential *-bira*, reported *-(ron)ki* and assumed *-mein*). In questions only the assumed evidential can be expressed (33a). In Shipibo-Konibo request questions, the use of this evidential conveys politeness (33b).

(33) Evidentials in Shipibo-Konibo (from Valenzuela 2003)
    a. *tso-a-mein*   *i-ti*   *iki?*
       who-ABS-ASSUM.EV   be-INF   AUX
       'Who could it be?'
    b. *mi-n-mein*   *e-a*   *nokon*   *wai*   *oro-xon-ai?*
       2-ERG-ASSUM.EV   1-ABS   POSS.1   garden.ABS   clear-BEN-INC
       'Would you please/perhaps clear my garden for me?'

In most natlangs, including Quechua and Jarawara, evidentials are not used in commands. When they are, they express a second-hand imperative ('do something as you were told'), as in Shipibo-Konibo (34).

(34) Evidentials in Shipibo-Konibo commands (from Valenzuela 2003)
    onpax-ki   *be-wé!*
    contained.water.ABS-QUOT.EV   bring-IMP
    '(S/he says that you must) bring water!'

Languages with morphological evidentials usually have two to six evidential distinctions. In some natlangs, one evidential is unmarked or default. The evidential distinction least likely to be marked morphologically/syntactically is the visual evidential (Aikhenvald 2004:73).

12.2.1 Evidentials in Conlanging

In Na'vi, the infix *-ats-* indicates indirect knowledge or uncertainty (Annis 2024: 21, 47). Láadan has a complex system of sentence-final evidential particles (35), exemplified in (36). Note that if the speaker refuses to include an evidential and the context is not redundant, 'that is allowed, but it cannot be easily overlooked' (Elgin et al. 2020:298).

(35) Láadan evidentials (adapted from Elgin et al. 2020: 298)

wa	[wɑ]	Perceived by speaker, externally or internally.
wáa	[wá.ɑ]	Assumed true since speaker trusts source.
waá	[wɑ.á]	Assumed false since speaker distrusts source.
waálh	[wɑ.áɬ]	Assumed false since source is not trusted and evil intent is assumed.
wo	[wo]	Imagined or invented by speaker, hypothetical.
wóo	[wó.o]	The speaker states lack of knowledge on the validity of the matter.
wi	[wɪ]	Known to speaker because self-evident.
we	[wɛ]	Perceived in a dream.
∅		No comment on validity, because of personal preference or because no comment is needed (as in sentences in connected discourse).

(36) Evidentials in Láadan (from Elgin et al. 2020:25)
   a. [bí.ɪ ɛ.ɹíl wí.ɪ ɹɑ mɪd wɑ]

Bíi	eril	wíi	ra	mid	wa.
DEC	PST	to.be.alive	NEG	creature	DIR.EV

   'The creature was not alive.'
   b. [bí.ɪ né.dɛ hɑl ɹɑ wɪθ wá.ɑ]

Bíi	néde	hal	ra	with	wáa.
DEC	want	work	NEG	woman	ASSUM.EV

   'The woman didn't want to work.'

The evidential system of Láadan served as inspiration for that in Lojban, which also has a rich system of evidential particles. Some examples include the direct evidential [za.ha], the quotative [ti.he], the internal experience evidential [ka.hu] (for information originating in dreams, visions or personal revelation) and the cultural knowledge evidential [se.ho] (for information originating in myths or customs). Evidential particles in Lojban are sentence-initial (Cowan 2016:302–304).

> **Your Turn**
>
> Which of the evidentials in Láadan corresponds to the categories we have discussed? Which are different?

12.3 Conlanging Practice: Negation in Deep Aqua

As you probably remember from Chapter 11, Deep Aqua has SVO word order, and statements, questions and commands are expressed via obligatory sentence-final particles. Sentence negation is expressed with the verbal suffix [-bi] across sentence types.

Taking into consideration your answers to the practice exercise in Section 11.4, translate the sentences below (remember: [disr] 'you (2SG)', [zi] 'ze' 'to.be.crazy, to.act.crazy', [sim] DEC). The first sentence is done for you.

1. 'You are not crazy.'   [disr   zi.'ze-bi   sim]
                                                  2SG   to.be.crazy-NEG   DEC
2. 'Aren't you crazy?'
3. 'Don't act crazy!'

12.4 Conlanging Practice: Evidentials in the Ur Languages

- What type of evidentials (if any) could the Fog/Aqua/Gem/Grass languages have? How could they be connected to the fictional world?
- Which of the Ur languages would be more likely to have a distinction between visual and auditory evidentials?
- Which of the Ur languages could have the evidential 'perceived in a trance'?

12.5 Negation and Evidentials in Muq

Sentential negation for statements and questions in muq is conveyed via the prefix [ə-] if the verb begins with a consonant, and [əɬ-] if the verb begins with a vowel. Examples of negative statements and questions are given in (37, 38).

(37)   Negation in muq statements
       a.   [ˈə-χeʁa-s-æ]   '(It) didn't break'
           NEG-break-PFV-REC.PST
       b.   [ˈəɬ-eza-m-a]   '(She) won't be swimming'
           NEG-swim-IMPF-REC.FUT

(38)   Negation in muq questions
       a.   [ˈə-χeʁa-s-æ-zos]   'Didn't (it) break?'
           NEG-break-PFV-REC.PST-INT
       b.   [zos   ˈəɬ-eza-m-a]   'Won't (she) swim?'
           INT   NEG-swim-IMPF-REC.FUT

As shown in Chapter 11, near and distant commands are formed with the preverbal particles [ei] and [ou], respectively. Prohibitives are formed by adding the negative prefix [ə-/əɬ-] to the verb, and the suffix [-d] to imperative particles (39).

(39) Prohibitives in muq

a. [ei-d]   'ə-χeʁa]   'Don't break (it) now!'
   IMP-PROH   NEG-break

b. [ou-d]   'ə-χeʁa]   'Don't break (it) later!'
   IMP.FUT-PROH   NEG-break

c. [ei-d]   'əɬ-eza]   'Don't swim now!'
   IMP-PROH   NEG-swim

The Salt language has only one evidential, quotative [ux] (40), used in the present and the past tense. [ux] is sentence initial in statements (40). [ux] follows command and interrogative particles, as shown in (41, 42).

(40) Muq evidentials: statements

a. ['χe.ʁa-s-æ]   '(It) broke.'
   break-PFV-REC.PST

b. [ux   'χe.ʁa-s-æ]   'It broke.' (somebody said)
   EV.QUOT   break-PFV-REC.PST

c. [ux   'ə-χe.ʁa-s-æ]   'It didn't break.' (somebody said)
   EV.QUOT   NEG-break-PFV-REC.PST

(41) Muq evidentials: commands

a. [ei   'χe.ʁa]   'Break (it) now!' (I'm/we're telling you)
   IMP   break

b. [ei   ux   'χe.ʁa]   'Break (it) now, as you were told!'
   IMP   QUOT.EV   break

c. [ou   'χe.ʁa]   'Break (it) later!' (I'm/we're telling you)
   IMP.FUT break

d. [ou   ux   'χe.ʁa]   'Break (it) later, as you were told!'
   IMP.FUT QUOT.EV   break

(42) Muq evidentials: questions

a. [zos   'χe.ʁa-m-æ]   'Did (it) break?'
   INT   break-PFV-REC.PST

b. [zos   ux   'χe.ʁa-m-æ]   'Did they say it broke?'
   INT   QUOT.EV   break-PFV-REC.PST

In the text conveying the origin myth of the Salt people, the first sentence requires the quotative [ux] since the text reports information that the Salt people have been told. The particle is omitted in the following sentences since it is understood to be part of the same story. [ux] is included in the last sentence as a rhetorical device to emphasize the fact that this is an origin myth passed on across generations. The translations of the first and last sentences of the text are given in (43).

(43) Salt language: fictional text (initial and final sentences)
    a. [ux   'xaɸ-m-i   'i.xi   ko-xa   'mei-m-i   'ɣeç]
       QUOT.EV sleep-IMPF-REM.PST world DEF.INAN-SG be-IMPF-REM.PST
                                                                   darkness
       '(It is said that) long ago the world slept; there was darkness'
    b. [ux   'ou.na-s-i   'muq.çem-xa]
       QUOT.EV   awaken-PFV-REM.PST our.island-SG
       'Thus (it is said that) our island awakened.'

12.6 Guide to Developing Negation and Evidentials

- Will your conlang encode negation with particles, affixes or negative auxiliaries?
  - If your conlang has negative particles, where do they occur in the sentence?
  - If your conlang has negative affixes, are they prefixes, suffixes, infixes? How are they ordered regarding other affixes of the same type?
  - Will your conlang have double negation? Why/why not?
  - Will there be prohibitives in your conlang?
- Will your conlang encode evidentials?
  - If so, which type of evidentials will be encoded (e.g., direct, indirect, visual)?
  - Will there be morphological or syntactic evidentials?
  - If morphological, will they involve suffixes, infixes, prefixes ...?
  - If syntactic, will they involve particles or auxiliary verbs?

To Learn More

For more information on negative statements and imperatives, see Dryer (2013g, h), van der Auwera and Lejeune (2013b), and Miestamo (2005). To learn more about evidentials, see Aikhenvlad and Dixon (1998), Aikhenvald (2004) and Barnes (1984), in addition to the WALS online chapters by de Haan (2013a, b). Other sources mentioned are listed in the reference section at the end of this book.

13 Complex Sentences

Chapters 10–12 discussed various aspects related to sentences, focusing mostly on simple sentences. This chapter examines complex sentences. Section 13.1 previews the most common types of complex sentences attested in languages. Section 13.2 focuses on coordinated sentences, and 13.3 on subordinated ones. Section 13.4 provides practice on complex sentences in Toki Pona, and 13.5 discusses coordination and subordination in muq. Finally, Section 13.6 provides a guided set of questions to help you build complex sentences in your conlang.

Key Words

Antecedent
Comitative conjunction ('with')
Coordination
   Adversative coordination
   Bisyndetic coordination
   Complementizers (COMP)
   Conjunctive coordination
   Coordinators (Coordinating conjunctions)
   Disjunctive coordination
   Juxtaposition (Asyndetic coordination)
   Syndetic coordination
Dependent clause
Finite verb
Non-finite verb
Main clause
Relative pronouns
Relativizer (REL)
Subordination
   Adjectival clauses (Relative clauses)
     Restrictive
     Non-restrictive
   Adverbial clauses
   Nominal clauses (Complement clauses)

13.1 Complex Sentences

Simple sentences only have one lexical verb, and thus one clause only, as in (1). Complex sentences, on the other hand, have more than one lexical verb; each is the center of a clause, a sentence-like constituent with its own subject and predicate. The sentences in (2) each have two or more lexical verbs and thus are complex. Each clause in (1, 2) is enclosed within square brackets.

(1) English: simple sentences
  a. [Yukiko has always hated snakes.]
  b. [What toppings does the pizza have?]
  c. [Malik would have really liked that!]
  d. [Don't turn now!]

(2) English: complex sentences (I)
  a. [Yukiko has always hated snakes] but [she never had a problem with alligators].
  b. [Turn now], or [face the consequences].
  c. [What toppings does the pizza have] and [how much does it cost]?

The clauses in (2) are linked with conjunctions (*but*, *or* and *and*, respectively). Conjunctions connect clauses (as above) and constituents (including noun phrases, as in *The planet and its moon*, or verb phrases, as in *twist and shout*).

In the complex sentences in (2), each clause can stand on its own, is structurally like the other clause in the sentence and contributes equally to the sentence meaning. Thus, each is a **main clause**. Sentences with two (or more) main clauses involve **coordination**. Now, consider the sentences in (3); each has two lexical verbs, and, therefore, two clauses. The second clause, enclosed within angle brackets, is a **dependent clause** because it completes the meaning of the sentence. In (3), dependent clauses act as the direct object of the main verb, but as we will see later they can fulfill other functions. Here and throughout, main clauses are enclosed within square brackets and dependent ones within angle brackets. Sentences with one or more dependent clauses involve **subordination**.

(3) English: complex sentences (II)
  a. [My friend confirmed < that Yukiko has always hated snakes >].
  b. [Malik would really like < to read that book >].
  c. [They told us < to turn now >].

Most natlangs use coordination and subordination to some extent. However, natlangs vary in how they treat complex sentences. One example was given in Chapter 10 for Dutch, where word order in main clauses is SVO, but SOV in dependent clauses. Another example is Swedish, where the negative particle follows the auxiliary verb in main clauses (4a) but precedes it in dependent clauses (4b).

(4) Swedish (adapted from Thompson et al. 2007:240)
   a. Vi   kunde inte   œpːna   kokosnøːten
      1PL   could NEG   open   coconut
      'We could not open the coconut.'
   b. Vi   var   ladsna < dɛrfor at: vi   inte kunde œpːna kokosnøːten.>
      1PL   were   sorry because that 1PL NEG could open coconut
      'We were sorry because we couldn't open the coconut.'

13.2 Coordination

Coordination is used to link words (5a), constituents (5b–e) and clauses (5f). The most common types of coordination are **conjunctive** (*and*), **disjunctive** (*or*) and **adversative coordination** (*but*).

(5) English: coordination of words, constituents and clauses
   a.   Verbs: [I cannot bake or buy a pecan pie.]
   b.   NPs: [I greeted all students and their spouses.]
   c.   APs: [His outfit was trendy but cheap.]
   d.   AdvPs: [The princess paused majestically and elegantly.]
   e.   VPs: [Louise reads books and writes papers.]
   f.   Clauses: [Abbot died], [Costello survived].

Coordination might involve conjunctions or affixes; in Kannada, for example, both coordinated nouns carry the suffix [-uː] (6). **Coordinating conjunctions** and affixes are referred to generally as **coordinators**.

(6) Coordination in Kannada (adapted from Sridhar 1990:106)
     narahariy-uː   soːmaʃeːkharan-uː   peːʈe-ge   hoː-d-aru
     Narahari-and   Somashekhara-and   market-DAT   go-PST-3PL
     'Narahari and Somashekhara went to the market'

Coordination involving conjunctions or affixes is known as **syndetic coordination**. Sometimes more than one conjunction or affix is involved, as in (6); this is termed **bisyndetic coordination**. If there are no overt coordinators, as in (5f), we have **juxtaposition** or **asyndetic coordination**. The following sections consider each in more detail.

13.2.1 Syndetic Coordination
13.2.1.1 Conjunction

Conjunctive coordination conveys addition ('and'). Natlangs might have only one conjunctive coordinator, as in English; or they might use different ones for different types of elements, most typically one for noun phrases and another for clauses or events. Examples from Korean, featuring different conjunctive suffixes, are given below.

(7) Conjunctive coordination in Korean (Haspelmath 2007:20)
    a. *yenphil-kwa*   *congi*
       pencil-and   paper
       'pencil and paper'
    b. *achim*   *mek-ko*   *hakkyo*   *ka-ss-eyyo*
       breakfast   eat-and   school   go-PST-IND
       '(I) ate breakfast and went to school.'

Conjunctions might be different in negative and affirmative sentences, as in (8); note that in (8b), the coordinator *or* indicates conjunction, not disjunction.

(8) English: coordinating conjunction in affirmative and negative statements
    a. I ate **and** drank.
    b. I didn't eat **or** drink.

In some natlangs the conjunctive coordinator linking nouns is the same as the **comitative conjuction ('with')**; one example from Samoan is given in (9). As we saw in Chapter 8, ALL stands for the allative case, indicating motion to/toward a place.

(9) Samoan comitative conjunction (Haspelmath 2007:29)
    a. *ia,*   *alu*   *atu*   *Sina*   *ma*   *le*   *ili-tea*
       well   go.SG   ALL   Sina   with   the   fan-white
       'Well, Sina went there with the white fan.'
    b. *ʔua*   *o:*   *atu*   *Sina*   *ma*   *Tigilau*
       PERF   go.PL   ALL   Sina   and   Tigilau
       'Sina and Tigilau left.'

In some natlangs conjunctions vary in male and female speech, as in Kukama-Kukamiria, where the coordinator 'and/or' is *yai* in female speech, but *riai* in masculine speech (10; note that MS indicates masculine speech).

(10) Kukama-Kukamiria (VO): coordination (adapted from Vallejos 2016:535)
     [*uri*   *yatsuk-ui*]   [*ta*   *riai*   *yatsuk-ui*]
     3SG.MS   swim-PST   1SG.MS   also/and   swim.PST
     'He swam, and so did I.'

There tends to be a relationship between word order and conjunctive coordinator placement. In both OV and VO languages, the conjunctive coordinator might appear between clauses; but in VO languages, it can occur after the first element of the second clause (as in 10), while in OV languages, it can occur after the last element (as in 11).

(11) Walapai (OV): coordination (Payne 2006:310, 311)
wàlpáikwáùk	háikùkwáùk-m	ítʃe
walapai.speech	white.man.speech-and	we.speak

'We speak Walapai and English.'

13.2.1.2 Disjunction

Disjunctive coordination involves a choice between words or constituents. It can be exclusive ('or') or inclusive ('or/and'). In English there is no overt difference between the two; context can help determine the specific interpretation. For example, if you are being offered food on a plane, *or* in (12a) would be exclusive, since you are expected to choose only one option. But if you are invited for dinner at your friend's house, *or* can be interpreted inclusively. In any case, the exclusive interpretation can be clarified with the addition of the conjunction *either* before the first coordinated element (12b), and the inclusive interpretation with the addition of *or both* (12c).

(12) English: disjunctive coordination
 a. Would you like pasta or chicken?
 b. Would you like either pasta or chicken?
 c. Would you like pasta, chicken, or both?

In some languages disjunctive coordinators differ in statements or questions, as in Finnish (13). As we saw in Chapter 8, ILL stands for the illative case, indicating motion into a location.

(13) Finnish: disjunctive coordination (Haspelmath 2007:25)
 a.
an:a-n	sinu-l:e	kirja-n	tai	albumi-n
give-1SG	you-ALL	book-ACC	or	album-ACC

 'I'll give you a book or an album.'
 b.
mene-t-kø	teat:eri-in	vai	lepo-puisto-on
go-2SG-Q	theater-ILL	or	rest-garden-ILL

 'Are you going to a theatre or to a park?'

13.2.1.3 Adversative Coordination

Adversative coordination is used to restrict or correct the meaning of the first coordinated element or to present a contrast, as in (14). While there is (technically) no limit on how many elements can be coordinated with conjunction and disjunction, only two can be coordinated adversatively (15).

(14) English: adversative conjunction
   a. Mark is handsome, but cocky.
   b. Jess is smart but has a horrible attitude.
   c. Otto doesn't love Marisol, but Sonia.
   d. Harry did not go back to school, he went into hiding instead.
   e. The girl studied so hard, yet she did not pass the wizarding test.

(15) English: multiple coordination
   a. Conjunction: Julia would like to travel to Iceland, Norway and Finland.
   b. Disjunction: Iratxe doesn't eat eggs, milk or seaweed.
   c. Adversative: I took piano lessons, but that was long ago (*but that was fun).

13.2.2 Juxtaposition

Juxtaposition, or asyndetic coordination, lacks overt coordinators. One famous example involving juxtaposition in Latin, attributed to Julius Caesar, is given in (16). In the Maricopa example in (17), juxtaposition links object NPs; in the English translation the conjunction needs to be stated explicitly, unlike in (17).

(16) Latin: juxtaposition
   veni,   vidi,   vici.
   come.3SG.PST   see.3SG.PST   conquer.3SG.PST
   'I came, I saw, I conquered.'

(17) Maricopa (Piipaash): juxtaposition (Gil 1991:99, cited in Haspelmath 2007:7)
   John   Bill   ɲi-ʔ-yu:-k
   John.ACC   Bill.ACC   PL.OBJ-1-see.SG-REAL
   'I saw John and Bill'

Juxtaposition can also occur with other meanings, including adversative (*Shanna did not come to school; she stayed home*) or causal, as in (18). The English translation uses juxtaposition but could be rendered with the causal coordinator *so*.

(18) Kukama-Kukamiria: juxtaposition (from Vallejos 2016:532)
   [ta   purepe   ikian   kitʃi-ui]   [ta   kuriki   upa]
   1SG.MS   buy   this   machete-PST1   1SG.MS   money   finish
   'I bought this machete; my money is gone.'

Natlangs with a long literacy history usually have overt coordinators, unlike those without. The reason is that coordination can be rendered easily via intonation in spoken speech, unlike in writing. Consider the examples below: in (19a) there are three different sentences, each ending in falling intonation. In (19b), there is one multiclausal sentence; the first two clauses have final rising intonation, unlike the third one. The presence of final rising intonation clues the hearer that the clause is coordinated, and thus part of the same sentence.

(19) English: Coordination and intonation

    a. I came. I saw. I conquered.   [ai 'kʰeim ‖ ai 'sɔ ‖ ai 'kʰɔŋ.kɪdl̩]

    b. [I came], [I saw], [I conquered].   [ai 'kʰeim | ai 'sɔ | ai 'kʰɔŋ.kɪdl̩]

13.2.3 Bisyndetic Coordination

Bisyndetic coordination involves coordinators in both combined elements. Examples occur in Kannada (6) and French (20). Most often the coordinator follows the elements combined. If the coordinators precede them, they tend to convey emphasis, as in French and English (20, 21).

(20) French: bisyndetic coordination

et	Marie	et	Latif	aiment	le	pop-corn.
and	Marie	and	Latif	like.3PL	the	popcorn

'Both Marie and Latif like popcorn.'

(21) English: bisyndetic coordination
    a. Conjunction: I like both reading books and listening to music.
    b. Disjunction: My neighbor has neither cats nor dogs.

13.2.4 Coordination in Conlanging

In Esperanto and Sindarin coordination involves a conjunction before the last coordinated element. Examples from Esperanto are given below.

(22) Esperanto: coordination (from https://lernu.net/en/gramatiko/konjunkcioj)

    a.

Petro	leg-is	la gazeto-n,	kaj	Karlo	rigard-is	televido-n.
Petro	read-PST	the paper-ACC	and	Karlo	watch-PST	TV-ACC

'Petro read the paper, and Karlo watched TV.'

    b.

Vi	pov-as	vojaĝi per	trajno,	buso,	aŭto	aŭ	biciklo.
You	can-PRS	travel by	train	bus	car	or	bicycle

'You can travel by train, bus, car or bicycle.'

    c.

Li	am-as	mi-n,	sed	mi	li.n	ne	am-as.
3SG.M	love-PRES	1SG-ACC	but	1SG	3SG-ACC	NEG	love-PRS

'He loves me, but I don't love him.'

In Sindarin, the coordinator *a* (*ah* before vowels) links different types of constituents (23). Other conjunctions include *egor* 'or, otherwise' and *sui* 'like, as' (Salo 2004:148).

(23) Sindarin: conjunctions (from Salo 2004:197, 207)
    a. *Taur*   *a*   *Perhael*
       Frodo   and   Samwise
       'Frodo and Samwise.'
    b. *ped-o*   *mel:on*   *a*   *min:-o.*
       say-IMP friend   and   enter-IMP
       'Say friend/Let a friend speak and enter.'

Na'vi and Klingon have different coordinators linking NPs and clauses. In Klingon, coordination in NPs is expressed via conjunctions placed after the final coordinated noun; disjunctive coordinators can be exclusive or inclusive (24).

(24) Klingon: noun coordination (Okrand 1985:55)
    a. *DeS*   *'uS*   *je*   [dɛʂ ʔuʂ dʒɛ]
       arm   leg   and
       'An arm and a leg'
    b. *DeS*   *'uS*   *ghap* [dɛʂ ʔuʂ ɣɑp]
       arm   leg   or
       'An arm or a leg (but not both)'
    c. *DeS*   *'uS*   *joq*   [dɛʂ ʔuʂ dʒoq]
       arm   leg   and/or
       'An arm or a leg or both'

Coordinated clauses in Klingon are linked with conjunctions placed between clauses (25). Note that the coordinators below involve the reversed segments of the nominal coordinators above!

(25) Klingon: clause coordination (Okrand 1985:61)
    a. [dʒɪ.ʂop.tax   ʔɛdʒ   qχoŋ.tax]
       jI-Sop-taH   *'ej*   *Qong-taH*
       1SG-eat-CONT and   3SG.sleep-CONT
       'I am eating, and he/she is sleeping.'
    b. [bɪ.ʂop.tax   qodʒ   bɪ.tɬutɬ.tax]
       bI-Sop-taH   *qoj*   *bI-tlhutlh-taH*
       2SG-eat-CONT and/or   2SG-drink-CONT
       'You are eating and/or (you are) drinking.'
    c. [bɪ.ʂop.tax   pɑɣ   bɪ.tɬutɬ.tax]
       bI-Sop-taH   *pagh*   *bI-tIhutIh-taH*
       2SG-eat-CONT or   2SG-drink-CONT
       'You are either eating or else (you are) drinking.'

High Valyrian expresses 'and' with the conjunction *se* or by lengthening the final syllable of the last conjoined word and shifting stress to the final syllable (26).

(26) High Valyrian coordination
(from https://wiki.dothraki.org/High_Valyrian_Syntax)
a. *vala*   ['va.la]   'the man'
b. *ābra*   ['aː.bra]   'the woman'
c. *vala ābrā* ['va.la aː.'braː] 'the man and the woman'

In Toki Pona, conjunction is expressed with *en* 'and' for subject nouns, disjunction with *anu* 'or' and adversative coordination with *taso* 'but.' Co-ordinated direct objects and adjectives/verbs are juxtaposed and involve the repetition of the accusative or sentence particle (27).

(27) Toki Pona coordination (Lang 2014:57, 61)
a. [ma ma.ma li li.li li le.te]
   ma   mama   li   lili   li   lete.
   earth ancestor PARTICLE small PARTICLE cold
   'The fatherland is small and cold.'
b. [o.na li se.li e so.we.li e pan]
   ona li   seli e   soweli e   pan.
   3   PARTICLE fire ACC animal ACC cereal
   'She cooks the hares and some rice.'
c. [mi ku.te e mi.je a.nu me.li]
   mi kute   e   mije anu meli.
   I   hear   ACC man   or   woman
   'I hear a man or a woman.'

> **Your Turn**
>
> a. Which of the coordinating strategies above do you consider most interesting, and why?
> b. Indicate whether juxtaposition, syndetic or bisyndetic coordination would be a good fit in the following scenarios:
>   - An alien conlang spoken on a different planet.
>   - A conlang emphasizing conciseness.
>   - A conlang emphasizing preciseness.

13.3 Subordination

Subordination involves a **main clause** and one or more dependent clauses. As we mentioned earlier, main and dependent clauses might have different

13.3 Subordination

word order. They can also differ in other ways, as we will see in this section. Subordinate clauses can be distinguished according to their function in the sentence: they can be **nominal**, **adjectival** or **adverbial**. We discuss each type in more detail below.

13.3.1 Nominal Clauses

Nominal (or **complement**) **clauses** function like NPs; as such, they can be the subject or direct object in a sentence. **Nominal clauses** are often introduced by subordinating conjunctions known as **complementizers** (COMP). Examples from English are given in (28).

(28) Nominal clauses in English
    a. [< That the climate is changing > is so obvious!]
    b. [It is clear < that Agatha loves him >.]
    c. [I would say < that this is a spaceship. >]
    d. [Charlotte asked George <if he would go to the party. >]
    e. [Charlotte doesn't know < whether George is going. >]

Examples (28a, b) have nominal clauses as subjects; both are introduced by conjunction *that*. In (28b), the subject nominal clause appears post-verbally. Nominal clauses tend to occur sentence-finally since they are long constituents; this is a general tendency in natlangs. Examples (28c–e) have nominal clauses as direct objects. Note that different complementizers introduce object-dependent clauses depending on the verb type (28d, e) and even whether the main verb is affirmative or negative (28d, e). A similar distinction is found in Spanish (29).

(29) Spanish object nominal clauses
    a. [Sé   < que es   una   nave espacial >.]
        know.1SG.PRS   that be.3SG.PRS INDEF.F   ship.from.space
        'I know that (it) is a spaceship.'
    b. [No sé   < si es   una   nave espacial>.]
        NEG know.1SG.PRS if   be.3SG.PRS INDEF.F   from.space
        'I don't know if (it) is a spaceship.'

Complementizers are sometimes not present; for example, in English it is common to omit *that* in object nominal clauses: *I would say (that) this is a spaceship*. This is also the case in Mualang (30).

(30) Apposition in Mualang (from Tija 2007:274)
    [ku   ndinga   < ia   udah   datay >.]
    1SG   hear   3SG   PFV   come
    'I heard (that) he has come.'

Examples (28–30) above involve nominal clauses with **finite verbs**, that is, verbs which have overt verbal morphology such as tense, aspect or agreement. **Dependent clauses** might involve **non-finite verbs**. This is the case in English when the main and nominal share the same subject (31a), or when the meaning conveyed is general (31b), for example. Similar examples occur in Italian (32); unlike in English, the non-finite clause is introduced by the preposition *di* 'of'. Note that 'she' in (32) refers to 'Chiara.'

(31) English: non-finite nominal clauses
   a. [I can't stand < losing you >].   (The Police)
   b. [< Breaking up > is hard to do].   (Neil Sedaka)

(32) Italian: non-finite nominal clauses
   [Chiara dic-e   < di   non   amare >].
   Chiara say-3SG.PRS   of   NEG   love
   'Chiara says she doesn't love.'

13.3.2 Adjectival Clauses

Adjectival or **relative clauses** modify nouns. They are usually introduced by **relativizers** (REL), which can be of two types: (i) complementizers (33a, b), or (ii) **relative pronouns** (33c, d). The latter introduces the relative clause and fulfills a role (such as subject or object) within the dependent clause. For example, in (33c), the relative pronoun 'which' is the object of the dependent verb 'loved,' and in (33d), 'who' is the subject of the dependent verb 'comes.' The nominal element modified by the relative clause is known as the **antecedent**; it is underlined below.

(33) English: relative clauses
   a. [I played the videogame < (that) you recommended >].
   b. [She met the influencer < (that) everyone is tweeting about >].
   c. [Ishiguro's new book, <which I absolutely loved>, is very futuristic].
   d. [The new diver, < who comes from Ecuador >, is incredibly skilled.]

Relative clauses can be **restrictive** (i.e., they narrow the referent; 33a, b), or **non-restrictive** (i.e, they add information; 33c, d). In English, restrictive relative clauses are optionally introduced by complementizer *that*, while non-restrictive adjective clauses are introduced by relative pronouns *which* if the antecedent is inanimate, and *who* if it is animate. This is not typical crosslinguistically; often natlangs employ the same relativizer in both types of relative clauses, regardless of animacy.

Relativizers can also be affixes, as in (34, 35) for Basque and Luganda. In addition, some natlangs lack overt relativizers, as in Alamblak (36). Note that the glosses REL and AUX in these examples refer to relativizer and auxiliary verb, respectively.

(34) Luganda: relativizer prefix (Payne 2006:303)
[omusaj:a   < omukazi   gwe-ya-kuba>]
man   woman   REL-she-hit
'The man that the woman hit.'

(35) Basque: relativizer suffix (from Hualde & Ortiz de Urbina 2003:764)
Pello-k   ekarri   du-en   diru-a   galdu   dut
Peter-ERG   bring   AUX-REL   money-DEF   lose   AUX
'I lost the money Peter brought.'

(36) Alamblak: No overt relativizer (from Bruce 1984:109)
[< ni   hik-r-fə >   yima-r]
2SG   follow-IRR-REC.PST   person-3SG.M
'A man (who) would have followed you.'

Relative clauses can occur after the noun they modify (as in English, Spanish or Luganda) or before (as in Alamblak and Basque); often this is connected to the relative order of nouns and adjectives. But as we saw above for nominal clauses, relative clauses tend to be placed sentence-finally since they are long constituents.

Like nominal clauses, relative clauses can include non-finite verbs. Examples from English involving gerunds are given below.

(37) English non-finite relative clauses
   a. The lady < holding the door > was Lyra's mom.
   b. One night I found my daughter < sleeping under the bed >.

It is important to note that not all natlangs allow relative clauses or relativize all types of nominal constituents. For example, natlangs might only relativize subjects, or not permit relative clauses for indirect objects.

13.3.3 Adverbial Clauses

Adverbial clauses are dependent clauses that function as adverbs. They can convey many different meanings, including location (38a), time (38b–d), manner (38e, f), purpose (38g), cause (38h), consequence (38i) and condition (38 j, k).

(38) English: adverbial clauses
   a. [There's a shoulder < where death comes to cry >] (Leonard Cohen)
   b. [< When you're unemployed >, there's no vacation.] (Flight of the Conchords)

c. [I'm gonna ride < 'til I can't no more >.] (Lil Nas X)
d. [<Since you've been gone> I can breathe for the first time.] (Kelly Clarkson)
e. [< As I told you earlier >, I lost Quiche Lorreine.]
f. [She acts < like she doesn't know>.]
g. [I went to the corner < just to ease my pain >.] (Ian & Sylvia)
h. [I can't buy a new car < because I'm saving for a house>.]
i. [We'll be on break next week, < therefore I won't be answering emails>.]
j. [Come with me < if you want to live >.] (from *Terminator*)
k. [< If you want him >, come and claim him.] (from *Lord of the Rings*)

In English, adverbial clauses can occur before the main verb (38b, d, e, k) or after (38a, c, f– j). In other languages they are positionally restricted; for example, in Korean they always precede the verb (39).

(39) Korean: preverbal adverbial clauses (from Thompson et al. 2007:240)
[< kwail-ul   sa-le>   kakey-ey   katta]
fruit-ACC   buy-to   store-at   went
'I went to the store to buy fruit.'

Adverbial clauses are typically introduced by conjunctions, most often clause-initial, as in English. In OV languages, adverbial clauses involve conjunctions in clause-final position, as shown for Japanese in (40).

(40) Japanese: adverbial clauses (adapted from Thompson et al. 2007:238)
[<ame ga   agaru to>,   Gon wa hotto ʃite   ana kara haidemaʃita]
rain   NOM stop   when Gon TOP relief performing   hole from snuck.out
'When the rain stopped, Gon got relieved and came out of the hole.'

In some natlangs, adverbial clauses have clause-internal conjunctions, as in Nkore-Kiga (41). Adverbial clauses can also be introduced by suffixes, as in Korean (39) or Basque (42). They do not appear to be introduced by prefixes in any natlang.

(41) Nkore-Kiga: adverbial clauses (adapted from Dryer 2013e)
[wa-kami   obu   y-a:-tu:riza   enjojo]
Mr.-Rabbit   when   3SG-HOD-challenge   elephant
'When Mr. Rabbit challenged the elephant.'

(42) Basque: temporal adverbial clauses
[<nahi duzu-nean>   hondartsa-ra joan-go gara.]
want   AUX.2SG.ERG.3SG.ABS-when   beach-ALL   go-FUT AUX.1PL.ABS
'We'll go to the beach when you want.'

13.3.4 Subordination in Conlanging

This section focuses on Láadan subordination, which is well described. Nominal clauses involve the subordinating suffix -hé [hɛ́] for statements (43a) or -hée [hɛ́.ɛ] for questions (43b); both are added to the last element of the dependent clause. Láadan relative clauses involve the clause-final relativizer suffix -háa [há.a] (44).

(43) Láadan: nominal clauses (from Elgin et al. 2020:69)
    a. [bí.ɪ lɪθ lɛ ɹa.ho.wa la.lɪ.hɛ́ wa]
        [Bíi   lith   le   < rahowa   lali-hé >   wa].
        DEC   think   1SG   be.cold   rain-COMP   DIR.EV
        'I think that the rain is cold.'
    b. [bí.ɪ lo.θɛl ɹa lɛ ɹa.ho.wa la.lɪ.hɛ́.ɛ wa]
        [Bíi   lothel   ra   le   < rahowa   lali-hée >   wa].
        DEC   know   NEG   I   be.cold   rain-COMP   DIR.EV
        'I don't know whether the rain is cold.'

(44) Láadan: adjectival clauses (from Elgin et al. 2020:73)
    [bí.ɪ dom lɛ hal wɪ.θɛ.há.a wá]
    [Bíi   dom   le   < hal   withe-háa >   wa].
    DEC   remember 1SG   work woman-REL   DIR.EV
    'I remember the woman that works.'

Láadan adverbial clauses are introduced by clause-initial conjunctions. *Widahath* [wɪ.da.haθ] 'when,' *widahoth* [wɪ.da.hoθ] 'where,' *widahuth* [wɪ.da.huθ] 'why' and *widaweth* [wɪ.da.wɛθ] 'how' are compounds from the verb *wida* [wɪ.da] 'carry' plus the words for time (*hath* [haθ]), place (*hoth* [hoθ]), reason (*huth* [huθ]) and way (*weth* [wɛθ]), respectively. Adverbial clauses can be preverbal or postverbal.

Láadan adverbial clauses indicating manner, cause and purpose are conveyed with subordinating affixes on the dependent verb, which is nominalized. These affixes are -*nal* [nal] 'manner', -*wan* [wan] 'purpose' and -*wáan* [wá.an] 'cause,' respectively. One example is given in (45); the gloss PRP stands for purposive case.

(45) Láadan: Adverbial clauses indicating purpose (from Elgin et al. 2020:59)
    [bí.ɪ ɛ.ɹil ʃá.ad bɛ bɛ.θɛ.dɪ ha.lɛ.wan wá.a]
    [Bíi   eril   sháad   be   beth-edi   < hale-wan>   wáa.]
    DEC   PST   go   3SG   home-ALL   work-PRP   ASSUM.EV
    'She went home in order to work.'

13.4 Conlanging Practice: Dependent Clauses in Toki Pona

Linguists are still analyzing complex sentences in the Ur languages. While they figure them out, let's consider complex sentences in Toki Pona instead. For each of the sentences in (46)–(49), indicate:

- The main and dependent clauses (using square and angle brackets, respectively).
- How subordination is expressed (such as using conjunctions, affixes, juxtaposition or rephrasing).

Note that in Toki Pona, the particle *la* separates context from main sentence and allows two sentences to be linked together.

(46) Toki Pona: object nominal clauses (adapted from Lang 2014:58)
[mi wi.le e ni jan me.la.ni li]
mi	wile	e	ni:	jan	Melani	li
1	want	ACC	this	person	Mélanie	PARTICLE

kama	tawa	tomo	mi.
come	toward	house	1

'I want the following: Melanie will come to my home'
('I want Melanie to visit me.')

(47) Toki Pona: relative clauses (adapted from Lang 2014:80)
[si.na so.na e to.ki wan ta.so la si.na]
sina	sona	e	toki	wan	taso,	la	sina
2	know	ACC	language	one	only	PARTICLE	2

[so.na a.la e to.ki ni]
sona	ala	e	toki	ni.
know	NEG	ACC	language	that

'The person who knows only one language does not truly know that language.' (from Goethe)

(48) Toki Pona: adverbial clause indicating condition (adapted from Lang 2014:75)
[si.na po.na e i.ke la si.na ka.ma jo e i.ke]
sina	pona	e	ike,	la	sina	kama	jo	e	ike.
2	give	ACC	bad	then	2	become	carry	ACC	bad

'If you give evil, you will receive evil.'

(49) Toki Pona: adverbial clause indicating time (adapted from Lang 2014:74)
[mi po.na e a.le mi la mi po.na e mi]

mi	pona	e	ale	mi,	la	mi	pona	e	mi.
1	good	ACC	all	1	then	1	good	ACC	1

'When I improve all areas of my life, I improve myself.'

13.5 Complex Sentences in Muq

Conjunction in muq is expressed via juxtaposition (50a). Emphatic conjunction is conveyed with the conjunction [ŋe] 'both' placed after the last coordinated element (50b).

(50) Conjunctive coordination in the Salt language
   a. *eza-m-a*   *yiam-m-a*
      swim-IMPF-REC.FUT   rest-IMPF-REC.FUT
      '(I) will be swimming and resting.'
   b. *eza-m-a*   *yiam-m-a*   *ŋe*
      swim-IMPG-REC.FUT   rest-IMPF-REC.FUT   both
      '(I) will be both swimming and resting.'

Disjunction is expressed with *ya* 'or'; and adversative coordination with *də* 'but'; both conjunctions precede the final element combined (51).

(51) Disjunctive and adversative coordination in the Salt language
   a. *eza-m-a*   *ya*   *yiam-m-a*
      swim-IMPF-REC.FUT   or   rest-IMPF-REC.FUT
      '(I) will be swimming or resting.'
   b. *eza-m-a*   *də*   *'ɘ-yiam-m-a*
      swim-IMPF-REC.FUT   but   NEG-rest-IMPF-REC.FUT
      '(I) will be swimming but not resting.'

Nominal clauses lack relativizers; consistent with the VOS word order, they are placed sentence-finally if they function as the subject, and immediately after the verb if they are the object. Restrictive and non-restrictive adjectival clauses involve the relativizer prefix [ˈziʁ-] on the first word of the relative clause.

Adverbial conjunctions have the same form as the corresponding interrogative words introduced in Chapter 11. The most frequent are listed in Table 13.1. Examples of adverbial clauses are given in (52).

Table 13.1 Salt language: subordinate conjunctions			
['ɑ.zos]	'when'	['ei.zos]	'where, where to'
['i.zos]	'because'	['ʁɑ.zos]	'how, the manner in which'
['ɬi.zos]	'to, in order to'		

(52) Adverbial clauses in muq
    a. ɘ-mæk-m   ei.zos   mistin-m-æ   'sæmʎu   ɬi-xa
       NEG-know-PFV where   travel-PFV-REC.PST archer   DET-AN
       '(I) don't know where the archer traveled to.'
    b. uʀ   'mistin-m-æ   'nia   'ɬizos tət 'penk-m-æ   'kust-je
       QUOT.EV travel-PFV-REC.PST mother to   gather-PFV-REC.PST salt-PAU
       'They say that Mother traveled to collect some salt.'

In the muq origin text, there are many instances of conjunctive coordination; two examples are given in (53). There is also one example of a temporal adverbial clause (54).

(53) Juxtaposition in the muq fictional text
    a. ['çis-s-i   'çis-s-i   'ŋuç-na]
       burn-PFV-REM.PST burn-PFV-REM.PST day-PL
       'It burned and burned for many days.'
    b. ['ʁa.li-s-i   'taʁ-s-i   'ʁouq-na 'ɲa.çen ko-xa]
       scream-PFV-REM.PST spew-PFV-REM.PST fire-PL   mountain DEF.INAN-SG
       'Then the mountain screamed and spewed much fire.'

(54) Temporal adverbial clause in the muq fictional text
    ['a.zos 'ɬam.xa-s-i   çem   ko-xa   'ou.sei-s-i]
    when dry.up-PFV-REM.PST island DEF.INAN-SG transform-PFV-REM.PST
    'When it stopped burning, the island had transformed.'

13.6 Guide to Developing Coordination and Subordination

- Indicate whether coordination in your conlang includes juxtaposition, syndetic coordination and/or bisyndetic coordination.
  - For juxtaposition, indicate if this is the default strategy or if it occurs in specific contexts. Provide glossed examples.
  - For syndetic coordination, list the coordinators. Are they conjunctions or affixes? Where are they placed? Provide glossed examples.
  - For bisyndetic coordination, list the coordinators used. Indicate whether they are conjunctions or affixes and their specific placement.

Does bisyndetic coordination indicate emphasis? Provide glossed examples.
- Indicate how your conlang conveys complement clauses for subjects and/or direct objects.
  - Do complement clauses precede or follow the verb? (Consider word order and the general tendency for long constituents to occur sentence-finally.)
  - Do complement clauses include overt complementizers? If so, list them, and indicate whether they are conjunctions or affixes, and their placement.
  - Provide glossed examples of subject and direct object complement clauses.
- Indicate how your conlang expresses relative clauses. Are they introduced by affixes or relativizers?
  - Do relative clauses precede or follow the head noun? (Consider the order between noun and adjectives in your conlang, and the tendency for long constituents to be sentence-final.)
  - Are restrictive and non-restrictive clauses conveyed similarly?
  - Provide glossed examples.
- Indicate how your conlang expresses adverbial clauses. Are they introduced via conjunctions or via affixes?
  - Indicate the position of adverbial clauses in the sentence.
  - Will adverbial and main clauses differ in mood, word order or other characteristics?
  - Provide glossed examples of sentences with adverbial clauses expressing time, location, manner and purpose.

To Learn More

Haspelmath (2007) is a detailed introduction to coordination in natlangs. For coordination, see Stassen (2013), and for nominal and clausal conjunction, Haspelmath (2013). Thompson et al. (2007) provides a great introduction to adverbial clauses, and Dryer (2013e) is a good summary of adverbial subordination across languages. Campos (1993) is a great, classic introduction to complex sentences in Spanish. Other sources mentioned in this chapter are listed at the end of this book.

14 Writing Systems

While a writing system is not essential for a conlang (not all natlangs have writing systems, after all), it can certainly enrich the fictional world associated with it. In many videogames, for example, constructed scripts (conscripts) are incorporated to make gaming more immersive. In addition, developing an original writing system can provide you with additional insights on the phonological structure of your conlang. This chapter previews the types of writing systems attested in natlangs, paying specific attention to how they fit the structure of the language. This chapter also introduces some noteworthy conscripts and provides you with a blueprint that will help you to design an original conscript for your conlang.

Section 14.1 introduces writing and previews writing systems, which are elaborated on in Sections 14.2 (logographic scripts) and 14.3 (phonographic scripts). Section 14.4 provides a short account of how writing originated. Section 14.5 introduces some notable constructed writing systems (conscripts), and Section 14.6 discusses the connection between writing, the fictional world, and the phonological and morphological structure of your conlang. Finally, Section 14.7 provides conscript practice, Section 14.8 introduces the muq writing system and Section 14.9 outlines the main steps in designing an invented script.

Key Words

- Boustrophedon
- Constructed scripts (conscripts or neographies)
- Cuneiform
- Glyph style and shape
- Graphemes
  - Characters (hanzi)
    - Radical
    - Phonetic determinative
  - Hieratic
  - Hieroglyph

Logogram (glyph, character)
Phonogram
Pre-writing
   Meaning extension
   Rebus principle
Semasiograph (ideograph)
Strokes
Writing (orthography)
Writing system
   Logographic (logo-syllabic)
   Logo-syllabary
   Mixed systems
   Phonographic
     Abjad (consonantal script)
     Abugida (alpha-syllabary)
     Alphabet
     Syllabary
   Semantic (semasiographic)

Before We Begin

- How many writing systems do you know of? Which is your favorite? Why?
- Have you ever made up a writing system? If so, how did you go about it?
- Do any of your favorite books, movies and/or videogames feature invented scripts? How do they enrich the fictional world and/or its experience?

14.1 What Is Writing?

Writing (or **orthography**) is the representation of language by graphic signs or symbols. Writing originated over 5,000 years ago; its appearance marks the boundary between prehistory and history. Writing and literacy facilitate the development of complex societies and the recording of an enormous amount of information (which is obvious from big library collections or the internet). **Writing systems** are closely connected to the communicative needs of the speakers and to the phonology and/or morphology of the language(s) they represent. Like language more generally, writing systems evolve and can be influenced by other writing systems and cultures. In fact, it is considered that writing arose independently only three times: first in Mesopotamia, then in China and later in Central America. An undeciphered script found in the Indus Valley, probably related to a Dravidian language, might provide evidence for a fourth independent invention of writing. However, writing is not crucial for communication. Many languages spoken in the past lacked writing; one example is the Kingdom of Kush (corresponding to modern Sudan). Hundreds of natlangs nowadays lack writing too.

The symbols used in a writing system are called **graphemes**. They can be visible, as the letters of the Latin alphabet, or tactile, as in the Braille system of writing and reading by touch. Depending on the units encoded, we can distinguish five main types of writing systems in natlangs (1). Note that the last four are **phonographic** since they represent sounds or sound combinations; most writing systems in use today are of this type.

(1) Natlang writing systems
- a. **Logo-syllabaries** convey words or morphemes. Examples include Ancient Chinese, Cuneiform and Mayan scripts.
- b. **Syllabaries** encode syllables via syllabograms. One example is the Cherokee script.
- c. **Abugidas (alpha-syllabaries)** have graphemes representing a consonant plus a (default) vowel, as in the Devanagari script used to write Hindi and other natlangs.
- d. **Abjads (consonantal scripts)** represent consonants, as in the Hebrew and Arabic scripts.
- e. **Alphabets** encode both consonants and vowels, as in the Greek or Latin scripts.

Semantic writing systems are those where graphemes represent units of meaning. They do not exist in natlangs, but are sometimes found in conscripts; examples are Blissymbolics and Heptapod B, to which we come back to in Section 14.5.

14.2 Logo-Syllabaries

In **logographic (logo-syllabic)** scripts, **logograms** (also referred to as **logographs, glyphs** or **characters**) represent words or morphemes. Most writing systems include a small number of logographs even if they are primarily phonographic. For example, English and other natlangs use number logograms like '7' or '9' in addition to additional ones such as $, & or @.

14.2 Logo-Syllabaries

> **Your Turn**
>
> Can you think of other logograms used in English writing?

Logo-syllabic scripts are best suited for languages with little or no inflectional morphology. Some writing systems began as logo-syllabic but adopted phonographic characteristics with time. Some of the best-known examples of logographic writing are found in **cuneiform** inscriptions from Ancient Mesopotamia; **hieroglyphs** from Ancient Egypt; primitive Chinese **characters**; and the Japanese Kanji script. Let's consider each in turn.

14.2.1 Cuneiform

Cuneiform is the oldest and longest-lasting written script on record: it was used continuously for over 3,000 years (from the fourth millennium BC to the first millennium BC). Cuneiform was used to write Sumerian and Akkadian in ancient Mesopotamia. It was typically written with reeds on soft clay tablets hardened in the sun or baked in an oven. Cuneiform symbols look triangular; their shape is formed of one to twelve wedges. This is the reason why this writing system is named 'Cuneiform' (which means 'wedge shaped'). In its earlier form, Cuneiform comprised 600 to 1,000 glyphs representing different words or parts of words.

Cuneiform was first and primarily used for accounting purposes, and eventually for literary and religious texts as well. Most Sumerian words were monosyllabic, and there were many homophones. Cuneiform used some symbols to convey words with different meanings but similar pronunciations. One example often cited is the use of the symbol for 'arrow' ([ti] in Sumerian) to write the word for 'life' (also pronounced [ti]).

Throughout time, the number of logograms in Cuneiform was greatly reduced while the number of graphemes for syllables increased. Eventually Cuneiform fell out of use and was replaced by Aramaic alphabetic writing.

14.2.2 Egyptian Hieroglyphs

Cuneiform might have served as inspiration for the development of Egyptian **hieroglyphs** although there is no visual similarity between the symbols used in both scripts. Egyptian hieroglyphs were originally logographic, but with time they could be read as logographs or **phonograms**. To distinguish between the two, logograms were marked with a vertical line. One interesting characteristic of Egyptian phonograms is that they represent consonants rather than syllables. Another remarkable aspect of this script is that it had two styles: (i) formal or monumental, separating strokes and highly pictorial, and (ii) cursive, for writing on papyrus; the latter is known as **hieratic**.

14.2.3 Primitive Chinese Script

Although primitive Chinese script (which developed around 1,000 BC) was logo-syllabic, Modern Chinese is only logographic in part. A small number of characters (hanzi) are logograms, but 99 percent comprise both a **radical** (semantic component), which provides a clue to the meaning of the character, and a **phonetic determinative** that indicates how the character is pronounced. Modern Chinese script includes about 200 **radicals** and 4,000 **phonetic determinatives**.

The Chinese writing system has over 50,000 characters, although 'only' 1,000 of them are present in 90 percent of non-technical writings, and 'only' about 5,000 are needed by most people. Chinese has little inflectional morphology, which makes a (partially) logo-syllabic system a good fit. Chinese writing was tried for both Korean and Japanese, but since both languages are more inflectional, it did not work as well, and other writing strategies were eventually used.

14.2.4 Japanese Kanji Script

Japanese probably has the most complex writing system currently in use today, since it involves three different scripts: Kanji, Katakana and Hiragana. Kanji, derived from Chinese characters, is logo-syllabic and it's used to write morphemes. Hiragana and Katakana are syllabic; Hiragana is employed to write morphological endings, and Katakana to convey foreign words and onomatopoeia.

> **Your Turn**
>
> What are the advantages and disadvantages of having multiple scripts to write one language?

14.3 Phonographic Systems

Graphemes in phonographic systems can convey syllables or sounds. Let's consider each of them in turn.

14.3.1 Syllabaries

Syllabaries use distinct graphemes for syllables, with no graphic similarity across phonetically similar syllables. For example, the Cherokee syllabary represents the syllables [la], [lo] and [lu] as 'W', 'G' and 'M,' respectively.

14.3 Phonographic Systems

The number of syllabograms depends on the number of contrastive consonants and vowels in a language and their possible combinations. For example, the Ethiopian syllabary has 182 syllabograms, Hiragana and Katakana have 48 syllabograms each, and Old Persian had 36.

The history behind the Cherokee syllabary is noteworthy. It was invented by Sequoyah in the first part of the nineteenth century after he noticed that people could communicate in English by reading and writing. Sequoyah devised a writing system for the Cherokee language that adopted some English graphemes and created additional ones. Sequoyah introduced his script to the Cherokee community around 1819. At first, it was considered witchcraft, but eventually the Cherokee decided to adopt it.

The Cherokee syllabary is a great fit to write the Cherokee language, since the language lacks codas. It consists of 86 syllabograms (Figure 14.1). Note that the first row of the syllabary lists symbols for vowels (which can be syllables in Cherokee). Although some graphemes are borrowed from English (such 'A', 'C' or 'R'), their phonetic value in Cherokee is unrelated.

> **Your Turn**
>
> Which Cherokee syllabograms in Figure 14.1 are based on graphemes from the English alphabet?

Another fascinating syllabary is Nüshu, a script used primarily by Chinese women in the Jiang Yong Prefecture of the Hunan Province in China from the sixteenth to the twentieth century. Nüshu (translated as 'women's

a			e			i			o		u		v [ə̃]	
D a			R e			T i			Ꮼ o		O u		i v	
Ꮜ ga	Ꮝ ka		Ꮄ ge			Ꮩ gi			A go		J gu		E gv	
Ꮳ ha			Ꮶ he			Ꮀ hi			Ꮂ ho		Γ hu		Ꮧ hv	
W la			Ꮷ le			P li			G lo		M lu		Ꮭ lv	
Ꮥ ma			Ꮋ me			H mi			Ꮭ mo		Ꮍ mu			
Θ na	Ꮏ hna	G nah	Ꮑ ne			h ni			Z no		Ꮕ nu		Ꮣ nv	
Ꮖ qua			Ꮝ que			Ꮗ qui			Ꮾ quo		Ꮙ quu		Ꮛ quv	
Ꮳ s	Ꮜ sa		4 se			Ꮃ si			Ꮀ so		Ꮒ su		R sv	
Ꮤ da	W ta		S de	Ꮷ te		Ꭰ di	Ꭱ ti		V do		S du		Ꭳ dv	
Ꮪ dla	Ꮭ tla		L tle			C tli			Ꮧ tlo		Ꮿ tlu		P tlv	
G tsa			V tse			Ꮳ tsi			K tso		Ꮣ tsu		Ꮢ tsv	
Ꮆ wa			Ꮩ we			Ꮝ wi			Ꮿ wo		9 wu		6 wv	
Ꮿ ya			Ꮾ ye			Ꮑ yi			Ꮩ yo		G yu		B yv	

Figure 14.1 Cherokee syllabary.

https://commons.wikimedia.org/wiki/File:Cherokee_Syllabary.svg#/media/File:Cherokee_Syllabary.svg writing' or 'women's script' in Chinese; cf. 'nashu' or 'men's writing,' referring to Standard Chinese characters) appears to be the world's only script created and used primarily by women. Nüshu was discovered in the late twentieth century. Nüshu survived despite a prohibition on local written languages, and although its use has declined, local and national authorities in China are working to revive it.

Nüshu was used and transmitted by village women, most of them illiterate in Chinese character script. It was used to write poems, ballads, stories and letters on books and on paper fans, and embroidered into belts, clothes and handkerchiefs. Nüshu was taught to young girls by their mothers and aunts, frequently by singing. When women were married and had to leave their hometown, Nüshu allowed them to be in touch with and convey private information to female friends and family members. Although it is commonly thought that Nüshu was a secret script for women only, some men were taught to read it, and texts written in Nüshu were designed to be chanted or sung. This means that the script could not be that secret. Few Nüshu manuscripts have survived, mainly because most were destroyed or buried with their owners so they could enjoy their favorite poems in the afterlife.

Nüshu has 600–1,000 characters; it is estimated that about 80 percent are adaptations of square Chinese characters, often by simplifying or italicizing them. The rest appear to have been invented. Nüshu characters are thick and elongated and look rhomboid. Traditionally, they were embroidered into cloth or written in ink with a sharpened stylus made of bamboo. Unlike Chinese Hanzi, Nüshu script is fully phonetic; characters convey full syllables of the local Chinese dialect (Chengguan Tuhua), including tones. Figure 14.2 shows how 'Nüshu' is written in Nüshu script.

Figure 14.2 Nüshu written in the Nüshu script. Public domain.
https://commons.wikimedia.org/wiki/File:Nu_shu.svg

14.3.2 Abugidas

Abugidas also represent syllables, but unlike syllabaries, they show graphical similarity across phonetically similar syllables. Specifically, syllables that begin with the same consonant have a constant shape. Syllable glyphs involve an 'inherent' or default vowel (often [a]); other vowels are indicated with diacritics. Abugidas vary in how they represent codas; options include adding a diacritic to indicate that the default vowel is not pronounced, writing the glyph with the inherent vowel even if not pronounced, or not writing the coda consonant at all.

Abugidas arose in India in the third century BC. A well-known abugida script is Devanagari, used to write Sanskrit, Hindi, Marathi and Nepali, among other languages. Devanagari glyphs are characterized by a horizontal line at the top ('shirorekha'). Base syllables involve the inherent vowel [a]. Other vowels are conveyed by diacritics placed around the basic glyph. The virama symbol [्] ('halant') is used to indicate that the base vowel is not pronounced. Examples of Devanagari glyphs for syllables beginning with /p/ and /t/ are shown in (2).

(2)　　Sample Devanagari glyphs
　　　a. [pa]　　[pa:]　　[pi]　　[pi:]　　[pu]　　[pu:]　　[p]
　　　　　प　　　पा　　　पि　　　पी　　　पु　　　पू　　　प्
　　　b. [ta]　　[ta:]　　[ti]　　[ti:]　　[tu]　　[tu:]　　[t]
　　　　　त　　　ता　　　ति　　　ती　　　तु　　　तू　　　त्

> **Your Turn**
>
> Identify the diacritics for /a/, /i/, /u/, and for /a:/, /i:/, /u:/ in (2).

14.3.3 Abjads

Abjads represent consonants only. They originated in Egypt and from there spread to other cultures. Languages written in abjad scripts include Hebrew, Arabic and Aramaic. The Arabic abjad is the most widely used consonantal script today, although it is not completely consonantal, as we will see.

Both the Hebrew and Arabic abjads are written from right to left. The Hebrew abjad has twenty-two consonant graphemes. Vowel diacritics are used in biblical texts, texts for children or Hebrew learners, and in some poetry; they constitute points or lines, usually written under the preceding consonant. Examples of Hebrew glyphs are given in (3).

(3)　　Sample Hebrew glyphs
　　　　a. [p] פ　　　[p] פַ　　　[b] ב　　　[b] בַ
　　　　b. [t] ת　　　[te] תֶ　　　[d] ד　　　[de] דֶ

The Arabic consonantal script has twenty-eight consonant graphemes, although three of them ('alif ا, 'waw' و, and 'ya' ي) can also be read word-medially or finally as the long vowels /aː iː uː/, respectively. Short vowels can be indicated with lines or points above or below the consonant they follow. There is also a diacritic ('šadda') that indicates long consonants. Some Arabic graphemes are given in (4).

(4) Sample Arabic glyphs (in isolation)
    a. [d] د   [t] ت   [b] ب
    b. [m] م   [n] ن   [l] ل

One interesting aspect of the Arabic script is that each consonantal grapheme has four different variants depending on whether the consonant occurs in isolation, or in the initial, middle or final position in a writing group. This might appear unusual, but consider that many written scripts, including the Latin alphabet, use different variants for capitalized and lowercase letters. However, other scripts, including Devanagari, do not.

14.3.4 Alphabets

Alphabets have graphemes for both consonants and vowels. Historically, alphabets developed from abjads; the ancient Greek adopted the Egyptian abjad and repurposed some of its graphemes to represent vowels. The Etruscans and then the Romans adapted the Greek alphabet, and now many natlangs have alphabetic scripts based on the Latin alphabet.

Alphabetic scripts inspired by or derived from the Greek one include the Georgian, Armenian and Cyrillic alphabets. The Georgian alphabet has an almost perfect correspondence between phonemes and graphemes; in comparison, the version of the Roman alphabet for English has twenty-six graphemes – perhaps a better alphabet would include up to forty.

Two interesting alphabetic systems are Futhark and Ogham; both appear to have been influenced by the Latin alphabet. Futhark (ᚠᚢᚦᚨᚱᚲ) is a runic alphabet which originated in Southern Europe and was carried north by Germanic tribes. Its oldest version ('Elder' or Germanic Futhark) has twenty-four runes. Elder Futhark is reproduced in (5), organized according to segment type (vowels, stops, fricatives, nasals and oral sonorants). The oldest Futhark inscription is from the first century AD, but most Futhark inscriptions date from the eleventh century. Runic alphabets tend to be associated with magic and mysticism, and have inspired many conscripts, including J. R. R. Tolkien's.

(5) Elder Futhark runes (organized according to segment type)
    a. [a] ᚨ   [æ] ᛇ   [e] ᛖ   [i] ᛁ   [o] ᛟ   [u] ᚢ
    b. [p] ᛈ   [b] ᛒ   [t] ᛏ   [d] ᛞ   [k] ᚲ   [g] ᚷ

c. [f] ⊵   [θ] ▷   [s] ⋸   [z] Y   [h] H
d. [m] M   [n] ┼   [ŋ] ◇
e. [l] ⌈   [r] R   [j] ⋄   [w] ⊵

Ogham was used by Celts of Britain and Ireland to write Old Irish from the fifth to the seventh century AD. Ogham has twenty main graphemes, written as short lines of one–five notches (for vowels) or **strokes** (for consonants). These notches and strokes touch or cross a horizontal line (6). Ogham also has five additional graphemes, mostly used to represent diphthongs in later manuscripts.

(6) The Ogham alphabet

╱	╱╱	╱╱╱	╱╱╱╱	╱╱╱╱╱		╶	╶╶	╶╶╶	╶╶╶╶	╶╶╶╶╶
[m]	[g]	[ŋ]	[z]	[r]		[a]	[o]	[u]	[e]	[i]
╲	╲╲	╲╲╲	╲╲╲╲	╲╲╲╲╲						
[b]	[l]	[f]	[s]	[n]		[h]	[d]	[t]	[k]	[kʷ]
✕	◇	⊔	✕	⊞						
[k]/[e]/[ea]	[oi]	[ia]	[ui]	[ae]						

Ogham graphemes are unusual in their shape; Ogham is also one of the few writing systems read and written vertically from bottom to top. It has been speculated that Ogham might be based on a secret finger language of Druidic priests. Ogham inscriptions are mainly found on boundary markers or gravestones.

Abjads and alphabets usually have fewer graphemes than syllabaries or abugidas; this generalization helps in script decipherment. For example, the Rongorongo script of Easter Island, discovered in 1860 and still undeciphered, has sixty symbols and is thought to be a syllabary or abugida. The reason is that it was used to write the Rapa Nui language, which has ten consonants and five vowels, and a simple (C)V syllable structure; this results in at most fifty-five syllable combinations. It is thought that the five additional Rongorongo glyphs could be phonetic determinatives.

> ### Your Turn
>
> Which writing system discussed so far would be a good fit for:
>
> - A language with few contrastive vowels?
> - A language with many contrastive vowels?
> - A language with simple syllables?
> - A language with complex syllables?

14.3.5 Mixed Systems

Some writing **systems** are **mixed**, that is, they incorporate characteristics of more than one type of writing. Examples include Cuneiform and Egyptian scripts, which involved both logograms and either syllabograms or consonantal graphemes, and Chinese Hanzi, combining logograms and phonograms. This section focuses on three scripts that combine aspects of alphabetic and syllable-based scripts: Korean Hangul, Mandombé and the Iberian script.

Commissioned by King Sejong in 1444, Hangul makes use of fourteen consonantal and ten vocalic graphemes organized into syllable blocks, which can be considered to combine alphabetic and syllabic characteristics. Since the consonants provide an iconic representation of the vocal tract, Hangul can also be analyzed as featural (the vowels represent heaven, earth and man). Many scholars consider Hangul one of the most sophisticated scripts ever devised for natlangs.

> **Your Turn: Hangul**
>
> You can see how consonant and vowel graphemes are combined in Hangul by using a multilingual keyboard such as Lexilogos (www.lexilogos.com/keyboard/korean.htm). For example, my name (Carolina) is written in Hangul as 가 로 리 나. Note that 'l' and 'r' are written with the same grapheme.

The Mandombé script was invented by David Wabeladio Payi in the late twentieth century. In this alphabetic system, the pronunciation changes according to how symbols are rotated (which is rare in natlang scripts). Mandombé has a religious goal: to convey religious texts in writing for the official languages of the Democratic Republic of Congo (i.e., Kikongo, Lingala, Tshiluba and Swahili). Like Hangul, Mandombé is written in syllabic blocks (Figure 14.3).

Figure 14.3 Mandombé in Mandombé script.
Public domain. https://commons.wikimedia.org/wiki/File:Mandombe_in_Mandombe.svg

The Iberian script was used in the Iberian Peninsula, the south of France and the Balearic Islands between the fourth century BC and the second century AD. It features graphemes for each vowel and for most consonants. Syllables beginning with stops are written with syllabograms, which is unusual in natlang scripts (7).

(7) Iberian script (North-East)
    a. Examples of alphabetic graphemes
        Vowels: ᚹ /a/   ᛂ /e/   ᛁ /i/   H /o/   ↑ /u/
        Nasals: ᛉ /m/   ᚱ /n/
    b. Examples of syllabograms
        X /da/~/ta/   ⊗ /de/~/te/   ᛟ /di/~/ti/
        ɯ /do/~/to/   △ /du/~/tu/

14.4 The Development of Writing

Writing is considered to have evolved from **pre-writing**, a way to convey specific information by making certain marks on surfaces. One example of pre-writing is the use of clay tokens for accounting purposes in ancient Mesopotamia. These tokens were enclosed in clay envelopes imprinted with seals featuring geometrical and figural designs. Numerous such tokens and envelopes marked with seals have been found, attesting to its widespread use for administrative purposes.

One remarkable type of writing system, considered pre-writing for a long time, is three-dimensional khipu, used for over 1,000 years by the Incas in the Andes in South America. Khipus were used for accounting and ritual purposes. They consist of knotted, colored string pendants hanging from a top cord. Khipus encode visual and tactile information in the type and color of fibers used for the strings, the type of knot and the direction of the ply, among others. Khipus could indicate how many animals or how much produce was owned, or the amount of labor performed by the members of a community. Different objects could be attached to khipu pendants or the end of the top cord, including dried beans, potatoes, feathers, figurines and clumps of wool. These objects were used iconically to indicate what was being recorded (e.g., ear tips from llamas and vicuñas identified the type of animals, perhaps the specific animals as well). Khipus also encoded the identity of the author (hair, feathers, genealogical trees), or the ritual actors (figurines could stand for ritual beings or spirits in ceremonial khipus or in calendars). Anthropologist Sabine Hyland indicates that khipus could also convey biographies, narratives and poetry, as well as religious myths. She has also discovered a narrative khipu based on phonetic writing, which she is currently deciphering.

Several insights contributed to the development of writing. One of them is **meaning extension**. For example, the symbol 👁 iconically represents the word 'eye.' This meaning can be extended to related concepts, including 'look,' 'see' or 'vision.' Another insight is the **rebus principle**, or sound extension; a symbol can be used to stand for an unrelated concept that sounds like it. For example, the symbol 👁 for 'eye' [ai] can stand for the homophones 'I' or 'aye,' since they sound the same. With time and use, iconic symbols tend to be simplified and thus further removed from their pictographic origin.

14.5 Conscripts

So far we have focused on natlang writing systems. In this section we explore **constructed scripts (conscripts or neographies)**, that is writing systems invented consciously, usually in connection with a conlang, and discuss what aspects to keep in mind when devising a script for your conlang. We consider examples of semantic, logographic and phonetic conscripts in turn.

Both Blissymbolics and Heptapod B are semantic. As we saw in Chapter 1, the main goal of Blyssymbolics was to serve as an international means of written communication and to convey ideas rather than words. Blissymbolics expresses ideas by combining different **semiographs (ideographs)** linearly. Heptapod B, the written language modality of the Heptapods in *Arrival* (2016), is also semantiic since it represents concepts and ideas not tied to a specific language. Heptapod B is written by squirting ink onto a transparent surface (at least in the movie!). Heptapod B features about 100 symbols and thus is not fully developed. These **semiograms** are circular and can be divided into twelve equal segments. Each has a meaningful shape; similar shapes have similar meanings. The thickness of the line denotes inflections, and an attached hook shape indicates a question. The end of this chapter suggests several resources to learn more about this conscript.

Toki Pona is most commonly written using Latin script but can also be conveyed in sitelen pona ('good, simple writing'), a logographic script; it is reproduced in its entirety in Figure 14.4.

In sitelen pona, two logograms can be combined when one is an adjective modifier; this logogram can be written above or inside the modified logogram. Figure 14.5 exemplifies this for sitelen pona.

14.5 Conscripts

Figure 14.4 Toki pona logograms.

Public domain. Sonja Lang, https://creativecommons.org/licenses/by-sa/4.0, via Wikimedia Commons. From Lang (2014: 104–110).

Perhaps the best-known conscripts are Tengwar and Angerthas, invented by J. R. R. Tolkien. While Angerthas is alphabetic and used for carvings in wood or stone, Tengwar can be used as an alphabet or abugida and is better suited for calligraphy with pen or brush. Angerthas graphemes are called cirth [ˈkirθ] (singular 'certh' [ˈkɛrθ]), usually translated as 'runes' because of their similarity to Futhark. Angerthas originated with the Beleriand Sindarin Elves, and later spread to other races, most notably the Dwarves. While

Figure 14.5 Toki Pona: *sitelen pona* 'good, simple writing,' in sitelen pona.

Public domain. Sonja Lang, via Wikimedia Commons. https://en.m.wikipedia.org/wiki/Sitelen_Pona#/media/File%3ASitelen_Pona.svg

Figure 14.6 Cirth /kirθ/ 'runes' in Angerthas script (Daeron mode).

Public domain. https://en.wikipedia.org/wiki/Cirth#/media/File:Cirth_word.png

the Dwarves of Moria used a modified runic alphabet called Angerthas Moria, the Dwarves of the Lonely Mountain used a version called the Mode of Erebor. Examples of Dwarf-runes are seen on Balin's tomb and the Book of Mazarbul in *The Lord of the Rings*. Figure 14.6 provides one example of Sindarin written using Angerthas in the mode of Daeron, before the end of the first age.

Tengwar ('letters' in Quenya) were invented by Fëanor, the most skilled craftsman of the Noldorin Elves. They were originally used for Quenya. Examples of Tengwar can be found in the inscriptions on the West-gate of Moria and in the One Ring – the latter convey Mordor's Black Speech. Tengwar was also adopted by other Elvish and non-Elvish peoples in Middle Earth.

Tengwar has twenty-four primary graphemes, formed by a stem (*telco*) and one or more bows (*lúva*). Graphemes are arranged in a grid of four columns (*témar* 'series') and six rows (*tyeller* 'grades'). Depending on the phonological inventory of the language, these columns and rows apply to

Figure 14.7 Tengwar /t ɛ ᵑgʷ a r/ 'letters' in Tengwar script.
Public domain. https://commons.wikimedia.org/wiki/File:Tengwar.svg

different sets of sounds. Diacritical marks (*tehtar* 'signs') indicate geminate consonants, preceding nasals or a following semivowel. They can also be used to indicate vowels. One example of Tengwar writing is given in Figure 14.7; note that the middle grapheme corresponds to the prenasalized labialized voiced velar /ᵑgʷ/, and that vowels are indicated by diacritics (*tehtar*) above the preceding onset consonant.

14.6 How to Design a Conscript

Now that we know the basics of writing systems, we can begin to develop a conscript. Although you can find inspiration in existing scripts, yours should be original and showcase your creativity. Unlike other aspects of language, writing systems are consciously devised by an individual or a group of people. Writing systems are efficient at first; as time goes by, their efficiency decreases because of the constant evolution of language. Think, for example, of the silent letters in English orthography, which used to be pronounced in earlier stages of the language. For simplicity, you can assume that your conscript is maximally efficient to begin.

Writing is tied to the fictional world: who writes, who reads and why writing takes place might determine or influence the shape of the script. Perhaps only the elite writes; or writing is within the purview of women or scribes. Perhaps writing is conducted in secret or restricted to certain uses such as record-keeping, ceremonies, magic or poetry. Record-keeping could involve chronicling historical information or conveying business transactions. Ceremonial and commemorative writing could be associated with religious documents or funeral inscriptions. The relative formality and durability of the written word might impact the **medium of writing** and the shape and style of the conscript glyphs.

The tools and surfaces used for writing should be available in the fictional world and be consistent with the purpose of writing, and the degree of technological advancement. For example, if there are trees or reeds, paper or papyrus might be available for writing. Other natural elements that offer writing possibilities are leaves, animal skins (e.g., parchment, leather), clay, rocks, bones or shells. Writing surfaces could be stationary (a monolith) or portable (a small clay tablet). They could be solid (walls) or flexible (fabric). Also consider the tools best suited for writing on the chosen medium; chisels, sharp stones, stylus, reeds, pigmented liquid paint or ink, pens, pencils and so on.

Ideally, your conscript should fit your conlang phonology. An abjad is well suited for a language with relatively few vowels; if your conlang has a larger vowel inventory, an alphabet is a better choice. If your conlang syllable structure is relatively simple, a syllabary or abugida could be a good fit, particularly if your conlang segmental inventory is not extensive. If your conlang lexicon is limited (perhaps around 100 words) and there is little or no inflectional morphology, you can consider a logographic script. A potential drawback is that as you develop the lexicon (the topic of the next chapter), you will need to add new glyphs, apply meaning extension and/or use the rebus principle to convey additional meanings.

How many graphemes does your conscript need? It depends on the phonemic inventory and the writing system. For a logographic script you need a glyph per morpheme/word. Alphabets require a grapheme for each phoneme (assuming a one-to-one correspondence between both), and abjads need a grapheme for each consonantal phoneme. For abjads you should consider (optional) vocalic diacritics. In syllabaries you need one glyph for each possible syllabic combination. Finally, for an abugida, you need to provide a base glyph for each possible onset, decide which vowel is default and consider how to represent other vowels. You also need to indicate how complex onsets or codas are written. Table 14.1 outlines the steps needed to develop each of these script types.

Let's now consider **glyph style** and **shape**. The medium of writing is a big consideration: angular characters can be more easily scratched on wood; writing on stone might be amenable to straight lines or wedges; and curved glyphs are a good choice for flexible surfaces such as paper or fabric.

Glyph style can also be connected to cultural aspects of the fictional world and/or to your own aesthetic preferences. While it might be ok to borrow some graphemes from already existing scripts (always acknowledging where they are coming from), it is better to create your own. Before you begin, consider that graphemes are composed of one of more **strokes** (writing movements). For example, in the Latin alphabet we use one stroke for 'o,' two for 'i' and 'x,' three for 'N' and 'R' and four for 'M' or 'W.' There is stylistic variation; you might write some of these letters with fewer or additional strokes. On average, graphemes are written with three different strokes.

You can use or combine vertical, horizontal or diagonal strokes, and you can play with their relative length (long/medium/short) and placement.

Table 14.1 Sketching a conscript

Abjads	Alphabets
• List all consonant phonemes. • Provide a grapheme for each. • [*Optional*] Indicate vowel diacritics.	• List all phonemes. • Provide a grapheme for each. • Consider listing consonant and vowel graphemes separately.
Syllabaries	**Abugidas**
• List all possible syllable combinations. • Provide a different glyph for each. • Indicate how complex syllables (e.g., CCV, CVC) are conveyed (if needed).	• List all syllables, organized by onset. • Provide a grapheme base for each onset. • Choose the default vowel. • Consider where vowel diacritics are placed: – Before/after/above/below/ around the base glyph • Indicate how complex syllables are conveyed (if needed). • How are onsetless syllables written?
Logographic system	
• Provide a logogram for each morpheme/word in your conlang. • Consider meaning extension and the rebus principle, particularly as you develop the lexicon.	

You can incorporate dots, circles or wavy lines; variations on squares, triangles or wedge shapes; arches (semicircles) and hooks. Nature is a common inspiration in the development of written scripts, particularly common vegetal elements (flowers, trees or leaves), certain animals (fish, turtles), widespread or relevant geographical features (mountains, bodies of water) and astronomical bodies (planets, stars). Some of my students used cloud shapes for a Fog conscript, and wavy lines for an Acqua writing system. Table 14.2 lists a few grapheme strokes and shapes to get you started.

Some conlangers design graphemes using specific software, but you can easily sketch yours using pen and paper or a tablet, which is less time-consuming. If you borrow from an existing font, you might be able to incorporate some symbols directly into a word-processing document. For proper citation, always keep a record of where the symbol came from.

An additional aspect to consider is the direction of writing. Most languages are written left to right, from top to bottom, but Hebrew and Arabic are written right to left; and some scripts are written in columns from top to bottom, left to right (as in Uyghur) or right to left (as in Lepcha of Sikkim). Some languages are written in **boustrophedon**, that is, from right to left,

Table 14.2 Grapheme strokes and shapes

Lines	Circular	Other geometrical	Natural
Vertical	Dots	Squares	Cloud-like
Horizontal	Circles	Triangles	Flower-like
Diagonal	Arches (semicircles)	Wedges	Zoomorphic
Wavy	Hooks	Rhomboids	Geographical

and from left to right, in alternate lines. Ancient Greek was sometimes written in this way; this is also the direction used in the Atlantean and Ithkuil conscripts. The Rongorongo script was written in reverse boustrophedon, beginning from the bottom left. The second line was written upside down right above; each line was turned 180 degrees. Writing from the bottom to the top is quite unusual, but this direction of writing was also attested in some Ogham inscriptions.

Finally, in English and many languages we leave spaces around words – but not all scripts work this way. In fact, the Latin alphabet lacked word spacing. Other scripts use word dividers, that is, symbols inserted to separate words. This is the case of the Old Persian and Iberian scripts. In the latter, a single or double dot separates words in writing. In the Aiha script of the Kesh conlang in Ursula Le Guin's *Always Going Home*, the diagonal line / is used in this way.

14.6.1 The Shizu Conscript

This section features a conscript designed by Gabrielle Isgar for her *Shizu* [ʃiː.zŏː] conlang (the fictional world and map were introduced in Chapter 2). Writing is vital in the fictional world; the medium of writing is a frozen metal scroll with liquid metal 'ink' (as depicted in the map in Figure 2.3). The metal is so precious that it leads to an attack by forces from another planet.

Shizu, which means 'the language of information,' has eighteen consonants, four vowels, a CV syllable pattern and five tones (three level and two contour). In the Shizu conscript, consonants are represented by different graphemes. Vowels are conveyed with circles or lines attached to the end of the consonant; if the vowel is long, circles or lines are also drawn at the beginning (Figure 14.8). The Shizu script is written left to right, and it is inspired by Braille and cursive writing.

The Shizu script conveys tonal information via diacritics placed syllable-finally (Figure 14.9). Tonal diacritics also act as connecting lines between the syllables of polysyllabic words, and as word dividers word-finally.

Grapheme placement	I Add ○ to consonant end	Iː Add ○ to consonant beginning and end	ʊ Add ⌒ from consonant end inwards	ʊː Add ⌒ from consonant beginning and end inwards
Examples (minimal set)	/pɪ/ QUOT.EV	/pɪː/ 'Death'	/pʊ/ PROG	/pʊː/ 'Crater'

Figure 14.8 Shizu vowel graphemes
(courtesy of Gabrielle Isgar).

Level tones	IPA	Shizu diacritic	Contour tones	IPA	Shizu diacritic
Low (L)	˩		Rising (LH)	ˇ	
Mid (M)	˧				
High (H)	˥		Falling (HL)	ˆ	

Figure 14.9 Shizu tonal diacritics
(courtesy of Gabrielle Isgar).

Figure 14.10 'Shizu' written in Shizu script
(courtesy of Gabrielle Isgar).

Figure 14.10 shows how the compound 'Shizu' [ʃɪ.zʊ̌] ('information language') is written in this conscript. The full script is given in Figure 14.11.

14.7 Conlanging Practice: Ur Scripts

A. Table 14.3 shows how the same words are written in various Ur scripts. Indicate which unit each grapheme corresponds to.

B. Now, write the following words in each of the scripts exemplified in Table 14.3 (for logogram writing, you will need to devise additional glyphs).

   [ki.biʃ] 'rug'   [ʃei.ka.bi] 'autumn'   [kbeʃ] 'to barter'

C. Examine Figure 14.11, which shows all possible syllable combinations in Shizu (tonal information is not provided). Is the Shizu conscript an abugida, like Devanagari, or a combined alphabetic–syllabic script, like Hangul?

14 Writing Systems

	/ɪ/		/iː/		/ʊ/		/uː/	
/p/	/pɪ/	Quotative (EVIDENTIAL)	/piː/	Death (NOUN)	/pʊ/	Progressive (ASPECT)	/puː/	Crater (NOUN)
/b/	/bɪ/	Non-visual (EVIDENTIAL)	/biː/	Alien (NOUN)	/bʊ/	Auditory (EVIDENTIAL)	/buː/	Species/race (NOUN)
/m/	/mɪ/	Perfective (ASPECT)	/miː/	Guide (NOUN)	/mʊ/	Imperfective (ASPECT)	/muː/	Tool (NOUN)
/n/	/nɪ/	Verbalizer*	/niː/	Possession (NOUN)	/nʊ/	Verbalizer*	/nuː/	Polar question
/ɲ/	/ɲɪ/	Technology* (CLASS)	/ɲiː/	Technology (NOUN)	/ɲʊ/	Technology* (CLASS)	/ɲuː/	Technologist (NOUN)
/t/	/tɪ/	Adjectivizer*	/tiː/	Rocket ship (NOUN)	/tʊ/	Adjectivizer*	/tuː/	Danger (NOUN)
/d/	/dɪ/	Enemy* (CLASS)	/diː/	Enemy (NOUN)	/dʊ/	Enemy* (CLASS)	/duː/	Conquest (NOUN)
/c/	/cɪ/	Semelfactive (ASPECT)	/ciː/	Water (NOUN)	/cʊ/	Iterative (ASPECT)	/cuː/	Food (NOUN)
/ɟ/	/ɟɪ/	Warrior* (CLASS)	/ɟiː/	War (NOUN)	/ɟʊ/	Warrior* (CLASS)	/ɟuː/	Warrior (NOUN)
/r/	/rɪ/	Other* (CLASS)	/riː/	Peace (NOUN)	/rʊ/	Other* (CLASS)	/ruː/	Metal (NOUN)
/f/	/fɪ/	Collective (PRONOUN)	/fiː/	Fear (NOUN)	/fʊ/	Singulative (marker)	/fuː/	Force (NOUN)
/v/	/vɪ/	Content questions	/viː/	Aura (NOUN)	/vʊ/	Content questions	/vuː/	Job/role (NOUN)
/s/	/sɪ/	Spirit* (CLASS)	/siː/	Spirit (NOUN)	/sʊ/	Spirit* (CLASS)	/suː/	Land (NOUN)
/z/	/zɪ/	Defensive* (CLASS)	/ziː/	Defense (NOUN)	/zʊ/	Defensive* (CLASS)	/zuː/	Information (NOUN)
/ʃ/	/ʃɪ/	'and' (CONJUNCTION)	/ʃiː/	Language (NOUN)	/ʃʊ/	'or' (CONJUNCTION)	/ʃuː/	Armor (NOUN)
/ʒ/	/ʒɪ/	Offense* (CLASS)	/ʒiː/	Offense (NOUN)	/ʒʊ/	Offense* (CLASS)	/ʒuː/	Leader (NOUN)
/l/	/lɪ/	Ally* (CLASS)	/liː/	Ally (NOUN)	/lʊ/	Ally* (CLASS)	/luː/	Unity (NOUN)
/ʎ/	/ʎɪ/	Must* (COMMAND)	/ʎiː/	Power (NOUN)	/ʎʊ/	Must* (COMMAND)	/ʎuː/	Knowledge (NOUN)

Figure 14.11 Shizu script
(courtesy of Gabrielle Isgar).

Table 14.3 Ur scripts

		Logogram	Abjad	Alphabet
[ki]	'moon'	○	𐎁	𐎁▸
[bek]	'sun'	⌘	Ж 𐎁	Ж ≈ 𐎁
[ʃa.ʃa]	'cloud'	☐	Ω Ω	Ω x Ω x

14.8 The Muq Conscript

Writing is central for the muq. Its most important context is ceremonial; it's performed in the muq council house to celebrate key seasonal events. These include the beginning of the salt harvest and the coming of age of young community members, when they are initiated in the secrets of salt cultivation and trade. The celebration of the salt harvest involves the ceremonial writing of the muq myth story, accomplished by carefully pouring salt on the floor of the council house. Since the salt has a pinkish hue and the council house floor is black, the aesthetic effect is striking.

Muq has twenty-nine consonants, nine vowels and a (C)V(C)(C) syllable structure, so an alphabetic system is a good fit. Its consonantal and vocalic graphemes are given in Tables 14.3 and 14.4 respectively. The direction of writing is left to right, from top to bottom.

Table 14.4 Muq consonant graphemes

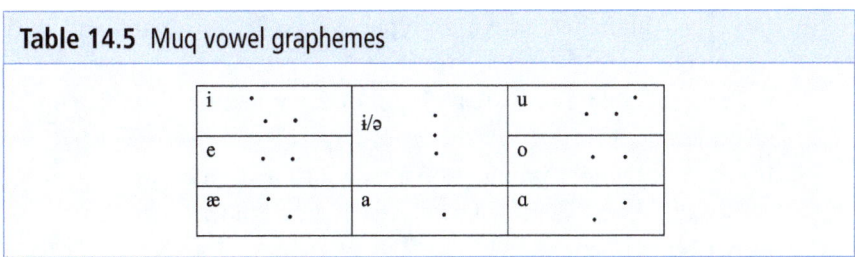

Table 14.5 Muq vowel graphemes

i		i/ə		u	
e				o	
æ		a		ɑ	

Double consonants are written vertically (Table 14.6). When doubled, graphemes consisting of double lines are written as three lines (rather than four). Examples of muq writing are given in Table 14.7. Vowels tend to be written inside the symbol of the onset consonant that precedes them. The first part of a diphthong is written within the symbol corresponding to the preceding onset consonant; the second part is written right after the onset.

Table 14.6 Identical consonants

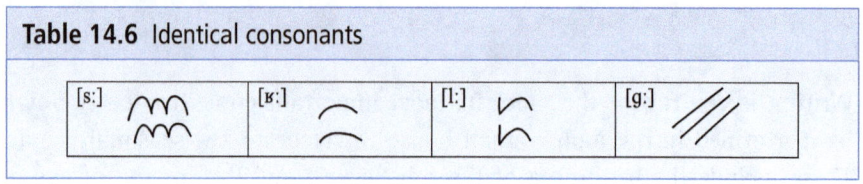

Table 14.7 Examples of muq writing

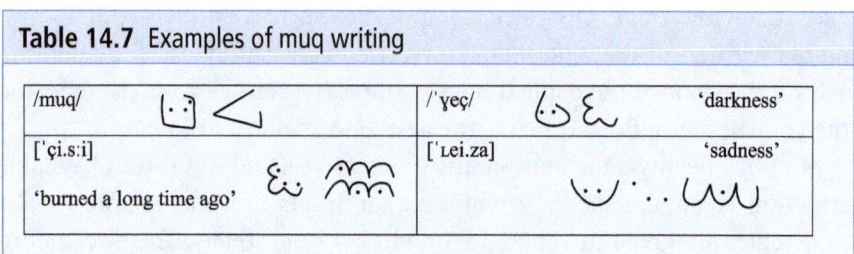

14.9 Guide to Developing Your Conscript

A. Connections to the fictional world
- What is writing used for in the fictional world?
- Who writes, and what types of documents are written?
- What is the writing medium? How does the medium influence glyph shape, dimensions or styling?
- What cultural elements could relate to glyph shape or style?
- Indicate any personal aesthetic preferences that will play a role in the script style.

B. Sketch the script
- What type of writing system is it (syllabary/abugida/abjad/alphabet)? How does it fit to the conlang phonology/phonology?
    o For an abjad, provide a glyph for each consonant.
    o For an alphabet, provide glyphs for each consonant and each vowel.
    o For a syllabary, provide a glyph for each possible syllable combination.
    o For an abugida, provide a base glyph for each consonant onset. Decide on the default vowel and indicate how other vowels are conveyed.
    o For a logographic system, provide a glyph for each word. Indicate if meaning extension and/or the rebus principle play a role.
- What is the direction of writing?
- Are there spaces between words?
- Are there additional writing conventions?
- Is your writing system inspired by existing scripts or artistic forms?

- Write the conlang name and either a few words or a full sentence using your conscript (provide an IPA transcription including syllabification and stress/tone).
- Go back to your fictional map and write the names of geographical locations depicted using your conscript (see Section 2.3.2 for examples).

To Learn More

This chapter draws from Comrie et al. (2013), Daniels (2001, 2018), Rogers (2005) and Ferrara (2022). The website *Omniglot: The Online Encyclopedia of Writing Systems and Languages* (https://omniglot.com/) provides detailed information on written scripts. Also recommended is the *Atlas of Endangered Alphabets,* with information about endangered and minority writing script: www.endangeredalphabets.net/. Thoth's Pill by Rudder (2015) is an entertaining account of the history of writing: www.youtube.com/watch?v=PdO3IP0Pro8.

To learn more about Nüshu, see Idema (2009) and chapter 19 in Li (2020). Nüshu features prominently in Lisa See's novel *Snow Flower and the Secret Fan* (2006). This novel was made into a film with the same title in 2011, directed by Wayne Wang. Online resources for Nüshu include Sala (2018), Chen (2018) and Orie Endo's *World of Nushu* website at http://nushu.world.coocan.jp/home.htm (2001).

For Tolkien conscripts, see Appendix E in *Lord of The Rings*, Måns Björkman Berg's webpage, *Amanye Tenceli: The Writing Systems of Aman*, at https://at.mansbjorkman.net/ (2021) and *Guides for Tengwar and Runes* by Per Lindberg at www.forodrim.org/daeron/md_teng_primers.html (2023). For Heptapod B, watch *Arrival* (Villeneuve 2016), based on the novella *Story of Your Life* (Chiang 1998). You might also find the insights of *Arrival*'s screenwriter Eric Heisserer (2016) on the creative process used to develop Heptapod B of interest. Lapointe (2022) is also recommended if you are a fan of *Arrival* and/or Heptapod B.

15 Semantics and Pragmatics

This chapter focuses on expanding your conlang lexicon by considering aspects of **semantics** (word and sentence meaning) and **pragmatics** (the meaning of words in context). The former include denotation and connotation (Section 15.1), polysemy (Section 15.2), metaphor (Sections 15.3) and the development of word networks (Section 15.4).

Section 15.5 focuses on words whose meaning depends on personal, social, spatial, temporal and textual contexts. Section 15.6 provides some conlanging practice, and Section 15.7 exemplifies semantic and pragmatic aspects in muq. Section 15.8 offers a step-by-step guide to expand your lexicon taking into consideration the information covered in this chapter.

Key Words

Deictic (indexical)
Deixis
  Personal
    Exclusive (EXCL)
    Inclusive (INC)
  Social ('politeness')
    Familiar (FAM)
    Honorific (HON)
    Extra-polite (HHON)
  Spatial
    Proximal (PROX)
    Medial (MED)
    Distal/remote (DIST)
  Temporal
  Textual
Doublespeak
Euphemism
Homonym
Homophone
Homograph
Hypernym

Hyponym
Idiom
Kinship term
Meaning
  Affective meaning
  Connotation
  Denotation
  Social meaning
Metaphor
Pejoration
Polysemy
Pragmatics
Semantic field
Semantics
Synonym
Taboo

15.1 What Is Meaning?

Morphemes, words and expressions have **meaning**, that is, semantic content associated with them. For example, in English the morpheme *-ing* indicates action in progress, the word *asteroid* refers to a lump of rocky minerals orbiting the Sun, and the expression *with flying colors* means 'with distinction.'

There are two types of semantic content: **denotative**, or literal meaning, and **connotative**, or non-literal meaning. The latter involves meaning associated with the referent or the context in which the word is used. It also relates to **social meaning**, since the use of certain words conveys social characteristics of the speaker.

Let's begin by considering **affective meaning**. In English, the word *moist* has as its literal meaning 'damp' or 'humid.' For many English speakers, this word has negative connotations, most likely because it is associated with bodily functions deemed disgusting (unlike the words *humid* or *damp*). The **denotation** of two or more words might be similar, but their **connotations** might vary: compare, for example, *assertive* vs. *aggressive*, and *frugal* vs. *cheap*. While the first word in each word pair has a neutral or positive connotation, the second has a negative one.

Connotations are often idiosyncratic: they might not be shared by all speakers of a language or dialect. Thus, certain words might have negative connotations for you but not for your friends, or vice versa. For example, I don't have a problem with the word *moist*, but I do with the word *curated*.

This word, previously used in the context of museums or art collections, has been increasingly used in recent years to describe any collection of things. I find this word pretentious, and a quick search online tells me that other speakers feel the same way (deeming it 'precious' and associating it with 'hipster speech').

Taboo words have very strong negative connotations. They are considered so offensive that they are avoided in polite company, or not used at all. Taboo words usually relate to death, birth, religion or certain bodily functions. Taboo words can change with time. For example, the word *pregnant* was considered taboo a few decades ago, so much so that it was impossible to say it on TV.

Since people need to refer to concepts denoted by taboo words, these are often replaced by **euphemisms**, that is, words with non-negative connotations. Euphemisms for 'pregnant' include *expecting* (and in the past, *enceinte* or *with child*). The euphemisms *to pass away* or *to go to heaven* (the latter with religious connotations) are often used to avoid mentioning the word *death*. Euphemisms are often used by children and in child-directed speech (*poop*, *pee*); they are often used to soften curses as well (*shoot!*). In Spanish, *¡Miércoles!* (literally, 'Wednesday') is a euphemism for a curse word beginning with 'm' in this language; and in Esperanto, *maltrinki* (literally 'to undrink') is used euphemistically to refer to urination. A specific type of euphemism is **doublespeak**, a word or expression that deflects or hides the true meaning of what is conveyed. Examples include *collateral damage*, used to refer to civilian casualties in a military attack, and *alternative facts*, to refer to lies or misinformation.

With the passage of time, euphemisms might fall out of use (as 'enceinte' did in English) or acquire negative connotations. If so, they are replaced by new euphemisms. Stephen Pinker named this process 'the euphemism treadmill'; it's one example of **pejoration**, a semantic drift toward negative connotations that is behind language change.

Connotation, taboo words and euphemisms can enrich the fictional world and add layers of complexity to the conlang lexicon. For example, 'Sauron' in *Lord of the Rings* and 'Lord Voldemort' in *Harry Potter* are taboo, referring to beings who are pure evil. Euphemisms used to avoid mentioning these names include 'The Dark Lord' for the former, and 'You-Know-Who' or 'He-Who-Must-Not-Be-Named' for the latter.

Connotation varies across languages and cultures; thus, you should avoid transferring particularly salient connotations of words from natlangs you know well into your conlang (such as *moist*). You should also think of which words might have specific affective connotations in the fictional world, and/or which words might be favored or used exclusively by specific groups.

Social meaning is also part of a word's connotation; it can convey formality and social identity. For example, in Peninsular Spanish the adjective *mono/a* means 'cute' or 'adorable.' This word is used informally and is favored by female speakers. Some words might be used by members of a specific social class, ethnicity, or religious or political group. For example, the terms *Father* and *Sister* are associated with the Catholic faith, while the terms *Rabbi* or *Imam* are associated with Judaism and Islam, respectively.

> **Your Turn**
>
> - Do *moist* or *curated* have negative connotations for you?
> - Are there any words in English (or other languages) that have specific affective connotations?
> - Can you think of additional words in English that have social meaning?

15.1.1 Connotations in Conlanging: Láadan

The Láadan dictionary clarifies whether certain words have specific connotations. For example, the word *mahanal* [mɑ.hɑ.nɑl] 'lustfully, desiringly' lacks negative connotations, and *nithedimethóo* [nɪ.θɛ.dɪ.mɛ.θó.o] 'refrigerator guest, a guest who shows up unannounced and helps herself to the contents of the fridge,' has positive connotations (Elgin et al. 2020:116, 121).

In Láadan the lateral fricative /ɬ/ evokes a negative connotation in words such as *lha* /ɬa/ 'sin' or *lhoho* [ɬo.ho] 'shame' (Elgin et al. 2020:172, 323). In addition, the pejorative affix /-ɬ-/ can be prefixed or suffixed to convey pejorative overtones (1).

(1) Láadan pejorative affix (from Elgin et al. 2020:130, 172, 323, 324)
    a. *rile* [rɪ.lɛ] 'silence' *rilelh* [rɪ.lɛɬ] 'malicious silence'
    b. *áada* [á.ɑ.dɑ] 'smile' *lháada* [ɬá.ɑ.dɑ] 'to smirk'
    c. *doyu* [do.ju] 'apple' *doyulh* [do.juɬ] 'repugnant apple'
    d. *ana* [ɑ.nɑ] 'food' *analh* [ɑ.nɑɬ] 'disgusting food'
                                                                            lhana [ɬɑ.nɑ]

15.2 How Many Meanings?

Polysemy refers to words that have more than one denotation. One example of a polysemous word is the noun *space*, which according to the *Merriam-Webster Online Dictionary* has the meanings listed in (2):

(2) Meanings of *space*
   a. A period of time or its duration
   b. A blank area separating words or lines
   c. The region beyond the earth's atmosphere or beyond the solar system; and
   d. Accommodations on a public vehicle

Natlangs vary in how they encode polysemy. For example, in Czech and Russian, *ruka* means 'hand, arm'; and in Hungarian, *ujj* means both 'finger' and 'toe.' Polysemy is crosslinguistically common for certain body parts. In fact, about half of natlangs have one single word referring to both 'eye' and 'face,' and about 39 percent have a word indicating both 'foot' and 'leg.' Polysemy is also common in other areas of the lexicon; for example, two thirds of natlangs have a single word conveying both 'tree' and 'wood.'

Some instances of polysemy appear to be connected to culture. Thus, languages of hunter-gatherers or cultures who have not made a complete transition to agriculture tend to have polysemy for 'finger' and 'hand,' unlike agriculture-dependent societies (Brown 2013b). Similarly, the number of words for 'hand/arm' and 'foot/leg' appears to be related to climate and culture. Polysemy for these terms tends to occur in languages spoken in warm climates close to the equator; their speakers rely on articles of clothing to a lesser extent than in other places.

Conlangs vary in their use of polysemy. Toki Pona, featuring only 120 words originally, relies heavily on it. For example, *jo* [jo] means 'to have, to contain, to carry' and *kili* [ki.li] both 'fruit' and 'vegetable.' On the other hand, Lojban and Ithkuil avoid polysomy since their goal is to avoid ambiguity.

Polysemy is a great way to enrich your conlang lexicon. You can add related **meanings** to words you have already created, and/or you can consider polysemy when developing new words. Both allow you to extend the web of related meanings that words can take on. Remember, however, that polysemy generally varies across languages; it is important to avoid transferring polysemic meanings from English or other languages you are familiar with to your conlang.

Polysemous words are distinguished from **homonyms**, that is, words with different meanings but identical pronunciation and/or spelling. There are two types of homonyms: **homophones** and **homographs**. Homophones are words that sound the same (*knight, night* [nait]; *I, eye* [ai]). Homographs are spelled the same but pronounced differently: (*to*) *convict*, (*a*) *convict*; (*to*) *record*, (*a*) *record*. The verbs in both pairs have final stress, unlike the nouns, and the vowels are pronounced differently as well.

It might be useful to incorporate homonyms in your conlang, particularly if the phonological inventory is small. If you do, remember that they should be specific to your conlang. For example, in Klingon, the noun *ram* 'night' and the verb *ram* 'to be trivial, trifling, unimportant' are homonyms (both are pronounced [rɑm]); and so are the adverb *reH* 'always' and the verb *reH* 'to play' (both pronounced [rɛx]) (Okrand 1985:105).

> **Your Turn**
>
> - Sort your conlang lexicon alphabetically. Are there polysemous words? If so, list all their related meanings under the same entry.
> - If any lexical entry has several meanings and at least one of the meanings is unrelated, you are dealing with homonyms. In this case, list the homonyms and their translations separately.
> - Check that the meanings of polysemous words are not identical with similar English words. For example, if you have a word for outer space, this word should not also refer to a period of time or its duration, or as separation between words or lines, as in English.
> - Check that any homonyms in your conlang are different from those in English or other natlangs you are familiar with.

15.3 Metaphor and Multiplicity of Meaning

Polysemy frequently originates from extending meaning. In many natlangs, color terms are used not only to describe the hue of an object or how it emits or reflects light, but also to describe emotion. Thus, if you feel 'blue' you are sad; you turn 'red' with shame, and 'green' with envy. The meaning of **kinship terms** (i.e., words referring to how individuals are related in a family or kinship unit) can also be extended to refer to non-kinship relationships. For example, consider the use of *mother* in 'Mother Teresa,' 'Mother Earth,' 'motherland' or 'motherload.'

The extension of non-literal meaning is termed **metaphor**. Using colors and kinship terms metaphorically might be universal. However, although metaphor is pervasive across languages and part of our creative use of language, it is often culturally and linguistically dependent. For example, in Spanish you turn yellow, not green, with envy (*amarillo de envidia*); and in Italian, if you are *al verde* 'in the green,' you are broke.

Many language-specific expressions or **idioms** are metaphoric; one example is to *recharge one's batteries*, based on an electrical metaphor and meaning to rest and relax to recover one's strength. The meaning of an idiom cannot always be predicted from the words that compose it, although it might originate from metaphor. For example, *to hear it through* *the grapevine* means to hear a rumor about something. This is a very English-specific idiom, and its literal translation into other languages does not make much sense. Similarly, the Spanish expression *tener monos en la cara*, literally 'to have monkeys in one's face,' translates into English as 'you're looking at me as if I was from another planet' (although the Spanish expression has a connotation of suspicion or a challenge).

Metaphor is useful in conlanging to build polysemy and/or develop culturally specific idioms. Care needs to be taken to not transfer metaphoric meanings from natlangs; creating your own metaphors and idioms will make your conlang more vivid and unique, and enrich the fictional world.

15.3.1 Metaphor in Conlanging

The Esperanto verb *krokodili* [kro.ko.di.li] 'to crocodile' is metaphoric; it indicates that someone is speaking their native language instead of Esperanto. Also metaphoric is *volapukaĵo* [vo.la.pu.ka.ʒo] (related to the name of the conlang Volapük), meaning 'gibberish, incomprehensible.'

In Dothraki, there are two ways to say 'you are my loved one' depending on whether they refer to a male or female; both are metaphoric and related to Dothraki mythology (3).

(3) Dothraki: 'You are my loved one' (Peterson 2014:30)
 a. Yer   shekh ma shieraki   anni.
   [jer   ʃex   ma ʃieɾak-i   anːi]
   2SG.FAM sun.NOM and star-NOM.PL.AN 1SG.GEN
   'You are my sun and stars.'
 b. Yer   jalan   atthirari anni.
   [jer   dʒalan aθːiɾaɾ-i a.nːi]
   2SG.FAM moon.NOM life-GEN.INAN 1SG.GEN
   'You are the moon of my life'.

Klingon has several idioms based on metaphoric extension. One of them is *naH jajmey* [naχ dʒadʒ.mɛɪ] 'vegetable/fruit days,' referring to the time when you are young and therefore not of an age appropriate to marry (Okrand 1997:110). Another is *Hoch nuH qel* [xotʃ nux qɛl] 'consider every weapon,' meaning 'consider every possibility/option' (Okrand 1997:108, 109).

15.4 Word Networks: Semantic Fields

Your conlang lexicon can expand via networks of words related in meaning, that is, **semantic fields**. Examples include color terms (*black, white, pink*), emotions (*happiness, anger, hatred*) and verbs of motion (*walk,* *run, jump*). Unless semantic fields are narrowly defined (such as 'verbs of motion'), they can encompass words from different class types. For example, the semantic field 'weaponry' can include nouns (*arrow, ax, sword*) and verbs (*to shoot, to throw, to draw*).

Semantic fields differ across languages, partly because not all languages partition experience in the same way, as we mentioned in Chapter 7. We've also seen earlier that words encoding certain objects, relationships or abstractions are not present in all languages. One example of how Klingon partitions some aspects of experience involves food terms. The Klingon verb *vut* [vut] 'to cook' rarely involves heat (unlike its closest English translation). Klingon also distinguishes the verbs *Sop* [ʂop] 'to eat,' *tlhutlh* [tɬutɬ] 'to drink' and *'ep* [ʔɛp] 'to consume (thick) soup' (Okrand 1997).

Two terms related to semantic fields are **hypernym** and **hyponym**. Hypernyms are terms for general categories. For example, the hypernym *flower* encompasses various types of flowers (e.g., violets, roses, daisies); these flower types are hyponyms. All natlangs have hypernyms and hyponyms, but they might not pattern similarly. For example, K'iche' Maya lacks the hypernym 'to break'; instead, it has twelve different lexical words encoding nuances of this general meaning.

Considering **synonyms** (words with similar meanings, like *thin* and *skinny*) is useful when developing semantic fields. True synonyms are rare, since semantically similar words tend to have different connotations (this is the case for *thin, skinny* and *slender*, and also for *pretty* and *beautiful*). In addition, synonyms are often used in different contexts. For example, you can have *beautiful men, beautiful women* and *pretty women*; but not *pretty men* (unless perhaps metaphorically). In addition, although 'pretty' can modify *girl* and *boy*, *pretty boy* has negative connotations for many speakers (being vain, silly and perhaps quite vacuous). Note that *beautiful boy* lacks this negative connotation.

Adjectives often have antonyms: *wet/dry, empty/full; nervous/relaxed*. So do adverbs: *happily/sadly, fortunately/unfortunately, quickly/slowly*. Some nouns and verbs do too: *sadness/happiness, poverty/wealth, come/go, give/take*. Derivational morphology is a great way to form antonyms (*fortunately/unfortunately; happy/unhappy*). Antonyms are subject to cross-linguistic variation; for example, in Samoan the verb *fuʔatau* means both 'buy' and 'sell.'

One semantic field relevant to all or most languages is kinship terms. All languages express sex, generational, biological and marriage relations, albeit in different ways. For example, while most natlangs have separate words for 'mother' and 'father,' Pirahã only has one term for both. In Japanese, there is a word for 'grandchild' (*mago*), but not for 'granddaughter' or 'grandson.' In some languages, the sex of the (connected) relative or of the speaker is relevant; compare *son* vs. *daughter* or *aunt* vs. *uncle* in English. In Basque there are four sibling hyponyms according to the gender of the sibling and that of their brother/sister (4). To denote the hypernym 'siblings' the compound *anai-arrebak* is used. Age and whether a relative is dead or alive can also play a role in kinship terms.

(4) Basque sibling terms
    a. *anaia*   [a.'na.ja]   'male sibling to a male'
    b. *neba*   ['ne.ba]   'male sibling to a female'
    c. *arreba*   [a.'re.ba]   'female sibling to a male'
    d. *ahizpa*   ['ais.pa]   'female sibling to a female'

15.4.1 Word Networks in Conlanging

Peterson (2014) organizes basic Dothraki vocabulary according to semantic fields for people, war, the human body, horses, food, hunting, nature and colors. Okrand (1997) also uses semantic fields to discuss specialized Klingon vocabulary, most notably warfare, music, food and the visual arts. Láadan includes rich semantic fields for female-centered feelings and experiences, including love, pregnancy and cleanliness. Words related to the latter, most derived via compounding, are given below.

(5) Láadan: cleanliness semantic field (adapted from Elgin et al. 2020:109)
    a. *éthe*   [ɛ́.θɛ]   'to be clean'
    b. *huhéthe*   [hu.hɛ́.θɛ]   'boss-clean'   (highest level of clean)
    c. *háawithéthe*   [há.a.wɪ.θɛ́.θɛ]   'child-clean'   (level of room cleanliness for a child)
    d. *onidahéthe*   [o.nɪ.da.hɛ́.θɛ]   'family-clean'   (usual state of affairs)
    e. *thóohéthe*   [θó.o.hɛ́.θɛ]   'guest-clean'   (level of cleaning you do for guests)
    f. *mudahéthe*   [mu.da.hɛ́.θɛ]   'pig-clean'   (state of your teenager's room)

15.5 Meaning in Context

Some words are **deictic** or **indexical**, that is, their meaning depends on context. This is the case of personal pronouns such as *me, you* and adverbs like *there* or *later*. Deictic words appear to be universal across languages. Including deictic words in your conlang will expand your lexicon (particularly the set of pronouns, determiners and adverbs) and are useful when translating your fictional text, as we will see later. The next sections introduce five main types of deixis: **personal, social, spatial, temporal** and **textual**.

15.5.1 Personal Deixis

Words whose meaning changes depending on who is talking to whom involve **personal deixis**. Natlangs tend to have first person pronouns corresponding to the speaker ('I', 'me') and second person pronouns referring to the addressee ('you'). Most natlangs also have third person pronouns ('they', 'them'). In some languages, third person pronouns are used mostly or only for emphasis or contrast (as in Spanish). In languages without third person pronouns, the referent is understood from context or expressed by demonstratives ('this', 'that').

Deictic pronouns (and determiners) can encode number, gender and case. In Spanish, all personal pronouns have different forms for singular and plural (6). In English, the second person pronoun does not encode number differences, although in some dialects *you guys, you all/y'all* or *youse* are used to refer to the second person plural (Table 15.1).

(6)   Deictic pronouns in Spanish

	SG	PL
1	yo	nosotras, nosotros
2	tú	vosotras, vosotros
3	ella, él	ellas, ellos

Pronouns can indicate additional number distinctions. One example is Fijian, with singular, dual, trial and plural pronouns. Fijian also has **inclusive (INC)** and **exclusive (EXCL)** pronouns that include and exclude the addressee, respectively. Other natlangs with this distinction include Hawaiian and Quechua.

About 33 percent of natlangs encode gender in pronouns, particularly in the third person, and in the singular (as in English). Fewer than 5 percent of natlangs encode gender in both third person and either first person or second person pronouns, as in Arabic or Peninsular Spanish (6). Very rarely, languages convey gender in second person pronouns, as in Burunge and Irawq.

Examples of natlangs which don't encode gender in pronouns include Turkish (where the third person pronoun *o* is used for 'he/she/it') and Pirahã. Indeed, Pirahã has the simplest pronoun system attested in natlangs; the third person pronoun *hi* /hi/ can refer to any gender or number depending on context (7). Pirahã also lacks a separate pronoun for the second person plural, which is conveyed by juxtaposing the pronouns for the first person and the second person singular.

(7)   Pirahã: Third person pronoun (Everett 2005:623)

hiaitíihí	*hi*	*kaoáíbogi*	*bai*	*-aagá*
Pirahã.people	3	evil.spirit	fear	be

'The Pirahã are afraid of evil spirits.' / 'A Pirahã is afraid of an evil spirit.'
'The Pirahã are afraid of an evil spirit.' or 'A Pirahã is afraid of evil spirits.'

Table 15.1 English pronouns and case

	NOM		ACC		GEN	
	SG	PL	SG	PL	SG	PL
1	I	we	me	us	mine	ours
2	you	you	you	you	yours	yours
3	she/he/it	they	her/him/it	them	hers/his/its	theirs

Pronouns can indicate case, as in English (Table 15.1) and Basque, from which some representative examples are given in (8).

(8)   Basque: pronouns and case (1st person)
     a.   ERG   *nik*   [nik]   'I'
     b.   ABS   *ni*   [ni]   'I, me'
     c.   DAT   *niri*   [ni.ɾi]   'to me'
     d.   GEN   *nirena*   [ni.ɾe.na]   'mine'

15.5.1.1 Personal Deictics in Conlanging

Pronouns in Esperanto have singular and plural forms; they mark gender only in the third person singular (Table 15.2). Some speakers use the gender-neutral pronoun *ri* [ri] when the gender is unknown, irrelevant or non-binary. The pronoun *ci* [tsi] 'thou' is used in solemn registers, including poetry. Like nouns, Esperanto pronouns take the accusative suffix *-n*.

Table 15.2 Esperanto pronouns in the nominative case (adapted from Kellerman Reed 2003)

	SG			PL
1		mi [mi]		ni [ni]
2			vi [vi]	
3	li [li] (M)	ŝi [ʃi] (F)	ĝi [dʒi] (INAN)	ili

Láadan pronouns encode person, number and case (9). Toki Pona has pronouns marked for person: *mi* [mi] 'I, me, we,' *sina* [si.na] 'you,' *ona* [o.na] 's/he/it/they.' Number is conveyed with the modifiers *wan* [wan] 'one,' *to* [to] 'two' and *mute* [mu.te] 'many.' *mije* [mi.je] 'man, male' and *meli* [me.li] 'woman, female' can be added to indicate gender, and *kulupu* [ku.lu.pu] 'community' to indicate an exclusive interpretation. In case you are wondering, *mi tu* can be used by Siamese twins or people possessed by spirits, for example (Lang 2014).

(9)   Láadan neutral pronouns in the nominative (adapted from Elgin et al. 2020:315)

	SG		PAU		PL	
1	le	[lɛ]	lezh	[lɛʒ]	len	[lɛn]
2	ne	[nɛ]	nezh	[nɛʒ]	nen	[nɛn]
3	be	[bɛ]	bezh	[bɛʒ]	ben	[bɛn]

15.5.2 Social Deixis, aka 'Politeness'

Politeness is closely tied to culture. Some societies are more hierarchical than others, and some favor polite speech or directness. Politeness can be expressed in various ways; from using specific titles, to avoiding direct commands or using specific euphemisms. In many natlangs, certain words convey contextual politeness (i.e., **social deixis**) as well. For example, in French the second singular pronoun *tu* is used in intimate or informal contexts, and *vous* indicates respect. A similar distinction is conveyed in several Spanish dialects in the second person singular (informal *tú* and formal *usted*). In addition, Peninsular Spanish distinguish *vosotros* (informal) and *ustedes* (polite) in the plural. A different distinction is encoded in Basque, where the second person singular pronoun *zu* [su] (in the absolutive case) is neutral, and *hi* [i] very familiar.

French, Spanish and Basque are within the 25 percent of natlangs where second person pronouns express a binary distinction between **familiar** (or intimate) and **honorific** (or respectful) forms of address (glossed as FAM and HON respectively). Multiple politeness distinctions occur in 7 percent of natlangs, including Tagalog and Marathi. For example, Marathi distinguishes among familiar, formal and **extra-polite (HHON)** pronouns, as shown below.

(10)   Social deixis in Marathi pronouns (from Helmbrecht 2013; IPA)
   /tu/   you.SG.FAM   Family members and intimate persons
   /te/, /he/ you.SG,.HON   People of higher social status
   /apaŋ/   you.SG.HHON   Priests and teachers, and in very formal contexts

In 3 percent of natlangs, pronouns are avoided in contexts of politeness and are substituted with other polite expressions such as titles or kinship terms. For example, in Indonesian, the kinship term *saudara* 'sibling' is used to informally address speakers of the same generation or younger; while *bapak* 'father' and *ibu* 'mother' are used among marriageable adults and to respectfully address older speakers (Velupillai 2012:371).

15.5.2.1 Politeness in Conlanging

Esperanto pronouns do not encode politeness except for *ci* [tsi] 'thou,' used in poetry and the Bible. In Toki Pona, politeness is conveyed with the modifier *sewi* [se.wi] 'awe-inspiring.' Toki Pona can also convey a derogative nuance with the modifier *jaki* [ja.ki] 'disgusting' (Lang 2014).

Dothraki has a three-way distinction among *shafka* [ʃaf.ka] (2.HON, both singular and plural), *yer* [jer] 2SG.FAMM and *yeri* [je.ɾi] 2PL.FAM (Peterson 2014: 35, 36). Láadan distinguishes four degrees of politeness in pronouns, as exemplified in (11).

(11) Láadan: politeness in pronouns (1SG.NOM; adapted from Elgin et al. 2020:315)
  a. Neutral   *le*   [lɛ]   Beloved   *la*   [lɑ]
  b. Honored *li*   [lɪ]   Despised *lhele* [ɬɛ.lɛ]

15.5.3 Spatial Deixis

Spatial deixis refers to relative location. It tends to be conveyed via demonstrative pronouns and determiners (*this, that*) or adverbs (*here, there, up, down*). It usually involves distance relative to the speaker and/or the hearer, although elevation or visibility can play a role as well.

Most often, languages distinguish between relative closeness (**proximal**) and relative distance (**distal** or **remote**), as in English (*this* vs. *that, here* vs. *there*). Medium distance from the speaker (**medial**) is also common, as in Spanish, which distinguishes proximal *este, esta* 'this,' medial *ese, esa* 'that' and distal *aquel, aquella* 'that over there' for demonstrative pronouns and determiners, and proximal *aquí* 'here,' medial *ahí* 'over there' and distal *allí* 'way over there' for adverbs. Proximal, medial and distal deixis are glossed as PROX, MED and DIST, respectively.

Speaker-relative and hearer-relative deictic distinctions are found in Japanese and Kambera among other languages. Japanese distinguishes demonstrative determiners *kono* (near the speaker), *sono* (near the hearer) and *ano* (away from both the speaker and the hearer). Kambera has four spatially deictic contrasts of this kind (12).

(12) Kambera distance contrasts (from Klamer 1998:55–56)
  a. *ni*   /ni/   'near/at speaker'
  b. *nai*   /nai/   'middle distance from speaker'
  c. *na*   /na/   'near/at addressee'
  d. *nu*   /nu/   'far from both speaker and addressee'

Natlangs with four or more deictic distinctions incorporate other aspects in addition to distance. For example, Sanzhi Dargwa demonstratives refer to relative elevation (above or below the speaker), while Yup'ik encodes visibility (visible or obscured/not in sight by the speaker from the place of speaking).

15.5.3.1 Spatial Deixis in Conlanging

Láadan distinguishes proximal and distal demonstrative pronouns (Elgin et al. 2020:133). Klingon has *naDev* [nɑ.ɖɛv] 'here, hereabouts' and *pa'* [pɑʔ] 'there, over there, thereabouts,' which are nouns rather than adverbs (Okrand 1985:96, 99).

Lojban and Dothraki distinguish proximal, medial and distal demonstrative pronouns. In Lojban, these are realized as [ti], [ta], [tu] respectively; all refer to something pointed at. Lojban lacks demonstrative articles (Cowan 2016:141, 142).

Dothraki demonstrative pronouns are marked for number, animacy and case; Table 15.3 lists their nominative forms. Demonstrative determiners are unmarked for number or animacy: *jin* [dʒin] 'this/these,' *haz* [haz] 'that/those,' *rek* [rek] 'that/those over there.' Deictic adverbs derive from the latter by gemination of the last consonant and the suffix [-e]: *jinne* [dʒi.nːe] 'here,' *hazze* [ha.zːe] 'there,' *rekke* [re.kːe] 'over there' (Peterson 2014:79, 80).

Table 15.3 Dothraki demonstrative pronouns (nominative; from Peterson 2014:81)

	AN			INAN		
	PROX	MED	DIS	PROX	MED	DIS
SG	jinak [dʒi.nak]	hazak [ha.zak]	rekak [re.kak]	jini [dʒi.ni]	hazi [ha.zi]	reki [re.ki]
PL	jinaki [dʒi.na.ki]	hazaki [ha.za.ki]	rekaki [re.ka.ki]			

15.5.4 Temporal Deixis

Temporal deixis refers to relative time, most often expressed with adverbs (*now, before*) or adverbial expressions (*last night, tomorrow morning*). Natlangs vary in how they convey temporal deixis. For example, the Spanish adverb *anteayer* is 'the day before yesterday,' *anoche* 'last night' and *esta noche* 'tonight' in English.

15.5.4.1 Temporal Deixis in Conlanging

Láadan expresses temporal deixis via auxiliary verbs, as we saw in Chapter 9. The Láadan dictionary does not list entries for temporal deictic terms such as 'tomorrow,' 'tonight' or 'yesterday,' but it includes *hihath* [hɪ.haθ] '(right) now,' a compound from *hi* 'this' and *hath* 'time' as well as *dideshá* [dɪ.dɛ.ʃá] 'hours between dawn and rising' and *honáal* [ho.ná.ɑl] 'hours between midnight and dawn.'

15.5.5 Textual Deixis

Textual deixis refers to information mentioned or forthcoming. It is usually conveyed via pronouns and adverbs. Examples include the adverbs *earlier* and *later*. Although these adverbs are most often used temporally in English, they can be used to refer to preceding or following text, that is, as textual deictic adverbs.

Personal or demonstrative pronouns such as *it*, *this* or *that* are used in this way in some languages, as in English. Other languages have dedicated textual deictic pronouns; examples in Spanish are pronouns *ello* 'it,' *esto* 'this' and *eso* 'that,' used exclusively to refer to a previous clause or sentence, as exemplified below.

(13) Spanish: textual deixis
  Quier-o   aprobar. Por   eso,   estudiar-é   mucho
  want-1SG.PRS pass   for   that   study-1SG.FUT   a.lot
  'I want to pass. For that reason, I'll study a lot.'

15.5.5.1 Textual Deixis in Conlanging

Lojban has an extensive textual deictic system referring to information that is, was or will be conveyed in speech or writing (Table 15.4). Lojban distinguishes among close, medium-distance and distant utterances. Examples of sentences with textual deictic pronouns are given in (14).

Table 15.4 Textual deixis in Lojban (Cowan 2016:142; IPA)

di'u [di.hu]	'the previous utterance'	*de'e* [dɛ.hɛ]	'a later utterance'
de'u [dɛ.hu]	'an earlier utterance'	*da'e* [da.hɛ]	'a much later utterance'
da'u [da.hu]	'a much earlier utterance'	*dei* [dɛi]	'this very utterance'
di'e [di.hɛ]	'the next utterance'	*do'i* [do.hi]	'some utterance'

(14) Lojban: textual deixis examples (Cowan 2016:143; IPA)
  a. *dei*   *jetnu*   *jufra*
      [dɛi   ʒɛt.nu   ʒu.fra]
      this.utterance   is.a.true   sentence
      'What I am saying (at this moment) is true.'
  b. *do'i*   *jetnu*   *jufra*
      [do.hi   ʒɛt.nu   ʒu.fra]
      some.utterance   is.a.true   sentence
      'That's true (where "that" is not necessarily what was just said)'.

15.6 Conlanging Practice: Semantics and Pragmatics in the Ur Languages

A. Match the Ur language to the most likely taboo area.

Fog	Death
Grass	Birth
Gem	Religion
Aqua	Body parts and functions

B. Think of euphemisms that could work in the Ur languages to avoid taboo words.
C. Which Ur language is most likely to have the following deictic systems?
- A system distinguishing proximal, medial and distal pronouns and adverbs.
- A system incorporating degree of visibility.
- A system incorporating degree of elevation.
- Another system that could be relevant to the fictional world.

15.7 Semantics and Pragmatics in Muq

15.7.1 Polysemy and Metaphor

Polysemous words in muq include [ouˌna] 'to begin, to awake,' and [ˈtæk.ɸu] 'warrior, noble, brave.' The extension of meaning from 'to begin' to 'to awake' is metaphorical; so is the extension of meaning from 'warrior' to 'brave, noble.'

Two additional examples of metaphors specific to the muq fictional world involve the words [ˈkus.tːei] 'heir, firstborn' and [ˈgli.mæ] 'sea snail.' [ˈkus.tːei], a compound from 'salt' [ˈkust] and 'to hold' [ˈtei], literally means 'salt holder.' The meaning was extended to refer to firstborn daughters and sons, who hold main rights to salt making within family units. The noun [ˈgli.mæ] 'sea snail' also means 'slow and beautiful,' two prized qualities associated with this life form in the fictional world. Examples of homonyms in muq will be discussed in Section 16.7.

15.7.2 Connotations, Taboos and Euphemisms

The word [kust] 'salt' has a positive connotation, as do derived words such as [kus] 'salty, worthy.' The word for 'night' [ˈɸuç] is used as a euphemism for 'death' [ˈqur.mur], which is taboo; similarly, 'to sleep' [ˈxaɸ] is a euphemism for 'to be dead' [ˈʟou].

15.7.3 Semantic Fields

Section 7.6 introduced muq words related to the semantic fields of size, temperature, value and color. So far the lexicon also includes vocabulary pertaining to flora, fauna, and verbs of motion, utterance and emotion, among others. An important semantic field relates to salt making, which is accomplished by holding seawater in a series of ponds so that water evaporates and salt can be harvested. Muq words related to these ponds are given in (15). Salt is harvested with a rake; three different types of salt are distinguished, depending on their quality and when they are harvested. These and other salt-related terms are given in (16, 17).

(15)　　Muq words related to salt-making ponds
　　　　a. [ˈse.ja]　　　'lagoon'
　　　　b. [ˈsa.siq]　　 'unripe'
　　　　c. [ˈtei]　　　　'to hold'
　　　　d. [ˈba.χi]　　　'to flake'
　　　　e. [ˈtei.se.ja]　'holding pond' (seawater first held here to begin evaporation process)
　　　　f. [ˈsa.siq. se.ja] 'evaporating pond' (seawater turns to brine here as it evaporates on)
　　　　g. [ˈba.χi.se.ja] 'crystalizing pond' (salt flakes are formed here, and are then harvested)

(16)　　Muq words related to salt
　　　　a. [ˈkig]　　　　'rake'
　　　　b. [ˈkust]　　　 'salt'
　　　　c. [ˈre.na]　　　'harvest'
　　　　d. [ˈmis.tə]　　 'dawn'
　　　　e. [ˈder]　　　　'noon'
　　　　f. [ˈa.ja]　　　 'evening'
　　　　g. [ˈmi.bæ]　　　'water'
　　　　h. [ˈlei]　　　　'sea, ocean'
　　　　i. [ˈŋum.ɫe]　　 'shallow'
　　　　j. [ˈlein]　　　 'to float'
　　　　k. [ˈɢoʁ]　　　　'to trade'
　　　　l. [tət.ˈpenk]　 'to gather, to collect'

(17)　　Types of salt in muq
　　　　a. [ˈmis.tə.kust] 'fleur de sel'　 (delicate salt, the first and most difficult to harvest)
　　　　b. [ˈder.kust]　 'sel gris'　　　 (fine salt, harvested after fleur de sel)
　　　　c. [ˈa.ja.kust]　'traditional salt' (coarser salt, last and easiest to harvest)

Table 15.5 lists kinship terms, many formed via compounding. Note that hypernym terms are also used for non-binary kinship.

Table 15.5 Kinship terms					
Hypernym		Female		Male	
[ˈcei.ni.a]	'parent, grandparent'	[ˈni.a.ni.a]	'maternal grandmother'	[ˈni.a.cei]	'maternal grandfather'
		[ˈcei.ni.a]	'paternal grandmother'	[ˈcei.ˈcei]	'paternal grandfather'
		[ˈni.a]	'mother'	[ˈcei]	'father'
[ˈsuʁ]	'spouse, life partner'	[ˈna.ja]	'wife'	[ˈpei]	'husband'
[ˈɢup.tə.sæʁ]	'offspring'	[ˈsæʁ]	'daughter'	[ˈɢup.tə]	'son'
[ˈkus.tːei]	'first born, heir (keeper of the salt)'	[ˈkus.tːei sæʁ]	'eldest daughter, female heir'	[ˈkus.tːei. ɢup.tə]	'eldest son, male heir'
[ˈɟi.ɟe.mi.ɣen]	'sibling'	[ˈɣen]	'sister'	[ˈɟi.ɟe.mi]	'brother'
[ˈmaʁ]	'aunt/uncle'	[ˈni.a.ɣen]	'maternal aunt'	[ˈni.a.ɟi. ɟe.mi]	'maternal uncle'
		[ˈcei.ɣen]	'paternal aunt'	[ˈcei.ˈɟi. ɟe.mi]	'paternal uncle'

15.7.4 Personal, Social and Textual Deixis

The Salt language has a set of personal pronouns indicating person and number (Table 15.6). The prefix [ne-] is used for the paucal, and [ma-] for the plural. The textual deictic pronoun [çei] is used to refer to a previous sentence or comment.

Table 15.6 Personal pronouns			
	SG	PAU	PL
1	[ˈbri]	[ˈne.bri]	[ˈma.bri]
2	[ˈχa]	[ˈne.χa]	[ˈma.χa]
3	[ˈzu]	[ˈne.zu]	[ˈma.zu]

The muq hold their elders in great regard; polite terms for them are [ˈni.a] 'mother' (if female), [ˈce.i] 'father' (if male) and [ˈcei.ni.a] 'parent' (for more than one elder, or for a non-binary one).

15.7.5 Spatial Deixis

Muq distinguishes three degrees of spatial deixis for adverbs, determiners and pronouns (Table 15.7). Determiners and pronouns have the same forms; both take number suffixes. Like articles, deictic determiners follow the noun.

Table 15.7 Spatial deixis

	Adverbs		Determiners and pronouns	
Proximal	[ˈɣe]	'here'	[ˈmɨn]	'this, this one'
Medial	[ˈŋim]	'there'	[ˈmɨk]	'that, that one'
Distal	[ˈŋi.me]	'way over there'	[ˈmɨk.mɨk]	'that (one) over there'

15.7.6 Temporal Deixis

Temporal deictic adverbs include [ˈʙei] 'now,' [ˈxus] 'soon' and [ˈŋou] 'later.' Adverbs referring to days or parts of days are shown in Table 15.8. The words for 'today' and 'tonight' are compounds (from [ˈmɨn] 'this' plus the noun for 'day' and 'night,' respectively). The words for 'the day after tomorrow' and 'the day before yesterday' involve reduplication of the first syllable of the words for 'tomorrow' and 'yesterday.'

Table 15.8 Temporal adverbs

Before today		Same day		After today	
[ˈde.bi]	'yesterday'	[ˈŋuç.mɨn]	'today'	[ˈsim.ti]	'tomorrow'
[ˈde.de.bi]	'day before yesterday'	[ˈɸuç.mɨn]	'tonight'	[ˈsim.sim.ti]	'day after tomorrow'

15.7.7 Semantics and Pragmatics in the Fictional Text

The text on the muq origin myth includes several examples of the deictic pronoun [zu] 3SG, and also the temporal deictic adverb [ˈŋou] 'later, then.' Chapter 18 shows how both are incorporated in the full text translation.

15.8 Guide to Expanding Your Conlang Lexicon

- Consider words in the conlang lexicon that have affective or social connotations.
- What topics/words are taboo in the fictional world (e.g., death, birth, bodily functions, religion)?

15.8 Guide to Expanding Your Conlang Lexicon

- What words are euphemisms? Indicate specific contexts in which they would be used.
- Check for words that might be polysemous or homonymous (such as words that refer to more than one body part).
- For polysemous words, consider if any of the meanings arise through metaphor.
- Consider adding related meanings to selected words via metaphorical extension (such as certain adjectives and/or kinship terms).
- Develop one or two idioms in your conlang. Are they based on metaphor?
- Organize your lexicon according to word networks (semantic fields). Consider adding a column to your lexicon spreadsheet to indicate this information.
- Fill out obvious lexical gaps in semantic fields, ideally connected to the fictional world. Identify or create hypernyms (general terms) for each category, as relevant.
- Sort your lexicon by word type. Are there synonyms? If so, consider whether they have different affective or social connotations. Expand or clarify their translations if necessary.
- Add antonyms for some adjectives and adverbs (if relevant).
- Can you think of additional semantic fields? (Some possibilities include fauna, flora, dwellings, hunting, gathering, verbs of motion and verbs of emotion).
- Work out the kinship system of your conlang, considering its connection to the fictional world.
- If there are pronouns, indicate whether they indicate number, gender and/or case. Even if your conlang has no or minimal nominal morphology, your pronoun system might still encode some (of all) these distinctions. Consider listing these pronouns in table form.
- Will pronouns encode politeness? If so, indicate how, and provide examples. Consider other lexical words or expressions that can encode politeness.
- Will your conlang have demonstrative pronouns and/or determiners? If so, indicate how many distinctions they involve.
- Work out the main spatial adverbs or lexical expressions for your conlang.
- Will your conlang include temporal deictic expressions such as *now, later, before, after*. If so, how are they formed?
- Are there words or expressions for 'last night,' 'tomorrow morning' or similar meanings?
- Are there textual deictic pronouns or adverbs?

To Learn More

Lakoff (1990) and Lakoff and Johnson (2003 [1980]) are classic studies on metaphors in language and the mind. Jeannette Littlemore (2019) discusses sources of variation in metaphor, including the shape and size of one's body, gender, religious beliefs and ideology, among others.

For polysemy, particularly concerning body parts, see Brown (2013a, b) and Witkowski and Brown (1985). For kinship terms, see Brian Schwimmer's kinship tutorial website:

www.umanitoba.ca/faculties/arts/anthropology/tutor/kinterms/toc.html

To learn more about deixis, see Anderson and Keenan (1985), Fillmore (1982), Levinson (2006), Diessel and Coventry (2020) and Post (2019). For politeness and honorifics, see Helmbrecht (2013) and Shibatani (1998).

More details on Esperanto can be found in Kellerman Reed (2003). The information on Pirahã comes from Everett (2005), and on Kambera from Klamer (1998).

16 Variation in Space and Time

This chapter addresses aspects of language variation and change, since both can enhance a conlang and make it more naturalistic. Sections 16.1 and 16.2 address dialectal and gender variation, respectively, and Section 16.3 covers variation in conlanging. Section 16.4 focuses on historical change in natlangs, and 16.5 discusses it in various conlangs. In addition, Section 16.6 provides some conlanging exercises, 16.7 describes some examples of dialectal variation and historical change in muq, and 16.8 is a list of guided questions to help you incorporate variation in your conlang. As usual, the chapter ends with a list of sources to explore these topics further.

Key Words

Assimilation
Dialect
   Ethnolect
   Genderlect
   Geolect
   Sociolect
   Standard
   Vernacular (non-standard)
Diminutive (DIM)
Extrinsic factors
   Cultural changes
   Language contact
   Prestige
Group identity
Intrinsic factors
   Context extension
   Semantic change
      Amelioration
      Pejoration

Semantic extension
Semantic narrowing
Sound change
Deletion
Metathesis
Lateralization
Mutual intelligibility
Rhotacization

16.1 Dialects

Sometimes people assume that they speak a 'language' and speakers from other geographical areas a '**dialect**.' But truly, everyone speaks at least one **dialect** or variety of a language.

I speak Basque Spanish, a variety of Spanish in contact with the Basque language in Northern Spain. Like most Spaniards, I use the pronouns *tú* 'you (SG)' and *vosotros* 'you (PL),' and I distinguish the phonemes /θ s/, as in the minimal pair *masa* ['ma.sa] 'mass, dough,' *maza* ['ma.θa] 'mace.' In other Spanish-speaking countries *vosotros* is not used, and /θ/ is not a phoneme (*masa, maza* are homonyms instead). My native dialect, however, differs from Peninsular Spanish in some ways. For example, I use some Basque borrowings (such as *simiriri* 'light rain' or *sagutxu* 'small mouse'), and I also tend to not use the subjunctive (irrealis) in conditional sentences.

Because I've lived in the United States for many years and I have interacted with speakers of Spanish from other countries, my native dialect has changed in some ways. I use some words and expressions that are frequent in Latin American Spanish, and I avoid using Spanish words that have negative connotations in other countries. Because I'm immersed in an English-speaking culture, I also borrow words from English, and I sometimes code-switch when I talk to English–Spanish bilinguals. Since I don't go back to Spain often, I am not as up to date with the current way my native Spanish dialect is spoken. For these reasons, my Spanish has neutralized. Other Spanish speakers can usually tell that I'm from Spain but might not be able to pinpoint exactly where from. Indeed, in recent years, some Spaniards have even complimented me on how well I speak the language, assuming I learned it as a foreign language. In sum, whether we like it or not, the way we speak changes with time and with the influences from other languages and dialects. For different reasons, speakers slowly but surely change how they speak through their lifetime.

> **Your Turn**
>
> - What is your first language?
> - Do you speak one or more dialects?
> - Do you have trouble understanding speakers from other geographical areas?
> - Have you ever been told that you have an 'accent'?

With centuries or millennia, languages change so much that varieties become different languages altogether. It's not always clear, however, when two dialects become two different languages. One criterion used often is that of **mutual intelligibility**. When speakers from two different varieties understand each other without prior familiarity or special effort, these speakers are considered to speak dialects of the same language. When they do not, these speakers speak different languages. Mutual intelligibility is not foolproof, however, since it tends to be affected by language contact and people's willingness to understand each other.

Group identity is another criterion used to distinguish between language and dialect: if a group of people says they speak a different language, then they do. One example concerns Hindi and Urdu, spoken in India and Pakistan, respectively. Although mutually intelligible, Hindi and Urdu have lexical differences (Hindi has many words from Sanskrit, and Urdu from Farsi) and are written with different scripts (Devanagari and Perso-Arabic script, respectively). Despite their mutual intelligibility, Hindi and Urdu are considered different languages for political and religious reasons.

The flip side is that some ways of speaking are deemed dialects of the same language even if not mutually intelligible. Examples include varieties of Arabic, such as Moroccan, Egyptian and Lebanese. Arabic varieties share the same writing script, but they differ phonologically, morphologically and/or syntactically, impeding mutual intelligibility of spoken speech. However, a shared written script and a sense of cultural and religious unity contribute to being considered different dialects.

Languages usually involve multiple dialects. **Geolects** are dialects determined geographically (such as Canadian English or Indian English), and **genderlects** are language variants associated with a specific gender (as we'll discuss further in Section 17.2). **Sociolects** are associated with a particular social class (such as Cockney English, spoken by working-class and lower-middle class Londoners), and **ethnolects** are dialects spoken by a specific ethnic group (such as Chicano English in the US). Dialects can also be **standard** or **vernacular**. **Standard dialects** tend to be prestige varieties connected to official business, writing and the media, while **vernacular** or

non-standard dialects are used for ordinary, day-to-day communication. Speakers can typically shift between the two depending on degree of formality and who they are talking to.

Which dialect is considered 'standard' boils down to political, geographical and/or cultural accident. Consider, for example, standard British English (also known as 'Received pronunciation'). Historically, English in the British Isles comprised many different dialects (it still does). London was (and is) the center of power and the cultural and economic hub of the country. In addition, since the fifteenth century, it was the center of manuscript copying/printing. London English was associated with political, cultural and economic prestige, and was written more often than other dialects. These factors contributed to it becoming the standard and the variety most often taught to second-language learners in Europe and other parts of the world.

Vernacular dialects tend to be associated with minorities, those with lower educational backgrounds and rural populations. They are often considered 'degenerations' from the standard. This negative perception arises from prejudice; non-standard dialects, like standard ones, have full, rich grammatical systems, and contrary to what many people think they do not originate from standard dialects. Let's consider two examples: Puerto Rican Spanish, and African American Vernacular English (AAVE).

Puerto Rican Spanish is a Spanish geolect from Puerto Rico. It can be heard frequently in parts of the US, particularly New York and Florida. Speakers of other Spanish dialects often consider it 'bad Spanish,' 'ugly' or 'ghetto.' One particularly maligned trait is the pronunciation of syllable-final 'r' as [l]. Thus, the word *mar* 'sea' is pronounced as [mal], the verb *beber* 'to drink' as [be.bel] and *puerto* 'port' as [pwel.to]. You might have heard these and similar pronunciations in reggaeton songs by Puerto Rican artists Ozuna and Bad Bunny, among others.

The pronunciation of 'r' as [l] is termed **lateralization** (since 'r' is pronounced as a lateral). Lateralization is also attested in other areas of the Caribbean, including parts of Cuba. One important aspect is that lateralization only occurs syllable-finally. It is instructive to compare it to **rhotacization** (pronunciation as a rhotic) of /l/ in Andalusian Spanish, where *mal* 'evil' is pronounced [mar], and *alma* 'soul' is [ar.ma]. Rhotacization is criticized by speakers of other Peninsular Spanish dialects, but neither lateralization nor rhotacization are 'bad'; they just result from the articulatory and acoustic similarities between [l] and [r] (both voiced alveolar consonants), which causes them to be misperceived, particularly in perceptually weak positions such as codas. In fact, 'l' and 'r' frequently substituted each other in the development of Romance languages. For example, the Latin word *peregrinus* 'pilgrim' underwent lateralization of the first 'r' in Italian *pellegrino*, French *pèlerin* and even in English 'pilgrim,' since this word was borrowed into English via French and Latin.

Let's now turn to AAVE. Widely considered to be a 'bad' way of speaking English, AAVE is a full linguistic system with differences from other English dialects. These include a complex, unique system of tense and aspect. Some examples are given in (1); capitalization indicates that the word is pronounced with stress, and SE stands for 'Standard English.'

(1) AAVE aspect: Present tense (from Rickford & Rickford 2000:119)
    a. He runnin. (progressive; SE 'He is running')
    b. He be runnin. (habitual progressive; SE 'He is usually running')
    c. He be steady runnin. (intensive habitual progressive; SE 'He is usually running in an intensive, sustained manner')
    d. He been runnin. (perfect progressive; SE 'He has been running')
    e. He BEEN runnin. (perfect progressive with remote inception; SE 'He's been running for a long time, and still is')

AAVE is a systematic, rule-governed dialect of English. It is perfectly good English: it just has different grammatical 'rules' from Standard American English or other English dialects.

16.2 Gender Variation

In all languages, there are ways in which men and women's ways of speaking differ. Sometimes gender variation is extensive, and the language can be said to have genderlects. Gender differences can be phonological. For example, in Karajá, women have the phoneme /k/, unlike men. Thus, Karajá women will say [dɪ.ka.rɜ̃] for 'I' and [ka.wa.ɾu] for 'horse,' while men will say [dɪ.a.rɜ̃] and [a.wa.ɾu] (Aikhenvald 2016:138). Another example is Pirahã, where men contrast the fricatives /h s/ but women only have /h/ (Everett 2005:178–179).

Voice quality, intonation and airstream mechanisms can also be associated with gender. For example, in Tohono O'odham women use pulmonic ingressive airstream to convey intimacy in discourse. In American English, uptalk (rising intonation at the end of statements) and creaky voice are associated with women; in British English, creaky voice is more prevalent for men. In Japanese, women tend to have a breathier voice quality than men.

Female and male forms of speech might be characterized by lexical or morphological differences as well. For example, in English, women supposedly use words like *lovely* or *really* more than men; and in A'aninin (Gros Ventre) 'hello' is *wahei* in men, and *næhæ* in women (Aikhenvald 2016:140). In Kukama-Kokamilla men and women use different personal pronouns, demonstratives, conjunctions and morphemes. For example, the plural suffix is [-nu] for women and [-kana] for men.

The differences considered so far relate to speakers' gender, but in some natlangs, they might be related to the gender of addressees. For example, in Tunica, pronouns and nominal affixes vary according to whether the addressee is female or male. For example, 'you (PL/DU)' is *wi'nima* for male addressees, and *hi'nima* for female ones. In the extinct isolate Yana, formerly spoken in Northern California, 'male' forms were used by men speaking to men; and 'female' forms in all other cases (Aikhenvald 2016:141–142).

In some languages gender is intertwined with politeness and honorifics. One example is Japanese, which has formal, plain and informal or deprecatory politeness levels. Politeness is not symmetrical, since a socially inferior person addresses a superior using formal language, even if addressed informally by them. Women tend to use the honorific prefix deference marker *o-* to refer to objects belonging to a respected person. If they use it to refer to their own belongings, this conveys elegance and grace. Men do not use this marker in this way (Shibatani 1990:374).

Japanese women also use more honorific forms than men, while men use words with derogatory connotations. Men also use the deprecatory pronouns *ore* and *omae/kisama* (for 'I' and 'you,' respectively), unlike women (Ide 1991:73). Men also use the particles *ze* and *zo* in rough speech; women use the particle *wa*, which softens a statement.

Men and women might use the opposite genderlect for specific purposes. Using the 'wrong' gender forms in a language might characterize foreign and/or children's speech; it might also be associated with being a more feminine man or a more masculine woman, or be used for specific purposes (quoting a person from the opposite gender, treating women as equals, making people pay attention, expressing affection or conveying authority, among others).

Why are there gender differences in some languages? Some gender variation is related to biology: women tend to have shorter vocal folds, and therefore their pitch tends to be higher than men's. Women also have narrower, shorter vocal tracts, which impacts the way in which sounds are produced. Other gender differences might be based on asymmetric language contact due to conquest or warfare. One example is the mixed language ancestor of Garifuna, spoken in Belize and Honduras. In the fifteenth century, the Ineri (Arawak) speaking population of the Lesser Antilles were invaded by Carib-speaking intruders. The latter killed all adult Arawak men and married the Arawak women they conquered. While the women hang on to their Arawak language, the men spoke Carib. They communicated in simplified Carib: the women using more Arawak words and morphology, and the men using more Carib ones. With time, the differences between male and female language diminished, but Garifuna now still has pairs of words and expressions reflecting 'men only' and 'women only' speech. For example, the command 'come here' is rendered as *abo ie* by men, and as *bugabu ia* by women.

Cultural practices might also bear on men-only and women-only forms. For example, Suri women used to have a wooden plate, between 1 and 6 inches in diameter, inserted into their lower lip. Having a stretched lower lip made bilabial consonants difficult to pronounce, so women replaced them with velars. For example, 'water' was *mà* for men, but *ŋà* for women. Even if the lip plates are no longer used, the pronunciation differences remain (Yigezu 1998:97–99). Another example involves Japanese: with the growing gender equality in Japan, Japanese genderlects are becoming less strict, and women use more male forms (such as the masculine form of 'I' *boku*) and men use more female forms (such as the particle *wa*).

16.3 Variation in Conlanging: The Case of Klingon

Klingon might be the conlang for which we have the most information regarding regional and social variation. Much of it is described in entertaining detail in Okrand (1997).

There are eighty dialects of Klingon. The 'official' or standard dialect changes with each new emperor. Klingons who wish to keep or gain power learn several Klingon dialects, since failing to properly speak the official dialect results in being judged as stupid or subversive. Most dialectal variation in Klingon is lexical or phonological. Lexical variation is extensive in words related to food, clothing and the body. For example, most Klingon dialects have different words for 'forehead.' Some words might be considered perfectly innocent in one dialect but insulting in another. One example is the word *ghaw'* /ɣɑwʔ/, used extensively across the empire to refer to a liver soup. In Vospeg Klingon, this word is slang for 'insecure, full of self-doubt,' obviously a terrible insult.

Dialects might vary phonologically as well. For example, Standard Klingon has both /b m/, but Krotmag Klingon only /m/. Thus, the Standard Klingon words *qab* /qɑb/ 'face' and *qam* /qɑm/ 'foot' are homonyms in Krotmag Klingon; so are *boH* /box/ 'be impatient' and *moH* /mox/ 'be ugly.' To avoid ambiguity or 'catastrophic misunderstanding,' Krotmag Klingon speakers disambiguate such words via compounding. Thus, 'foot' can be rendered as *uS qam* /uṣ qɑm/ ('leg foot') and 'face' as *nach qab* /natʃ qɑb/ ('head face'). The verbs 'be impatient' and 'be ugly' might be clarified with additional linguistic context, for example with the Klingon equivalent for 'calm down' after the former, or 'my eyes ache' after the latter.

In the Star Trek universe, English is used as the lingua franca for intergalactic communication. Klingon coexists with other languages, particularly in the capital and other big cities in Kronos. This might explain some of its regional variation. Although it is considered offensive to speak other languages in the presence of people who might not know them, words from these languages are borrowed into Klingon. One example is *qajunpaQ* [qɑ.dʒun.pɑqχ], referring to surprising or unexpected, perhaps even reckless, courage. This is a borrowing from a language spoken in Krios, where it meant 'glowing' or 'flowing lava.'

An ancient form of Klingon, known as *no' Hol* [noʔ.xol] ('ancestor's language') is heard mostly in songs, particularly those associated with rituals (myths, ceremonies and most opera). Also, 'Proper' Klingon is distinguished from 'Clipped' Klingon, used in combat or often day-to-day. For example, in Clipped Klingon the imperative is formed with the verb root only, leaving the imperative prefix out.

Klingon also shows age-dependent variation. For example, Klingon children tend to pronounce 'j' /dʒ/ as [j] and 'q' /q/ as [k]. Children also tend to use the **diminutive (DIM)**, as in *SoSoy* /ʂoʂ-oj/ 'mommy (mom-DIM)' or *targhoy* /tɑrɣ-oj/ 'targy, pet targ' (targ-DIM). Klingon children also regularize irregular plural nouns (as children learning natlangs often do). Younger and older Klingons also use different words. Those used by young people are 'fresh words' (i.e., 'slang') while those used by older Klingons are 'tired words.' Examples of slang include *Igh* /ɪɣ/ 'be cursed, jinxed' (which can be quite insulting); and *SIj* /ʂɪdʒ/ 'be insightful, clever, have a keen mind,' literally meaning 'slash, slit (with a blade).' The tag question *qar'a'* [qɑr.ʔɑʔ] 'is it accurate?' is favored among younger speakers.

Klingon also has sociolects. The honorific verbal suffix *-neS* /-nɛʂ/ is used to address Klingons of high military rank or power. Klingons of high-status use more archaic words, particularly relating to food; lower classes use more slang, particularly if younger. In addition, high-ranked government and military officials often use English to talk to each other as a mark of rank or status and to keep 'the general populace' uninformed in certain contexts.

16.4 Language Change

Nobody knows for sure how or when language originated, although estimates place its origin 150,000–30,000 years ago in East Africa. Babbling and a genetic predisposition to acquire and use language might have facilitated it. Language could have originated via a mutation before human groups split, subsequently spreading and changing into the (approximately) 7,000 languages spoken today.

Language is dynamic; it is constantly changing. At the same time, because linguistic change is slow, it gives the impression that language is static. New and old forms of speech frequently coexist, even in the same dialect. New stages of a language change might be considered 'mistakes' at first. However, when enough people use the 'wrong' word, sound or grammatical construction, it is accepted as part of the language. In any case, language does not degenerate; it changes to serve the communicative and expressive needs of speakers.

Languages change due to **extrinsic factors** including **language contact, prestige** and **cultural changes,** and because of **intrinsic factors** such as **changes in sounds, meaning** and **context extension.** Let's consider each in turn.

16.4.1 Extrinsic Factors

When two languages come into extensive contact, borrowings become common. For example, English has borrowed 'taco' and 'siesta' from Spanish, 'tsunami' and 'emoji' from Japanese, 'wiki' and 'taboo' from Hawaiian, and 'latte' and 'paparazzi' from Italian. These languages also have English loanwords. For example, 'hamburger', 'gangster' and 'stress' are *hamburguesa*, *gánster* and *estrés* in Spanish. Borrowings are also used in conlanging. For example, Na'vi has the English loanwords [ˈkun.sɪp] 'gunship' and [puk] 'book,' and Lojban borrowed various evidentials from Láadan, as mentioned in Chapter 12.

Borrowings are typically adapted to sound more native-like. For example, since Na'vi lacks voiced stops, loanwords with these consonants are pronounced as voiceless stops, as in the examples above. Borrowings can also adopt native morphology; for example, 'to flip out' is rendered as *flipar* in Spanish in the infinitive form. Borrowings can involve a change in word category; for example, the English noun *fashion* has been borrowed as the slang adjective *fashion* (pronounced [fa.si̯on]) 'trendy, fashionable' in Peninsular Spanish.

In addition to showing group allegiance (as with slang), language can be used to convey status. Consider, for example, the difference between *café* vs. *coffee shop*; *à la mode* vs. *served with ice cream*, and *vintage* vs. *second hand*. In all these examples, the first word/expression has connotations of elegance, culture and trendiness, unlike the second. Words with prestigious connotations often displace ordinary words with similar denotations.

As culture, technology and the economy evolve, new concepts come to life, and new words enter the language. Some recent examples in English include *shrinkflation, metaverse* and *nomophobia*. In Na'vi, contact with humans results in the new words *human* [ˈtaw.tu.tɛ] (literally, 'sky person') and *computer* [ˈɛl.tu lɛ.ˈfŋap] (literally 'metal brain'), among others. In addition, words might become obsolete because the objects they refer to are no longer in use (*floppy disk, walkman*), or because they are replaced by other words. For example, *flight attendant* has replaced *stewardess* to avoid gender bias. Examples of archaic or obsolete words in English are given in (2).

(2) Obsolete and archaic words in English
    a. *methinks*   'it seems to me'
    b. *eyen*   'eyes'
    c. *hagride*   'to afflict with worry; to torment'
    d. *elflock*   'hair matted as by elves'
    e. *scamander*   'to wonder about without a settled purpose'
    f. *grimalkin*   'Domestic cat, especially an old female one'

16.4.2 Intrinsic Changes

We might not realize in our lifetime, but pronunciation is constantly in flux. After a few generations, some sounds might change or disappear, and new sounds might enter the language. For example, *house* and *mouse* have diphthongs now, but in Old English they were pronounced [hus] and [mus], respectively. On the other hand, some diphthongs are disappearing; for example, in American English the word *new* is often pronounced as [nu] instead of [nju].

Common types of **sound changes** involve **deletion** (i.e., not pronouncing a sound) and **metathesis** (reversing the linear order of two sounds). Deletion can affect vowels, consonants and even syllables. It is particularly common in syllable or word positions that are not prominent, including codas and final and unstressed syllables. Sounds in these positions are hard to articulate and/or perceive fully. Examples of deletion in the history of English are found in words such as *knee* and *knight*, whose first sound was [k] in Middle English, unlike today.

> **Your Turn**
>
> Consider the Latin word *peregrinus* 'pilgrim' and its modern descendants in Spanish and French. Which sounds were deleted historically, and in which contexts?
>
> Latin   *peregrinus*   [pe.ˈre.gri.nus]
> Spanish   *peregrino*   [pe.re.ˈɣri.no]
> French   *pèlerin*   [pɛl.ˈʁɛ̃]

Metathesis occurs more sporadically than deletion; one typical context is consonant clusters. For example, the words *dusk* and *ask* used to be pronounced with word-final [ks] rather than [sk], as is standard today (*ask* is still pronounced [æks] in AAVE). There are many other types of sounds changes; we will discuss some in relation to the muq language in Section 16.7.

Words can also change their meaning. If word meaning becomes broader, it is considered **semantic extension**; if it becomes narrower, it is considered **semantic narrowing**. Examples of the former include *dog*, formerly meaning a type of dog only; and *aunt*, previously denoting a father's sister. Examples of semantic narrowing include *hound*, which used to refer to all dogs, but now only refers to a specific hunting dog breed, and *girl*, which in Middle English was used to refer to children regardless of sex.

The meaning of a word or expression can become more positive (**amelioration** or negative (**pejoration**). The word *knight*, for example, used to refer to a boy but now denotes an honorary title. Amelioration is commonly found in slang; for example, *sick* and *wicked* convey that something or someone is awesome. One example of historical pejoration is the word *wench*, which used to refer to a girl but now indicates a 'wanton woman' (at least in some dialects). Another example is *witch*, which used to have a neutral connotation, but now it is associated with evil. Unfortunately, many words relating to women undergo pejoration historically.

Certain words or expressions might be extended to new contexts, causing language to change. This is sometimes due to mislearning or reanalysis of a word or grammatical structure. For example, consider the word *hamburger*, which originally indicated something from Hamburg ('Hamburg' plus an *-er* suffix indicating provenance). This word became reanalyzed as 'ham' plus 'burger' and now serves as a model for other food items, including *cheeseburger*, *chicken burger* or *black bean burger*, among others.

Negation in French is a good example of change via **context extension**. In Early French, negation was conveyed with the particle *ne* 'not' before the verb (3), as mentioned in Chapter 12. If negation was emphatic, an additional word, such as *pas* 'step,' *mie* 'crumb' or *goutte* 'drop,' was added after the verb (4).

(3) Neutral negation in Early French (adapted from McWorther 2001:26)

    a. *Il*   *ne*   *marche.*   'He does not walk.'
        he   NEG   walk.3SG.PRS

    b. *Il*   *ne*   *mange.*   'He does not eat.'
        he   NEG   eat.3SG.PRS

    c. *Il*   *ne*   *boit*   'He does not drink.'
        he   NEG   drink.3SG.PRS

(4) Emphatic negation in Early French (adapted from McWorther 2001:26)
    a. Il ne marche pas. 'He does not walk a step.'
       he NEG walk.3SG.PRS step
    b. Il ne mange mie. 'He does not eat a crumb.'
       he NEG eat.3SG.PRS crumb
    c. Il ne boit goutte 'He does not drink a drop.'
       he NEG eat.3SG.PRS crumb

The word *pas* prevailed over other emphatic words in negative sentences, eventually losing its emphasis and becoming associated with the expression of neutral negation. Currently, it is the main negation marker, since *ne* is usually dropped in informal speech (5).

(5) Neutral negation in Modern French
    a. Il (ne) marche pas. 'He does not walk.'
       he NEG walk.3SG.PRS NEG
    b. Il (ne) mange pas. 'He does not eat.'
       he NEG eat.3SG.PRS NEG
    c. Il (ne) boit pas. 'He does not drink.'
       he NEG walk.3SG.PRS NEG

16.5 Conlangs and Historical Change

Conlangs can change over time; when this happens, it's often because new conlang versions are proposed, either by the original inventor or by conlang users. One example is Loglan, invented by James Cooke Brown in 1955. In later years, a group of Loglan followers implemented several revisions, which Brown refused to accept. In 1987, these followers decided to take the revised Loglan, changed the lexicon to avoid copyright issues and named the resulting variant Lojban. As Cowan (2016:10) states, Loglan is the ancestral version of Lojban.

    Another example is Esperanto, created by Ludwik Lejzer Zamenhof in the late nineteenth century. Zamenhof published the first Esperanto book in 1887. Since then, there have been dozens of proposed revisions, known as 'Esperantidos' (*ido* in Esperanto means 'offspring'). One of them is reformed Esperanto, proposed by Zamenhof himself; it involved discarding the accusative suffix and adjective–noun agreement, among others (Garvía 2016:134). This revision was not accepted by the Esperanto community. Other Esperantidos include Antido (from 1907) and Esperanto II (from 1937), both devised by mathematician René de Saussure (brother of the famous linguist Ferdinand de Saussure). The best-known Esperantido is Ido (from 1907), proposed by Louis de Beaufront and championed by mathematician Louis Couturat and linguist Otto Jespersen. Ido incorporates some of Zamenhof's 1894 proposed reforms. Ido was subject to many changes; making it as 'perfect' as possible was prioritized over building a community of speakers. This contributed to Ido not taking off in the same way Esperanto did. One relatively recent revision of Esperanto is Ayola (from 2002).

If a conlang is taken on by a large community of speakers and becomes the native language of a new generation of speakers, then it becomes a natlang and will be subject to language change. This is the case with Esperanto. It is hard to know exactly how many Esperanto speakers there are; estimates vary from 300,000 to 10 million. There are about 350 documented cases of children being taught Esperanto as their first language together with another mother tongue.

The original description of Esperanto included sixteen rules and over 900 words. In 1970 the lexicon already comprised more than 16,000 words. Several new words were included via borrowings and derivation. Others have changed meaning and/or been replaced by new ones. For example, *malsanulejo* [mal.sa.nu.le.jo] originally meant 'hospital' but changed its meaning to 'sick house'; *hospitalo* [ho.spi.ta.lo] is the common word for 'hospital' now. Grammatical change is also taking place in Esperanto, including having SVO as preferred word order and a diminishing use of the accusative case (Gledhill 2000:117–119).

Historical change can be inextricably linked to conlanging and the development of a fictional word; this was the case for J. R. R. Tolkien, who devoted decades developing the conlangs showcased in his writings. Historical change and dialectal variation were prominent in Tolkien's conlanging and were tightly connected to his world building. Tolkien describes the languages and dialects of Elves, Men, Hobbits and other races in Appendix F in *Lord of the Rings*. Common Eldarin, originally spoken by the Eldar, was spoken by three different clans, each having a distinct dialect. With time, these dialects evolved and became different languages. The most enduring were Quenya ('High-Elven') and Sindarin ('Grey-Elven'). Examples of both are given in (6).

(6) Words in Quenya and Sindarin (Noel 1980:72, 73; IPA)

	Quenya		Sindarin		Translation
a.	*arda*	[ˈar.da]	*arth*	[ˈarθ]	'realm, earth'
b.	*carne*	[ˈkar.nɛ]	*caran*	[ˈka.ran]	'red'
c.	*isil*	[ˈi.sil]	*ithil*	[ˈɪ.θɪl]	'moon'
d.	*nor*	[ˈnɔr]	*dor*	[ˈdɔr]	'land'

Quenya is more archaic than Sindarin and was the first Elvish language to appear in written form. Quenya had different regional dialects, including Valinorean (spoken by Valinor Elves). In Middle Earth, Quenya is used by the High Elves for ceremony, lore and song; it is not used in daily speech. If you are a Tolkien fan, you might have come across Quenyan names such as *Sauron* 'the Abhorred,' *Eärendil* 'Lover of the Sea' and *Telcontar* 'Strider' (Aragorn's nickname). Sindarin developed from Doriathrin and Old Noldorin; it was the main language of Elves in different regions from Middle Earth and had different dialects and accents. Some proper names in Sindarin you might recognize include *Aragorn* 'having royal valor,' *Arwen* 'noble maiden' and *Elrond* 'dome of stars' (Salo 2004, appendix 5).

Sindarin was also spoken by other peoples, including the Dúnedain and Faramir, and his men. The former, who were Númenoreans, were friends of the Elves and had learned a variation of Sindarin transmitted from generation to generation but changing little throughout time (similar to how Ladino was transmitted in the Jewish diaspora from the fifteenth century to our days). Their 'men of wisdom' also learned Quenya, considered prestigious and used to name important places and people. However, their native speech was Adûnaic, also referred to as 'Mannish' or the 'Language of the West.' As time went by, the Dúnedain population dwindled; most stopped using Sindarin, although several Sindarin words were borrowed into Adûnaic.

16.6 Conlanging Practice: Variation in the Ur Languages

A. Match the Ur language to the most likely dialect differentiation in the fictional world.

Fog	Geolect
Grass	Sociolect
Gem	Genderlect
Aqua	Ethnolect

B. Taking into consideration the map you created in Chapter 2, indicate the most likely locations for geolects in your conlang.

16.7 Variation in the Salt Language

The Salt language has a standard dialect that is used in ceremonial situations and to communicate with muq people from different regions. Everyone can speak the standard dialect; it is quite formal and sounds tend to be fully articulated, with little or no sound reduction or deletion.

There are also geolects connected to different regions of the island (the coast, the valley, the forest and the mountains). The coastal dialect is spoken by people living close to the shore, who tend to work in fishing and salt making. In this dialect, long words (three syllables or longer) used frequently tend to be reduced (via deletion of unstressed syllables, particularly word-medially; 7a, b). In addition, word-final consonant clusters are simplified to one consonant (7c, d).

(7) Geolectal variation in muq

	Standard muq	Coastal muq	Translation
a.	[ˈsɑ.siq. se.ja]	[ˈsɑ.se.ja]	'evaporating pond'
b.	[ˈba.χi.se.ja]	[ˈba.se.ja]	'crystalizing pond'
c.	[ˈmis.tə.kust]	[ˈmis.kus]	'fleur de sel'
d.	[ˈder.kust]	[ˈder.kus]	'sel gris'

Coastal muq is also known for palatalizing /n/ to [ɲ] before front vowels. This is a type of **assimilation**, that is, a sound change that makes one sound more similar to another in its vicinity. Assimilation often occurs because it is easier to articulate adjacent sounds if they are similar, particularly in fast speech. In Coastal muq, /n/ palatalization results in the 'absorption' of a front vowel into the palatal nasal; the word becomes shorter as a result (8).

(8) Palatalization in Coastal muq

	Standard muq	Coastal muq	Translation
a.	[ˈni.a.cei]	[ˈɲa.cei]	'maternal grandfather'
b.	[ˈni.a.ɣen]	[ˈɲa.ɣen]	'maternal aunt'
c.	[ˈni.a.ni.a]	[ˈɲa.ɲa]	'maternal grandmother'

In Coastal muq, the words for [ˈmis.tə] 'dawn,' [ˈder] 'noon' and [ˈa.ja] 'evening' can be used as adjectives to refer to people. The first conveys that the person is beautiful and elegant, the second that a person is solid and straightforward, and the third that the person is rough around the edges. This meaning extension originates from the inclusion of these words in compounds referring to salt quality (as explained in Chapter 16).

The Salt people usually keep to themselves. Traders transport salt and other merchandise through the mountains or across the sea several times a year. They sometimes bring back novelty food and items; words to refer to them are borrowed from languages spoken in other regions. Two borrowings from a language from across the sea (pronounced [dan] by the muq) are [ˈsol] 'lavender spice' and [ˈmur] 'silk tunic.' In the *dan* language, these words were pronounced [ˈtsoːl] and [ˈᵐburː], respectively. The beginning consonant was substituted by the closest equivalent in muq, and long sounds were pronounced as short (as we've seen, muq lacks long vowels, and long consonants can only occur medially in compounds).

Muq has nine contrastive vowels, as we saw in Chapter 3. A change in progress is observed whereby /ɨ/ and /ə/ are slowly merging (i.e., losing their contrast). For example, the minimal pair /ˈʎunər/ 'outside,' /ˈʎunɨr/ 'to lie down' tend to be pronounced by younger muq speakers as [ˈʎu.nər] in both cases (which means these words are becoming homonyms). The reason for this merging is that central vowels are perceptually similar and tend to occur in unstressed syllables.

Ancient muq was an ergative-absolutive language, with a tendency for the verb to come first, but with relative freedom in the order between subject and object. With time, the ergative and absolutive case endings were dropped and word order became VOS.

16.8 Guide to Incorporating Variation in Your Conlang

A. Dialectal Variation
   Does your conlang have dialects associated with various social classes, genders, ethnicities or geographical locations? (Revise your answers to 2.5.2 if needed).
   - If so, provide examples of phonological, lexical, morphological and/or syntactic variation.
B. Historical Change
   - Consider the history of the fictional group. Did the conlang speakers migrate from another area, or have they remained in the same area for centuries or millennia?
   - Indicate how cultural changes and/or technological advances could have resulted in language change (for specific words or morphological, and/or syntactic characteristics).
   - Think of how some sounds and/or meanings have changed, or ways in which morphological and/or syntactic characteristics have been extended to other contexts.
   - If the fictional group had prolonged contact with another group in the fictional world, what words could have been borrowed into the conlang? Think, for example, of food-related words, and words and phrases connected to cultural or technological innovation.

To Learn More

To learn more about dialectal variation, see Simpson (2019). For a comprehensive introduction to American English dialects, see Wolfram and Schilling (2016). Bailey and Thomas (1998) is a short introduction to AAVE phonology; accessible book-length sources on this dialect include Rickford

(1999), Green (2002) and McWhorter (2017). Rickford and King (2016) is advanced reading but highly recommended. Also recommended is the documentary *Talking Black in America* (2017) and the International Dialects of English Archive (IDEA) (www.dialectsarchive.com).

For a short TED talk on language change, see Alex Gendler's 'How Languages Evolve', available here: https://youtu.be/iWDKsHm6gTA. Ostler (2005) is a highly engaging account of the rise and fall of languages through history. To learn more about how languages change, see Janson (2012) and McWhorter (2001). For more about language evolution in conlanging, see chapter 3 in Peterson (2015). Also recommended is the board game Dialect from Thorny Games: https://thornygames.com/pages/dialect.

The discussion of gender in this chapter draws from Aikhenvald (2016). The examples of obsolete and archaic words in English are sourced from Forsyth (2012), dictionary.com and the *Merriam-Webster Online Dictionary*. For more information on Quenya and Sindarin, see Appendix E in Tolkien's *Lord of the Rings*, in addition to Noel (1980), Salo (2004) and Farrugia (2018).

The Klingon information discussed in this chapter comes from Okrand (1997). For more information on Esperanto, see Gledhill (2000), Garvía (2015), and Fiedler and Brosch (2022); the last of these includes a chapter on language change. For Loglan, see Brown (1975), and for Lojban, see Cowan (2016). A good summary of how Loglan changed into Lojban is given in Okrent (2010).

17 Language Channels and Modalities

This chapter goes beyond spoken languages and considers various language modalities and communication channels, since these are part of language and present interesting opportunities for conlanging. A brief preview of language modalities is given in Section 17.1; Section 17.2 covers attested communication channels in spoken natlangs, and Sections 17.3 and 17.4 focus on manual-visual and tactile language modalities. The remainder of the chapter discusses communication in non-human species, including plants (Section 17.5), animals (Section 17.6) and aliens (Section 17.7). Section 17.8 provides some opportunities for conlang practice, and Section 17.9 presents some information on communication channels in muq. Section 17.10 provides a guided set of questions to help you incorporate communication channels and language modalities in your conlang. This chapter includes an extensive list of sources to continue your exploration of these topics.

Key Words

CODAs (children of deaf adults)
Communication channels
  Hum speech
  Modal speech
  Musical speech
  Whistled speech
  Yell speech
Emerging sign languages
Hand orientation
Handshape
Homesign
Language modalities
  Manual-visual
  Oral-aural
  Tactile
    Tactile fingerspelling
    Tracking

    Tracing
    Written
  Manual articulations
    Handshape
    Location
    Movement
  Manual articulators
  Non-manual articulators
    Non-manual features
  Pidgin
  Sign languages
  Whistled languages
  Xenolinguistics (astrolinguistics, exolinguistics)

17.1 Language Modalities

Languages have different **modalities**, that is, physical channels in which they are conveyed and perceived. The main modalities attested in natlangs are **oral-aural** (articulated by the mouth and perceived by the ears), **manual-visual** (articulated by the hands and other body parts and perceived by the eyes) and **tactile** (articulated and perceived by the hands or other body parts). Most natlangs use the oral-aural modality. Sign languages use the manual-visual modality, and tactile **sign languages**, used by people with both vision and hearing impairments, make use of the tactile modality. In addition, many natlangs use the **written** language modality, as we saw in Chapter 14.

17.2 Communication Channels in Spoken Languages

A **communication channel** refers to the specific medium in which a message is conveyed. In spoken languages, the most common channel of communication is called **modal speech**. However, some natlangs use additional oral-aural channels for specific purposes or in certain situations. The most frequent of these is **whistled speech**, attested at least in eighty cultures throughout the world (Mayer 2021). Whistled speech is used to convey messages across large distances, usually in dense forests, rugged, mountainous terrain or around roaring rivers. Most forms of whistled speech (often referred to as **whistled languages**) are endangered, but some are still used in remote areas with little access to roads and/or technology.

For example, the whistled language Silbo, spoken in the Canary Islands of El Hierro and La Gomera in Spain, is used among farmers and shepherds to communicate across long distances. In addition, Pirahã hunters use whistled speech to locate and help each other in dense forests without scaring off prey, and the Hmong in the Himalayas use whistled language for poetic and romantic purposes when engaged in secret courtship. Other examples include the Amazigh in the Atlas Mountains, who used whistled speech to convey secret messages in war during their resistance to French colonial forces; and the Inuit communities in the Bering Strait, which used it to convey commands in whale hunting.

In whistled speech, the frequency, amplitude and duration of sounds is modified to increase perceptibility across long distances and/or in noisy environments. Whistled speech conveys most information between 1,000 and 4,000 Hz, a range of frequencies that allows for the discrimination of most speech sounds while standing out from (most) ambient noise. Whistling involves increased loudness, ranging from 80 to 120 dB (louder than a car horn). This helps the message to be understood at least ten times further away than shouting would, with little or no tiredness or damage to the vocal folds. In fact, whistled speech can carry information up to 5 miles away (in the absence of dense vegetation). Whistled speech conveys messages 10–50 percent more slowly than in **modal speech**, increasing the chances that the message will be decoded correctly.

Whistled speech works differently in tonal and non-tonal languages. In tonal languages, whistling is pitch-based since it conveys the tonal make-up of words. In non-tonal languages, whistling mimics the way vowels are distinguished from each other in terms of frequency. For example, in whistled Spanish, Greek and Turkish, /i/ is whistled at the highest pitch and /o/ at one of the lowest. Consonants are recognized by how whistles slide or jump across notes.

In Pirahã, modal speech is unmarked and used by default, while whistled speech is employed exclusively for males in (play) hunting, warring and aggressive male play. Pirahã also has three additional channels of communication: **hum speech, musical speech** and **yell speech**. Hum speech involves humming suprasegmentals at low volume. It is used for privacy, intimacy, and to disguise the message or one's identity. Hum speech is also used when there is an oral obstruction (such as eating), and by mothers and caregivers when talking to children. Musical speech is used in flirting, dancing, discussing important new information, and in communications by/with spirits. In musical speech, the tonal differences between high and low tones are emphasized, and the rhythm of words and phrases is changed to create a melody. Finally, yell speech is used to convey messages across long distances, particularly across the river, or when there is a lot of noise (such as during a thunderstorm). In yell speech, the pitch goes up, reaching falsetto. Vowels are typically replaced by a partially nasalized [ã], and consonants by either [k] or [ʔ]. Hum, musical and yell speech have not yet been attested in other natlangs.

> **Your Turn**
>
> Can you think of communication channels that could be employed by non-human beings?

17.3 Manual-Visual Languages

Sign languages are natlangs based on the manual-visual language modality. Sign languages are independent of spoken languages. The most recent edition of the *Ethnologue* lists over 150 documented sign languages, including American Sign Language, British Sign Language and Dominican Sign Language, among others. Note that the name of the sign language typically refers to the country or region where it is used; it does not mean that the sign language is related to the main language spoken in the area. For example, although American and British English are mutually intelligible, American Sign Language (ASL) and British Sign Language are not. In fact, their origins differ. British Sign Language, documented as far back as the fifteenth century, emerged in the British Isles. On the other hand, ASL is considered to have developed in the 1900s from the creolization of local sign varieties used in Martha's Vineyard (Massachusetts) with French Sign Language.

Sign languages are minority languages in the country or region where they are spoken, which partly explains the fact that they are understudied and misunderstood. An interesting example is Plains Indian Sign Language (also known as First Nation Sign Language or Plains Sign Talk), documented as far back as the sixteenth century in what is now Texas and the north of Mexico. Plains Sign Talk was used as a lingua franca for deaf and hearing speakers of about forty different languages in the Plains area of Canada, the US and northern Mexico. In the 1880s, it had reportedly 100,000 users. Although Plains Indian Sign Language is still in use among native American peoples such as the Navajo and the Blackfoot, only elderly people use it nowadays, and it is considered nearly extinct (Eberhard et al. 2024).

How do sign languages evolve? Usually when a deaf child is born in a hearing household, the family comes up with an ad-hoc manual-visual communication system; this is referred to as **homesign**. Homesign is like a **pidgin**, that is, a simplified form of language used in situations where two communities come into contact but don't share a common language. In time, local educational programs or a school for the deaf are established. Homesigns used by different children merge into a new communal system and linguistic structure evolves. Often, the teachers in these programs or schools are trained in a national sign language, and some of its characteristics are blended in the emerging system. A famously documented example is Nicaraguan Sign Language (Idioma de Señas de Nicaragua) in the 1970s and 1980s.

It is important to note that sign languages are not just used by deaf people. Hearing **children of deaf adults (CODAs)** are typically fluent in both a spoken language and a sign language. Other people might choose to learn a sign language as a second (or multiple) language as well. In addition, sign languages might be used by deaf and hearing people in communities with a high incidence of deafness (usually hereditary). These sign languages are sometimes referred to as **emerging sign languages**. Examples include Adamorobe Sign Language in Ghana and Ban Khor Sign Language in Thailand.

For a long time, sign languages were considered less complex than spoken languages; indeed, they were believed to lack systematic linguistic structure and expressive power. But in the mid-twentieth century, Barnard T. M. Terwoort and William Stokoe demonstrated that sign languages show the same linguistic complexity as aural-oral natlangs. Like spoken languages, sign languages involve articulators; unlike spoken languages, these can be manual and non-manual. **Manual articulators** include the shoulder, the elbow, the radio-ulnar joint (which allows for forearm rotation), the wrists, the base knuckles and the interphalangeal joints. **Non-manual articulators** encompass the torso, the head and the face. These articulators can move in a complex manner to convey meaning: for example, the torso can lean or rotate, the head can tilt or nod, and the eyebrows can raise or lower.

Akin to basic consonant and vowel classification, signs can be described according to three **basic manual articulations: handshape, location** and **movement. Handshape** comprises the shape of the hand; for example, whether the hand is shaped into a fist or whether the fingers are together or spread. **Location** refers to where the hand is in space or on the body. The default location is the area in front of the signer's torso. Other locations include the chin, the mouth or the opposite hand. Finally, **movement** describes the action performed by the hand (most commonly left or right, up or down, or away from or towards the signer).

Additional articulations are relevant for some signs. These include **hand orientation**, that is, the way the palm of the hand is facing, and **non-manual features**, that is, movements and expressions of other parts of the body. Hand orientation may be absolute (up, down), relative to the signer (inward, outward) or relative to a particular body part (such as the face or the other hand). Non-manual features can include body posture, facial expressions and gaze.

Signs may differ in just one property, which can create minimal pairs. For example, the signs for SORRY and PLEASE in ASL have similar location (chest) and movement (circular motion). However, they differ in handshape: in SORRY, the thumb is up and the other fingers hidden, while in PLEASE, the fingers are extended.

Most sign languages that have been investigated are in Western Europe and North America. There is much we don't know about sign languages in other parts of the world, but research reveals some tendencies. For example, Zeshan (2013b) finds that most sign languages lack question markers, possibly because they are in the process of being grammaticalized. This does not mean that questions cannot be asked – sign language users can use tag questions or lexical expressions for this purpose, for example.

Sign languages with question markers tend to have only one, used either in yes–no questions or in all question types; it tends to be sentence-final. Examples of question markers include PALM-UP in Finnish Sign Language; a nod in Lengua de Señas Española (the official language of the Deaf community in Spain); and the compound sign HAVE-NOT HAVE in Taiwanese Sign Language.

Sign languages can involve dialectal variation. For example, Black American Sign Language is a dialect of ASL that originated in historically segregated African American Deaf communities. One extreme example of dialectal variation occurred with Irish Sign Language, which developed distinctly for girls and boys in deaf schools in Ireland beginning in the late nineteenth century. After leaving the school, both varieties of Irish Sign Language were in contact, but men derided women's signs. While men used their signs in all contexts, women started using the men's signs in public, reserving female signs for private communication with other women. This gave rise to two very different dialects. Female Irish Sign Language became used less and less and is now almost extinct.

17.3.1 What about Gestures?

Chances are that if you speak an oral-aural natlang, you also use non-verbal communication to express your feelings or to clarify your meaning. For example, you might hold up your hand with the palm out to request that someone stops moving or talking. You might raise your eyebrows to express incredulity or disapproval; or stick out your tongue in disgust or mockery (or in playfulness, as many children do). Non-verbal communication can even override speech; when in conflict, non-verbal communication is considered a more reliable indicator of the speaker's intent.

Non-verbal communication can range from quite deliberate (such as the hand sign for 'stop') to subconscious (such as blushing in embarrassment). Non-verbal communication is not necessarily universal because gestures are codified and interpreted differently across cultures. For example, the hand gesture used for 'ok' in English refers to money in Japan, to something worthless in France, and it is used as an insult in some parts of Germany.

Using gestures is important in human communication, but doing so does not constitute a different language by itself. The reason is that gestures by themselves are not linguistically structured. It is only when there is a community of people large enough to extend the use of gestures to expand communication into codified signs that sign languages can emerge. Typically, this occurs when educational programs or schools for the deaf are established (as in Nicaraguan Sign Language), or when there is a high incidence of (hereditary) deafness in a community (as in Adamorobe Sign Language in Ghana). Unlike gestures, signs are not depictive, they are linguistically structured, and thus, they constitute language.

> **Your Turn**
>
> - Which gestures/facial expressions do you use (e.g., winking, pouting, frowning)? When do you use them?
> - Have you observed cultural differences in non-verbal communication (e.g., regarding smiling or looking overtly serious)?

17.3.2 Sign Languages and Gestures in Conlanging

Sign languages are gaining ground in conlanging. Examples include Tusken Sign Language, developed by Troy Kotsur for *The Mandalorian* and *The Book of Boba Fett*, and the House Atreides and Fremen sign languages in *Dune: Part I and Part II*, developed by David and Jessie Peterson. While the Fremen Sign Language is the main sign language used in Arrakis, House Atreides Sign Language is more of a secret code.

Luka pona is a naturalistic sign language devised by jan Olipija and used by the Toki Pona community (Lang 2021:11). Its vocabulary is similar to that of Toki Pona, but it has a different grammar. An earlier manual-visual version of Toki Pona (called *toki pona luka*) that included signs for Toki Pona letters and vocabulary was conceived by Sonja Lang in 2014. She suggested that it could be used when speaking is a no-no (such as in a quiet library or at a house of worship) and in playful contexts including "covert ninja operations," "diving underwater for treasure" and "taunting rival Lojbanists with gang signs" (Lang 2014:92). Unlike Luka pona, Toki pona luka is a manually coded form of Toki Pona rather than a true sign language, since it is based on Toki Pona vocabulary and grammar.

The conlang Belter in the show *The Expanse*, which we introduced in Section 2.2, incorporates the use of gestures (as you might recall from Chapter 2, Belter is spoken by marginalized people living in the Asteroid Belt). Hand signs and gestures are part of this conlang and partly compensate for possible failure of communication devices in space. Some examples of gestures/signs in Belter are given in (1).

(1) Belter gestures
      a. Folding both arms across chest: No, negative, stop!
      b. Lifting a fist: Affirmative, nodding, greeting
      c. One or both palms up: Shrugging

> **Your Turn**
>
> Have you come across other examples of gestures or sign languages in conlanging?

17.4 Tactile Languages

The tactile language modality is used for communication by visually and auditorily impaired people. The tactile language modality makes use of touch to convey and receive information. It is involved in **tactile fingerspelling**, used by Laura Dewey Bridgman (1829–1889) and Helen Keller (1880–1968). Tactile fingerspelling relies on **written** and spoken language. Other methods to convey information by touch include **tracking** (involving placing hands over the wrists or forearms of the signer) and **tracing** signs (or letters) on the palm or body.

Unlike sign languages, tactile sign languages are not very common, and we know very little about them. One example of a tactile sign language that emerged spontaneously is Bay Islands Sign Language (French Harbour Sign Language) in Honduras. The village of French Harbour has a high incidence of Usher Syndrome, a rare genetic disorder that causes hearing loss and visual impairment. Bay Islands Sign Language originated in the deaf-blind community of French Harbour in the island of Roatán and then spread to the neighboring island of Guanaja.

One example of a tactile conlang is the gripping language developed by Sai Emrys and Alex Fink, used to communicate covertly in the presence of other people. This conlang, devised to be used by two people at a time, is based on pressing various parts of the hand.

17.5 Plant Communication

Trees communicate with each other; they create communities in which they help each other with nutrients and information. They do so olfactorily and via chemical and electrical signals. For example, when giraffes feed on acacia trees in the African savannah, the acacia trees emit ethylene to warn other trees close by of the danger. This way acacia trees can prepare themselves for the upcoming danger by pumping toxins into their leaves. Trees also pass information to other trees about insects, droughts and other dangers with chemical and electrical signals transmitted via the fungal networks that grow around the tips of their roots.

There is some evidence that trees also use sound to communicate. In an experiment with grain seedlings, researchers found that roots were crackling at a frequency of 220 Hz. Intriguingly, when the roots of seedlings not involved in the experiment were exposed to this crackling, they oriented their tips in that direction, suggesting that they were registering this frequency.

Plant and tree communication features in several fictional works. A recent example is Kenneth Opel's *The Overthrow* trilogy, where cryptogenic seeds rain down on Earth. These alien seeds grow rapidly into plants that spread toxic pollen. The alien plants in this fictional world communicate with each other via electrical signals.

In *The Overstory* by Richard Powers, one of the central characters is Dr. Patricia Westerford, a tree scientist who discovers that trees communicate among themselves. Her character is partly inspired by real-life scientist Suzanne Simmard, who made key discoveries on tree communication, particularly regarding underground fungal networks. Simmard also discovered that forests have 'Mother Trees' that serve as hubs for sharing information and regulating resources.

If this reminds you in any way to the hyperconnected forest in Pandora and to the Tree of Souls, this is because Simmard's work was an important influence in James Cameron's *Avatar*. The 'Tree of Souls' (*Vitraya Ramunong* in Na'vi) is of the highest importance to the Na'vi because it is closely associated with Eywa. Pandora is interconnected; the Na'vi use their neural queues to connect with their mates, and the flora and fauna of Pandora.

J. R. R. Tolkien also drew on tree communication in *The Hobbit* and *Lord of the Rings*. In Tolkien's fictional world there are three different types of tree-like beings: trees, Ents and Huorns. Ents are tree-protecting spirits, the oldest beings surviving into the Third Age in Middle Earth. They speak Entish, which takes a very long time, partly because Entish words are very long. The word for 'hill,' for example, is *a-lalla-lalla-rumba-kamanda-lindor-burúme*. Old Entish, mostly forgotten in Middle Earth, was slow and sonorous, and had multiple tonal and vowel distinctions. It was an exceedingly complex language which not even Elves could learn. New Entish kept Old Entish grammatical structure, but its vocabulary comes from Elvish languages.

Huorns are Ent-like ancient trees and tree-like Ents that have become less animated. They live in Fangorn and in the Old Forest. Most Huorns are tended by Ents. One exception is Old Man Willow, who, to prevent the further encroachment of other sentient beings in its territory, enchants the Old Forest with its song.

One example of a conlang used by trees is Ifuhuxu. This language is used by the fictional Nifu trees, which move their leaves and vibrate their twigs to communicate. The closest sounds to those of human speech are rendered as fricatives, labiodental and alveolar affricates, and a glottal stop. Ifuhuxu also has four vowels, two of them voiceless: /i ɯ i̥ ɯ̥/. Ifuhuxu has OVS word order and lacks questions – these are rendered as requests for information instead. Examples of Ifuhuxu words are given in (2).

(2)   Ifuhuxu words (from https://conlang.fandom.com/wiki/Ifuhuxu#Phonology)
    a. *husu*   [hɯ̥.sɯ̥]   'to whisper, to speak a language'
    b. *yfw*   [i.fɯ]   'Nifu tree'
    c. *hi'w*   [hi̥.ʔɯ]   'sun'
    d. *hwxw* [hɯ.xɯ]   'the wind; a language; a word or phrase'

17.6 Animal Communication

Animal species use various communication channels, including auditory, visual, olfactory and electrical. Bird calls are used to threaten, court or warn other birds about dangers. Dolphins and other sea mammals communicate using ultrasound (sounds with frequencies of 20,000 Hz or higher) or infrasound (sounds with frequencies of 20 Hz or lower). Although many animal species use sound, they tend to communicate a limited range of messages, and their sounds tend to be continuous (such as pitch sliding in dolphins' whistling) rather than discrete, as in human language.

Simian species use both verbal and non-verbal communication. Other visually based communication attested in animal species include bee 'dances,' performed to let other bees in the beehive know about the location and quality of nearby flowers, and their distance and orientation from the beehive. Cephalopods use color, aided by chromophores (cells that can change color) to communicate their mood and to confuse their prey.

Several works of fiction include animal communication (both real and fictional). In Adrian Tchaikovsky's novel *Children of Time*, sentient spiders use a combination of sign language and ground-patting to provoke meaningful vibrations and communicate with each other. In *Lord of the Rings*, the big spiders in Mirkwood talk to each other in a language that can be understood only if you wear the One Ring. The demon spider Shelob is also able to talk to Gollum (even when he's not wearing the Ring). In *The Hobbit*, the dragon Smaug talks, and some ravens and thrushes can understand and talk to humans and/or dwarves. In Harry Potter, snakes and other serpent-like creatures such as the Basilisk (and Runespoor) speak in Parseltongue; those who can talk to them (such as Voldemort and Harry Potter) are known as Parselmouths.

Another example is Lapine, the rabbit language in Richard Adams's novel *Watership Down*, which includes several dozen words related to rabbit life meant to sound 'wuffy, fluffy'; several are onomatopoeic. Examples are given in (3); see also Section 2.1.1 for additional examples.

(3) Lapine words (Adams 2005:475–476)
   a. *elil*   '(Natural) enemies of rabbits (foxes, stoats, badgers ... and humans); evil'
   b. *frith*   'the sun (personified as a God for the rabbits)'
   c. *pfeffa* 'cat'
   d. *sil*   'outside, outdoors'
   e. *tharn*   'tonic immobility; stupefied'
   f. *thlay*   'fur'

Another example is the C'ąąr conlang by Alex Hailman. C'ąąr is a language spoken by fictional dawns (a type of crow) and tailored to their specific anatomical characteristics. C'ąąr has rostral sounds made with the beak (/m r/); palatal sounds, and choanal (uvular) sounds. C'ąąr lacks alveolar sounds since birds lack alveolar ridges. There are front and central vowels, but not back ones. This conlang also features clicks, a rich tonal system and a contrast among oral, nasal and creaky vowels.

The C'ąąr vocabulary tries to capture how dawns view their world. One interesting word in this conlang is the adjective [rê] 'the color of some flowers including dandelions; some things we perceive as dark-colored, including blueberries, obsidian; etc.' This word reflects avian color vision and could be translated as 'ultraviolet' in English.

17.7 Xenolinguistics

The field of **xenolinguistics** (also referred to as 'astrolinguistics' or 'exolinguistics') explores what alien languages would be like. This word was coined for Star Trek; the Star Fleet Academy had a xenolinguistics department.

Until communication with aliens is established, xenolinguistics is speculative. Given the tremendous distances among solar systems and galaxies, it is not certain that even if there are alien languages out there we will ever learn about them. There have been different attempts to send messages to intelligent alien civilizations far from us. These messages consider the commonalities that alien cultures might have with us, such as mathematics. However, it is not clear if mathematics is truly universal. The Pirahã lack numbers; intelligent alien life might lack them too.

What would an alien language be like? Some of the conlangs devised for aliens assume human-like articulatory-perceptual mechanisms; this is the case of Klingon and Na'vi. Klingons and Na'vis share many physical characteristics with humans. Both conlangs have sounds and linguistic structures that are unusual but possible in natlangs.

Alien languages might feature linguistic systems like those used by animal species on Earth; for example, dolphins and whales communicate using complex calls, and octopuses and squid communicate using changes in color, shape, size and texture. The heptapods in *Arrival* have an oral language modality ('Heptapod A'), rendered in the movie by splicing sounds from whales and big cats. In the exolang Rikchik, the tentacled rikchiks communicate using a sign language; and in Ilish, the fish-like il of Fithia communicate via electric shocks. Other alien conlangs/alien conlang modalities assume different articulatory, perceptual and/or cognitive systems. This is the case of Heptapod B in *Arrival*, which is connected to the non-linear experience of time.

There is much to learn about how animal (and plant) species communicate; advancement in this area might give us a better starting point if or when contact with alien species becomes a reality.

17.8 Conlanging Practice: Language Modalities and Speech Channels in the Ur Languages

A. Which Ur languages are more likely to have one of the following language modalities/speech channels?
- Whistled speech
- Musical speech
- Yelled speech
- Tactile language
- Secret sign language

B. Consider the fictional maps showcased in Section 2.3.2. In which geographical areas do you think whistled or yelled speech would be more likely to arise?

17.9 A Note on Language Channels in Muq

The muq language has musical speech, which all muqs learn before they come of age. Musical speech is used for ceremonial purposes, mostly connected to the salt harvest.

As you can see in the map in Section 2.6, part of the muq island is covered by dense vegetation. In the forest closest to the volcano live some muq people who mostly keep to themselves. There is a rumor that they can communicate using whistled speech. However, when asked about it, muq forest dwellers deny such a thing and change the subject. This is certainly an intriguing area of investigation for muq scholars.

17.10 Guide to Incorporating Language Channels and Modalities

- Do you envision communication channels in your conlang beyond modal speech (such as whistled speech, musical speech, hum speech, yell speech or other)?
    - If so, how are these communication channels connected to the fictional world?
- Are sign languages relevant in the fictional world? If so, indicate how.
- Does your conlang include specific, culturally dependent gestures?
    - If so, in which contexts or for which purposes?

To Learn More

Robson (2017) and Holmes (2021) are good introductions to whistled languages and include audio and/or video examples. For an in-depth discussion of whistled speech in humans and animal species, see Meyer (2015, 2021). Meyer et al. (2021) discuss the relevance of human whistled language in decoding dolphin whistled speech.

To learn more about Pirahã and its communication channels, see Everett (1985, 2008). A concise summary of Pirahã's communication channels is found in O'Neill (2014); video clips are available at http://daneverettbooks.com/radiopublications/film-clips/.

For an introduction to sign languages, see Taylor (1996), Sandler (2006) and Zeshan (2013a). For a recent monograph on this topic, see Brentari (2020). Zeshan (2013b) addresses the typology of questions in natlang sign languages. Zeshan and de Vos (2013) is a fascinating volume on emerging sign languages (also referred to as 'rural' or 'indigenous' sign languages in the literature).

LeMaster (2006) discusses gender differences in Irish Sign Language. For Black American Sign Language, see Bayley et al. (2020) and McCaskill et al. (2020). The documentary *Signing Black in America* is also highly recommended. A list of additional resources can be found in Joseph Hill's website: www.josephchill.com/black-asl. For more information on Bay Islands Sign Language, see *The Endangered Languages Archive* (www.elararchive.org/).

Information on toki pona kuka (signed Toki Pona) is available in Lang (2014) and in the website http://tokipona.net/tp/janpije/signlanguage.php. For a dictionary of signs in luka pona (Toki Pona Sign Language), see www.youtube.com/watch?v=rE_crkyRPhQ. For more information on the Gripping conlang by Sai Emrys and Alex Fink, see https://conference.conlang.org/lcc3/talks/Alex_and_Sai.pdf.

To learn more about tree communication, see Jabr (2020). Book-long overviews can be found in Wohlleben (2016) and Simard (2021). Simard's (2016) TED talk is also recommended. Powers (2019) is a thought-provoking Pulitzer Prizewinning novel featuring tree communication.

Information about Entish can be found in Appendix F in Tolkien's *Lord of the Rings*. In *Guardians of the Galaxy*, there is an Ent-like character Groot, from the Flora Colossi alien species, famous because he can only say 'I am Groot.' More details on the Ifuhuxu conlang are available at https://conlang.fandom.com/wiki/Ifuhuxu.

Kershenbaum (2020) speculates on aliens and alien communication, taking as a starting point animals and animal communication on Earth. For Lapine, see Adams's novels (2005, 1996); Rosen's (1978) movie adaptation is also worth watching. Murray (1985) writes about Lapine words that have crossed over to some dialects of American English. For more information about Rikchik, see https://suberic.net/~dmm/rikchik/intro.html.

For xenolinguistics, see the *Diaphanes* article 'From Xenolinguistics to Cephalopods,' a conversation between Mário Gomes and a group of experts representing various fields (www.diaphanes.net/titel/xenolinguistics-5623). Book-length treatments of this topic are Ollongren (2013), Oberhaus (2019), and Vakoch and Punske (2024). Moro (2016) explores what is possible and impossible in human languages, and McKenzie and Punske (2020) write about language change in interstellar travel. If you like board games, you might also enjoy playing Xenolanguage and Sign, from Thorny Games: https://thornygames.com/.

18 Wrapping Up and Moving Forward

In this chapter, we recap the conlanging journey we undertook in this book, we discuss ways to build our conlangs further, and we reflect on the extent to which conlangs need to be consistent with natlang patterns (Sections 18.1–18.3). We also provide the full translation of the fictional muq text introduced in Chapter 2 (Section 18.4) and suggest additional sources to continue exploring conlanging.

18.1 What We Have Accomplished So Far

Throughout this book we have explored how to build a naturalistic, typologically plausible conlang from the ground up. We started by setting conlanging goals and devising a fictional world (Chapters 1–2). Our world building included sketching a map and composing a text related to the fictional culture associated with our conlang. Ideally, the characteristics of the fictional world you envisioned will have inspired some of your conlanging decisions, and possibly your aesthetic ideas of what the conlang would sound like will have done so as well.

You chose a set of vowels and consonants and decided on a stress or tone pattern and used them as building blocks for the syllables and words in your conlang (Chapters 3–6). While minimal pairs helped to get your conlang vocabulary started, your conlang lexicon grew by incorporating words relevant to the fictional world – including those needed to translate your fictional text – and meanings that tend to be expressed in natlangs (Chapter 7). Considering connotation, polysemy, metaphorical extension and semantic fields, as well as deictic pronouns, determiners and adverbs helped expand the conlang vocabulary further (Chapter 15).

Your language might include nominal and verbal morphology, concisely integrating functional meaning, such as number and tense, and helping 'glue' words together in constituents and sentences (particularly if your conlang features case or inflection) (Chapters 8–9). You decided on fixed or flexible word order for your conlang, worked out the expression of sentential negation and decided how different sentence types (questions, commands, statements) and complex sentences were formed, perhaps even incorporating evidentials (Chapters 10–13). Along the way, the translation of your fictional text showcased some of the morphological and syntactic characteristics of your conlang. Your translation might have also revealed new connections between the lexicon and the fictional culture, and pointed to lexical, morphological and syntactic areas that could be revised or expanded on.

Throughout this book you have also considered the context of writing in the fictional world and invented a novel conscript fitting the phonological/morphological characteristics of the conlang (Chapter 14). You also considered ways in which your conlang varied, either because it was spoken in different regions and/or because it was spoken by different genders, ethnicities and social classes (Chapter 16). Considering some ways in which your conlang might have changed through time also enriched the conlang and might have revealed areas to revise or explore further. The book also addressed speech channels, language modalities and forms of communication for non-humans, which you might have incorporated into your conlang to some extent and which might have caused an expansion of the fictional world (Chapter 17).

The (fictional) world keeps on changing, and conlangs, like natlangs, are never 'done' – they can always grow and change. To further expand your conlang, you might (i) try to convince a group of people to learn it and practice it with you, (ii) compose or translate additional texts into your conlang, and/or (iii) continue to expand its vocabulary and grammar. I wish you luck with the first option; I attempted it years ago with very limited success (but then, I was only twelve years old and knew next to nothing about conlanging). The next section addresses the second and third options, which are much more doable and could perhaps, after a while, even help you to successfully achieve the first one.

18.2 Expanding Your Conlang

18.2.1 Composing and Translating Fictional Texts

Throughout this book we have used a fictional text as an aid in world building and to expand and showcase our conlang lexicon and grammar. After working through your conlang text, you might want to compose additional ones or translate already existing texts into your conlang. Let's consider translations first. Since the sixteenth century, certain texts have been translated into different natlangs to exemplify how these languages work; some are commonly used in conlang translations as well. For example,

Zamenhof's *Unua libro*, the first book written on Esperanto, includes a translation of both the Lord's Prayer and the creation account in Genesis. A typical religious text used in conlang translations is the Babel text (Genesis 11:1–9), reproduced in (1).

(1) The Babel text (Genesis 11:1–9; New International version)
¹Now the whole world had one language and a common speech. ² As people moved eastward, they found a plain in Shinar and settled there. ³ They said to each other, 'Come, let's make bricks and bake them thoroughly.' They used brick instead of stone, and tar for mortar. ⁴ Then they said, 'Come, let us build ourselves a city, with a tower that reaches to the heavens, so that we may make a name for ourselves; otherwise we will be scattered over the face of the whole earth.' ⁵ But the Lord came down to see the city and the tower the people were building. ⁶ The Lord said, 'If as one people speaking the same language they have begun to do this, then nothing they plan to do will be impossible for them. ⁷ Come, let us go down and confuse their language so they will not understand each other.' ⁸ So the Lord scattered them from there over all the earth, and they stopped building the city. ⁹ That is why it was called Babel – because there the Lord confused the language of the whole world. From there the Lord scattered them over the face of the whole earth.

Other good options to use for conlang translations include proverbs and/or famous quotations (as shown in Lang 2014 for Toki Pona) and certain fables. Examples (2–4) reproduce the first article of the Universal Declaration of Human Rights, Aesop's fable 'The North Wind and the Sun' (included often in phonetic natlang descriptions), and August Schleicher's fable 'The Sheep and the Horses,' written originally to give an idea of how Proto-Indo European would have sounded (4).

(2) Universal Declaration of Human Rights: Article One
All human beings are born free and equal in dignity and rights. They are endowed with reason and conscience and should act towards one another in a spirit of brotherhood.

(3) Aesop's fable: 'The North Wind and the Sun' (as rendered in Ladefoged 1999:44)
The North Wind and the Sun were disputing which was the stronger, when a traveler came along wrapped in a warm cloak. They agreed that the one who first succeeded in making the traveler take his cloak off should be considered stronger than the other. Then the North Wind blew as hard as he could, but the more he blew the more closely did the traveler fold his cloak around him; and at last the North Wind gave

up the attempt. Then the Sun shined out warmly, and immediately the traveler took off his cloak. And so the North Wind was obliged to confess that the Sun was the stronger of the two.

(4) Schleicher's fable: 'The Sheep and the Horses' (adapted from Beekes 2011:287)
A sheep that had no wool saw horses, one of them pulling a heavy wagon, one carrying a big load, and one carrying a man quickly. The sheep said to the horses: 'My heart pains me, seeing a man driving horses.' The horses said: 'Listen, sheep, our hearts pain us when we see this: a man, the master, makes the wool of the sheep into a warm garment for himself. And the sheep has no wool.' Having heard this, the sheep fled into the plain.

Conlang translations do not need to be literal; they can reflect 'the spirit of the meaning' (Lang 2014:72). Ideally, they will be adapted to reflect the worldview associated with a conlang, as Suzette Elgin recommends (5).

(5) Translations in conlanging (Elgin et al. 2020:259)
Take some simple text – a short folktale is a good choice – and start translating it into your language. This serves as a diagnostic probe to let you know what you need to add or change. For the Láadan language, which was constructed to express the perceptions of women, I began by translating the Twenty-Third Psalm, because the King James Bible is one of the most masculine-perception-expressing books I know of and that psalm is the right size.

When translating the Twenty-Third Psalm, Elgin made key lexical and grammatical choices reflecting Láadan's female-centered point of view. These included non-masculine pronouns to convey a more gender-neutral divine being and adapting expressions (such as 'anointing my head with oil' or 'Thy rod and thy staff they comfort me') to reflect a more female perspective ('braiding my hair with thine own hand,' 'Thy word and Thine eye comfort me'). You can read the full translation of this psalm in Elgin et al. (2020:223–226).

Let's now turn to composing additional original texts. Most likely, the fictional text you started with in Chapter 2 is a short narrative. You could decide to expand it or to write additional texts related to the fictional world if you prefer. This could involve retelling a story or myth. For example, Elgin et al. (2020:241–246) includes a Láadan retelling of the nativity story written from Mary's point of view; the English version is given in (6).

(6) The Birth-Giving of Mary the Beloved (Elgin et al. 2020:242)
Long ago, a woman gave birth in the wintertime. She had a baby boy, and she named him 'Jesus'. The baby pleased her, and she said to her spouse, 'If this baby doesn't do well, I'll be very surprised'. And then – suddenly – there arrived many shepherds, many angels, and several wise men. They said, 'May we please see the baby?'.

'What a horrible time for a baby-viewing!', the woman said to herself. 'They have no common sense and no manners! –and she was disgusted. But aloud she said, 'Please come and see'. As would be obvious to any thinking person, the Baby Jesus was hungry and wet. He started crying, and he kept on crying. Nevertheless, the crowd stayed on. 'What a lot of blind, deaf, dumb, thick-headed creatures!', the woman thought.

And she held the baby close and rocked him. Time went by ... and more time went by. At last the woman said to herself, 'All of you, please think! You're not guests any longer, you're nothing but trouble! Don't you know anything? Your parents would be ashamed.' And she stood up and took the baby and took care of him. The woman's name was Mary.

Several of the texts Elgin created or translated into Láadan are about religion. This might be connected to the plot of *Native Tongue*, the trilogy associated with Láadan. In the first novel, women linguists in a dystopian future construct Láadan in secret, using another conlang as decoy to make sure men are not privy to their true intent: to create and pass down a language that will free humanity from male domination. In the second novel (*The Judas Rose*), Láadan is passed on from linguist women to non-linguist women, mostly using the religious grapevine.

When composing original texts for your conlang, you can consider poetry and other genres. Several conlangers have written original poems in their conlangs, including L. L. Zamenhof and J. R. R. Tolkien. Zamenhof featured different types of texts (including translations, as we saw earlier) in the first published Esperanto book. His poem *Ho, mia kor'* ('Oh, My Heart') is considered the first literary text composed in Esperanto. The first stanza and its English translation are given in (7).

(7) First stanza of *Ho, mia kor'* (Zamenhof 1889:23; trans. Richard H. Geoghegan)

Ho, mia kor', ne batu maltrankvile,	Oh, my heart, don't beat so uneasily,
El mia brusto nun ne saltu for!	Do not leap from my chest now!
Jam teni min ne povas mi facile,	I can barely hold myself now,
Ho, mia kor'!	Oh, my heart!

As you probably know, for Tolkien, language invention was primarily about phono-aesthetics; thus, it's not too surprising that poetry was his preferred way to showcase his conlangs. In his essay 'A Secret Vice,' based on a lecture on language invention he gave in 1931, he shared for the first time poetry in Qenya (an early version of Quenya) and Noldorin (which later developed into Sindarin). One of the poems included was *Oilima Markirya* 'The Last Ark.' The first stanza and its English translation are given in (8).

(8)   *Oilima Markirya* 'The Last Ark' (Tolkien 1931; in Fimi & Higgins 2016:27, 28)

Man kiluva kirya ninqe   Who shall see a white ship
oilima ailinello lúte,   leave the last shore,
níve qímari ringa ambar   the pale phantoms
ve maiwin qaine?   in her cold bosom
                                like gulls wailing?

Tolkien's choice of poetry is a good fit within the fictional world as well, since the Elves relish beauty, nature, poems and song. Inspired by Tolkien's Elvish languages, Enya's lyricist, Roma Ryan, invented Loxian, mostly conveyed in poems (as songs). Loxian can be heard in several songs in Enya's albums *Amarantine* and *Dark Sky Island*.

You could also consider dialogues, which are good ways to show how a conlang is spoken in a more naturalistic, informal way. For example, Peterson's (2014) book on Dothraki includes several Dothraki dialogues (one featuring a conversation between a Dothraki warrior and a visitor). The development of Dothraki involved translating dialogue for the *Game of Thrones* show, so it makes sense that some of the available texts in this conlang are of this type.

You could even compose original comics (as Russ Williams did for Toki Pona; see Lang 2014:71) or even an opera if you are feeling particularly ambitious. The first Klingon opera, titled *'u'* [ʔuʔ] 'universe,' written by Eef van Breen, Kees Ligtelijn and Marc Okrand, premiered in The Hague in 2010, after all.

18.2.2   Building Vocabulary and Grammar Further

This book covered a lot of ground, but, for simplicity and reasons of space, many things had to be left out. This section indicates some avenues to explore if you are interested in developing your conlang lexicon and grammar further.

We set out to build a conlang lexicon of 100–200 words. This is a very modest goal; Dixon (2016:172) estimates that natlangs have 5,000–10,000 words on average. You might have reached your initial 200-word goal or gone over. At the time of writing this chapter, my muq lexicon database has just reached 300 words, and I am aware of many words that should be added. Expanding semantic fields further and building up the derivational morphology of your conlang are two ways to make your conlang lexicon grow.

For conlang phonology, we focused on contrastive vowels and consonants. We discussed allophones (variant pronunciations) briefly in Chapter 4. In speech, sounds relentlessly run into each other, causing them to assimilate, dissimilate, merge and undergo many other fascinating transformations. If you want to expand your conlang and make it more naturalistic, I certainly recommend exploring allophonic variation further.

Our morphological and syntactic discussion mostly focused on regular patterns – but we know that languages are full of irregularities. English has several irregular plurals (*geese* and *children* come to mind) as well as a wealth of irregular past and past participle forms (such as *saw, seen*, or *hit, hit*). Unless one of your conlanging goals is regularity (as in Toki Pona or Esperanto), adding irregularities will make your conlang more realistic.

There are several advanced topics that I would have liked to cover in this book, and additional linguistic characteristics of natlangs and conlangs that I would have liked to share with you. If you want to continue to expand your conlang (or perhaps invent another one), it is very helpful to delve deeper into existing conlangs and natlangs to learn more about what language can do. I also recommend that you read Okrent (2010), Peterson (2015) and Rosenfelder (2010, 2012, 2013) if you haven't yet, since they offer great perspectives on conlanging and conlangers.

18.3 A Final Question

On working through this book, perhaps you have asked yourself to what extent your conlang needs to follow natlang tendencies. We've maintained that conlangs need to be plausible, but the best conlangs are unique and push the limits of what language can (or could) do. Consider, for example, Toki Pona, with fewer than 200 words; Kēlen, which lacks verbs; or Ilish, which has no nouns but thousands of pronouns. Could a conlang with only contrastive nasal vowels work? How about a conlang that has infixes but no other affix types? Conlangs like these could certainly work as engelangs and/or if there is a compelling backstory behind such typologically unattested characteristics. The specific anatomy of the beings speaking the conlang, unusual characteristics of the fictional world and/or quirks of language contact or historical evolution might be conducive to unusual linguistic patterns. In any case, conlanging is an exercise in analysis and creativity: a willingness both to learn from natlangs and existing conlangs and to think outside of the box is important.

I do hope that you enjoyed conlanging, and that whatever stage your conlang is at, you are proud of your effort. Perhaps you are not completely happy with how your conlang turned out. If you were to do it over, perhaps you would do it differently. This is a normal part of the conlanging process. After all, Tolkien worked on his Elvish languages for decades, and even Toki Pona, which was designed with the goal of having just 120 words, has been expanded to include a few more words since it was invented in 2001.

I leave you with a full gloss and translation of the fictional muq text introduced in Chapter 2. You will notice that the final English rendering is not identical to the initial version; this is to be expected. The final part of the chapter includes some sources to check if you would like to pursue conlanging further. I hope that you found conlanging exhilarating (and not too nerve-racking), and I wish you the best in your future conlanging endeavors!

18.4 Translation of the Muq Fictional Text

Here is the final translation and glossing of the muq origin text. For each section of the text, the first line conveys the muq language; the second line provides the morpheme-by-morpheme gloss and the third line a free English translation.

(9) Muq fictional text: Salt people origin story

a. [ux   ˈxaɸ-m-i   ˈi.xi   ko-xa   ˈmei-m-i   ˈyeç]
   QUOT.EV sleep-IMPF-REM.PST world DEF.INAN-SG be-IMPF-REM.PST darkness
   'It is said that long ago the world slept; there was darkness.'

b. [ˈmei-m-i   ˈseʁ-xa   ˈɫu.ma   ko-xa]
   be-IMPF-REM.PST silent-SG wind DEF.INAN-SG
   'The wind was silent'

c. [ˈxi.ma-m-i   ə.ˈɬei.za   ˈɬei   ko-xa]
   whisper-IMPF-REM.PST sad ocean DEF.INAN-SG
   'The ocean whispered sadly.'

d. [ˈŋou ˈʁa.li-s-i   ˈtaʁ-s-i   ˈʁouq-na ˈŋa.çen ko-xa]
   then scream-PFV-REM.PST spew-PFV-REM.PST fire-PL mountain DEF.INAN-SG
   'Then the mountain screamed and spewed much fire,'

e. [ˈçis-s-i   çem   ko-xa]
   burn-PFV-REM.PST island DEF.INAN-SG
   'and the island burned.'

f. [ˈçis-s-i   ˈçis-s-i   ˈzu   ˈŋuç-na]
   burn-PFV-REM.PST burn-PFV-REM.PST   3SG   day-PL
   'It burned and burned many days.'

g. [ˈa.zos ˈɫam.xɑ-s-i   ˈçem ko-xa   ˈou.sei-s-i   ˈzu]
   when   dry.up-PFV-REM.PST   island DEF.INAN-SG   transform-PFV-REM.PST   3SG
   'When the island stopped burning it had transformed.'

h. [ˈɸiθ-s-i   ˈzu   ˈɬei   ko-xa]
   soothe-PFV-REM.PST   3SG   ocean   DEF.INAN-SG
   'The ocean had soothed it'

i. [ˈnei-s-i   ˈzu   ˈsi.an-je]
   give-PFV-REM.PST   3SG   life.force-PAU
   'and gave it some life force.'

j. [ˈχe.ʁa-s-i   ˈɣeç   ko-xa   ˈsi.an   ˈmɨk-xa]
   destroy-PFV-REM.PST   darkness DEF.INAN-SG   life.force   MED-SG
   'That life force destroyed the darkness,'

k. [ˈmeq.ze-s-i   ˈmis.tə-xa]
   return-PFV-REM.PST   dawn-SG
   'and dawn returned.'

l. [ux   ˈou.na-s-i   ˈmuq.çem-xa]
   QUOT.EV   awaken-PFV-REM.PST   our.island-SG
   'Thus (it is said that) our island awakened.'

To Learn More

To learn more about natlangs, see Andresen and Carter (2016) and Lyovin et al. (2017). Parkwall (2008) is a fun compilation of unusual natlang characteristics. Translations of different types of texts are available for several conlangs, including one in Toki Pona for L. Frank Baum's 'The Wonderful Wizard of Oz' (Lang 2024). For Klingon, there are even translations for Shakespeare's *Hamlet* (aka *The Tragedy of Khamlet, Son of the Emperor of Qo'noS*; Nicholas & Strader 2020), *Much Ado About Nothing* (or 'The Confusion is Great because of Nothing' (Nicholas 2003), the *Tao Te Ching* (Solska 2008) and the *Epic of Gilgamesh* (Cheesbro 2003), among others. Additional Klingon texts and translations are listed in the Klingon Institute website (https://www.kli.org/).

The complete text of the Universal Declaration of Human Rights can be found in the United Nations' website: www.un.org/en/about-us/universal-declaration-of-human-rights. The versions of the fables 'The Sheep and the Horses' and 'The North Wind and the Sun' included in this chapter are from Beekes (2011) and Ladefoged (1999).

18.4 Translation of the Muq Fictional Text

Tolkien's essay 'A Secret Vice' appears in Tolkien (1983). A recent critical edition of this essay, in addition to Tolkien's 'Essay on Phonetic Symbolism' can be found in Fimi and Higgins (2016). The Loxian fictional world is described in Roma Ryan's book *Water Shows the Hidden Heart*, which was included in Enya's *Amarantine* deluxe boxed set. For more information on Loxian, see http://enya.sk/roma-ryan/loxian/. There are three Loxian songs in Enya's album *Amarantine* (2005) (Less Than a Pearl – Heah Viiya,' 'The River Sings – Ea Hymm Llay Hey' and 'Water Shows The Hidden Heart – Syoombrraya'). Their lyrics and English translations are available at http://enya.sk/lyrics.php. Enya's album *Dark Sky Island* (2015) also includes two Loxian songs: 'The Forge of the Angels' and 'The Loxian Gates'; lyrics and English translations are found here: http://enya.sk/roma-ryan/lyrics/dark-sky-island/.

APPENDIX A
Natlangs Mentioned

Language	ISO	Classification	Country/region	Chapters
!Xóõ	nmn	Tuu	Botswana, Namibia	4
A'aninin (Gros Ventre)	ats	Algonquian	Montana, (US)	16
Abkhaz	abk	Abkhaz-Adyghe	Georgia	4
Acholi	ach	Nilo-Saharan	Uganda, Sudan	11
Adamorobe Sign Language	ads	Shared sign language	Ghana	17
Ainu	ain	Isolate	Japan	1, 4, 6, 7
Akan	aka	Niger-Congo	Eastern Ghana, Ghana	1
Alamblak	amp	Sepik	Papua New Guinea	13
Alutor	alr	Chukotko-Kamchatkan	Russia	8
Alqosh (Assyrian) Aramaic	aii	Afro-Asiatic, Semitic	Alqosh, Iraq	10
Amazigh	tia, tjo	Afro-Asiatic, Berber	Algeria	17
American Sign Language (ASL)	ase	Deaf community sign language	United States	17
Andoke	ano	Isolate	Colombia	4
Arabic	ara	Afro-Asiatic, Semitic	Middle East	1, 2, 4, 8, 9, 10, 11, 14, 15, 16
Armenian	hye	Indo-European,	Armenia	14
Ban Khor Sign Language	bfk	Shared sign language	Thailand	17
Barngarla	bjb	Pama-Nyungan	Australia	8
Basque	eus	Isolate	Spain	6, 8, 9, 10, 11, 12, 13, 15
Bay Islands Sign Language	–	Deaf/blind/Usher syndrome community sign language	Honduras	17
Berber	ber	Afro-Asiatic	North Africa	4, 5, 6, 8

Appendix A: Natlangs Mentioned

Language	ISO	Classification	Country/region	Chapters
Biak	bhw	Austronesian	Papua New Guinea, Indonesia	8
Biloxi	bll	Siouan	United States	11
Black American Sign Language	ase	Dialect of American Sign Language	United States	17
British Sign Language	bfi	Deaf community sign language	United Kingdom	17
Burunge	bds	Afro-Asiatic, Cushitic	Tanzania	15
Capanahua	kaq	Panoan	Peru	6, 11
Cherokee	chr	Iroquoian	Oklahoma and North Carolina (US)	1, 3, 5, 11, 14
Chickasaw	cic	Muskogean	Oklahoma (US)	11
Chinese	zho	Sino-Tibetan	China	8, 14
Choctaw	cho	Muskogean	Louisiana, Mississippi, Oklahoma, Tennessee (US)	1
Coast Tsimshian	tsi	Tsimshian	Canada; Alaska, Hawaii (US)	11
Comanche	com	Uto-Aztecan	Oklahoma (US)	6
Cornish	cor	Indo-European, Celtic	United Kingdom	1
Czech	ces	Indo-European, Balto-Slavic	Czech Republic	15
Dahalo	dal	Afro-Asiatic, Cushitic	Kenya	4
Dakota	dak	Siouan-Catawban	Minnesota, Montana, Nebraska, South Dakota (US)	6
Danish	dan	Indo-European, Germanic	Denmark	2, 3
Dutch	nld	Indo-European, Germanic	The Netherlands	1, 6, 8, 10, 12, 13
Dyirbal	dbl	Australian, Pama-Nyungan	Australia	7, 9
Eipo	lek, eip	Trans-New Guinea	Papua, Indonesia	12
English	eng	Indo-European, Germanic	United Kingdom	*All*
Estonian	est	Uralic	Estonia	6, 12
Éwé	ewe	Niger-Congo	Ghana	7
Ewondo	ewo	Bantu	Cameroon	12
Fanti (Akan)	aka	[See Akan]	Ghana	11

Language	ISO	Classification	Country/region	Chapters
Farsi (Persian)	fas	Indo-European, Indo-Iranian	Iran, Afghanistan, Tajikistan	16
Fasu	faa	Trans-New Guinea	Papua New Guinea	12
Female Irish Sign Language	isg	Deaf community sign language	Ireland	17
Fijian	fij	Austronesian	Fiji	5, 9, 15
Finnish	fin	Uralic	Finland	4, 6, 7, 11, 12, 13
Finnish sign language	fse	Deaf community sign language	Finland	17
French	fra	Indo-European, Italic	France	1, 3, 4, 6, 7, 8, 11, 12, 13, 15
French sign language	fsl	Deaf community sign language	France	17
Fula/Fulfulde	ful	Niger-Congo	Camaroon, Guinea, Nigeria, Sudan	4, 8
Garifuna	cab	Maipurean	Belize, Honduras, Guatemala	16
Georgian	kat	Kartvelian	Georgia	5, 14
German	deu	Indo-European, Germanic	German	1, 2, 3, 4, 7, 8, 11, 15
Gimira (Bench)	bcg	Afro-Asiatic	Ethiopia	6
Grebo	grb	Niger-Congo	Liberia	11
Greek	ell	Indo-European, Greek	Greece	6, 14, 17
Gujarati	guj	Indo-European, Indo-Iranian	India	3, 11
Harar Oromo	orm	Afro-Asiatic	Ethiopia	9
Hausa	hau	Afro-Asiatic	Nigeria	1, 7
Hawai'i Creole English	hwc	Pacific	Hawaii (US)	8
Hawaiian	haw	Austronesian	Hawaii, Alaska (US)	1, 3, 5, 6, 7, 8, 10, 12, 15, 16
Hebrew	heb	Afro-Asiatic, Semitic	Israel	1, 4, 7, 8, 10, 11, 14
Hindi	hin	Indo-European, Indo-Iranian	India	1, 4, 14, 16
Hmong	hmn	Hmongic	Himalayas	17
Huariapano	pno	Panoan	Peru	6
Hungarian	hun	Uralic	Hungary	7, 8, 11, 15

Appendix A: Natlangs Mentioned

Language	ISO	Classification	Country/region	Chapters
Icelandic	isl	Indo-European, Germanic	Iceland	8, 11
Igbo	ibo	Niger-Congo	Nigeria	1, 4, 6, 7
Ik (Icetot)	ikx	Nilo-Saharan	Uganda	3
Indonesian	ind	Austronesian	Indonesia	8, 9, 15
Ineri (Kalinago)	crb	Arawakan	Lesser Antilles	16
Inga	inb	Quechuan	Colombia	6
Irish	gle	Indo-European, Celtic	Ireland	14
Irish Sign Language	isg	Deaf community sign language, related to French Sign Language	Ireland	17
Italian	ita	Indo-European, Italic	Italy	1, 2, 3, 4, 5, 7, 8, 11, 13, 15, 16
Izii	izz	Niger-Congo	Nigeria	12
Jahai	jhi	Austro-Asiatic	Malaysia	2
Jalapa Mazatec	maj	Otomanguean	Mexico	3
Jalé (Yali)	yli, nlk, yac	Papuan	Papua New Guinea	2
Jaminjung	djd	Jaminjungan	Australia	11
Japanese	jpn	Japonic	Japan	1, 2, 3, 7, 10, 11, 13, 14, 15, 16, 17
Jarawara (Madí)	jaa	Arawan	Brazil	11, 12
K'ekchi (Q'eqchi')	kek	Mayan, K'ichean	Guatemala, Belize, El Salvador	4
Kambaata	ktb	Afro-Asiatic, Cushitic	Ethiopia	4
Kambera	xbr	Austronesian	Indonesia	15
Kannada	kan	Dravidian	Southern India	13
Karajá (Iny rybè)	kpj	Macro-Je	Brazil	16
Kisi	kiz	Mel	West Africa	8
Koasati	cku	Muscogean	Southeastern US	12
Kukama-Kukamiria (Kokama-Kokamilla)	cod	Tupí-Guaraní	Peru	13
Kolyma (Southern) Yukaghir	yux	Yukaghir	Yukaghir, Siberia, Russia	9, 12
Korean	kor	Koreanic	Korea	3, 11, 13, 14, 15
Kresh	krs	Nilo-Saharan	Sudan	12

Appendix A: Natlangs Mentioned

Language	ISO	Classification	Country/region	Chapters
Kwuakw'ala	kwk	Wakashan	Canada	4
Lakhota	lkt	Siouan-Catawban	United States, Canada	4
Larike	alo	Austronesian	Indonesia	8
Latin	lat	Indo-European, Italic	Vatican State	1, 4, 6, 8, 10, 14, 16
Latvian	lav	Indo-European, Balto-Slavic	Latvia	11
Lavukaleve	lvk	Solomos East Papuan	Soloman Islands	8, 11
Lepcha	lep	Sino-Tibetan	India, Bhutan, Nepal	14
Limbu	lif	Tibeto-Burman	Nepal	11
Lokaa	yaz	Niger-Congo	Nigeria	12
Luganda	lug	Niger-Congo	Uganda	13
Maasai	mas	Nilo-Saharan	Kenya	8
Macushi	mbc	Carib	Brazil	9
Malagasy	mlg	Austronesian	Madagascar	10
Maori	mri	Austronesian	New Zealand	1, 12
Mandarin Chinese	cmn	Sino-Tibetan	China	6, 10, 11
Marathi	mar	Indo-Aryan	India	14, 15
Marshallese	mah	Austronesian	Marshall Islands	4
Mapudungun	arn	Mapudungu	Argentina, Chile	6, 7
Matsés	mcf	Panoan	Peru, Brazil	9
Mixtec	mim, xta, mpz, mip	Otomanguean	Mexico	6
Mualang	mtd	Austronesian	Indonesia	13
Nama	nmx	South-Central Papuan	Papua New Guinea	4
Navajo (Diné Bizaad)	nav	Eyak-Athabaskan	Arizona, Colorado, New Mexico, Utah (US)	4, 6, 17
Nepali	npi	Indo-European, Indo-Aryan	Nepal	14
Ngiti	niy	Nilo-Saharan	Democratic Republic of Congo	8
Nicaraguan Sign Language	ncs	Deaf community sign language	Nicaragua	17
Nkore-Kiga	nyn, cgg	Niger-Congo, Bantu	Uganda	13
Saami	sme	Uralic	Denmark, Finland, Norway, Sweden	4, 12

Language	ISO	Classification	Country/region	Chapters
Norwegian	nor	Indo-European, Germanic	Norway	2, 4
Nuer	nus	Nilo-Saharan	Djibouti, Etritrea and Ethiopia, South Sudan	8
Oromo	orm	Afro-Asiatic, Cushitic	Ethiopia, Kenya	9, 12
Maricopa (Piipaash)	mrc	Yuman	US Southwest	13
Pirahã	myp	Muran	Central Brazil	2, 4, 7, 8, 15, 16, 17, 18
Plains Cree	crk	Algic	Canada	6
Plains Indian Sign Language	psd	Shared sign language	United States, Canada	17
Portuguese	por	Indo-European, Italic	Portugal, Brazil	1, 3, 7, 12
Quechua	que	Quechuan	Peru	3, 6, 7, 12, 15
Rama	rma	Chibchan	Nicaragua	9, 12
Rapa Nui	rap	Austronesian	Chile	14
Rotokas	roo	North Bougainville	Papua New Guinea	4
Russian	rus	Indo-European, Balto-Slavic	Russian Federation	4, 6, 10, 15
Samoan	smo	Austronesian, Polynesian	Samoan Islands	13, 15
San Carlos Apache	apw	Eyak-Athabaskan	San Carlos and Fort Apache Reservations in Arizona (US)	11
Sanskrit	san	Indo-European, Indo-Iranian	India	14, 16
Sanzhi Dargwa	dar	Nakh-Daghestanian	Russian Federation	15
Saynáwa	sya	Panoan	Peru	6
Scots Gaelic	gla	Indo-European, Celtic	Ireland, United Kingdom	11
Sénufo	–	Niger-Congo	Burkina Faso	5
Shawã	–	Panoan	Brazil	12
Shipibo-Konibo	shp	Panoan	Peru	3, 11, 12
Silbo (Gomero)	spa	Whistle register of Spanish	Canary Islands, Spain	17
Slovak	slk	Indo-European, Balto-Slavic	Slovakia	5
Southern Barasano	bsn	Tucanoan	Colombia	8
Spanish	spa	Indo-European, Italic	Latin America, Spain	*All*

Language	ISO	Classification	Country/region	Chapters
Supyire	spp	Niger-Congo	Mali	8
Suri	suq	Nilo-Saharan, Surmic	Ethiopia	16
Swahili	swa	Niger-Congo	Democratic Republic of the Congo	1, 2, 4, 5, 8, 10, 11, 14
Swedish	swe	Indo-European, Germanic	Denmark, Finland, Norway, Sweden	1, 7, 13
Taba (East Makian)	mky	Austronesian	Indonesia	4
Tagalog	tgl	Austronesian	Philippines	4, 8, 15
Takelma	tkm	Takelman (Unclassified)	Oregon (US)	12
Tamashek	taq	Afro-Asiatic, Berber	Algeria, Mali	12
Tamil	tam	Dravidian	India, Sri Lanka	8
Tashlhiyt	shi	Afro-Asiatic, Berber	Southern Morocco	5, 11
Tauya	tya	Trans-New Guinea	Papua New Guinea	9
Tawala	tbo	Oceanic	Papua New Guinea	9
Thai	tha	Kra-Dai	Thailand	6, 12
Tiwi	tiw	Australian, Tiwian	Northern Australia	8
Tlingit	tli	Eyak-Athabaskan	Alaska	4
Tohono O'odham	ood	Uto-Aztecan	United States, Mexico	16
Toqabaqita	mlu	Austronesian	The Solomon Islands	7
Trique	trs, trc	Otomanguean	Mexico	6
Tuareg	tmh	Afro-Asiatic	Niger	5
Tunica	tun	Isolate	Louisiana (US)	16
Turkish	tur	Turkic	Turkey	3, 4, 5, 12, 15, 17
Tuyuca	tue	Tucanoan	Brazil, Colombia	12
Ukrainian	ukr	Indo-European, Balto-Slavic	Ukraine	6, 10
Urarina	ura	Isolate	Peru	10, 11
Urdu	urd	Indo-European, Indo-Iranian	Pakistan	16
Uyghur	uig	Turkic	China	14
Walapai	yuf	Cochimí-Yuman	Western US	13
Warao	wba	Isolate	Venezuela	9, 10
Wardaman	wrr	Yangmaniac	Australia	9
West Greenlandic	kal	Eskimo-Aleut	Greenland	11
Xhosa	xho	Niger-Congo	South Africa	4
Yaaku	muu	Afro-Asiatic	Kenya	1

Language	ISO	Classification	Country/region	Chapters
Yagua	yad	Yaguan	Peru, Colombia, Brazil	9
Yaminahua	yaa	Panoan	Peru	9
Yana	ynn	Isolate	Northern California, (US)	16
Yawa	yva	Isolate	Papua New Guinea, Indonesia	9
Yimas	yee	Ramu-Lower Sepik	Papua New Guinea	3
Yoruba	yor	Niger-Congo	Nigeria	1, 5
Zapotec	zap	Otomanguean	Mexico	6, 8
Zulu	zul	Niger-Congo	Lesotho, Eswatini, South Africa, Mozambique,	2

APPENDIX B
Conlangs Mentioned

Language	Type	World/Series/Origin	Creator	Chapters
Adûnaic	Artlang	Language spoken by the Men of Númenor	J. R. R. Tolkien	16
Afrihili	Auxlang	Swahili, Akan, and other African languages	K. A. Kumi Attobrah	1
Aiha	Conscript	Kesh conscript in Ursula Le Guin's *Always Going Home*	Ursula K. Le Guin	14
Angerthas (Cirth)	Conscript	Semi-artificial script based on runic alphabets	J. R. R. Tolkien	14
Atreides Sign Language	Artlang	Sign language used as a secret code in *Dune*	David J. Peterson	17
Babigo	Ludling	Japanese language game	N/A	1
Balaibalan	Auxlang	Persian, Turkish, and Arabic; A priori language, written in Arabic script	Fazlallah Astarabadi	1
Belter (Creole)	Artlang/ Auxlang	*The Expanse*, vocabulary and grammar of Chinese, English, Germanic, Japanese, Slavic, Romance, Zulu	Nick Farmer	1, 2, 17
Blissymbolics	Conscript	An ideographic writing system consisting of many basic symbols; used to educate people with communication difficulties	Charles K. Bliss	1, 14
Brithenig	Altlang	Romance language in the British Isles with Celtic development	Andrew Smith	1
C'ą̂ą̂r	Artlang	An a priori language spoken by a fictional species of corvids (birds) called 'daws'	Alex Hailman	17

Appendix B: Conlangs Mentioned

Language	Type	World/Series/Origin	Creator	Chapters
Common Eldarin	Artlang	Spoken by the Eldar or West Elves in *Lord of the Rings*; the last common ancestor of all Elvish languages	J. R. R. Tolkien	16
Doriathrin	Artlang	Language of Doriath; a form of Sindarin used in the First Age	J. R. R. Tolkien	16
Dothraki	Artlang	Language in *Game of Thrones*	David Peterson	1, 2, 3, 4, 5, 6, 8, 9, 10, 11, 12, 15, 18
Elvish	Artlang	Languages in *Lord of the Rings*	J. R. R. Tolkien	1
Eskayan		Boholano, Spanish, and English		1
Esperanto	Auxlang	Romance, Germanic, and Slavic	L. L. Zamenhof	1, 3, 4, 5, 7, 8, 9, 10, 11, 12, 13, 15, 16, 18
Fith	Exolang	Languages of centauroid sapient marsupials on planet Fithia	Jeffrey Henning	1
Fremen Sign Language	Artlang	*Dune*; the main sign language used in Arrakis	David J. Peterson	17
Gripping language	Artlang	A touch-mediated language designed for exactly 2 people to use for communication	Sai Emrys and Alex Fink	17
Guosa	Auxlang	Hausa, Yoruba, and Igbo	Alex Igbineweka	1
Heptapod A	Fictional	Oral modality of the Heptapods' languages in Denis Villaneuve's *Arrival* (2016), based on Ted Chiang's novella *The Story of Your Life*	Morgan and Dave Whitehead	2, 17
Heptapod B	Exolang/Engelang	Written modality of the Heptapods' language in Denis Villaneuve's *Arrival* (2016), based on Ted Chiang's novella *The Story of Your Life*	Martine Bertrand and Patrice Vermette	1, 2, 14, 17

Appendix B: Conlangs Mentioned

Language	Type	World/Series/Origin	Creator	Chapters
High Valyrian	Artlang	*Game of Thrones*	David Peterson	1, 2, 3, 8, 10, 13
Ido	Auxlang	Derived from Reformed Esperanto to be used as a universal second language	Louis de Beaufront	8, 16
Idrani	Artlang	A personal language derived from Navajo, Chinese, Xhosa, and Finish	Trent Pehrson	1
Ifuhuxu	Artlang	A tree language	Sraemoyes (Shanna Moyes)	17
Ilish	Exolang	Electric shock language without nouns but with thousands of pronouns	Jeffrey Henning	17, 18
Ithkuil	Engelang/philosophical	A mix between an a priori philosophical language and a logical language; designed to express nuanced levels of human cognition, particularly about human categorization	John Quijada	1, 4, 6, 8, 15
Jana'ata	Naming	Alien language in *The Sparrow* and *Children of God*	Mary Doria Russell	1
Jerizonga	Ludling	Spanish language game	N/A	1
Kēlen	Engelang	Language without verbs	Sylvia Sotomayor	1, 4, 7
Klingon	Artlang	Alien language in *Star Trek* series	Marc Okrand	1, 2, 3, 4, 5, 6, 7, 8, 9, 10, 11, 12, 13, 15, 16, 17, 18
Láadan	Engelang	Language based on female experience	Suzette Haden Elgin	1, 2, 3, 4, 5, 6, 7, 8, 9, 10, 11, 12, 13, 15, 16, 18
Lapine	Naming	Rabbit language in *Watership Down*	Richard Adams	1, 2, 7, 17

Appendix B: Conlangs Mentioned

Language	Type	World/Series/Origin	Creator	Chapters
Lingua Ignota	Naming	Vocabulary only, no known grammar; one text with words embedded in Latin	St. Hildegard von Bingen	1
Loglan	Loglang	Logical language	James Cooke Brown	1, 7, 16
Lojban	Loglang	Loglan's successor	James Cooke Brown	1, 12, 15, 16
Centauran	Artlang	Centaur language	Daniel Bates	2
Loxian	Artlang	Language used in Enya's albums *Amarantine* and *Dark Sky Island*	Roma Ryan	1, 18
Luka pona	Artlang	Naturalistic sign language used by the Toki Pona community	Jan Olipija	17
Lunfardo	Secret language	Secret language used among Argentinian criminals	N/A	1
Na'vi	Artlang	Language of the Na'vi in Pandora (*Avatar* 2009, 2022)	Paul Frommer	1, 2, 3, 4, 5, 6, 7, 8, 9, 10, 11, 12, 13, 16, 17
Noldorin	Artlang	Elvish dialect that was a precursor to Sindarin	J. R. R. Tolkien	16, 18
Philosophical Language	Philosophical	Language to facilitate international communication among scholars, outlined in *An Essay Towards a Real Character, and a Philosophical Language* (1668)	John Wilkinson	1
Pig Latin	Ludling	English language game	N/A	1
Polari	Secret language	Secret language used by queer people in Britain	N/A	1
Parseltongue	Fictional	Language of the Basilisk and Parselmouths in *Harry Potter*	Francis Nolan	17
Quenya (High-Elven)	Artlang	Language of the Elves	J. R. R. Tolkien	1, 2, 3, 4, 5, 6, 8, 14, 16, 18
Rikchik	Exolang	Alien sign language	Denis Moskovitz	17

Language	Type	World/Series/Origin	Creator	Chapters
Rövarspråket	Ludling	Swedish language game	Astrid Lindgren	1
Runa	Naming	Alien language in *The Sparrow* and *Children of God*	Mary Doria Russell	1
Shizu	Artlang	Language spoken by the spiritual guides on the planet Suushiizuu	Gabrielle Isgar	2, 14
Sindarin (Grey-Elven)	Artlang	Language of the Elves	J. R. R. Tolkien	1, 2, 3, 6, 8, 9, 10, 11, 13, 14, 16
Axon	Artlang	Secret lingua franca in the prison moon Talasa	Robert Curran and Matt Anderson	2
Teonaht	Artlang	Language spoken by the Teonim, a race of polydactyl humans that worship catlike deities	Sally Caves (Sarah Higley)	1, 10
Tengwar	Conscript	Script used to write Elvish languages	J. R. R. Tolkien	14
Toki Pona	Philosophical language	Minimalistic language aimed to simplify thoughts and communication	Sonja Lang	2, 3, 4, 5, 6, 7, 8, 9, 11, 12, 13, 14, 15, 17, 18
Tusken Sign Language	Artlang	Language used by the Tusken Raiders of Tatooine in *The Mandalorian* and *The Book of Boba Fett* within the *Star Wars* series	Troy Kotsur	18
Volapük	Auxlang	The first constructed auxlang	Johann Martin Schleyer	1, 15

References

Adam, Michael. (2003). *Slayer Slang: A Buffy the Vampire Slayer Lexicon*. Oxford: Oxford University Press.

Adam, Michael. (2011). *From Elvish to Klingon: Exploring Invented Languages*. Oxford: Oxford University Press.

Adams, Richard. (1996). *Tales from Watership Down*. New York: Random House.

Adams, Richard. (2005). *Watership Down*. London: Rex Collings Ltd.

Aikhenvald, Alexandra Y. (2004). *Evidentiality*. Oxford: Oxford University Press.

Aikhenvald, Alexandra Y. (2010). *Imperatives and Commands*. Oxford: Oxford University Press.

Aikhenvald, Alexandra Y. (2016). *How Gender Shapes the World*. Oxford: Oxford University Press.

Aikhenvlad, Alexandra Y. & Dixon, R. M. W. (1998). Evidentials and areal typology: A case study from Amazonia. *Language Sciences, 20*(3), 241–257.

Almasi, Oswald, Fallon, Michael David, & Wared, Nazish Pardhan. (2014). *Swahili Grammar for Introductory and Intermediate Levels. Sarufi Ya Kiswahili Cha Ngazi Ya Kwanza Na Kati*. Lanham, MD: University Press of America.

Amika, Felix. (1992). Interjections: The universal yet neglected part of speech. *Journal of Phonetics, 18*, 101–118.

Anderson, Stephen R. & Keenan, Edward L. (1985). Deixis. In T. Shopen (ed.), *Language Typology and Syntactic Description*, Vol. III: *Grammatical Categories and the Lexicon, 259–308*. Cambridge: Cambridge University Press.

Andresen, Julie Tetel & Carter, Phillip M. (2016). *Languages in the World*. Chichester: Wiley Blackwell.

Annis, William S. (2024). *Horen Li'fyayä leNa'vi: A Reference Grammar of Na'vi*. Version 1.34. https://files.learnnavi.org/docs/horen-lenavi.pdf

Bailey, Guy & Thomas, Erik. (1998). Some aspects of African-American Vernacular English phonology. In G. Bailey, J. Baugh, S. S. Mufwene & J. R. Rickford (eds.), *African-American English: Structure, History, and Use*, 85–109. London: Routledge.

Bailey, Richard. (2003). *Rogue Scholar: The Sinister Life and Celebrated Death of Edward H. Rulloff*. Ann Arbor: University of Michigan Press.

Bailyn, John F. 2012. *The Syntax of Russian*. Cambridge: Cambridge University Press.

Baker, Paul. (2019). *Fabulosa! The Story of Polari, Britain's Secret Gay Language*. Chicago: Reaktion Books.

Barnes, Janet. (1984). Evidentials in the Tuyuca verb. *International Journal of American Linguistics, 50,* 255–271.

Barrett, Edward R. (1999). *A Grammar of Sipakapense Maya.* Ph.D. dissertation, University of Texas at Austin.

Bat-El, Outi. (1996). Selecting the best of the worst: The grammar of Hebrew blends. *Phonology, 13,* 283–328.

Bauer, W. A. (1981). *Aspects of the Grammar of Maori.* Edinburgh: University of Edinburgh Press.

Bauer, Winifred (with William Parker and Evans). (1993). *Te Kareongawai. Maori.* London: Routledge.

Bayley, R., Lucas, C., Hill, J. & McCaskill, C. (2020). The sociolinguistic ramifications of social injustice: The case of Black ASL. In R. Blake & I. Buchstaller (eds.), *The Routledge Companion to John Rickford,* 133–141. New York: Routledge.

Beekes R. S. P. (2011). *Comparative Indo-European Linguistics: An introduction* (2nd ed.). Amsterdam; Philadelphia: John Benjamins.

Bennett, Michael Eric. (1986). *Aspects of the Simple Clause in Malagasy: A Stratificational Approach.* Ph.D. dissertation, Michigan State University.

Bickel, B. & Nichols, J. (2007). Inflectional morphology. In T. Shopen (ed.), *Language Typology and Syntactic Description,* Vol III: *Grammatical Categories and the Lexicon* (2nd ed.), 169–240. Cambridge: Cambridge University Press. [1st ed. 1985].

Bickel, B. & Nichols, J. (2013a). Fusion of selected inflectional formatives. In M. S. Dryer & Martin Haspelmath (eds.), *The World Atlas of Language Structures Online.* Leipzig: Max Planck Institute for Evolutionary Anthropology. http://wals.info/chapter/20

Bickel, B. & Nichols, J. (2013b). Exponence of selected inflectional formatives. In M. S. Dryer & M. Haspelmath (eds.), *The World Atlas of Language Structures Online.* Leipzig: Max Planck Institute for Evolutionary Anthropology. http://wals.info/chapter/21

Blake, Barry J. (2001). *Case* (2nd ed.). Cambridge: Cambridge University Press. [1st ed. 1994].

Blando, Jared. (2015). *How to Draw Fantasy Art and RPG Maps: Step by Step Cartography for Gamers and Fans.* Cincinnati, OH: Impact Press.

Booij, Geert. (2016). Dutch. In P. Müller, I. Ohnheiser, S. Olsen & F. Rainer (eds.), *Word-Formation: An International Handbook of the Languages of Europe,* 2427–2451. Berlin; Boston: De Gruyter Mouton.

Botne, R. 2012. Remoteness distinctions. In R. I. Binnick (ed.), *The Oxford Handbook of Tense and Aspect,* 536–562. Oxford: Oxford University Press.

Bowden, John & Hajek, John. (1999). *Taba.* In *Handbook of the International Phonetic Association: A Guide to the Use of the International Phonetic Alphabet,* 143–146. Cambridge: Cambridge University Press.

Boye, Kaspar. (2016). The expression of epistemic modality. In J. Nuyts & J. van der Auwera (eds.), *The Oxford Handbook of Modality and Mood*, 117–140. Oxford: Oxford University Press.

Brentari, Diane. (2020). *Sign Language Phonology*. Cambridge: Cambridge University Press.

Brown, Cecil H. (2013a). Hand and arm. In M. S. Dryer & M. Haspelmath (eds.), *The World Atlas of Language Structures Online*. Leipzig: Max Planck Institute for Evolutionary Anthropology. http://wals.info/chapter/129

Brown, Cecil H. (2013b). Finger and hand. In M. S. Dryer & M. Haspelmath (eds.), *The World Atlas of Language Structures Online*. Leipzig: Max Planck Institute for Evolutionary Anthropology. http://wals.info/chapter/130

Brown, James C. 1975. *Loglan 1: A Logical Language*. Gainesville, FL: The Loglan Institute.

Bruce, Les. (1984). *The Alamblak Language of Papua New Guinea (East Sepik)*. Canberra: The Australian National University.

Burgess, Anika. (2017). Mapping Dante's Inferno, one circle of hell at a time: A topography of torment. *Atlas Obscura*. www.atlasobscura.com/articles/mapping-dante-hell-inferno-satan-divine-comedy

Campos, Héctor. (1993). *De la oración simple a la oración compuesta: Curso superior de gramática española*. Washington, DC: Georgetown University Press.

Catford, J. C. (2001). *A Practical Introduction to Phonetics* (2nd ed.). Oxford: Oxford University Press.

Cheesbro, Roger. (2003). *Gilgamesh: A Klingon Translation*. Cabin John, MD: Wildside Press.

Chen, Xiaorong. (2018). Nüshu: From tears to sunshine. *UNESCO*, 23 Feb. 23, 2018. en.unesco.org/courier/2018-1/nushu-tears-sunshine

Chiang, Ted. (1998). *Story of Your Life and Others*. Northampton: Vintage Books.

Coey, Christopher, Esling, John H. & Moiski, Scott R. (2014). *University of Victoria, iPA Phonetics*, Version 1.0 [2014]. Department of Linguistics, University of Victoria. http://web.uvic.ca/ling/data/IPAlab/IPAlab.htm

Comin, Neil F. (2011). *What if the Earth Had Two Moons?* New York: St. Martin's Press.

Comin, Neil F. (2012). *What if the Moon Did Not Exist?* New York: HarperCollins Publishers.

Comrie, Bernard. (1976). *Aspect*. Cambridge: Cambridge University Press.

Comrie, Bernard. (1985). *Tense*. Cambridge: Cambridge University Press.

Comrie, Bernard (ed.). (1990). *The World's Major Languages*. Oxford: Oxford University Press.

Comrie, Bernard. (2013). Alignment of case marking of full noun phrases. In M. S. Dryer & M. Haspelmath (eds.), *The World Atlas of Language Structures Online*. Leipzig: Max Planck Institute for Evolutionary Anthropology. http://wals.info/chapter/98

Comrie, Bernard, Haspelmath, Martin & Bickel, B. (2008). *The Leipzig Glossing Rules: Conventions for Interlinear Morpheme-by-Morpheme Glosses.* Department of Linguistics of the Max Planck Institute for Evolutionary Anthropology & the Department of Linguistics of the University of Leipzig. www.eva.mpg.de/lingua/pdf/Glossing-Rules.pdf

Comrie, Bernard, Matthews, Stephen & Polinsky, María (eds.). (2003). *The Atlas of Languages: The Origin and Development of Languages Throughout the World.* New York: Facts on File.

Coogler, Ryan. (Director). (2018). *Black Panther* [Film]. Marvel Studios.

Cook, Guy. (2000). *Language Play, Language Learning.* Oxford: Oxford University Press.

Corbett, Greville G. (2000). *Number.* Cambridge: Cambridge University Press.

Corbett, Greville G. (2013a). Number of Genders. In M. S. Dryer & M. Haspelmath (eds.), *The World Atlas of Language Structures Online.* Leipzig: Max Planck Institute for Evolutionary Anthropology. http://wals.info/chapter/30

Corbett, Greville G. (2013b). Sex-based and non-sex-based gender systems. In M. S. Dryer & M. Haspelmath (eds.), *The World Atlas of Language Structures Online.* Leipzig: Max Planck Institute for Evolutionary Anthropology. http://wals.info/chapter/31

Couto, Cláudio. (2010). *Análise fonológica do Saynáwa (Pano): A língua dos índios da T. I. Jamináwa do Igarapé Preto.* MA thesis, Universidade Federal de Pernambuco (UFPE), Recife, Brazil.

Cowan, John. (2016). *The Complete Lojban Language.* N.p.: Logical Language Group, Inc.

Crystal, David. (1998). *Language Play.* Chicago: University of Chicago Press.

Dahl, Östen & Velupillai, Viveka. (2013a). The past tense. In M. S. Dryer & M. Haspelmath (eds.), *The World Atlas of Language Structures Online.* Leipzig: Max Planck Institute for Evolutionary Anthropology. https://wals.info/chapter/66

Dahl, Östen & Velupillai, Viveka. (2013b). The future tense. In Dryer, Matthew S. & Haspelmath, Martin (eds.), *The World Atlas of Language Structures Online.* Leipzig: Max Planck Institute for Evolutionary Anthropology. https://wals.info/chapter/67

Dahl, Östen & Velupillai, Viveka. (2013c). Tense and aspect. In M. S. Dryer & M. Haspelmath (eds.) *The World Atlas of Language Structures Online.* Leipzig: Max Planck Institute for Evolutionary Anthropology. http://wals.info/chapter/s7

Dahl, Östen & Velupillai, Viveka. (2013d). Perfective/imperfective aspect. In M. S. Dryer & M. Haspelmath (eds.), *The World Atlas of Language Structures Online.* Leipzig: Max Planck Institute for Evolutionary Anthropology. Available at https://wals.info/chapter/65

Dalrymple, Mary & Mofu, Suriel. (2013). Semantics of number in Biak.

Journal of the Linguistic Society of Papua New Guinea, 31(1), 42–55.

Daniels, Peter. (2001). *Writing Systems*. In M. Aronoff and J. Rees-Miller (eds.), *The Handbook of Linguistics*, 43–80. Hoboken, NJ: Wiley-Blackwell.

Daniels, Peter. (2018). *An Exploration of Writing*. Sheffield: Equinox.

Davie, Jim. (2018). *Slang across Societies: Motivations and Construction*. New York: Routledge.

De Beaufront, L. (2004). *Kompleta Gramatiko Detaloza di Ido*. Ponferrada, Spain: Krayono. www.ido-vivo.info/kgd.pdf

de Haan, Ferdinand. (2013a). Semantic distinctions of evidentiality. In M. S. Dryer & M. Haspelmath (eds.), *The World Atlas of Language Structures Online*. Leipzig: Max Planck Institute for Evolutionary Anthropology. http://wals.info/chapter/77

de Haan, Ferdinand. (2013b). Coding of evidentiality. In M. S. Dryer & M. Haspelmath (eds.), *The World Atlas of Language Structures Online*. Leipzig: Max Planck Institute for Evolutionary Anthropology. http://wals.info/chapter/78

Deutscher, Guy. (2005). *The Unfolding of Language*. New York: Henry Holt.

Deutscher, Guy. (2010). *Through the Language Glass: Why the World Looks Different in Other Languages*. New York: Metropolitan Books.

Diessel, Holger, & Coventry, Kenny R. (2020). Demonstratives in spatial language and social interaction: An interdisciplinary review. *Frontiers in Psychology, 11*. https://doi.org/10.3389/fpsyg.2020.555265

Dixon, R. M. W. (2002). *Australian Languages: Their Nature and Development*. Cambridge: Cambridge University Press.

Dixon, R. M. W. (2016). *Are Some Languages Better than Others?* Oxford: Oxford University Press.

Dryer, Matthew S. (2013a). Order of subject, object and verb. In M. S. Dryer & M. Haspelmath (eds.), *The World Atlas of Language Structures Online*. Leipzig: Max Planck Institute for Evolutionary Anthropology. http://wals.info/chapter/81

Dryer, Matthew S. (2013b). Order of adposition and noun phrase. In M. S. Dryer & M. Haspelmath (eds.), *The World Atlas of Language Structures Online*. Leipzig: Max Planck Institute for Evolutionary Anthropology. http://wals.info/chapter/85

Dryer, Matthew S. (2013c). Position of polar question particles. In M. S. Dryer & M. Haspelmath (eds.), *The World Atlas of Language Structures Online*. Leipzig: Max Planck Institute for Evolutionary Anthropology. http://wals.info/chapter/92

Dryer, Matthew S. (2013d). Position of interrogative phrases in content questions. In M. S. Dryer & M. Haspelmath (eds.), *The World Atlas of Language Structures Online*. Leipzig: Max Planck Institute for Evolutionary Anthropology. http://wals.info/chapter/93

Dryer, Matthew S. (2013e). Order of adverbial subordinator and clause. In M. S. Dryer & M. Haspelmath (eds.), *The World Atlas of Language Structures Online*. Leipzig: Max Planck Institute for Evolutionary

Anthropology. http://wals.info/chapter/94

Dryer, Matthew S. (2013f). Negative morphemes. In M. S. Dryer & M. Haspelmath (eds.), *The World Atlas of Language Structures Online.* Leipzig: Max Planck Institute for Evolutionary Anthropology. http://wals.info/chapter/112

Dryer, Matthew S. (2013g). Polar questions. In M. S. Dryer & M. Haspelmath (eds.), *The World Atlas of Language Structures Online.* Leipzig: Max Planck Institute for Evolutionary Anthropology. http://wals.info/chapter/116

Dryer, Matthew S. (2013h). Order of negative morpheme and verb. In M. S. Dryer & M. Haspelmath (eds.), *The World Atlas of Language Structures Online.* Leipzig: Max Planck Institute for Evolutionary Anthropology. http://wals.info/chapter/143

Eberhard, David, Simons, Gary & Fennig, Charles (eds.). (2024). *Ethnologue: Languages of the World* (27th ed.). Dallas, TX: SIL International. Available online at www.ethnologue.com

Eco, Umberto. (1997). *The Search for the Perfect Language.* Hoboken, NJ: Wiley-Blackwell.

Eddington, David & Turner, Michael. (2017). In search of cowboy B: Bilabial implosives in American English. *American Speech*, 92(1), 41–51.

Edwards, Harold T. (2003). *Applied Phonetics: The Sounds of American English* (3rd ed.). Clifton Park, NY: Delmar Cengage Learning.

Eklund, Robert. (2008). Pulmonic ingressive phonation: Diachronic and synchronic characteristics, distribution and function in animal and human sound production and in human speech. *Journal of the International Phonetic Association*, 38(3), 235–324.

Elbert, Samuel H. & Pukui, Mary Kawena. (1979). *Hawaiian Grammar.* Honolulu: University of Hawaii Press.

Elgin, Suzette Haden, Gomoll, Jeanne & Martin, Diane. (2020). *A Third Dictionary and Grammar of Láadan.* N.p.: Union Street Press.

Endo, Orie. (2019). *Inscribing Intimacy: The Fading Writing Tradition of Nüshu* (trans. Hidejo Abe). Scotts Valley, CA: CreateSpace Independent Publishing Platform.

Everett, Daniel. (1985). Syllable weight, sloppy phonemes, and channels in Pirahã discourse. In M. Niepokuj, D. Feder, V. Nikiforidou & M. Van Clay (eds.), *Proceedings of the Eleventh Annual Meeting of the Berkeley Linguistics Society*, 408–416. Berkeley, CA: Berkeley Linguistics Society.

Everett, Daniel L. (2005). Cultural constraints on grammar and cognition in Pirahã: Another look at the design features of human language. *Current Anthropology*, 46(4), 621–646.

Everett, Daniel L. (2008). *Don't Sleep, There Are Snakes.* New York: Pantheon Books.

Everett, Daniel L. (2012). *Language: The Cultural Tool.* London: Profile Books.

Everett, Caleb. (2023). *A Myriad of Tongues: How Languages Reveal Differences in How We Think.*

Cambridge, MA: Harvard University Press.

Ezard, Bryan. (1997). *A Grammar of Tawala, an Austronesian Language of the Milne Bay Area, Papua New Guinea.* Canberra: Australian National University.

Farrugia, Lindsay M. (2018). *Ónë tengwelë: Elvish and English Sound Symbolism and Ethnocentrism in J. R. R Tolkien's Constructed Languages.* MA dissertation, University of British Columbia.

Fauskanger, Helge. (2002). *Quenya Course.* https://ardalambion.net/qcourse.htm

Faust, Norma & Loos, Eugene E. (2002). *Gramática del Idioma Yaminahua.* Lima: Instituto Lingüístico de Verano.

Ferrara, Silvia. (2022). *The Greatest Invention: A History of the World in Nine Mysterious Scripts* (trans. from Italian by Todd Portnowitz). New York: Farrar, Straus & Gireaux.

Fiedler, Sabine & Brosch, Cyril Robert. (2022). *Esperanto- Lingua Franca and Language Community.* Amsterdam; New York: John Benjamins.

Fillmore, Charles J. (1982). Towards a descriptive framework for spatial deixis. In R. J. Jarvell & W. Klein (eds.), *Speech, Place and Action: Studies in Deixis and Related Topics*, 31–59. London: Wiley.

Fimi, Dimitra & Higgins, Andrew (eds.). (2016). *A Secret Vice: Tolkien on Invented Languages.* London: Harper Collins.

Fleck, David W. (2003). *A Grammar of Matses.* Ph.D. dissertation, University of Rice.

Fleck, David W. (2007). Evidentiality and double tense in Matses. *Language, 83*, 589–614.

Forsyth, Mark. (2012). *Horologicon: A Day's Jaunt through the Lost Words of the English Language.* New York: Berkley Books.

Garvía, Roberto. (2015). *Esperanto and Its Rivals: The Struggle for an International Language.* Philadelphia: University of Pennsylvania Press.

Gendler, Alex. (2014). How languages evolve [TED Talk]. https://youtu.be/iWDKsHm6gTA.

Gerdts, D. (1998). Incorporation. In A. Spencer & A. Zwicky (eds.), *The Handbook of Morphology*, 84–100. Oxford: Blackwell.

Gil, David. (2013). Para-linguistic usages of clicks. In M. S. Dryer & M. Haspelmath (eds.), *The World Atlas of Language Structures Online.* Leipzig: Max Planck Institute for Evolutionary Anthropology. http://wals.info/chapter/142

Gilliver, Peter, Weiner, Edmund & Marshall, Jeremy. (2006). *The Ring of Words: Tolkien and the Oxford English Dictionary.* Oxford: Oxford University Press.

Gledhill, Christopher. (2000). *The Grammar of Esperanto: A Corpus-Based Description.* Munich: Lincom Europa.

Goddard, C. (2014). Interjections and emotions (with special reference to "surprise" and "disgust"). *Emotion Review, 6*(1), 53–63.

Goedemans, R. & van der Hulst, H. (2013a). Fixed stress locations. In M. S. Dryer & M. Haspelmath (eds.), *The Word Atlas of Language Structures*

Goedemans, R. & van der Hulst, H. (2013a). Fixed stress locations. In M. S. Dryer & M. Haspelmath (eds.), *The Word Atlas of Language Structures Online*. Max Planck Institute for Evolutionary Anthropology. https://wals.info/chapter/14

Goedemans, R. & van der Hulst, H. (2013b). Weight-sensitive stress. In M. S. Dryer & M. Haspelmath (eds.), *The Word Atlas of Language Structures Online*. Max Planck Institute for Evolutionary Anthropology. https://wals.info/chapter/15

Goedemans, R. & van der Hulst, H. (2013c). Weight factors in weight-sensitive stress systems. In M. S. Dryer & M. Haspelmath (eds.), *The Word Atlas of Language Structures Online*. Max Planck Institute for Evolutionary Anthropology. https://wals.info/chapter/16

Goedemans, R. & van der Hulst, H. (2013d). Rhythm types. In M. S. Dryer & M. Haspelmath (eds.), *The Word Atlas of Language Structures Online*. Max Planck Institute for Evolutionary Anthropology. https://wals.info/chapter/17

Goodall, Grant. (2023). Constructed languages. *Annual Review of Linguistics, 9*, 419–437.

Gordon, Lynn. (1986). *Maricopa Morphology and Syntax*. Berkeley: University of California Press.

Gordon, Matthew. (2016). *Phonological Typology*. Oxford: Oxford University Press.

Green, Lisa. (2002). *African American English: A Linguistic Introduction*. Cambridge: Cambridge University Press.

Grinevald, Colette G. (1988). *A Grammar of Rama (Report to National Science Foundation BNS 8511156)*. Université de Lyon.

Gunn James. (Director). (2014). *Guardians of the Galaxy* [Film]. Marvel Studios.

Hagège, Claude. (2008). Towards a typology of interrogative verbs. *Linguistic Typology, 12*, 1–44.

Hajek, John. (2013). Vowel nasalization. In M. S. Dryer & M. Haspelmath (eds.), *The World Atlas of Language Structures Online*. Leipzig: Max Planck Institute for Evolutionary Anthropology. http://wals.info/chapter/10

Harlow, Don. (1995). *The Sixteen Rules of Esperanto Grammar*. University of California, Santa Cruz. https://babel.ucsc.edu/~hank/105/Esperanto16.pdf

Harrison, David K. (2007). *When Languages Die: The Extinction of the World's Languages and the Erosion of Human Knowledge*. Oxford: Oxford University Press.

Haspelmath, Martin. (2007). Coordination. In Timothy Shopen (ed.), *Language Typology and Syntactic Description*, Vol. II: *Complex Constructions* (2nd ed.), 1–51. Cambridge: Cambridge University Press. [1st ed. 1985].

Haspelmath, Martin. (2013). Nominal and verbal conjunction. In M. S. Dryer & M. Haspelmath (eds.), *The World Atlas of Language Structures Online*. Leipzig: Max Planck Institute for Evolutionary Anthropology. http://wals.info/chapter/64

Hayes, Bruce. (2009). *Introductory Phonology*. Hoboken, NJ: Wiley-Blackwell.

Helmbrecht, Johannes. (2013). Politeness distinctions in pronouns. In M. S. Dryer & M. Haspelmath (eds.), *The World Atlas of Language Structures Online*. Leipzig: Max Planck Institute for Evolutionary Anthropology. http://wals.info/chapter/45

Heisserer, Eric. (2016). How I wrote *Arrival* (and what I learned doing it). *Talkhouse*, November 10, 2016. www.talkhouse.com/how-i-wrote-arrival/

Higgins, Jackie. (2022). *Sentient: How Animals Illuminate the Wonder of Our Human Senses*. New York: Atria Books.

Higley, Sarah. (2007). *Hildegard of Bingen's Unknown Language: An Edition, Translation, and Discussion*. London: Palgrave Macmillan.

Holmes, Bob. (2021). *Speaking in whistles. Knowable Magazine*. https://knowablemagazine.org/article/mind/2021/whistled-languages

Hualde, José Ignacio (2005). *The Sounds of Spanish*. Cambridge: Cambridge University Press.

Hualde, José Ignacio & Ortiz de Urbina, Jon. (2003). *A Grammar of Basque*. Berlin; New York: Mouton de Gruyter.

Hyman, L. (2018). What tone teaches us about language. *Language*, 94, 698–709.

Ide, Sachiko. (1991). How and why do women speak more politely in Japanese? In Ide Sachiko & Naomi McGloin (eds.), *Aspects of Japanese Women's Language*, 63–79. Tokyo: Kurosio.

Idema, Wilt. (2009). *Heroines of Jiangyong: Chinese Narratives Ballads in Women's Script*. London; Seattle: University of Washington Press.

Iggesen, Oliver A. (2013a). Number of cases. In M. S. Dryer & M. Haspelmath (eds.), *The World Atlas of Language Structures Online*. Leipzig: Max Planck Institute for Evolutionary Anthropology. http://wals.info/chapter/49

Iggesen, Oliver A. (2013b). Chapter position of case affixes. In M. S. Dryer & M. Haspelmath (eds.), *The World Atlas of Language Structures Online*. Leipzig: Max Planck Institute for Evolutionary Anthropology. http://wals.info/chapter/51

Jabr, Ferris. (2020). The social life of forests. *The New York Times*. www.nytimes.com/interactive/2020/12/02/magazine/tree-communication-mycorrhiza.html

Janson, Tore. (2012). *The History of Languages: An Introduction*. Oxford: Oxford University Press.

Jones, Wesley. (2020). *Fantasy Mapping: Drawing Worlds*. N.p.: WTJones.

Kay, Paul & Maffi, Luisa. (2013). Number of non-derived basic colour categories. In M. S. Dryer & M. Haspelmath (eds.), *The World Atlas of Language Structures Online*. Leipzig: Max Planck Institute for Evolutionary Anthropology. http://wals.info/chapter/132

Kellerman Reed, Ivy. (2003). *A Complete Grammar of Esperanto the International Language*. www.gutenberg.org/files/7787/7787-h/7787-h.htm

Kelly, Piers. (2022). *The Last Language on Earth: Linguistic Utopianism in the Philippines*. Oxford: Oxford University Press.

Kershenbaum, Arik. (2020). *The Zoologist's Guide to the Galaxy: What Animals on Earth Reveal about Aliens – and Ourselves*. New York: Penguin Press.

Kim, M., Martin, J. R., Shin, G.-H. & Choi, G. H. (2023). *Korean Grammar: A Systemic Functional Approach*. Cambridge: Cambridge University Press.

Kimball, Geoffrey. (1985). *A Descriptive Grammar of Koasati*. Ph.D. dissertation, Tulane University.

Klamer, Marian. (1998). *A Grammar of Kambera*. Berlin; New York: Mouton de Gruyter.

Konnelly, Lex, Conrod, Kirby & Bradley, Evan D. (2023). Non-binary singular they. In Laura L. Paterson (ed.), *The Routledge Handbook of Pronouns*, 450–464. London; New York: Routledge.

König, Ekkehard & Siemund, Peter. (2007). Speech act distinctions in grammar. In Timothy Shopen (ed.), *Language Typology and Syntactic Description*, 276–324. Cambridge: Cambridge University Press.

Kurlansky, Mark. (2003). *Salt: A World History*. New York: Penguin Books.

Kutsch Lojenga, Constance. (1994). *Ngiti: A Central Sudanic Language of Zaire*. Cologne: Rüdiger Köpp.

Ladefoged, Peter. 1999. American English. In *Handbook of the International Phonetic Association: A Guide to the Use of the International Phonetic Alphabet*, 41–44. Cambridge: Cambridge University Press.

Ladefoged, Peter & Maddieson, Ian. (1996). *The Sounds of the World's Languages*. Oxford: Blackwell.

Ladefoged, Peter & Ferrari, Sandra. (2012). *Vowels and Consonants* (3rd ed.). Hoboken, NJ: Wiley-Blackwell.

Lakoff, George. (1990). *Women, Fire and Dangerous Things: What Categories Reveal about the Mind*. Chicago: University of Chicago Press.

Lakoff, George & Johnson, Mark. (2003). *Metaphors We Live By*. Chicago: University of Chicago Press. [Originally published in 1980].

Laidig, Wyn & Laidig, Carol. (1990). Larike pronouns: Duals and trials in a Central Moluccan language. *Oceanic Linguistics*, 28(2), 87–109.

Lang, Sonja. (2014). *Toki Pona: The Language of Good*. St. Paul, MN: Tawhid Press.

Lang, Sonja. (2021). *Toki Pona Dictionary*. St. Paul, MN: Tawhid Press.

Lang, Sonja. (2024). *The Wonderful Wizard of Oz (Toki Pona Edition)*. St. Paul: Tawhid Press.

Lapointe, Tanya. (2022). *The Art and Science of Arrival*. London: Titan Books.

Lawson, E., Stuart-Smith, J., Scobbie, J. M. & Nakai, S. (2018). *Seeing Speech: An Articulatory Web Resource for the Study of Phonetics*. Glasgow: University of Glasgow Press. www.seeingspeech.ac.uk/

Lee, Hyun-bok. (1999). An IPA illustration of Korean. In *Handbook of the International Phonetic Association: A Guide to the Use of the International Phonetic Alphabet*, 120–123. Cambridge: Cambridge University Press.

LeMaster, Barbara. (2006). Language contraction, revitalization, and Irish Women. *Journal of Linguistic Anthropology, 16*(2), 211–228.

Levinson, Stephen C. (2006). Deixis. In Laurence R. Horn & Gregory L. Ward (eds.), *The Handbook of Pragmatics*, 97–121. Malden, NJ: Blackwell Publishing.

Lewis-Jones, Huw. (2018). *The Writer's Map: An Atlas of Imaginary Lands.* Chicago: University of Chicago Press.

Li, Yu. (2020). *The Chinese Writing System in Asia: An Interdisciplinary Perspective*, 169–178. Oxford; New York: Routledge.

Li, Charles & Thompson, Sandra. (1990). *Mandarin Chinese: A Functional Reference Grammar.* Berkeley: University of California Press.

Littlemore, Jeannette. (2019). *Metaphors in the Mind: Sources of Variation in Embodied Metaphor.* Cambridge: Cambridge University Press.

Loos, Eugene. (1969). *The Phonology of Capanahua and Its Grammatical Basis.* Norman: Summer Institute of Linguistics, University of Oklahoma.

Loos, Eugene & Loos, Betty. (1998). *Diccionario Capanahua-Castellano.* Yarinacocha, Peru: Instituto Lingüístico de Verano. www.sil.org/resources/archives/30091

Lyovin, Anatole V., Kessler, Brett & Leben, William R. (2017). *An Introduction to the Languages of the World* (2nd ed.). Oxford: Oxford University Press. [1st ed. 1997].

MacDonald, Lorna. (1990). *A Grammar of Tauya.* Berlin: Mouton de Gruyter.

McGloin, Naomi Hanaoka. (2014). *Modern Japanese Grammar: A Practical Guide.* London: Routledge.

Maddieson, Ian. (1984). *Patterns of Sounds.* Cambridge: Cambridge University Press.

Maddieson, Ian. (2013a). Vowel quality inventories. In M. S. Dryer & M. Haspelmath (eds.), *The World Atlas of Language Structures Online.* Leipzig: Max Planck Institute for Evolutionary Anthropology. http://wals.info/chapter/2

Maddieson, Ian. (2013b). Front rounded vowels. In M. S. Dryer & M. Haspelmath (eds.), *The World Atlas of Language Structures Online.* Leipzig: Max Planck Institute for Evolutionary Anthropology. http://wals.info/chapter/11

Maddieson, Ian. (2013c). Consonant inventories. In M. S. Dryer & M. Haspelmath (eds.), *The World Atlas of Language Structures Online.* Leipzig: Max Planck Institute for Evolutionary Anthropology. http://wals.info/chapter/1

Maddieson, Ian. (2013d). Syllable Structure. In M. S. Dryer & M. Haspelmath (eds.), *The World Atlas of Language Structures Online.* Leipzig: Max Planck Institute for Evolutionary Anthropology. http://wals.info/chapter/12

Maddieson, Ian. (2013e). Tone. In M. S. Dryer & M. Haspelmath (eds.), *The World Atlas of Language Structures Online.* Leipzig: Max Planck Institute for Evolutionary Anthropology. http://wals.info/chapter/13

Majid, Asifa & Kruspe, Nicole. (2018). Hunter-gatherer olfaction is special. *Current Biology, 28*(3), 409–413.

Majid, Asifa & Burenhult, Niclas. (2014). Odors are expressible in language, so long as you speak the right language. *Cognition, 130*(2), 266–270.

Mandala, Susan. (2010). *Science Fiction and Fantasy: The Question of Style.* London: Continuum.

Martin, J. B. (2010). How to tell a Creek Story in five past tenses. *International Journal of American Linguistics, 76*(1), 43–70.

Marušič, Franc. (2023). Circumfixation. In Peter Ackema, Sabrina Bendjaballah, Eulàlia Bonet & Antonio Fábregas (eds.), *The Wiley Blackwell Companion to Morphology*, Vol. I, 419–444. Hoboken, NJ: Wiley-Blackwell.

Maslova, Elena. (2003). *A Grammar of Kolyma Yukaghir.* Berlin; New York: Mouton de Gruyter.

McCaskill, Carolyn, Lucas, Ceil, Bayley, Robert & Hill, Joseph. (2020). *The Hidden Treasure of Black ASL: Its History and Structure.* Washington, DC: Gallaudet University Press.

McKenzie, A. & Punske, J. (2020). Language development during interstellar travel. *Acta Futura*, 123–132. https://zenodo.org/record/3747353

McIlwaine, Catherine. (2018). *Tolkien: Maker of Middle-Earth.* University of Oxford: The Bodleian Library.

McWhorter, John. (2001). *The Power of Babel: A Natural History of Language.* New York: Times Books.

McWhorter, John. (2013). Are Elvish, Klingon, Dothraki and Na'vi real languages? [TED Talk]. http://ed.ted.com/lessons/are-elvish-klingon-dothraki-and-na-vi-real-languages-john-mcwhorter

McWhorter, John. (2017). *Talking Back, Talking Black: Truths about America's Lingua Franca.* New York: Bellevue Literary Press.

Merlan, Francesca C. (1994). *A Grammar of Wardaman, a Language of the Northern Territory of Australia.* Berlin: Mouton de Gruyter.

Meyer, Julien. (2015). *Whistled Languages. A Worldwide Inquiry on Human Whistled Speech.* Springer: Berlin.

Meyer, Julien. (2021). Environmental and linguistic typology of whistled languages. *Annual Review of Linguistics, 7*(1), 493–510.

Meyer, Julien, Magnasco, Marcelo & Reiss, Diana. (2021). The relevance of human whistled languages for the analysis and decoding of dolphin communication. *Frontiers in Psychology, 12*, 1–22.

Miestamo, Matti. (2005). *Standard Negation: The Negation of Declarative Verbal Main Clauses in a Typological Perspective.* Berlin: Mouton de Gruyter.

Miestamo, Matti. (2007). Symmetric and asymmetric encoding of functional domains, with remarks on typological markedness. In Matti Miestamo & Bernhard Wälchli (eds.), *New Challenges in Typology: Broadening the Horizons and Redefining the Foundations*, 293–314. Berlin; New York: Mouton De Gruyter.

Moir, Bruce & Kingsbury, Bob. (Directors). (1974). *Mr. Symbol Man* [Film]. ONF | NFB / Film Australia.

Moran, Steven & McCloy, Daniel. (eds.) (2019). *PHOIBLE 2.0*. Jena: Max Planck Institute for the Science of Human History. http://phoible.org

Moro, Andrea. (2016). *Impossible Languages*. Cambridge, MA: MIT Press.

Müller, Stefan G. (2024). *An Annotated Na'vi Dictionary: Aysikenonghu a Li'upuk leNa'vi*. http://ivongnavi.info/AnnotatedDictionary.pdf

Munro, Patricia. (2012). Interrogative verbs in Takic. *UCLA Working Papers in Linguistics 17*: *Theories of Everything*, 274–284.

Murray, Thomas E. (1985). Lapine lingo in American English: Silflay. *American Speech*, 60(4), 372–375.

Neely, Kelsey C. (2019). *The Linguistic Expression of Affective Stance in Yaminawa (Pano, Peru)*. Ph.D. dissertation, University of California, Berkeley.

Nicholas, Nick. (2003). *Much Ado About Nothing: The Restored Klingon Version*. Flourtown, PA: The Klingon Institute.

Nicholas, Nick & Strader, Andrew. (2020). *The Klingon Hamlet: The Restored Klingon Version*. Flourtown, PA: The Klingon Institute.

Noel, Ruth S. (1980). *The Languages of Tolkien's Middle-Earth*. Boston: Houghton Mifflin Company.

Nuyts, Jan & van der Auwera, Johan (eds.). (2016). *The Oxford Handbook of Modality and Mood*. Oxford: Oxford University Press.

O'Neill, Gareth. (2014). Humming, whistling, singing, and yelling in Pirahã context and channels of communication in FDG. *Pragmatics*, 24, 349–375.

Oberhaus, Daniel. (2019). *Extraterrestrial Languages*. Cambridge, MA: MIT Press.

Ohala, Manjari. (1999). Hindi. In *Handbook of the International Phonetic Association: A Guide to the Use of the International Phonetic Alphabet*, 100–103. Cambridge: Cambridge University Press.

Okrand, Marc. (1985). *The Klingon Dictionary*. New York: Pocket Books.

Okrand, Marc. (1997). *Klingon for the Galactic Traveler*. New York: Gallery Books.

Okrent, Anika. (2010). *In the Land of Invented Languages*. New York: Random House.

Okrent. Anika. (2013). *The Pig Latins of 11 other languages. Mental Floss*. http://mentalfloss.com/article/50242/pig-latins-11-other-languages

Okrent, Anika. (2021). *Highly Irregular: Why Tough, Through, and Dough Don't Rhyme – And Other Oddities of the English Language*. Oxford: Oxford University Press.

Olawsky, Knut. (2006). *A Grammar of Urarina*. Mouton de Gruyter.

Ollongren, Alexander. (2013). *Astrolinguistics: Design of a Linguistic System for Interstellar Communication Based on Logic*. New York: Springer.

Ostler, Nicholas. (2005). *Empires of the Word: A Language History of the World*. New York: Harper Perennial.

Oostendorp, M. van. (1999). Syllable structure in Esperanto as an instantiation of universal phonology. *Esperantologio Esperanto Studies 1*, 52–80.

Owens, Jonathan. (1985). *A Grammar of Harar Oromo (Northeastern Ethiopia)*. Hamburg: Helmut Buske Verlag.

Palmer, F. R. (2001). *Mood and Modality* (2nd ed.). Cambridge: Cambridge University Press. [1st ed. 1986].

Parker, Steve. (1994). Coda epenthesis in Huariapano. *International Journal of American Linguistics, 60*, 95–119.

Parker, Steve. (1998). On the phonetic duration of Huariapano rhymes. *Work Papers of the Summer Institute of Linguistics, University of North Dakota Session, 42*(1), Article 4. https://commons.und.edu/sil-work-papers/vol42/iss1/4

Parkwall, Mikael. (2008). *The Limits of Language: Almost Everything You Didn't Know You Didn't Know about Language and Languages*. Willsonville, OR: William, James & Company.

Payne, Doris L. and Payne, Thomas. (1990). Yagua. In Desmond C. Derbyshire and Geoffrey K. Pullum (eds.), *Handbook of Amazonian Languages*, Vol. II, 249–474. Berlin: Mouton de Gruyter.

Payne, Thomas E. (2006). *Exploring Language Structure: A Student's Guide*. Cambridge: Cambridge University Press.

Peterson, David. (2003–2023). *The Conlang Manifesto*. https://dedalvs.com/notes/manifesto.php

Peterson, David. (2014). *Dothraki: A Conversational Language Course Based on the Hit Original HBO Series Game of Thrones*. New York: Living Language.

Peterson, David. (2015). *The Art of Language Invention*. London: Penguin.

Pompino-Marschall, Bernd, Steriopolo, Elena & Żygis, Marzena. (2017). Ukrainian. *Journal of the International Phonetic Association, 47*: 349–357.

Post, Mark. (2019). Topographical deixis in Trans-Himalayan (Sino-Tibetan) languages. *Transactions of the Philological Society, 117*, 234–255.

Powers, Richard. (2019). *The Overstory*. New York: W. W. Norton & Company.

Rice, Keren & de Reuse, Willem. (2017). The Athabaskan (Dene) language family. In Alexandra Aikhenvald & R. M. W. Dixon (eds.), *The Cambridge Handbook of Linguistic Typology*, 707–746. Cambridge: Cambridge University Press.

Rickford, John. (1999). *African American Vernacular English*. Oxford: Blackwell.

Rickford, John R. & King, Sharese. (2016). Language and linguistics on trial: Hearing Rachel Jeantel (and other vernacular speakers) in the courtroom and beyond. *Language, 92*(4), 948–988.

Rickford, John R. & Rickford, Russell J. (2000). *Spoken Soul: The Story of Black English*. New York: John Wiley & Sons.

Ridouane, Rachid. (2014). Tashlhiyt Berber. *Journal of the International Phonetic Association, 44*, 207–221.

Ritchart, Amanda & Arvaniti, Amalia. (2014). The form and use of uptalk in Southern Californian English. *Proceeding of the International Conference on Speech Prosody*, 331–336.

Robson, David. (2017). *The beautiful languages of the people who talk like birds*. BBC Future. www.bbc.com/future/article/20170525-the-people-who-speak-in-whistles

Rogers, H. (2005). *Writing Systems: A Linguistic Approach*. Malden, NJ: Blackwell.

Romero-Figueroa, Andres. (1985). OSV as the basic order in Warao. *Linguistics*, 23, 105–121.

Rosen, Martin. (1978). *Watership Down* [Film]. Nepenthe Production.

Rosenfelder, Mark. (2010). *The Language Construction Kit*. Chicago: Yonagu Books.

Rosenfelder, Mark. (2012). *Advanced Language Construction*. Chicago: Yonagu Books.

Rosenfelder, Mark. (2013). *The Conlanger's Lexipedia*. Chicago: Yonagu Books.

Rudder, Joshua. (2015). *Thoth's Pill: An Animated History of Writing* [YouTube video]. www.youtube.com/watch?v=PdO3IP0Pro8.

Russell, Mary Doria. (1996). *The Sparrow*. New York: Villard Books.

Russell, Mary Doria. (2007). *Children of God*. New York: Ballantine Books.

Sala, Ilaria Maria. (2018). *Nushu: What the world's fascination with a female-only Chinese script says about cultural appropriation*. Quartz. https://qz.com/1271372/what-the-worlds-fascination-with-nushu-a-female-only-chinese-script-says-about-cultural-appropriation/

Salo, David. (2004). *A Gateway to Sindarin*. Salt Lake City: Utah University Press.

Sandler, W. (2006). Sign language: Overview. In K. Brown (ed.), *Encyclopedia of Language and Linguistics* (2nd ed.), 328–338. Oxford: Elsevier.

Sanders, Nathan. (2020). A primer on constructed languages. In Jeffrey Punske, Nathan Sanders and Amy V. Fountain (eds.), *Language Invention in Linguistics Pedagogy*, 6–26. Oxford: Oxford University Press.

Schachter, Paul and Otanes, Fé T. (1972). *Tagalog Reference Grammar*. Berkeley: University of California Press. [Repr. 1983].

Schultze-Berndt, Eva. (2000). Simple and complex verbs in Jaminjung: A study of event categorisation in an Australian language. Ph.D. dissertation, Radboud University.

See, Lisa. (2006). *Snow Flower and the Secret Fan*. New York: Random House.

Shibatani, Masayoshi. (1990). *The Languages of Japan*. Cambridge: Cambridge University Press.

Shibatani, Masayoshi. (1998). Honorifics. In Jacob L. Mey (ed.), *Concise Encyclopedia of Pragmatics*, 341–350. Amsterdam: Elsevier.

Siewierska, Anna. (2013a). Verbal person marking. In M. S. Dryer & M. Haspelmath (eds.), *The World Atlas of Language Structures Online*. Leipzig: Max Planck Institute for

Evolutionary Anthropology. http://wals.info/chapter/102.

Siewierska, Anna. (2013b). Order of person markers on the verb. In M. S, Dryer & M. Haspelmath (eds.), *The World Atlas of Language Structures Online*. Leipzig: Max Planck Institute for Evolutionary Anthropology. http://wals.info/chapter/104

Simard, Suzanne. (2016). How trees talk to each other [TED Talk]. www.ted.com/talks/suzanne_simard_how_trees_talk_to_each_other?language=en

Simard, Suzanne. (2021). *Finding the Mother Tree: Discovering the Wisdom of the Forest*. New York: Knopf.

Simpson, Andrew. (2019). *Language and Society: An Introduction*. Oxford: Oxford University Press.

Sneddon, James. (1996). *Indonesian Reference Grammar*. St. Leonards, Australia: Allen and Unwin.

Solska, Agnieska. (2008). *Tao Te Ching: A Klingon Translation*. Flourtown, PA: The Klingon Institute.

Souza, Emerson Carvalho de. (2012). *Aspectos de uma gramática Shawã (Pano)*. Ph.D. dissertation, Universidade Estadual de Campinas, Brazil.

Sridhar, S. N. (1990). *Kannada: Descriptive Grammar*. London: Routledge.

Stassen, Leon. (2013). Noun phrase conjunction. In M. S. Dryer & M. Haspelmath (eds.), *The World Atlas of Language Structures Online*. Leipzig: Max Planck Institute for Evolutionary Anthropology. http://wals.info/chapter/63

Tadmor, Uri. (2009). Loanwords in the world's languages: Findings and results. In Martin Haspelmath & Uri Tadmor (eds.), *Loanwords in the World's Languages: A Comparative Handbook*, 55–75. The Hague: De Gruyter Mouton. http://udel.edu/~pcole/fieldmethods2010/The%20Leipzig-Jakarta%20Word%20List.pdf

Taylor, Allan R. (1996). Nonspeech communication systems. In I. Goddard (ed.), *Handbook of North American Indians, Vol. 17: Languages*, 275–289. Washington, DC: Smithsonian Institution.

Terrill, Angela. (1999). *A Grammar of Lavukaleve: A Papuan Language of the Solomon Islands*. Ph.D dissertation, Australian National University.

Thompson, Sandra A., Longacre, Robert E. & Hwang, Shin Ja J. (2007). Adverbial clauses. In Timothy Shopen (ed.), *Language Typology and Syntactic Description*, Vol. II: *Complex Constructions* (2nd ed.), 237–300. Cambridge: Cambridge University Press. [1st ed. 1985].

Tija, Johnny. (2007). *A Grammar of Mualang: An Ibanic Language of Western Kalimantan, Indonesia*. Utrecht: LOT.

Tingsabadh, Kalaya & Abramson, Arthur. (1999). Thai. In *Handbook of the International Phonetic Association: A Guide to the Use of the International Phonetic Alphabet*, 147–150. Cambridge: Cambridge University Press.

Tolkien, J. R. R. (2004). *Lord of the Rings*. 50th anniversary edition. London: Harper Collins.

Tolkien, J. R. R. (1983). *The Monsters and the Critics, and Other Essays*, ed. C. Tolkien. London: Allen and Unwin.

Toutios, Asterios, Lingala, Sajan Goud, Vaz, Colin, Kim, Jangwon, Esling, John, Keating, Patricia, Gordon, Matthew, Byrd, Dani, Goldstein, Louis, Nayak, Krishna & Narayanan, Shrikanth. (2016). Illustrating the production of the International Phonetic Alphabet sounds using fast real-time magnetic resonance imaging. Paper presented at *Interspeech 2016*, September 8–12, 2016, San Francisco. 2428–2432. https://sail.usc.edu/span/pdfs/toutios2016illustrating.pdf

Travis, Catherine. (2006). Dizque: A Colombian evidentiality strategy. *Linguistics*, 44, 1269–1297.

Uys Jamie. (Director). (1980). *The Gods Must be Crazy* [Film]. C. A. T. Films.

Vakoch, Douglas & Punske, Jeffrey (eds.). (2024). *Xenolinguistics: Towards a Science of Extraterrestrial Language*. London; New York: Routledge.

Valenzuela, Pilar. (2003). *Transitivity in Shipibo-Konibo Grammar: A Typologically Oriented Study*. Ph.D. dissertation, University of Oregon.

Valenzuela, P. & Castro Soares de Oliveira, S. (2021). Degrees of temporal remoteness in Pano: Contribution to the cross-linguistic study of tense. *LIAMES*, 22, e022014. https://doi.org/10.20396/liames.v22i00.8668622

Vallejos, Rosa. (2016). *A Grammar of Kukama-Kukamiria: A Language from the Amazon*. Leiden; Boston: Brill.

van der Auwera, Johan & Lejeune, Ludo (with Umarani Pappuswamy & Valentin Goussev). (2013a). The morphological imperative. In M. S. Dryer & M. Haspelmath (eds.), *The World Atlas of Language Structures Online*. Leipzig: Max Planck Institute for Evolutionary Anthropology. http://wals.info/chapter/70

van der Auwera, Johan & Lejeune, Ludo (with Valentin Goussev). (2013b). The prohibitive. In M. S. Dryer & M. Haspelmath (eds.), *The World Atlas of Language Structures Online*. Leipzig: Max Planck Institute for Evolutionary Anthropology. http://wals.info/chapter/71

van der Auwera, Johan & Ammann, Andreas. (2013). Epistemic possibility. In M. S. Dryer & M. Haspelmath (eds.), *The World Atlas of Language Structures Online*. Leipzig: Max Planck Institute for Evolutionary Anthropology. http://wals.info/chapter/75

Villeneuve, Denis (Director). (2016). *Arrival* [Film]. Paramount.

Velupillai, Viveka. (2012). *An Introduction to Linguistic Typology*. Amsterdam: John Benjamins.

von Trotta, Margarethe (Director). (2009). *Vision* [Film]. Zeitgeist Films.

Wang, Wayne (Director). (2011). *Snow Flower and the Secret Fan* [Film]. Fox Searchlight.

Warren, Paul. (2016). *Uptalk: The Phenomenon of Rising Intonation*. Cambridge: Cambridge University Press.

Watkins Britton (Director). (2017). *Conlanging: The Art of Crafting Tongues* [Film]. Filmhub.

Wells, John. (1994). Esperanto. In R. E. Asher (ed.), *The Encyclopedia of Language and Linguistics*, Vol. III, 1143–1145. Oxford: Pergamon.

Witkowski, Stanley R. & Brown, Cecil H. (1985). Climate, clothing, and body-part nomenclature. *Ethnology*, 24, 197–214.

Wohlleben, Peter. (2016). *The Hidden Life of Trees: What They Feel, How They Communicate – Discoveries from a Secret World*. Munich: Ludwig Verlag.

Wolf, Mark. (2018). *The Routledge Companion to Imaginary Worlds*. New York: Routledge.

Wolfram, Walt & Natalie Schilling. (2016). *American English: Dialects and Variation* (3rd ed.). Hoboken, NJ: Wiley Blackwell.

Wolfram, Walt. (2020). *Signing Black in America: The Story of Black ASL*. Raleigh, NC: The Language & Life Project at North Carolina State University.

Yamamoto, Motoi. (2012). *Return to the Sea: Saltworks*. Columbia: University of South Carolina Press.

Yavaş, Mehmet. (2020). *Applied English Phonology* (4th ed.). Hoboken, NJ: Wiley-Blackwell. [1st ed. 2005]

Yigezu, Moges. (1998). Women in society and female speech among the Suri of south-western Ethiopia. In Gerrit Jan Dimmendaal & Marco Last (eds.), *Surmic Languages and Cultures*, 83–102. Cologne: Rüdiger Köppe Verlag.

Yip, Moira. (2002). *Tone*. Cambridge: Cambridge University Press.

Yu, Alan. (2004). Infixing with a vengeance: Pingding Mandarin infixation. *Journal of East Asian Linguistics*, 13(1), 39–58.

Yu, Alan. (2007). *A Natural History of Infixation*. Oxford: Oxford University Press.

Zamenhof, Ludwig Lazarus. (1887). *Dr. Esperanto's International Language. Introduction and Complete Grammar (Unua libro)*. English edition by Richard H. Geoghegan. Warsaw: Chaim Kelter.

Zeshan, Ulrike. (2013a). Sign languages. In M. S. Dryer & M. Haspelmath (eds.), *The World Atlas of Language Structures Online*. Leipzig: Max Planck Institute for Evolutionary Anthropology. http://wals.info/chapter/s9

Zeshan, Ulrike. (2013b). Question particles in sign languages. In M. S. Dryer & M. Haspelmath (eds.), *The World Atlas of Language Structures Online*. Leipzig: Max Planck Institute for Evolutionary Anthropology. http://wals.info/chapter/140

Zeshan, Ulrike & de Vos, Connie (eds.). (2013). *Sign Languages in Village Communities. Anthropological and Linguistic Insights*. Berlin: De Gruyter Mouton-Ishara Press.

Zhang, Jie. (2002). *The Effects of Duration and Sonority on Contour*

Tone Distribution. New York: Routledge.
Zimmer, Karl & Orham, Orgun. (1992). Illustrations of the IPA: Turkish. *Journal of the International Phonetic Association, 22*, 43–45.
Zottola, Angela. (2023). Gender binaries in constructed languages. In Laura L. Paterson (ed.), *The Routledge Handbook of Pronouns*. London; New York: Routledge. 437–449.
Zingler, Tim. (2022). Circumfixation: A semasiological approach. *Word Structure, 15*, 55–113.
Zsiga, Elizabeth C. (2024). *The Sounds of Language: An Introduction to Phonetics and Phonology*. Hoboken, NJ: Wiley-Blackwell.
Zuckermann, Ghil'ad. (2020). *Revivalistics: From the Genesis of Israeli to Language Reclamation in Australia and Beyond*. Oxford: Oxford University Press.

Websites

Amanye Tenceli: The Writing Systems of Aman (Måns Björkman Berg 2024)	https://at.mansbjorkman.net/
Atlas of Endangered Alphabets	www.endangeredalphabets.net/
Brian Schwimmer's kinship tutorial website	www.umanitoba.ca/faculties/arts/anthropology/tutor/kinterms/toc.html
Dothraki–English Dictionary	https://docs.dothraki.org/Dothraki.pdf
Doulos font	https://software.sil.org/doulos/
Eklund's Ingressive Speech Page	http://ingressivespeech.info/
The Endangered Languages Archive	www.elararchive.org/
English–Dothraki Dictionary	https://theunlikelyassembly.org/Shared%20Documents/Dothraki%20Dictionary.pdf
Fiat Lingua	www.fiatlingua.org/
From xenolinguistics to cephlopods	www.diaphanes.net/titel/xenolinguistics-5623
Gripping conlang	https://conference.conlang.org/lcc3/talks/Alex_and_Sai.pdf
Guides for Tengwar and Runes (Per Lindberg 2023)	www.forodrim.org/daeron/md_teng_primers.html
Houma Language Project	www.houmalanguageproject.org/
Ifuhuxu	https://conlang.fandom.com/wiki/Ifuhuxu
Interactive IPA chart	www.internationalphoneticassociation.org/IPAcharts/inter_chart_2018/IPA_2018.html
Interactive Sagittal Section	http://smu-facweb.smu.ca/~s0949176/sammy/

Interlanguages	http://interlanguages.net/
International Dialects of English Archive (IDEA)	www.dialectsarchive.com/
IPA Chart (2020)	www.internationalphoneticassociation.org/content/ipa-chart
Joseph Hill's website	www.josephchill.com/black-asl
Lexilogos	www.lexilogos.com/keyboard/ipa.htm
Linguistic Atlas Project (LAP)	www.lap.uga.edu/
Messaging Extraterrestrial Intelligence (METI)	www.meti.org/
Omniglot	https://omniglot.com/
Pig Latin Translator by LingoJam	https://lingojam.com/PigLatinTranslator
Pirahã video clips	http://daneverettbooks.com/radiopublications/film-clips/
Real-time MRI IPA charts	https://sail.usc.edu/span/rtmri_ipa/
Rikchik	https://suberic.net/~dmm/rikchik/intro.html
Searching for Extraterrestrial Intelligence (SETI) Institute	www.seti.org/
Stresstyp2	http://st2.ullet.net/
Teonaht Language	www.concavities.org/teonaht/contents.html
Toki Pona Luka	http://tokipona.net/tp/janpije/signlanguage.php
The Smiley Award	http://dedalvs.com/smileys/
The World of Nushu (Orie Endo 2001)	http://nushu.world.coocan.jp/home.htm
TypeIt	https://ipa.typeit.org/
UCLA Phonetics Lab	http://phonetics.ucla.edu/
UIowa Sounds of Speech	https://soundsofspeech.uiowa.edu/

Index

A posteriori conlangs, 8
A priori conlangs, 8, 12
abjads, 263, 265, 272
abstract nouns, 122
abugidas, 263, 265, 272
accompaniment, 81
adjective phrases (APs), 193
adjectives, 125
adpositions, 133, 198
adverbial phrases (AdvPs), 193
adverbs, 129
adversative coordination, 240, 242
affective meaning, 81, 281
affixation, 139, 148
airstream mechanisms, 79
alien languages, 6
allomorphs, 153
allophones, 73
alphabets, 264, 265, 272
alternative languages (altlangs), 7
amelioration, 311
A-not-A construction, 209
antonyms, 125
articulators, 66
artistic languages (artlangs), 7
aspect, 178–181
　completive, 180
　comtemplative, 180
　continuative, 180
　habitual, 180
　imperfect, 179
　inceptive, 180
　iterative, 180
　perfective, 179
　progressive, 178
　semelfactive, 180
　strong perfective, 179
aspiration, 77, 78
associate plural, 156
astrolinguistics, 328
auxiliary languages (auxlangs), 7

blends, 138
borrowings, 22, 120, 309
boustrophedon, 273
breathy voice, 79

case, 161, 199
　ablative, 162
　absolutive, 163
　accusative, 161
　allative, 163
　aversive, 164
　benefactive, 163
　comitative, 163
　dative, 162
　ergative, 163
　evitative, 164
　genitive, 162
　instrumental, 163
　malefactive, 164
　nominative, 161
　vocative, 162
children of deaf adults (CODAs), 322
chronoception, 25
circumfixes, 149
clauses, 239
　adjectival, 248–249
　adverbial, 249–250
clicks, 79, 80, 130, 328
clitics, 174
closed class, 121, 125
codas, 92
collective, 157
color terms, 126, 127, 143, 285
commands, 215, 216
common nouns, 123
communication channel, 319
complementizers, 247, 248
compounding, 120, 127, 137, 138, 288, 297, 307
compounds, 14, 116, 137, 298, 323

conjunctions, 107, 133, 239, 240, 241, 247
connotation, 281, 282, 283, 287, 302, 309, 311
consonant inventories, 73
consonants
　non-pulmonic, 79
　pulmonic, 79
　voiced, 67
　voiceless, 67
constituency tests, 192, 193
constituents, 189, 191, 194, 224, 239
constructed languages (conlangs), 2
constructed scripts (conscripts), 256–279
content questions, 210
content words, 105, 120
contour tone, 110
coordination, 240
　adversative, 242
　asyndetic, 240
　bisyndetic, 240, 244
　conjunction, 241
　disjunctive, 242
　juxtaposition, 240
　syndetic, 240
coordinators, 240
count nouns, 123
creaky voice, 78, 305
creole, 26
culture, 19
Cuneiform, 259

degree of exponence, 152
　agglutinative languages, 152
　cumulative languages, 152
　separative languages, 152
degree of flexion, 153
　flexive languages, 153
　non-flexive languages, 153

degree of fusion
  concatenative languages, 152
  isolating languages, 152
  non-concatenative languages, 152
degrees of remoteness, 176
deixis, 288
  distal, 292
  medial, 292
  proximal, 292
  remote, 292
  spatial, 292
  temporal, 293
  textual, 294
deletion, 310
derivational morphology, 137, 146, 148, 287, 338
determiners, 133
dialects
  ethnolects, 303
  genderlects, 303
  geolects, 303
  sociolects, 303
  standard, 303
  vernacular (non-standard), 303
diphthongs, 45, 93, 97, 109, 310
disjunction, 240, 242
do support, 209
double negatives, 224
dual, 155, 289
duration, 54, 55, 75
dystopia, 24

echo questions, 211
egressive sounds, 79
ejectives, 79, 85
engineered languages (engelangs), 7, 338
epiglottis, 43
equilibrioception, 25
euphemisms, 282
evidentials, 231
  assumed, 232
  auditory, 231
  direct, 231
  indirect, 231
  inferential, 232
  non-visual, 231
  quotative, 232
  reported, 231
  visual, 231

exolinguistics, 328

fantasy, 23, 135
Fantasy Frequency Wordlist, 135
fictional languages, 7, 8
fictional map, 26, 27, 123
fictional world, 24
fronting, 76, 211

geminates, 75, 76, 271
gender, 158, 174
gestures, 21, 324, 325
glossing, 150, 167, 185, 339
grammar, 3
  descriptive, 3
  prescriptive, 3
grammatical words, 121, 132, 135
graphemes, 258, 259, 260, 261, 263, 264, 272
group identity, 303

head-final languages, 198
head-initial languages, 198
hiatus, 95, 97, 98
hieratic script style, 260
hieroglyphs, 259
homesign, 321
homographs, 284
homonyms, 284, 285, 302, 316
homophones, 259, 284
honorific, 291, 306, 308
hortative, 218
hum speech, 320
hypernyms, 287, 288
hyponyms, 287, 288

ideograms, 268
idioms, 285, 286
imperatives, 216
implosives, 79, 80, 81
in situ questions, 211, 214
infixes, 149, 338
ingressive sounds, 79
interjections, 79, 130, 131, 132
International Phonetic Alphabet (IPA), 43–45
interrogative quantifiers, 213
intonation, 113, 205, 207, 209, 210, 213, 215, 244, 305

inversion, 208, 209, 213
irrealis, 182

juxtaposition, 240, 243

kinship terms, 140, 285, 287, 291, 297

language contact, 83, 303, 309, 338
language games (ludlings), 5, 6
larynx, 42, 43, 66, 77, 79
lateralization, 304
Leipzig–Jakarta word list, 135
level tone, 110
lexicon, 22, 25, 120, 124
lexicon building
  building block approach, 137
  corpus list approach, 135
  dictionary approach, 134
  lexicon-generator approach, 136
  proto-language approach, 136
  text approach, 140
lingua franca, 26, 33, 37, 308
linguistic relativity, 20
linguistic systems, 3, 10
lip rounding, 45, 46, 47, 50, 52, 76
loanwords, 309
logical languages (loglangs), 7
logograms, 258, 259, 260, 266, 268
logo-syllabaries, 258
lungs, 42, 73

main clause, 197, 239, 240, 246
main stress, 105
manner of articulation, 67
  affricate, 67
  approximant, 68
  fricative, 67
  nasal, 67
  obstruent, 68
  plosive, 67
  rhotic, 69
  sibilant, 69
  sonorant, 68

stop, 67
tap, 69
trill, 69
manual articulators, 322
manual-visual languages, 321–325
mass nouns, 123
meaning extension, 268, 272, 315
metaphor, 285, 286
metaphoric extension, 127, 295
metathesis, 310, 311
minimal pairs, 48, 61, 76, 88, 108, 302, 323
minimal sets, 48, 49, 62
modality, 181, 183
   assumptive, 182
   deductive, 182
   dubitative, 182
   speculative, 182
monophthongs, 45, 93, 116
mood, 181–183
   irrealis, 181, 217
   realis, 181
morphemes, 3, 4, 148
morphological typology
   degree of exponence, 151
morphology, 4, 14, 146–170, 171–188
morpho-phonology, 187
musical speech, 320
mutual intelligibility, 303, 321

naming languages, 6
nasal cavity, 42
natural languages (natlangs), 2
near-minimal set, 49
negation, 224
negative affixes, 226
negative auxiliaries, 227
nominal clauses, 247
nominalizer, 157
non-manual articulators, 322
noun phrases, 132, 191, 241
noun subclasses, 123
nouns, 122
number, 154

onsets, 92
open class, 120, 129
oral cavity, 42

paucal, 156
pejoration, 282, 311
person marking, 172, 173
personal deixis, 289
pharyngealization, 77
pharynx, 42, 66, 77
philosophical languages, 7, 8
phonemes, 48, 83, 264, 302
phonetic determinative, 260
phono-aesthetics, 85, 337
phonology, 4, 161, 272
phonotactics, 91, 99, 130
phrases, 191
pitch accent, 110
place of articulation, 67, 69
   alveolar, 71
   alveo-palatal, 71
   bilabial, 70
   dental, 71
   dorsal, 71
   epiglottal, 73
   glottal, 72
   interdental, 70
   labiodental, 70
   labio-velar, 70, 72
   laryngeal, 72
   lateral fricative, 68, 73
   palatal, 71
   palato-alveolar, 71
   pharyngeal, 72
   post-alveolar, 71
   radical, 72
   retroflex, 71
   uvular, 72
   velar, 72
polar questions, 207
politeness, 217
polysemy, 283
postpositions, 133, 198
pragmatics, 199, 280
predicate, 192, 194, 205
prefixes, 139
prepositional phrases (PPs), 193
prepositions, 107, 133, 197, 198
pre-writing, 267
primary stress, 105
prohibitive, 228
pronouns, 132
   exclusive, 289
   inclusive, 289
proper nouns, 123

questions, 206

radical (semantic component), 260
rebus principle, 268, 272
reduplication, 154
relative clauses, 197, 248
relative pronouns, 248
relativizers, 248
rhotacization, 304
rhyme, 92
romanization, 43
rounded vowels, 46

science fiction, 23
secondary articulation, 76
secondary stress, 105, 106
secret languages, 5
semantic extension, 311
semantic field, 286
semantic narrowing, 311
semantics, 161, 280
sentences, 190
   complex, 238–255
   intransitive, 193
   questionable, 195
   simple, 238
   transitive, 193
   ungrammatical, 195
sentences, parts of
   clause, 239
sign languages, 321–325
singulative, 154, 157
slang, 5, 6, 121, 307, 311
social, 283
sonority, 99
sonority scale, 99
speech sounds, 42–43
statements, 113, 190, 205
stem changes, 154
stress, 104–117
stress clash, 106, 116
stress lapse, 106
stress systems, 107
   fixed, 108
   lexical, 107
   morphological, 108
   quantity-sensitive, 108
subject, 15, 161, 192, 194
subordinate clauses, 247
subordination, 239, 246
superplural, 156
Swadesh list, 135
syllabaries, 260, 272
syllable margins, 92

syllable peak, 92
syllables, 91–103
syntax, 4, 189

taboo words, 282
tactile fingerspelling, 325
tactile sign languages, 325
tags, 208, 209
tense, 124, 175–178
tense, aspect, and mood (TAM), 171–188
thermoception, 25
tonal changes, 227
tone, 104–117
tongue height, 51
trachea, 42
trial, 155, 156, 289
triphthongs, 45, 93, 95, 100

unrounded vowels, 46
uptalk, 113, 305
utopia, 24

velarization, 77
verb phrases, 191, 192

verbal agreement, 172, 173, 174, 198, 200
verbs, 124
  action, 124
  auxiliary, 133
  cognition, 124
  ditransitive, 173
  emotion, 124
  factive, 124
  finite, 248
  modal, 134, 224, 233
  motion, 124
  non-finite, 248
  position, 124
  process, 124
  transitive, 173
  utterance, 124
vocal folds, 42, 43
vocalic inventories, 48, 51
voice quality, 57
voicing, 67
vowel advancement, 45
vowel classification, 45
vowel dispersion, 51
vowel height, 45
vowels, 45

breathy, 57
close, 46
corner, 51, 54
creaky, 57
modal, 57
murmured, 57
nasal, 56
non-modal, 57
open, 46
oral, 56
voiceless, 57
whispered, 57

whistled languages, 319
whistled speech, 319
word order, 189–203, 227
world building, 23
writing systems
  ideographic, 258, 268
  mixed, 266–267
  phonographic, 258, 260

xenolinguistics, 328

yell speech, 320

For EU product safety concerns, contact us at Calle de José Abascal, 56–1°, 28003 Madrid, Spain or eugpsr@cambridge.org.

www.ingramcontent.com/pod-product-compliance
Lightning Source LLC
LaVergne TN
LVHW081527060526
838200LV00045B/2026